仲裁与法律

ARBITRATION AND LAW

第142辑

主办

中国国际经济贸易仲裁委员会
中国海事仲裁委员会
中国国际商会仲裁研究所

法律出版社
LAW PRESS·CHINA

仲裁与法律

第142辑

编辑部地址：北京市西城区桦皮厂胡同2号国际商会大厦6层

邮 政 编 码：100035

电　　话：(010)82217788　64646688

传　　真：(010)82217766　64643500

电 子 信 箱：law@ cietac. org

网　　址：http://www. cietac. org

目 录

·专论 争鸣·

·第五届"中伦杯"获奖论文选登·

·热点 时评·

·域外 参考·

专论　争鸣

试论商事仲裁自裁管辖权的现状与中国的改进

张玉卿*

摘要：法院与仲裁庭在决定仲裁庭管辖权方面如何分工，仲裁庭是否具有决定自身管辖权的权力，这是长期以来在仲裁理论与实践中不断争论的问题，尤其是在中国。本文从分析仲裁庭自裁管辖权的概念及分类、法律渊源、仲裁的三个阶段入手，总结概括国际上广泛通行的理念与做法。同时，结合中国立法与实践，以《联合国国际贸易法委员会国际商事仲裁示范法》为模本提出改进设想，以促进仲裁为"一带一路"倡议服务，提高中国仲裁在国际上的公信力。文章集中论述仲裁管辖权，在阐述商事仲裁管辖权分类、释明积极与消极自裁管辖权、仲裁三段性，主张中国应采取积极自裁管辖权机制方面，具有一定的特点和创新。

关键词：自裁管辖权　商事仲裁　"三段论"　分离原则　《UNCITRAL 仲裁示范法》

尽管一个国际商事合同订有仲裁条款，但在出现纠纷或一方提起仲裁时，仲裁程序往往不一定能顺利开展，因为纠纷的另一方往往会因仲裁条款的存

* 张玉卿，中国政法大学兼职教授、博士研究生导师；仲裁员，WTO 争端解决专家组成员，国际投资争端解决中心（International Centre for Settlement of Investment Disputes，ICSID）在册仲裁员。

在、效力、适格主体以及仲裁范围等问题挑战仲裁的管辖权。① 这种质疑的理由,有的是出于当事方对自身合法权利的维护,有的是基于法律理由,当然也不乏拖延、阻碍仲裁程序,或试图扰乱对方诉讼策略,或拟另觅能更好维护自身利益的场合解决争议的情况。一个好的仲裁制度应探求消除对仲裁程序的阻碍,在充分维护仲裁的核心价值"仲裁功效"(arbitration's efficacy)的同时,又能维护对仲裁持异议当事方的"合法权益"(legitimacy interests)。如何处理好这对"竞争价值",②不仅涉及一国仲裁制度是否合理,也涉及一国法院与仲裁的职责分工问题。

本文拟通过对仲裁庭的自裁管辖权理论的介绍,通过对中国目前的立法与实践的评论,阐明中国在国际商事仲裁的自裁管辖权方面应如何改进与发展,以期促进建立中国的国际仲裁中心的路程。

---

① 一方当事人可能会质疑仲裁庭管辖权的理由包括:(1)主体合同不存在;(2)仲裁条款无效,或不可执行,或不存在书面仲裁协议;(3)被申请人未签署仲裁协议,仲裁协议是被申请人的兄弟公司、母公司,或集团公司签署,被申请人不应受到拘束;(4)代理人只被授权签署合同但并未被授权签署仲裁条款,故仲裁条款对被申请人无拘束力;(5)合同已转让给第三方,作为被申请人的第三方从未同意通过仲裁解决有关争议;(6)合同当事方的公司经过分立或合并,新公司称不受原来合同仲裁条款的约束;(7)所涉争议不属仲裁管辖范围,或强制性法律不允许争议事项通过仲裁解决;(8)提交仲裁的前提条件未满足,如未到提起仲裁的期限,未履行前置协商程序等;(9)仲裁违反"一事不二审"原则;(10)不存在协议约定的仲裁机构(如仲裁机构写成"在日内瓦的国际商会仲裁");(11)申请人已放弃仲裁解决争议的权利;(12)仲裁涉及"国家主权豁免",拒绝仲裁庭有管辖权,等等。See John J. Barceló,"Who Decides the Arbitrators' Jurisdiction? Separability and Competence-Competence in Transnational Perspective", *Vanderbilt Journal of Transnational Law*, p. 1118; Sigvard Jarvin, Chapter7, "Objection to Jurisdiction" in Lawrence W. Newman, Richard D. Hill (ed.), *The Leading Arbitrators'Guide to International Arbitration*, Second Edition, Juris Publish ing, Inc., 2008.

② 美国康奈尔大学教授约翰·J. 巴塞罗(John J. Barceló)认为,一个法律裁决应当确定如何权衡这些相互冲突的法律价值以及如何构建将价值最大化的程序:既能减少当事人恶意阻挠仲裁进程的机会,又能保护当事人的合理快捷司法决定的合法诉求,仲裁条款的分离性原则和自裁管辖权原则,正是在这样一个临界点上运行的。See John J. Barceló "Who Decides the Arbitrators' Jurisdiction? Separability and Competence-Competence in Transnational Perspective", *Vanderbilt Journal of Transnational Law*, p. 1119.

一、自裁管辖权的由来与发展

自裁管辖权是指仲裁庭有权裁定其自身的管辖权,①它是一项被国际公认的准则。② 自裁管辖权理论的发展由来已久,早在18世纪末期英国法官就曾提到仲裁员有权决定其对案件的审理范围问题。③ 早期使用"自裁管辖权"的德文为Kompetenz-Kompetenz,其含义是德国法允许当事方可让仲裁庭决定仲裁协议的存在、效力以及仲裁范围等问题,而且在仲裁庭作出关于管辖权的裁决后,就不再允许法院做事后审查。德国在1998年接受《联合国国际贸易法委员会国际商事仲裁示范法》(UNCITRAL Model Law on International Commercial Arbitration,以下简称《UNCITRAL 仲裁示范法》)后,才改变了这一制度。④ 这一原则后来体现在一系列的国际条约之中,如1945年《国际法院规约》(Statute of the International Court of Justice)规定:"关于法院有无管辖权之争端,由法院裁决之。"⑤1961年的《欧洲国际商事仲裁公约》(European Convention on International Commercial Arbitration)甚至禁止法院在仲裁庭作出管辖权裁决之

---

① "自裁管辖权"德文为Kompetenz-Kompetenz,法文为compétence-compétence,现多用英文competence-competence表示。See Emmanuel Gaillard, John Savage (ed.), *Fouchard Gaillard Goldman On International Commercial Arbitration*, Kluwer Law International, 1999, para. 651, p. 396. 加里·B.博恩(Gary B. Born)建议使用"管辖权权力"(jurisdictional competence)一词来取代Competence-Competence. See Gary B. Born, *International Commercial Arbitration*, 2nd ed., Kluwer Law International, 2014, p. 1049.

② "自裁管辖权原则,一般来说,是指国际仲裁庭有权考虑并裁决有关其自身管辖权的争议。这个原则与仲裁庭和法院之间在管辖权分配上考虑与决定管辖冲突密切相关","几乎所有国家的法律制度都认可自裁管辖权原则"。See Gary B. Born, *International Commercial Arbitration*, 2nd ed., Kluwer Law International, 2014, pp. 1047, 1050.

③ "自裁管辖权原则历史悠久,早期自裁管辖权观点是由洛夫保洛夫大法官在1794年有关杰伊条约争议时提出的,他说'怀疑仲裁员(commissioners)有权决定其自身管辖权是荒唐的,他们必须能具有案件可以审理或不能审理的决定权'。"See Gary B. Born, *International Commercial Arbitration*, 2nd ed., Kluwer Law International, 2014, Chapter7.

④ See Emmanuel Gaillard, John Savage (eds.), *Fouchard Gaillard Goldman On International Commercial Arbitration*, Kluwer Law International, 1999, para. 651, p. 396.

⑤ 1945年《国际法院规约》第36.6条规定:"对于法院是否具有管辖权争议的事项,应由法院决定之。"(In the event of a dispute as to whether the Court has jurisdiction, the matter shall be settled by the decision of the Court.)

前审理仲裁庭的管辖权问题。[①] 仲裁庭有权决定其自身管辖权后来被联合国国际贸易法委员会（Unite Nations Commission on International Trade Law, UNCITRAL）制定的《UNCITRAL 仲裁示范法》和《UNCITRAL 仲裁规则》（UNCITRAL Arbitration Rules）采纳，正式成为国际规范。《UNCITRAL 仲裁示范法》规定，“仲裁庭可以对其管辖权作出裁定，包括对与仲裁协议的存在或效力有关的任何异议作出裁定”；《UNCITRAL 仲裁规则》也规定，“仲裁庭有权力对其自身管辖权作出裁定，包括对与仲裁协议的存在或效力有关的任何异议作出裁定”。[②] 目前，国际上的主要公约、国际上的主要贸易国家国内立法均已接受了仲裁庭自裁管辖权原则。[③] 尽管仲裁庭关于是否具有管辖权的裁决会受到法院的审查，但对这一统一的、已被广泛认可的原则不容置疑。

二、自裁管辖权的分类

对于自裁管辖权的分类，国际上通常存在两种理论，即积极自裁管辖权理论和消极自裁管辖权理论，现分别予以介绍。

---

① 1961年《欧洲国际商事仲裁公约》第6.3条规定：“当仲裁协议的任何一方在争端提交法院之前，已启动了仲裁程序，缔约国法院被要求处理相同当事人之间的相同内容的争议，或被要求判定仲裁协议是否不存在、是否无效或是否已过期时，法院在仲裁员作出裁决之前，应停止审理仲裁员的管辖权，除非有正当且实质性的理由不这么做。”

② 《UNCITRAL 仲裁示范法》第16(1)条规定，仲裁庭对其管辖权作出裁定的权力包括仲裁庭可以对其管辖权，包括对关于仲裁协议的存在或效力的任何异议作出裁定。为此目的，作为合同一部分的仲裁条款应当视为独立于合同其他条款的一项协议。仲裁庭作出关于合同无效的决定，在法律上不导致仲裁条款无效。

《UNCITRAL 仲裁规则》对仲裁庭管辖权的抗辩，见第23.1条的规定。仲裁庭有权力对其自身管辖权作出裁定，包括对与仲裁协议的存在或效力有关的任何异议作出裁定。为此目的，构成合同一部分的仲裁条款，应视为独立于合同中其他条款的一项协议。仲裁庭作出合同无效的裁定，不应自动造成仲裁条款无效。

③ “自裁管辖权已被主要国际仲裁公约，众多国内法和大多国际仲裁规则所认可。”See Emmanuel Gaillard and John Savage (eds.), *Fouchard Gaillard Goldman On International Commercial Arbitration*, Kluwer Law International, 1999, para. 653, p. 397. “如下面所讨论的，实际上所有的法律制度都认可自裁管辖权原则”，“如果现代仲裁学者能同意一件事，那就是必须允许仲裁员决定其自身的管辖权”。See Gary B. Born, *International Commercial Arbitration*, 2nd ed., Kluwer Law International, 2014, Chapter 7, pp. 1047, 1048, fn. 3.

(一)积极自裁管辖权理论

积极自裁管辖权理论是指仲裁案件提起后,仲裁庭具有首先决定其自身的管辖权的权力。[①] 当事人在法院对起诉称仲裁条款不存在或无效,该司法程序并不阻止仲裁程序的正常进行。这一原则在《UNCITRAL 仲裁示范法》中体现得最为明显,该示范法第 8 条第 2 款规定:"提起本条第 1 款所指诉讼后,在法院对该问题未决期间,(仲裁庭)仍然可以开始或继续进行仲裁程序,并可作出裁决。"仲裁庭如果首先作出了具有管辖权的初步裁决后,不服裁决的当事人将管辖权问题又诉诸法院时,根据积极自裁管辖权的理论和实践,在法院未作出明确要求终止仲裁的命令时,仲裁庭无须中止仲裁程序等待法院对其初步裁决的审理结果,而是可继续审理案件,直至作出最终裁决。这一理论要求仲裁庭一旦启动程序就要自行决定包含管辖权在内的一切涉案问题。这种对解决管辖权及安排仲裁程序的方法具有"积极功效"(the positive effect),已被国际仲裁统一法和世界绝大多数国家的仲裁法所接受,成为国际商事仲裁的一项基本准则和惯常做法。[②]

如果论及积极自裁管辖权理论的不足,那就是有时会造成仲裁庭与法院同时审理仲裁庭管辖权事项的情形,出现平行诉讼(parallel proceedings)。另外,法院毕竟是行使最终决定权的机关,如果法院裁定仲裁庭不具管辖权,仲裁程序就要终止。

(二)消极自裁管辖权理论[③]

消极自裁管辖权理论主要指在仲裁提起前,由谁(是法院还是仲裁庭)来

---

① 加里·B. 博恩教授称:"积极自裁管辖权就是仲裁庭有权考虑和决定对管辖权的质疑问题。"See Gary B. Born, *International Commercial Arbitration*, 2nd ed., Kluwer Law International, 2014. 另外,在该书注脚 133 中,他引用了美国第三巡回法院的裁决,该裁决写道,当事人就管辖权审查的争议,应当允许仲裁员在第一时间对可仲裁性和管辖范围作出决定,而不是要求当事人停止仲裁、要求去法院解决。换句话说,应视仲裁庭有能力对案件是否有管辖权这一争议的问题作出初步决定。

② See Emmanuel Gaillard, John Savage (eds.), *Fouchard Gaillard Goldman On International Commercial Arbitration*, Kluwer Law International, 1999, para. 660, p. 671. 另见《UNCITRAL 仲裁示范法》第 16 条第 1 款和第 3 款规定。

③ 这一概念和理论最早由伊曼纽尔·盖拉德(Emmanuel Gaillard)教授提出。Emmanuel Gaillard, Yas Banifatemi, *Enforcement of Arbitration Agreement and International Arbitral Awards: The New York Convention in Practice*, Cameron May Ltd., 2008, Chapter 8, Negative Effect of Cmpetence-Competence: The Rule of Priority in Favour of The Arbitrators fn. 4.

决定仲裁庭的管辖权问题。具体讲,是指法律如何克服阻碍仲裁的策略以及促使已同意仲裁的当事方通过仲裁去解决商事纠纷的问题。消极自裁管辖权,是从仲裁庭在受理案件后即可一直审理案件的积极管辖权理论与做法引申出来的。“消极”一词是针对法院而言,即要求法院在仲裁庭组成之前,对一方当事人对仲裁协议的“门槛挑战”(gateway issue or challenge)要进行自我限制,即除仲裁协议属不存在或不明显存在无效外,法院要放弃管辖,要让仲裁庭起码能够先有机会和权力决定其自身的管辖权问题。[①] 正如伊曼纽尔·盖拉德所言,“消极作用同样重要,仲裁员虽然不是唯一的‘法官’,但在管辖权决定上是首先的裁判者。因此,自裁管辖权的原则要求法院在面对一项有关仲裁庭管辖权的请求时(例如,仲裁庭的组成或仲裁协议的效力),在仲裁员有机会就管辖权作出裁决之前,不要就仲裁员管辖权的实体辩论进行听证”。[②] 这一理论体现仲裁庭对其管辖权具有排他性的决定权。消极自裁管辖权不但具有积极特性(positive dimension),即在仲裁开始时由仲裁庭决定其管辖权;还具有消极特性(negative dimension),即排除法院在仲裁开始之前或在仲裁开始时,对仲裁庭的管辖权进行审理。消极自裁管辖权理论实际是要求在仲裁庭与法院之间针对仲裁管辖权裁定的时间确定一个先后顺序,仲裁庭具有第一审理、决定其自身管辖权的机会与权力,法院只有在仲裁庭作出有管辖权的初步裁决或最终裁决后,应不服仲裁庭具有管辖权决定的当事人的请求,才可就仲裁协议存在、效力或范围进行司法审查。实行消极自裁管辖权的功能和意义主要是能更有效阻止可能存在的一方当事人对仲裁程序的拖延甚至破坏的策略,避免仲裁庭与法院就同一管辖权问题并行、重复诉讼,浪费司法资源。该理念要求法律和法院相信仲裁庭对管辖权审理、裁决的能力,要求法院将司法审查推迟到仲裁庭作出管辖权的裁决之后,或者在败诉方要求撤裁或拒绝承认与执行裁决时再行使。另外,对于以主张不存在有效仲裁协议,或无法实施、超出仲裁协议范

---

① See Gary B. Born, *International Commercial Arbitration*, 2nd ed., Kluwer Law International, 2014, p. 1069.

② Emmanuel Gaillard, John Savage (eds.), *Fouchard Gaillard Goldman On International Commercial Arbitration*, Kluwer Law International, 1999, para. 660.

围而反对仲裁的当事方来说,其完全可以向仲裁庭提出该类主张。如其主张未被仲裁庭接受且仲裁庭作出具有管辖权的临时裁决或最终裁决,该当事人依然有机会诉诸司法审查。① 由于法院只有在应当事方请求,在撤销或承认、执行仲裁庭裁决时才会进行司法审查,此时有管辖权的法院又相对集中,层级较高,审判裁决水平更为可靠,有利于维护仲裁制度的严肃性。② 消极自裁管辖权的理论认为,"仲裁功效"应优于对质疑仲裁当事方的"合法利益"的考虑,因为毕竟后者还具有司法救济的机会,可以从司法诉讼中追索其在仲裁中失去的利益。实行消极自裁管辖权原则以体现在《UNCITRAL 仲裁示范法》和《欧洲国际商事公约》中的规定的国家目前主要有法国、瑞士、印度。③ 另外,该原则还被加拿大安大略法院以及我国香港特别行政区法院所接受。④

消极自裁管辖权的缺点是反对仲裁的当事方必须参加仲裁程序,有可能浪费时间与费用,但客观上这种现象很少,问题并不严重。正如帕克教授所说言,

---

① 帕克(Park)教授在评论法国消极自裁管辖权时说:"这一理论似乎是,相比一个错误地加入仲裁的当事方来说,一个被错误地阻止提起仲裁的当事方更值得关注。为了解决后者的风险(扰乱仲裁的拖延策略),法院在仲裁开始前只能够有限地审查仲裁条款的有效性,并且在仲裁开始后,无权审查任何问题。" William W. Park, "Arbitrator's Jurisdiction to Determine Jurisdiction, V. Items for Further Consideration", in Albert Jan van den Berg (ed.), *International Arbitration* 2006: *Back to Basics? ICCA Congress Series*, Vol. 13, KluwerLawInternational, 2007, pp. 112-144.

② See Emmanuel Gaillard, John Savage (eds.), *Fouchard Gaillard Goldman On International Commercial Arbitration*, Kluwer Law International, 1999, para. 681.

③ 见《UNCITRAL 仲裁示范法》第 16(1)(3)条及 *Fouchard Gaillard Goldman On International Commercial Arbitration*, Kluwer Law International, 1999, paras. 680-682。1961 年《欧洲国际商事公约》第 6.3 条规定:当仲裁协议的任何一方在争端提交法院之前,已启动了仲裁程序,缔约国法院被要求处理相同当事人之间的相同内容的争议,或被要求判定仲裁协议是否不存在、是否无效或是否已过期时,法院在仲裁员作出裁决之前,应停止审理仲裁员的管辖权,除非有正当且实质性的理由不这么做。

④ 参见加拿大安大略法院案例:Ontario Court of Justice, Mar. 1, 1991, Rio Algom Ltd. v. Sammi Steel Co. Ltd, XVIII Y. B. Com. ARB, 166(1993);香港高等法院案例:Hong Kong Supreme Court, July 30, 1992, Pacific International Lines(Pte)Ltd. v. Tsinlien Metals and Minerals Co. Ltd., XVIII Y. B. Com. ARB. 180(1993)。上述两案均接受了消极自裁管辖权原则。另见 Emmanuel Gaillard, John Savage (eds.), *Fouchard Gaillard Goldman On International Commercial Arbitration*, Kluwer Law International, 1999, para. 660, fn. 98。

仲裁法更关心的是仲裁程序的不被拖延。①

仲裁庭的自裁管辖权原则,是被《UNCITRAL 仲裁示范法》确定的国际仲裁法的原则。仲裁条款是仲裁庭确定其管辖权以及开展审理案件的工具与钥匙,也是仲裁庭处理自裁管辖权的依据。通过仲裁一个程序解决当事人之间的纠纷,包括仲裁协议的存在、效力以及仲裁范围问题,是对当事人意旨的尊重,可以节约诉讼成本,提高效率。如果仲裁条款约定的争议范围比较广泛,如约定"产生于合同或与合同有关的所有争议均提交仲裁解决",就应视为当事人同意将有关管辖权的争议首先交由仲裁庭裁决,法院在仲裁庭作出裁定后才能应申请进行司法审查。

总之,仲裁条款的自治原则是当事人之间达成的一项意在将已发生或将发生的商业纠纷,包括针对仲裁庭管辖权的纠纷,交由仲裁庭解决的独立合同。仲裁庭根据仲裁协议、适用仲裁的法律与规则,以及当事人的陈述与提交的证据,确定自己的管辖权,这是被广泛认可的国际规则与做法。

三、自裁管辖权的法理依据

仲裁庭具有自裁管辖权的法理依据,根据国际仲裁法学理论以及各国司法实践,可以归纳为如下几点。

(一)仲裁协议独立原则赋予仲裁庭自裁管辖权

仲裁条款的独立性原则,是指仲裁条款独立于含有仲裁条款的主合同。一个商事合同通常可分为两部分:一部分是约定当事人之间有关商事交易权利与义务的主合同(the underlying contract);另一部分是约定一旦当事人间就交易事项发生争议,应如何解决争议的仲裁条款,该条款独立于主合同,形成一个独

① See William W. Park, "Arbitrator's Jurisdiction to Determine Jurisdiction, V. Items for Further Consideration", in Albert Jan van den Berg (ed.), *International Arbitration* 2006: *Back to Basics? ICCA Congress Series*, Vol. 13, Kluwer Law International, 2007, pp. 112-144.

立的合同。欧洲国家特别是法国,倾向以“自治原则”(the principle of autonomy)①来表示仲裁条款独立性,而英美普通法系则倾向使用“分离原则”来表示仲裁条款独立性,②二者含义基本相同。仲裁条款独立性是仲裁理论一个十分重要的原则,在国际上被广泛认可。③ 仲裁条款的独立原则被视为仲裁

① 1963年法国最高法院曾裁决道:国际仲裁中,无论是分别达成还是包括在有关合同中的仲裁协议,应具有“完全的法律自治性”(full legal autonomy),不应受到前述合同可能无效事实的影响。See Caseleciv., May7, 1963, Ets. Raymond Gossetv. Carapelli, JCP, Ed. G., Pt. II, No. 13, 405(1963). 该判决但书部分曾含有“除例外情况”字样,后来法院判决均不再提该但书内容。See Emmanuel Gaillard, John Savage (eds.), *Fouchard Gaillard Goldman On International Commercial Arbitration*, Kluwer Law International, 1999, paras. 389-392. 福查德·盖拉德·高曼(Fouchard Gaillard Goldman)称:仲裁条款的“自治原则”是欧洲已经牢固确立的概念,英美法学者倾向于使用 severability、separability 或 detachment 的概念,担心使用 autonomy 会与传统的所谓仲裁条款独立于国内法的“独立原则”相混淆。基于这一原则,即便主合同是无效的或属可撤销的,也不直接影响仲裁条款的效力,不直接影响仲裁庭的管辖权,因为仲裁协议独立于主合同的原则足以对抗因主合同无效,进而使包含在主合同中的仲裁条款也无效的主张。另外,宋连斌称:其内容要而言之,即仲裁庭对当事人提出的管辖权异议有管辖权,因此被形象地称为管辖权/管辖权或权限/权限原则(Kompetenz-Kompetenz, Competence-Competence),理论上或称为管辖权/管辖权理论。参见宋连斌:《国际商事仲裁管辖权研究》,法律出版社2000年版,第208~214页。

② “分离原则”(the principle of separability or severability),在美国由美国最高法院在 Prima Paint 案确定,后来案件也一直遵循这一原则。See Prima Paint Corp. v. Flood & Conklin Mfg. Co., 388U. S. 395 (1967); John J. Barceló, “Who Decides the Arbitrators' Jurisdiction? Separability and Competence-Competence in Transnational Perspective”, *Vanderbilt Journal of Transnational Law*, pp. 1119-1122.

③ “自裁管辖权是对仲裁协议独立原则的一个推断。”[That principle (of compétence-compétence) is often presented as the corollary of the principle of the autonomy of the arbitration agreement.]“仲裁协议的独立性,自然是允许仲裁员能决定其自身仲裁管辖权的第一步。”(The principle of autonomy is of course the first stage of the process which results in the arbitrators being able to determine their own jurisdiction.)“正是由于仲裁条款的自治原则,才不使主合同在某种程度上无效或可撤销而直接影响仲裁协议以及仲裁员的管辖权问题。”(It is thanks to the autonomy of the arbitration agreement that any claim that the main contract is in some way void or voidable will have no direct on the arbitration agreement and on the jurisdiction of the arbitrators.) See Emmanuel Gaillard, John Savage (eds.), *Fouchard Gaillard Goldman On International Commercial Arbitration*, Kluwer Law International, 1999, para. 416. 加里·B. 博恩提道:“如上面所讨论的,有时自裁管辖权是来源于,或基于分离原则。特别是许多国家的仲裁法和仲裁机构的规则包含将分离原则与仲裁庭自裁管辖权的条联系在一起,学者有时也做如此联系。”(As discussed above, it is sometimes said that the competence-competence principle is derived from, or dependent on, the separability presumption. In particular, many national arbitration statutes and institutional rules contain provisions whose text links the separability presumption with the competence-competence of arbitral tribunals, while commentators sometimes make the same connection.)在引用了《UNCITRAL 仲裁示范法》第16条之后,加里·B. 博恩认为,“文本起码默示显示,仲裁条款的分离原则解释了仲裁庭具有裁决其管辖权的权力理由”。See Gary B. Born, *International Commercial Arbitration*, 2nd ed., Kluwer Law International, 2014, p. 1071. “情况是,自裁管辖权显示为仲裁协议自治原则的第二个后果。另外,当事人间就管辖权问题存在争议时,自裁管辖权授权仲裁员有权决定其权限的目标和限制。” See Gary B. Born, *International Commercial Arbitration*, 2nd ed., Kluwer Law International, 2014, fn. 142.

庭自裁管辖权的基础和前提条件,[①]自裁管辖权是仲裁协议独立原则的一个结果。如果没有仲裁条款的独立原则,仲裁庭就无法在宣告主合同无效的情况下继续行使其对该案争议的管辖权。[②] 然而,仅凭仲裁条款的独立原则仍无法支持仲裁庭解决其管辖权问题,因为独立原则根本未提仲裁庭的自裁管辖权,是自裁管辖权原则才赋予仲裁庭有权决定其自身的管辖权问题。因此,仲裁条款的独立原则与仲裁庭的自裁管辖权关系虽然密不可分,[③]但功能仍存在不同,前者为因,后者为果,两个原则在立法上应同时存在。

从总的功能上讲,两个原则具有共同的目标,即支持和维护仲裁的基本理

---

① "很明显,在解决管辖权争议上仲裁协议的独立性更可取,因为它给了仲裁员存在的基础,即便主张主合同因履行或依法被终止也是如此。" See Sigvard Jarvin, Chapter7, "Objection to Jurisdiction" in Lawrence W. Newman, Richard D. Hill (ed.), *The Leading Arbitrators'Guide to International Arbitration*, Second Edition, Juris Publish ing, Inc., 2008. 鲁本(Reuben)认为,"当仲裁条款包含在一个大的合同之中而且争议是关于大的合同的合法性问题时,传统的观点(起码是20世纪的后50年)是仲裁员,而不是法院,决定大合同的有效性。仲裁条款被视为是有效的协议,其分离于并独立于大的合同。这就是分离原则,是基于对可仲裁性的默示同意原则"。See Richard C. Reuben, "First Options, Concent to Arbitration, and The Demise of Separability: Restoring Access to Justice for Contracts with Arbitration Provisions", *S. M. U. L. Rev.*, 56, 2003, p. 838.

② 福查德·盖拉德·高曼认为,仲裁法的一项实质原则是仲裁员有权裁决其自身的管辖权(自裁管辖权)。仲裁条款的自治原则超出了"自裁管辖权"规则,"自裁管辖权"规则允许仲裁员审查其自身的管辖权。仲裁员如果发现主合同无效,仅依靠"自裁管辖权"规则就无其他选择,只能放弃管辖;"自裁管辖权"是对仲裁协议独立原则的一个推断。See Emmanuel Gaillard, John Savage (eds.), *Fouchard Gaillard Goldman On International Commercial Arbitration*, Kluwer Law International, 1999, para. 416. 谈到二者的关系,帕克教授说,尽管事后可能受到司法审查,自裁管辖权允许仲裁庭审理、裁定仲裁条款的效力,但如果没有分离原则,仅凭自裁管辖权,仲裁庭就无法宣告主合同无效,而其管辖权却不受到影响。See William W. Park, "Determining Arbitral Jurisdiction: Allocation of Tasks between Courts and Arbitrators", *American Review of International Arbitration*, 8, 1997.

③ 福查德·盖拉德·高曼认为,这两个原则(仲裁条款的自治原则和自裁管辖权)虽然紧密相连并具有相似目标,仅部分重叠。See Emmanuel Gaillard, John Savage (eds.), *Fouchard Gaillard Goldman On International Commercial Arbitration*, Kluwer Law International, 1999, para. 416.

念,尽量减少甚至杜绝司法的不当干预。①

应当指出的是,仲裁条款独立于主合同并非是当事人订立合同时的约定,而是仲裁法学家们出于有利于仲裁和纠纷解决的政策考虑对仲裁法理的创设。② 仲裁条款的独立原则为仲裁庭提供了一个全面审理当事人协议的方法,是支持仲裁、有利于仲裁的体现。③

（二）当事人授权赋予仲裁庭自裁管辖权

仲裁是商事纠纷解决的一种方式,完全由合同当事人通过合同约定决定。因此,当事人同意以仲裁方式解决纠纷,由仲裁庭决定仲裁管辖权的前提条件是当事人的意旨或授权。这是被国际条约、主要贸易国家的法律及实践所承认

---

① “首先,二者具有共同的目标,均在于支持仲裁,使仲裁程序能顺利开展。”See Gary B. Born, *International Commercial Arbitration*, 2nd ed. , Kluwer Law International, 2014, p. 1071, fn. 142. 帕克教授认为,分离原则与自裁管辖权只在一点上交叉,即当仲裁员裁决其管辖权时(就如同法院决定可否允许仲裁程序继续进行一样),其仅仅审查仲裁条款,而不是审查整个合同。See William W. Park, “Determining Arbitral Jurisdiction: Allocation of Tasks between Courts and Arbitrators”, *American Review of International Arbitration*, 8, 1997. 约翰·J. 巴塞罗称:“分离原则与自裁管辖权是国际商事仲裁中最重要的两个概念. 它们内涵不同,但经常联系在一起,因为它们具有共同的目标:阻止司法过早地对仲裁进行干预,破坏仲裁程序。两个概念都涉及谁决定的问题,即‘是法院还是仲裁员决定可仲裁性问题’”。See John J. Barceló, “Who Decides the Arbitrators' Jurisdiction? Separability and Competence-Competence in Transnational Perspective”, *Vanderbilt Journal of Transnational Law*, p. 1116. 格拉菲(Graffi)认为“自治概念与自裁管辖权原则紧密相连,因为……两个理论均在于保护仲裁,反对司法控制机制”。See Leonardo Graffi, “The Law Applicable to the Internation Arbitration”, in Franco Ferrari, Stepfen Kröll(ed.), *Conflict of Laws in International, Arbitration*, Earopean Law Publishers, 2011, pp. 19-62.

② “仲裁条款独立性理论是20世纪60年代以后流行起来的关于仲裁条款的有效性及自裁管辖权的学说,它已得到世界各国的广泛接受和采纳,成为现代仲裁的重要理论和实践。”“仲裁条款独立理论的产生与第二次世界大战后仲裁的发展以及各国对仲裁实行的自由、宽容和支持政策目标相关,没有这个大环境,这一理论也不可能出现。”参见黄进:《国际商事争议解决机制研究》,武汉大学出版社2010年版,第三章国际商事仲裁机制研究,第105~108页。前国际商会顾问西格瓦德·亚尔温(Sigvard Jarvin)认为,“这一理论或许远非商人签署合同时的想法(而是律师的产品),但现在成了被广泛接受的理论,因为否则仲裁程序就会无效”。See Sigvard Jarvin, Chapter7, “Objection to Jurisdiction” in Lawrence W. Newman, Richard D. Hill(ed.), *The Leading Arbitrators' Guide to International Arbitration*, Second Edition, Juris Publish ing, Inc. , 2008.

③ “近几十年来,司法创设的仲裁理论对国际商事仲裁的法律基础扮演了重要角色,促进了争议解决的自治与有效的平台,特别是‘分离原则’与‘自裁管辖权’理论在法院与仲裁庭之间就有效控制民间商事公正的门槛问题的权力分配作了划分。”See Philip D. O' Neill Jr. , *International Commercial Arbitration Case Studies and materials Exploring Where theory Meets Practice*, American Casebook Series, WEST, 2012, A Thomson Reuters Business, p. 195.

的基本原则,是仲裁庭权力的基础。自然,当事人的授权应当在法律允许的范围内。授权既可体现在仲裁员的指定函或仲裁协议之中,亦可体现在适用于仲裁程序的仲裁规则之中,二者自然均要受到适用法律的约束。① "而仲裁庭对其管辖权的决定权,则主要来源于当事人之间已存在的,选择以仲裁作为争议解决方式的有效仲裁协议。"②另外,当事人在仲裁协议中授权仲裁庭决定管辖权问题,既可以是明示的,也可以是默示的。明示是指当事人在指定仲裁员的文件中或在仲裁协议中明确赋予仲裁庭具有决定仲裁协议存在、效力及仲裁范围的权力;默示授权通常指依当事人之间的贸易过程所采用的惯例,探求当事人具有通过仲裁庭解决其管辖权问题的意旨。③

当然,当事人在签订仲裁协议时,鲜少明确授权仲裁庭自裁管辖权,仲裁庭大多是运用默示规则或通过对仲裁条款的解释来确定仲裁条款的存在、效力以及仲裁庭的职责范围,特别是当仲裁条款用语较为宽泛时就更是如此。例如,"凡因本合同引起的或与本合同有关的任何争议"的约定,就应被视为赋予了仲裁庭对管辖权的审理与裁决。

(三)法律赋予仲裁庭自裁管辖权

国际仲裁学者大多认为,仲裁庭的自裁管辖权还基于适用于仲裁条款或适用于仲裁地的法律、相关国际条约或公约,以及基于承认仲裁庭管辖权决定的

---

① 雷德芬(Redfern)将前者称为"直接授权",即指当事人明示仲裁庭收集证据、指定专家、举行听证会、传唤证人以及审理争议等;将后者称为"间接授权",指设立仲裁庭的仲裁机构的仲裁规则开展仲裁程序。See Nigel Blakaby, Constantine Partasides QC, Alan Redfern, Martin Hunter, Chapter 5: B. Power of Arbitrators, Powers, Duties, and Jurisdiction of AnArbitral Tribunal, *Redfern and Hunter on International Arbitration*, 6nd ed., Oxford University Press, 2015, p. 307.

② 赵秀文主编:《国际商事仲裁法》(第2版),中国人民大学出版社2014年版,第四章"仲裁庭及其管辖权限"。

③ 帕克教授列举了一个瑞士案例和一个德国案例。前一个案例显示,尽管货主并非提单的签字方,但长期的交易史证明货主接受了提单的仲裁条款;后一个案例是关于羊皮买卖的纠纷,买方在解除合同后要求卖方退回其已支付的货款,卖方要求仲裁,法院称贸易惯例足以证明双方当事人已经放弃了法院的管辖权。See William W. Park, "Determining Arbitral Jurisdiction: Allocation of Tasks between Courts and Arbitrators", *American Review of International Arbitration*, 8, 1997.

国家的法律。[①] 仲裁法学者认为,仲裁庭的自裁管辖权起初可能是来源于国际公法的“每个法庭是其自身管辖权的法官”的基本概念,如《国际法院规约》规定的关于法院有无管辖权之争端,“由法院裁决之”。《UNCITRAL 仲裁示范法》以及近代相关国际条约几乎都规定了仲裁庭的自裁管辖权制度。[②]《关于解决国家和他国国民之间投资争议公约》(以下简称《ICSID 公约》)第 41 条规定:“仲裁庭应是其本身权限的决定人。”

世界主要贸易国家的仲裁法也对仲裁庭有权决定管辖权进行了立法,为自裁管辖权机制在国内的适用提供了法源基础,特别是那些接受了《UNCITRAL

---

① 福查德·盖拉德·高曼认为:“答案很简单:自裁管辖权原则的基础并非依赖于仲裁协议,而是基于仲裁地的法律,更广泛地说,是基于有责任对仲裁员作出的有关管辖权的仲裁裁决的所有国家的法律。”See Emmanuel Gaillard, John Savage(eds.), *Fouchard Gaillard Goldman On International Commercial Arbitration*, Kluwer Law International, 1999, para. 658; John J. Barceló, “Who Decides the Arbitrators' Jurisdiction? Separability and Competence-Competence in Transnational Perspective”, *Vanderbilt Journal of Transnational Law*, p. 1132, fn. 82. 该脚注称:“有意思的是,法国的评论家们并不试图从当事方的协议来解释法国理论的源泉,而是从仲裁地或寻求对裁决的承认与执行地国家的仲裁法来解释其渊泉。”“仲裁,特别是国际仲裁的情况(与法院)不同,仲裁庭的权力、义务和管辖权产生于当事人意旨、管辖仲裁协议的法律、仲裁地法律,以及承认或寻求执行仲裁裁决地法律的发展混合体。” Nigel Blakaby, Constantine Partasides QC with Alan Redfern, Martin Hunter, *Redfern and Hunter on International Arbitration*, 6nd ed., Oxford University Press, 2015, pp. 133-145, Chapter 5: B. Power of Arbitrators, Powers, Duties, and Jurisdiction of An Arbitral Tribunal.

② 《UNCITRAL 仲裁示范法》第四章“仲裁庭的管辖权”第 16 条规定:“仲裁庭对其管辖权作出裁定的权力:(1)仲裁庭可以对其管辖权,包括对关于仲裁协议的存在或效力的任何异议作出裁定,为此目的,构成合同一部分的仲裁条款应当视为独立于合同其他条款的一项协议。仲裁庭作出关于合同无效的决定,在法律上不导致仲裁条款无效。”《ICSID 公约》第 41 条规定:“(1)仲裁庭应是其本身权限的决定人。(2)争端一方提出的反对意见,认为该争端不属于中心的管辖范围,或因其他原因不属于仲裁庭的权限范围,仲裁庭应加以考虑,并决定是否将其作为先决问题处理,或与该争端的是非曲直一并处理。”1961 年《欧洲国际商事仲裁公约》第 5 条关于仲裁管辖权的抗辩第 3 款规定:“以事后法院地司法审查为限,仲裁庭的管辖权受到质疑时,应有权进行仲裁,裁决其管辖权,决定构成合同一部分的仲裁协议的存在及效力。”第 6 条第 3 款规定:“仲裁协议一方在诉诸法院之前已启动仲裁程序,缔约方法院随后要求处理仲裁协议是否不存在、或无效、或已失效问题,法院在仲裁庭作出裁决之前,应停止对仲裁员管辖权的裁定,除非法院具有正当、重大的相反理由。”《世界知识产权组织仲裁规则》关于仲裁庭管辖权的抗辩的第 36 条规定:“(a)仲裁庭有权对关于仲裁庭管辖权的异议,包括依照第 61 条(c)款的规定提出的关于仲裁协议的形式、存在、效力或范围的任何异议,进行审理并作出决定;(b)仲裁庭有权对仲裁协议所属的或与仲裁协议有关的任何合同的存在或效力作出决定。”

仲裁示范法》的国家。[①] 在此应特别提到法国的理论,其认为仲裁庭的自裁管辖权原则是源于国内法,而非当事人之间的仲裁协议。

自然,凡是那些立法认可仲裁庭自裁管辖权以及那些接受了《UNCITRAL仲裁示范法》的国家的仲裁机构,也都于仲裁规则中定有仲裁庭自裁管辖权的条文。仲裁规则是仲裁机构所在地国国内立法的体现,然而,仅有仲裁规则对仲裁庭自裁管辖权的规定,无仲裁机构所在地法律的支撑,会导致仲裁规则缺乏法律基础,进而使仲裁庭的关于管辖权的裁决存在风险。

四、自裁管辖权决定的"三段式(接力棒)"理论

国际上通常按仲裁的整个流程,在管辖权的决定上分为三个阶段。第一阶段为合同当事人争议发生、仲裁尚未启动的阶段。此时如一方当事人不同意将纠纷交由仲裁解决,企图诉诸法院,要求法院确定仲裁条款的存在、效力问题。这时法院是唯一可以对这些问题进行审理、裁定的机构。依据《承认及执行外国仲裁裁决公约》(以下简称《纽约公约》)的规定,法院如果发现存在仲裁条款,应指令当事人通过仲裁解决争议。但法院如果发现仲裁条款不存在或无效,亦可直接进行管辖、审理争议。第二阶段指案件已提交仲裁或仲裁庭已经组成,仲裁庭可依据仲裁法律和仲裁规则下达程序令,确定当事人提交陈述意见与证据、开庭审理,直至作出裁决。对于管辖权问题,仲裁庭可以根据当事人的请求,首先就管辖权作出初步裁决,然后应当事人申请由法院进行司法审查。应当指出的是,即便当事人将仲裁庭具有管辖权的初步裁决诉诸法院,此时仲裁庭的程序亦应照常进行。如果判定管辖权问题与案件实体问题纠缠在一起,仲裁庭也可以在最终裁决时,就管辖权问题与实体问题一并作出裁决。仲裁庭对管辖权无论是作出初步裁决还是最终裁决,法院对管辖权都具有最终的审查与决定权。但应指出的是,在整个第二阶段,即便存在法院对自裁管辖权的审理程序,仲裁程序无须中止,可照常进行,除非法院作出仲裁庭无管辖权的决

---

① 至2017年4月,国际上有74个国家共在104个法域通过了以《UNCITRAL仲裁示范法》为基础的国内仲裁立法。

定。第三阶段为仲裁庭作出具有管辖权的初步裁决,或将管辖权问题与实体问题一起作出终局裁决后的阶段。此时,无论属于哪种裁决,依当事人的请求,法院应在当事人申请撤裁或申请拒绝承认与执行时,审查仲裁庭的管辖权问题。

“三段式”的理论与实践可以清晰、有效地解决仲裁庭与法院之间的权责划分问题。[①] 一旦一方当事人质疑仲裁庭的管辖权问题,依时间段可以清晰地确定由谁(是仲裁庭还是法院)来决定仲裁庭的管辖权问题。

在体现尊重仲裁庭关于具有管辖权裁决的问题上,法院如果认为仲裁庭关于管辖权的裁决合情合理,具有说服力,就可以核准仲裁庭的裁决;如果认为相反,亦可驳回仲裁庭关于管辖权的裁决,重新审查(de novo review)并作出最终决定。

“三段式”决定仲裁庭管辖权的理论与实践具有一定的积极意义。首先,在仲裁程序未开始的第一阶段,将仲裁管辖权问题交由法院决定是客观上的唯一可以选择的路径。其次,当事人可以在仲裁庭组成前求助法院裁定仲裁协议的存在、效力或仲裁范围问题,而不一定非得等待仲裁程序开始后再解决这些问题。体现当事人确想认真解决问题、具有诚实信用品质的行为,是法律应予鼓励的。另外,一旦组成仲裁庭,仲裁程序即应依规则顺利进行,可以提高仲裁的效率与功能,能体现仲裁程序的完整性。最后,仲裁庭可以在初步裁决或最终裁决中作出具有管辖权的决定。应当事人申请,法院依然是作出仲裁庭是否

---

① 约翰·J. 巴塞罗教授认为:第一阶段包括诉讼,一般来说是在纠纷开始之时,由法院决定是应当审理纠纷还是将案件移交给仲裁庭;第二阶段,则由仲裁员决定审理或拒绝审理案件;第三阶段,则由法院审查仲裁庭的裁决(包括撤销裁决或者对裁决的承认与执行),判定仲裁员对案件是否有正当管辖权。See John J. BarcelÓ, “Who Decides the Arbitrators’ Jurisdiction? Separability and Competence-Competence in Transnational Perspective”, *Vanderbilt Journal of Transnational Law*, p. 1118. 英国法官马克斯狄尔(Mustill)将仲裁庭和法院对仲裁庭管辖权决定权比喻为“接力棒赛”(relay race)。他说,理想的是,处理仲裁纠纷就如同一场接力赛。在开始阶段,在仲裁员处理纠纷之前,接力棒在法院手中,因为在这个阶段,没有其他组织机构能够采取措施阻止仲裁协议无效。当仲裁员接过案件后,就接过了接力棒。仲裁员接过接力棒并一直保留到他们作出裁决之时止。在此时间点上,仲裁员不再具有任何职能,将接力棒交还给法院,以使法院在需要时,能以强制力执行裁决。See Nigel Blakaby, Constantine Partasides QC with Alan Redfern, Martin Hunter, Chapter 5: B. Power of Arbitrators, Powers, Duties, and Jurisdiction of AnArbitral Tribunal, *Redfern and Hunter on International Arbitration*, 6nd ed., Oxford University Press, 2015, p. 418.

具有管辖权的最终决定机关,反对仲裁的当事人依然具有权利救济的机会。

因此,最理想的仲裁制度应是法院在第一与第三阶段行使对仲裁庭管辖权的司法审查权。案件只要进入第二阶段,仲裁案件就应掌控在仲裁庭手中,由其处理仲裁案件的管辖权问题。当然,一方当事人对仲裁庭关于具有管辖权的裁决持有不同意见的,其完全有权再寻求法院的救济,获得法院的最终裁决。

五、中国目前关于自裁管辖权的现状

(一)仲裁法认可分离原则

我国《仲裁法》承认仲裁条款的独立原则。该法第19条第1款规定:"仲裁协议独立存在,合同的变更、解除、终止或者无效,不影响仲裁协议的效力。"这体现了国际仲裁统一法与世界主要贸易国家关于自裁管辖权制度的基本原则,是值得肯定的,也为今后修改我国《仲裁法》以及正式确立自裁管辖权奠定了良好的基础。

(二)仲裁庭自裁管辖权授予了仲裁委员会或法院

我国《仲裁法》对仲裁庭的自裁管辖权规定由权仲裁机构或法院决定。我国《仲裁法》第20条第1款规定:"当事人对仲裁协议的效力有异议的,可以请求仲裁委员会作出决定或者请求人民法院作出裁定。一方请求仲裁委员会作出决定,另一方请求人民法院作出裁定的,由人民法院裁定。"

此条的含义是:(1)只有在中国依法设立的仲裁委员会或法院才具有决定仲裁协议效力的权力;(2)在决定管辖权问题上,法院具有强于仲裁委员会的权力;(3)法律并未述及仲裁庭有权决定其管辖权问题。

这一规定受到了国际学者的注意与评论。例如,有的学者在谈到仲裁庭自裁管辖权时说:"一个例外就是中国法,仲裁庭没有自裁管辖权,管辖权或由仲裁地的仲裁机构决定或由法院决定。"①

① Julian D. M. Lew, Loukas A. Mustelis, Stefan M. Kroll, *Comparative International Commercail Arbitration*, Kluwer Law International, 2003, p. 333. 加里·B. 博恩认为,中国的仲裁法继续对仲裁员的自裁管辖权表示怀疑,并将解决管辖权纠纷的权力,通常情况下保留给中国法院和仲裁机构。See Gary B. Born, *International Commercial Arbitration*, 2nd ed., Kluwer Law International, 2014, p. 1064.

（三）仲裁规则的规定

2015年《中国国际经济贸易仲裁委员会仲裁规则》第6条对仲裁协议及/或管辖权的异议规定："（一）仲裁委员会有权对仲裁协议的存在、效力以及仲裁案件的管辖权作出决定。如有必要，仲裁委员会也可以授权仲裁庭作出管辖权决定。（二）仲裁委员会依表面证据认为存在有效仲裁协议的，可根据表面证据作出仲裁委员会有管辖权的决定，仲裁程序继续进行。仲裁委员会依表面证据作出的管辖权决定并不妨碍其根据仲裁庭在审理过程中发现的与表面证据不一致的事实及/或证据重新作出管辖权决定。（三）仲裁庭依据仲裁委员会的授权作出管辖权决定时，可以在仲裁程序进行中单独作出，也可以在裁决书中一并作出。（四）当事人对仲裁协议及/或仲裁案件管辖权的异议，应当在仲裁庭首次开庭前书面提出；书面审理的案件，应当在第一次实体答辩前提出。（五）对仲裁协议及/或仲裁案件管辖权提出异议不影响仲裁程序的继续进行。（六）上述管辖权异议及/或决定包括仲裁案件主体资格异议及/或决定……"

在当前仲裁法律制度的基础上，这应是中国国际经济贸易仲裁委员会在仲裁规则中对我国《仲裁法》第20条最好的具体化和选择。除重申"仲裁委员会有权对仲裁协议的存在、效力以及仲裁案件的管辖权作出决定"外，提出了"也可以授权仲裁庭作出管辖权决定"的变通做法。同时，规定虽然一方当事人可能存在管辖权异议，但仲裁庭可继续开展程序。另外，对仲裁庭何时可作出管辖权裁决、当事人应何时提出管辖权异议、管辖范围等也作出了规定。首先，2015年《中国国际经济贸易仲裁委员会仲裁规则》关于"授权"这一规定并无仲裁法上的基础。其次，"也可以"字样说明仲裁庭有可能被授权，决定管辖权的权力依然握在委员会手中。客观情况是，仲裁机构从不直接开庭实体审理当事人之间关于管辖权的争议，难怪被加里·B.博恩讲"有点古怪"。[①]

① 少数例外之一，就是《中国国际经济贸易仲裁委员会仲裁规则》，该规则规定由仲裁机构（中国国际经济贸易仲裁委员会）而非仲裁庭来考虑对管辖权的异议。中国国际经济贸易仲裁委员会可以授权仲裁庭行使此项权力，但并不要求一定这么做。中国国际经济贸易仲裁委员会的做法和中国《仲裁法》对自裁管辖权的规定是一致的，但这种做法是古怪的，也无可取之处，同时该做法还要受到中国国际经济贸易仲裁委员会的内部审查。See Gary B. Born, *International Commercial Arbitration*, 2nd ed., Kluwer Law International, 2014, pp. 1066-1067.

(四)司法解释

1. 控制宣告仲裁协议无效的通知

1995年最高人民法院为控制地方法院在宣告涉外仲裁条款无效方面的随意性,曾发布了《关于人民法院处理与涉外仲裁及外国仲裁事项有关问题的通知》(以下简称《通知》),[①]意在限制受理和裁决“仲裁条款或者仲裁协议无效、失效或者内容不明确无法执行”。立意无疑是积极的,在于控制地方法院任意宣告仲裁条款无效的情况。但该《通知》未提及是在前文“三个阶段”中的哪个阶段的起诉。可以想象,如果仲裁程序已经开始,被申请人将管辖权问题既诉诸仲裁机构,又诉诸法院,在法院受理案件或在“暂不予受理”期间,仲裁程序如何进展?这是《通知》没有回答的问题。[②] 因此,如能明确诉讼应在第一个阶段,会更能体现支持仲裁的政策。另外,《纽约公约》第2条第3款规定:“当事人就诉讼事项订有本条所称之(仲裁)协定者,缔约国法院受理诉讼时应依当事人一造之请求,命当事人提交仲裁,但前述协定经法院认定无效、失效或不能实行者不在此限。”该条主旨含义是,法院要求当事人在合同存在仲裁条款的情况下通过仲裁解决纠纷,是以积极态度立法的。但书部分只是在法院发现仲裁协议“无效、失效或不能实行者”时,才可受理案件。[③] 因此,最高人民法院的《通知》并未把法院的时间程序问题规定清楚。例如,受案法院在多长时间内要作出决定,何时上报,高级人民法院多长时间内要作出“审查”,以及最高人

---

① 参见1995年8月28日最高人民法院《关于人民法院处理与涉外仲裁及外国仲裁事项有关问题的通知》,其中第1点规定:“凡起诉到人民法院的涉外、涉港澳和涉台经济、海事海商纠纷案件,如果当事人在合同中订有仲裁条款或者事后达成仲裁协议,人民法院认为该仲裁条款或者仲裁协议无效、失效或者内容不明确无法执行的,在决定受理一方当事人起诉之前,必须报请本辖区所属高级人民法院进行审查;如果高级人民法院同意受理,应将其审查意见报最高人民法院。在最高人民法院未作答复前,可暂不予受理。”

② 笔者了解的另一起仲裁案为,仲裁庭已作出具有管辖权和法律责任的部分裁决(未作救济方面的最终裁决)之后,被申请人在所在城市的中级人民法院起诉仲裁案外的某第三人(据称是仲裁案申请人的关联公司)。该中级人民法院裁定书称:不管法院判决结果如何都会对仲裁案的最终裁决有影响,认定“仲裁案有中止审理的必要”,裁定仲裁案件的申请人在3日内向仲裁机构申请中止仲裁庭对仲裁案作出最终裁决的审理程序。

③ 注意,《纽约公约》中文文本第2条第3款中,将“refer the parties to arbitration”译为“命当事人提交仲裁”。

民法院何时要作出“答复”等,均未作明确规定。[①]

2. 谁决定仲裁庭管辖权

1998年最高人民法院公布了《关于确认仲裁协议效力几个问题的批复》(以下简称《批复》),试图厘清仲裁委员会与法院在决定管辖权方面的关系。[②]由谁、在何时决定仲裁庭管辖权的问题无论在中国,还是在国际上都是十分重要的问题。最高人民法院在《仲裁法》未作修改的情况下,通过司法解释试图解决这个问题无疑是很好的尝试。

然而,从该《批复》第3点可以有如下理解:(1)如果一方当事人将管辖权异议申请到仲裁委员会,仲裁委员会则有权对仲裁案件的管辖权作出决定;(2)虽然一方当事人向仲裁委员会提出了管辖权异议,在仲裁委员会尚未作出具有管辖权裁决时,如果该当事人又同时向法院提出了同样的管辖权诉讼,此时法院可以受理此诉讼并作出裁决;(3)在前述第二种情况下,法院具有优先处理仲裁管辖权的权力并可通知仲裁委员会终止仲裁审理程序。

国内不少学者认为,这个《批复》大有改进的余地。首先,此《批复》未考虑仲裁申请人通过仲裁解决争议,包括由仲裁庭解决其管辖权问题的期待与其合法权益;其次,如果仲裁程序已经开始,《批复》未考虑仲裁程序的连贯进行问题;最后,《批复》在一定程度上是在鼓励和支持反对仲裁的当事人即便在仲裁程序开始后,依然可以在地方法院就仲裁协议的有效性或仲裁庭的管辖权提起诉讼。[③] 实际上,该《批复》间接拒绝了国际上被普遍认可的积极自裁管辖权的

---

① 笔者了解的某起仲裁案,仲裁程序已经开始,被申请人称仲裁协议约定适用《UNCITRAL仲裁规则》,属临时仲裁,而临时仲裁在中国属于非法,故该仲裁协议无效。被申请人诉至北京某中级人民法院,要求宣告仲裁协议无效。但法院长期不作判决,仲裁程序无法进行,最后当事人最终被迫私了结案。

② 参见1998年10月26日最高人民法院《关于确认仲裁协议效力几个问题的批复》(法释〔1998〕27号)。其中第3点规定:“当事人对仲裁协议的效力有异议,一方当事人申请仲裁机构确认仲裁协议效力,另一方当事人请求人民法院确认仲裁协议无效,如果仲裁机构先于人民法院接受申请并已作出决定,人民法院不予受理;如果仲裁机构接受申请后尚未作出决定,人民法院应予受理,同时通知仲裁机构终止仲裁。”

③ 笔者了解的某起仲裁案件,仲裁程序已经开始,被申请人之一在仲裁程序中提出管辖权异议,是年1月仲裁庭对管辖权问题开庭听证,但该被申请人几乎与此同时在本地中级人民法院提出了仲裁协议效力之诉,该中级人民法院决定是年8月开庭并向国外申请人发出传票,致使仲裁程序不得不中止。1年后,仲裁申请人通知仲裁委员会“我们正等候最高人民法院就此案作出的决定”。

理论与做法,体现了法院高于仲裁机构及仲裁庭的固有观念,缺乏对仲裁的信任与支持。

2006年最高人民法院公布了《关于适用〈中华人民共和国仲裁法〉若干问题的解释》,[①]该司法解释并未废止前面提到的法院的《通知》与《批复》。[②] 可见,仲裁庭的自裁管辖权问题仍然牢牢地掌控在法院的手中。

六、设想与建议

中国于1986年加入《纽约公约》,[③]中国在20世纪80年代曾积极参加UNCITRAL对《UNCITRAL仲裁示范法》和《UNCITRAL仲裁规则》的起草制定工作。[④] 21世纪初,中国仲裁法学者曾集中研究仲裁法的修改问题,并起草了《〈中华人民共和国仲裁法〉(建议修改稿)》。[⑤] 王利明教授主张:"我们要坚持改革。商事仲裁事业的发展,首先我们在理念上要不断革新,理念要与国际接轨……尽量减少行政化和行政干预,使仲裁机构真正成为名副其实的机构"。[⑥]

《UNCITRAL仲裁示范法》是国际商事仲裁发展的基石,代表了当前国际

---

① 参见最高人民法院2006年8月23日发布《关于适用〈中华人民共和国仲裁法〉若干问题的解释》,该解释于2005年12月26日由最高人民法院审判委员会第1375次会议通过,自2006年9月8日起施行。

② 在2017年的某起仲裁案中,某中级人民法院通知:根据最高人民法院《关于确认仲裁协议效力几个问题的批复》(法释〔1998〕27号)第4条之规定,特通知你会中止×××号仲裁案件。待我院审查终结后,将另行向你会送达相应裁定书。

③ 1986年12月2日第六届全国人民代表大会常务委员会第十八次会议决定中国加入《纽约公约》,同时作出"互惠"和"商事"(契约性和非契约性商事法律关系)保留。

④ 《UNCITRAL仲裁规则》,最初系依据1976年12月15日通过的《联合国大会第31/98号决议》颁布。2006年,UNCITRAL决定修订《UNCITRAL仲裁规则》,以适应仲裁实务在过去30年间的变化,提高按照《UNCITRAL仲裁规则》进行仲裁的效率,并保持该文书原有的结构、精神或文体不变。2010年12月6日,联合国大会以"65/22号决议"正式通过《UNCITRAL仲裁规则》2010年修订本,修订后的《UNCITRAL仲裁规则》自2011年8月15日起生效,其中:对多当事方仲裁、并入程序、赔偿责任、对仲裁庭所指定的专家提出反对的程序、修改后的仲裁员更换程序、合理性费用要求、仲裁费用审查机制以及临时措施等作了较为详细的规定。笔者和中国国际贸易促进委员会的唐厚志先生参加了关于《UNCITRAL仲裁示范法》和《UNCITRAL仲裁规则》的讨论、制定会议。

⑤ 参见宋连斌、黄进:《〈中华人民共和国仲裁法〉(建议修改稿)》,载《法学评论》2003年第4期(总第120期),第91~98页。

⑥ 王利明:《中国商事仲裁国际化水平亟待提升》,载《中国对外贸易》2016年第10期。

商事仲裁的基本原则与做法，具有时代的先进性和广泛的代表性，已成为国际商事纠纷解决的趋势，自然亦应是中国仲裁立法与实践追求的目标。①“仲裁庭的权力是当事人和国家法律授予的，并主要来源于当事人的授权。仲裁庭的权力范围是相当广泛的。在程序方面，仲裁庭可以确定其自身的管辖权，引导和管理仲裁程序的进行，确定仲裁程序事项。”②

本着前述精神与原则，就仲裁庭自裁管辖权问题，我国修改后的《仲裁法》与仲裁规则应体现下列原则：

(一)鼓励第一阶段交由法院处理的原则

当纠纷发生后但在仲裁庭组成前，即在前文提到的第一阶段，在有仲裁条款的情况下，法院应要求当事方通过仲裁解决纠纷，包括有关仲裁协议效力问题的争议，除非法院认定仲裁条款不存在、无效或无法实施。这是我国参加的《纽约公约》第2条第3款的要求，同时，如此规定可以鼓励对以仲裁解决争议，包括对仲裁协议存在、效力或仲裁范围持有异议的当事人，能在仲裁程序启动前，就诉诸法院解决，而不是在仲裁启动后再由法院来挑战这些问题，阻止仲裁程序。这有利于促进当事人的诚实信用，防止对仲裁程序的阻挠与破坏。

(二)实行积极自裁管辖权原则

一旦纠纷提交仲裁且仲裁庭业已组成，即进入第二阶段后，法律应采取积极的自裁管辖权制度，③包括授权仲裁庭受理、裁决有关当事人提出的管辖权

---

① 截至2016年7月，共72个国家在102个法域通过了以《UNCITRAL仲裁示范法》(1985年制定，2006年修正)基础的立法。参见2016年联合国国际贸易法委员会第四十九届会议文件：《各项公约和示范法的现状》(A/CN. 9/876)，第22~23页。截至2016年7月，共43个国家(地区)52家仲裁机构全部或部分采用了《UNCITRAL仲裁规则》。参见2016年联合国国际贸易法委员会第四十九届会议文件：《各项公约和示范法的现状》(A/CN. 9/876)，第26~28页。除其他问题外，起码中国在自裁管辖权问题上并未采纳统一法的标准。

② 黄进主编：《国际商事争议解决机制研究》，武汉大学出版社2010年版，第121页。

③ 《UNCITRAL仲裁示范法》采纳了积极的自裁管辖权原则，其中第16条第3款规定：仲裁庭可以根据案情将本条第2款(指质疑仲裁庭管辖权)所指抗辩作为一个初步问题裁定或在实体裁决中裁定。仲裁庭作为一个初步问题裁定其拥有管辖权的，任何一方当事人可在收到裁定通知后30天内请求第6条规定的法院对此事项作出决定，该决定不得上诉；在对该请求未决期间，仲裁庭可以继续进行仲裁程序和作出裁决。

另外，《UNCITRAL仲裁规则》第23条第3款也作了相应规定，即使法院审理对其仲裁庭管辖权的任何异议待决，仲裁庭仍可继续进行仲裁程序并作出仲裁裁决。

方面的异议,直至仲裁庭作出初步关于管辖权的裁决或案件的最终裁决。法院在此期间应拒绝受理、审理任何有关管辖权方面的争议。我们应接受《UNCITRAL 仲裁示范法》和《UNCITRAL 仲裁规则》,以提高中国仲裁在国际上的公信力。

（三）坚持必要的司法审查制度

如果仲裁庭先就管辖权作出具有管辖权的初步裁决,法院应不服裁决当事方的申请,可对该裁决进行司法审查。《UNCITRAL 仲裁示范法》给予当事人30天期限向法院提起诉讼,以及仲裁庭即便在法院诉讼期间也无须中止程序的规定,应予借鉴。[①] 当仲裁庭认为管辖权与实体问题紧密相关时,管辖权问题可以与争议的实体问题一并作出裁决。同样,法院依当事人申请,依然可对案件所涉及的管辖权问题进行司法审查,包括在撤销裁决,或对国际案件的拒绝承认与执行程序中进行审查。

中国是《纽约公约》的缔约方,曾积极参加了《UNCITRAL 仲裁示范法》和《UNCITRAL 仲裁规则》的制定和修改工作。目前,国际条约、世界主要贸易国家,包括大多数发展中国家,它们的国内仲裁立法、仲裁机构的仲裁规则以及仲裁裁决、法院的判例都承认仲裁庭的自裁管辖权,拒绝认可仲裁庭的管辖权只是个别的例外情况。[②] 我们不能仅满足、停止于例外的情况,应及时对中国《仲

---

① 参见《UNCITRAL 仲裁示范法》第16条第3款。

② 加里·B.博恩称,除非及少数例外情况(这些情况被广为批评),世界主要和其他大多数的立法机关和司法机关接受了某种版本的自裁管辖权原则。相似地,正如前面所讨论的,所有领先的国际仲裁公约都在一定程度上肯认了自裁管辖权原则。另外,据加里·B.博恩介绍,以色列、南非的法律规定只有仲裁协议的当事方明示授权时,仲裁庭才具有决定其自身管辖权的权力。See Gary B. Born, *International Commercial Arbitration*, 2nd ed., Kluwer Law International, 2014, p. 1059, pp. 1064-1065. 在该书的第1214页,加里·B.博恩提道,中国《仲裁法》还对自裁管辖权原则采取了限制性做法,规定管辖权的决定权会由仲裁机构(仲裁委员会)而非由仲裁庭,依法行使。不像许多欠发达国家或发展中国家,中国在其《仲裁法》中并未采纳《UNCITRAL 仲裁示范法》。中国基于其自身特殊的文化在仲裁法中形成了一些独特的特质。Michael Ostrove, Claudia T. Salomon, Bette Shifman (ed.), *Choice of Venue in International Arbitration*, Oxford University Press, 2014, p. 117.

裁法》作出修改,处理好仲裁庭与法院之间的关系。① 实现前述设想,起码在决定仲裁庭管辖权方面可以拉近中国《仲裁法》、仲裁规则与实践同国际通常做法的距离。国内法学界已经对中国《仲裁法》的修改提出过建议,我们有责任和历史使命为发展我国商事仲裁事业、为"一带一路"建设、为在中国建成名副其实的国际仲裁中心,做出不懈努力。

---

① 雷德芬认为,国家法院与仲裁庭的关系在强制共处和真实伙伴之间转换,仲裁依赖法院的基础支持,因为在一方当事人拟破坏仲裁时,只有法院才具有权力挽救仲裁制度。Nigel Blackaby, Constantine Partasides QC, Alan Redfern, *supra* note30. 贾科莫 · 马尔基西奥(Giacomo Marchisio)认为:"总之,在国家法院与仲裁庭就管辖权分工共存范围内,两个正常的机制,法院与仲裁员,身份应平等,是一个符合某种重要的机制性原则的趋势。" Giacomo Marchisio, Jurisdictional Matters in International Arbitration: Why Arbitrators Stand on an Equal Footing with State Courts, *Journal of International Arbitration*, Vol. 31, 2014.

Development of Commercial Dispute Resolution in China and the World

Lu Yahan　Zhao Jian *

Abstract: The closer economic exchanges and the implementation of the "Belt and Road" Initiative gave birth to a rising number of cross-border commercial disputes. Countries made innovative efforts to effectively resolve such disputes. The establishment of international commercial courts and the entry into force of the relevant Hague Conventions in international litigation, and the emergency arbitrator mechanism, *ad hoc* arbitration practice and the expedited procedure in international arbitration are all meaningful attempts to improve the efficiency and reduce the cost for dispute resolution. The aim is to meet the needs in international commercial transactions and to break the barriers in international economic and trade, promoting global economic development. Against this new backdrop, China closely followed the trend of international development, and made remarkable achievements by innovating mechanisms in litigation, arbitration and other fields of international dispute resolution.

Keywords: international commercial arbitration, dispute resolution

---

* Lu Yahan, Case Manager of China International Economic and Trade Arbitration Commission.

Dr. Zhao Jian, Vice President of the Arbitration Court of China International Economic and Trade Arbitration Commission.

1. Development in International Commercial Dispute Resolution

In recent years, some aspects in international commercial dispute resolution mechanism went through tremendous changes to break impediments to efficient resolution of cross-border disputes. Countries are working on a number of fronts to advance the existing regime for enforcement of foreign judgments in order to meet the need of the parties and to address the rising numbers of commercial disputes.

(1) Cross-border Litigation

In terms of litigation, the usual concerns for parties choosing national courts to resolve their disputes relate to the differences among jurisdictions during litigation, and the difficulties to enforce the judgments after litigation. A lot of efforts were made to address these concerns, including but not limited to the establishment of international commercial courts and the signing of international conventions.

a. International Commercial Courts

There is a visible shift to greater institutionalization as reflected in the European Union's establishment of an Investment Court System as well as the launch of about 10 international commercial courts, including the Dubai International Financial Centre Courts, the Singapore International Commercial Court, the Astana International Financial Center Court in Kazakhstan, the Netherlands Commercial Court, the International Chamber of the Court of Appeal in Paris, the Court of Chancery in Delaware, and of course the China International Commercial Court (the CICC). These international commercial courts have different markets and different selling points, but a challenge they face in common is the enforceability of their judgments.

b. The Entry into Force of the Convention on Choice of Court Agreements in 2015

The purpose of the Convention on Choice of Court Agreements (the Convention)[①] is to increase the enforceability of choice of forum clauses in which parties to international commercial contracts agree that their disputes will be decided by the courts of a specific nation. Under the treaty, the court that is selected contractually by the parties must hear the dispute; other courts must decline to hear the dispute; and the final judgment of the court selected by the parties must be recognized and enforced. Of course, these mandates apply only to the courts of those countries that have actually ratified the treaty. China has signed the Convention, but has yet to ratify it. Three years after its entry into force, the Convention now has 32 Contracting Parties, including the European Union, EU Member States, Montenegro, Mexico, and Singapore.

In addition, the Hague Conference on Private International Law, which developed the Convention, continues to work on negotiations for a "Judgement Project" for the recognition and enforcement of foreign judgments that would apply to a larger set of foreign judgments than the Convention. Still being drafted with good process, the Judgement Project could be another exciting step to increase the enforceability of judgements.

(2) International Commercial Arbitration

As an alternative means to resolve international commercial disputes, international commercial arbitration also provides the parties with innovative options in resolving cross-border disputes. Many attempts were made to facilitate more efficient procedures, such as the Emergency Arbitrator mechanism in the arbitration rules of the Stockholm Chamber of Commerce (SCC, 2010), the International Chamber of Commerce (ICC, 2012), the Hong Kong International Arbitration Centre (HKIAC, 2013) and China International Economic and Trade

---

① Full text is available at: https://assets.hcch.net/docs/510bc238-7318-47ed-9ed5-e0972510d98b.pdf, January 2, 2019.

Arbitration Commission (CIETAC, 2015), the Arb-Med procedure initiated by CIETAC, and the truncated tribunal mechanism established in multiple leading arbitration rules.

Another concern for the parties when choosing arbitration is the cost. Arbitration institutions provide a series of procedural arrangements that help the parties to reduce cost, such as the consolidation of arbitration proceedings, the arbitration of multiple contracts, and the most recent third-party funding mechanism, etc. All of the innovative procedural arrangements aim to allow the parties to take advantage of the arbitration to the largest extend and to address their disputes as efficiently as possible.

The innovations aim at improving the efficiency of international commercial arbitration and enabling fast and effective resolution of trade and investment disputes by arbitration.

(3) Mediation

Mediation in commercial cases is said to be effective in about 70% of cases. The United Nations Convention on International Settlement Agreements Resulting from Mediation (the Singapore Convention) will soon be open for signature. It addresses the concern for enforceability of settlement agreements reached by mediation and aims to provide guarantee for the cross-border enforcement of settlement agreements.

Allowing the parties to tailor their agreements, the Singapore Convention applies to settlement agreements that are "concluded in writing by parties to resolve a commercial dispute which, at the time of its conclusion, is international"①. Though issues such as false or deceptive mediation still need to be attended to, the approval of the Singapore Convention undoubtedly safeguards the agreements

① UN GA A/CN. 9/942.

reached by the parties in mediation and will encourage voluntary enforcement.

(4) Developments in Industrial Dispute Resolution

Another trend in international dispute resolution mechanism is the professionalization of dispute resolution service in specific industries. Usually involving large dispute amount, construction dispute resolution requires solid knowledge in both the practice of construction projects and the law. The amendment of International Federation of Consulting Engineers (FIDIC) provides further guidance to regulate the construction market. Other professional industries also developed its own arbitration rules and mediation procedures to resolve the disputes. For instance, the International Seeds Federation issued its own set of arbitration and mediation rules to address disputes arising out of the trade of seeds, and the National Equities Exchange and Quotations Limited Liability Company cooperated with CIETAC to resolve the disputes by means of CIETAC's mediation service.

2. Development of International Commercial Dispute Resolution in China

(1) China International Commercial Court

The CICC, as a "one-stop" destination for international dispute resolution which involves close coordination of litigation, arbitration, and mediation services, receives a lot of attention recently. The CICC is a permanent adjudication organ established by the Supreme People's Court (the SPC) to deal with international commercial disputes. It practices the "First Instance being Final". The judgments and rulings made by the CICC are final and binding on the parties with legal effect. In order to strengthen international exchanges and cooperation, facilitate and promote the trial work of CICC, support such diversified dispute resolutions as mediation, arbitration and litigation to resolve international commercial disputes, the SPC established the International

Commercial Expert Committee, composed of 32 Chinese and foreign experts.[①]

On October 24, 2018, the SPC established the Case Management Offices for the First and Second International Commercial Court, which is responsible for case registration, filing and management of related administrative work for the International Commercial Court. On 6 November 2018, The SPC appointed the persons in charge.[②]

One Oxford-based scholar recently characterized the consolidation of dispute resolution services by the CICC as falling within a larger tradition of the "multi-door courthouse".[③] It provides different means for dispute resolution and the parties may choose which door to go to.

(2) Nanning Statement and Memorandum of Guidance on the Mutual Recognition and Enforcement of Singaporean and Chinese Judgments

Countries are making efforts to enhance regional judicial cooperation to strengthen continuous judicial communication and cooperation in order to guarantee social security and economic prosperity in the region.

The Nanning Statement issued bythe Chief Justices of Association of Southeast Asian Nations (ASEAN) and the Chief Justice of the SPC of China sets a good example of a liberal regime for the recognition and enforcement of judgments. More recently, in August, the Chief Justices of China and Singapore entered into a Memorandum of Guidance on the mutual recognition and enforcement of Singapore and Chinese judgments. The Memorandum serves as a milestone for the mutual recognition of judgements, and lays out a clear procedure

① See "The Decision on the Establishment of International Commercial Expert Committee of the Supreme People's Court", http://cicc.court.gov.cn/html/1/219/235/243/index.html, January 2, 2019.

② See "The Supreme People's Court of China (SPC) Appointed the Persons in Charge and Established the Case Management Offices for the First and Second International Commercial Court", http://cicc.court.gov.cn/html/1/219/208/210/1096.html, January 2, 2019.

③ Matthew S. Erie, The China International Commercial Court: Prospects for Dispute Resolution for the "Belt and Road Initiative", Vol. 22 ASIL Insights Issue 11 (Aug. 31, 2018).

for the enforcement of remedies. With improved enforcement mechanism, it may encourage the parties to choose commercial courts in both countries to resolve their disputes.

According to the Nanning Statement,[①] it is important to build and strengthen continuous exchanges and cooperation in promoting the "Belt and Road" Initiative. Paragraph 7 of the Nanning Statement stipulates that, "Cross-border transactions and investments in the region require the mechanism of mutually recognizing and enforcing appropriate judgments as judicial guarantees. Within the scope permitted by the law in China, courts from participating countries will interpret their own laws to reduce unnecessary parallel litigation, and consider the appropriate promotion of mutual recognition and enforcement of civil and commercial judgments in different nations. In countries that have not yet concluded international treaties of recognizing and enforcing foreign civil and commercial judgments, if there is no precedent for refusing to recognize and enforce civil commercial judgments on the grounds of reciprocity in the judicial process of recognizing and enforcing the country's civil and commercial judgments, within the scope permitted by the law in China, it can be presumed that there is a reciprocal relationship between each other." It will have profound influences because the Statement will effectively reduce parallel proceedings by establishing a presumed reciprocal relationship among China and ASEAN courts. The parties involved would have the freedom to choose the most convenient forum to resolve their disputes and expect the judgments to be enforced.

Though there is still a long way to go, it shows a new pathway for future recognition and enforcement of foreign awards if negotiated appropriately. Countries are working on providing more enforceability and security for awards

① http://cicc.court.gov.cn/html/1/219/208/209/800.html, January 2, 2019.

rendered by national courts, increasing the credibility of litigation for cross-border disputes.

(3) International Commercial Arbitration

China's arbitration market underwent sharp increase in recent years. In 2017, 253 arbitration commissions across China accepted a total of 239360 cases, an increase of 30815 cases with the growth rate of 15% compared with 2016. The dispute amount of these cases totaled RMB 533.8 billion, growing by RMB 64.3 billion with the growth rate of 14% compared with 2016. Moreover, 6 arbitration commissions handled a total of 85399 cases by online arbitration, accounting for 36% of the total cases nationwide.① To better resolve the increasing disputes, China tried to optimize its arbitration environment by connecting its arbitration system with international practice, opening up its arbitration market and improving its arbitration procedures.

a. *Ad Hoc* Arbitration

China's legal system is becoming more and more friendly to international arbitration. The arbitration market becomes increasingly open as signaled by the SPC in its multiple opinions and interpretations. With its *Opinions on Providing Judicial Safeguard for the Construction of Pilot Free Trade Zones*② (FTZ), the SPC made meaningful attempts on the determination of the validity of arbitration agreements and the arbitration types. More specifically, the *Opinion* stipulates that where the enterprises registered in an FTZ reach an agreement to arbitrate at a specific place in mainland China, by specific arbitrator(s), and under a specific set of arbitration rules, it may be deemed valid.

The aforesaid stipulations are in line with general international practices of *ad*

① See CIETAC, "Annual Report on International Commercial Arbitration in China 2017", http://www.cietac.org.cn/Uploads/201810/5bd6d2e9b333e.pdf, January 2, 2019.

② FF [2016] No. 34.

hoc arbitration, showing positive support to the development of international arbitration in China and injecting new drive for rule of law into further implementation of the "Belt and Road" Initiative.

To respond to the SPC's support towards arbitration, and to meet the needs of the parties in different jurisdictions, Zhuhai Hengqin New Area Administrative Committee and Zhuhai Arbitration Commission jointly issued the *Ad Hoc Arbitration Rules of Hengqin Pilot Free Trade Zone* on March 23, 2017; CIETAC adopted the *Rules for CIETAC Hong Kong Arbitration Center to Serve as the Appointing Authority*; Shijiazhuang Arbitration Commission published the *Arbitration Rule* on June 2, 2017, defining the *ad hoc* arbitration as mentioned in the said judicial opinions. China Internet Arbitration Alliance released the *Rules for Bridging Ad Hoc Arbitration and Institutional Arbitration* (hereinafter the "Rules for Bridging") on September 19, 2017, and Guangzhou Arbitration Commission amended its arbitration rules accordingly, indicating the recognition and acceptance of the Rules for Bridging. So far, arbitration institutions in China have made many helpful attempts in the *ad hoc* arbitration rules.

b. Opening the Arbitration Market and Reaching Out

In April 2015, the State Council issued the*Notice on Issuing the Plan for Further Deepening the Reform and Opening-up of China (Shanghai) Pilot Free Trade Zone*, clearly pointing out that "FTZs shall support international well-known commercial dispute resolution institutions to have their offices therein so that China can keep in line with international commercial dispute resolution rules, optimize arbitration rules in Pilot FTZs and enhance the internationalization of commercial arbitration. The establishment of a nationwide FTZ arbitration legal service alliance shall be explored and the construction of an Asia-Pacific arbitration center for the world shall be accelerated". By the end of 2016, internationally renowned commercial dispute resolution institutions such as the HKIAC, SIAC and the ICC had set up offices in the Shanghai Pilot FTZ.

In practice, the SPC also demonstrated a positive support to the validity of arbitration awards in the cases. For instance, in *Shanghai Golden Landmark Co. Ltd v. Siemens International Trade Co. Ltd*, the SPC gave a broad definition to the elements that constitute "foreign related"① by allowing the enforcement of the arbitration award made by SIAC between parties registered in Shanghai FTZ with foreign company as sole shareholders. In *Anhui Longlide Wrapping and Printing Co., Ltd. v. BP Agnati S. R. L*, the SPC upheld the validity of an arbitration award rendered by ICC with the seat in Shanghai after citing Article 16 of the 2006 SPC Interpretation of the PRC Arbitration Law. With more and more cases, the SPC demonstrated stronger support for an open market for international commercial arbitration.

Against this backdrop, Chinese arbitration institutions are reaching out to explore larger market and to provide local service for Chinese parties in cross-border transactions. Following the establishment of CIETAC Hong Kong Arbitration Center in 2012, CIETAC landed its North America Arbitration Center in Vancouver in July 2018 and its European Arbitration Centre in September 2018, expanding its oversea network.

c. Improved Mechanisms in Arbitration

By accelerating the development of arbitration market and opening up to international practice, China is building a business-friendly environment. The SPC issued a series of Opinions and judicial interpretations regulating the review of

① https://www.chinacourt.org/article/detail/2017/05/id/2863098.shtml, January 2, 2019.

arbitration awards by establishing a centralized handling mechanism.① The SPC also limits the lower courts' power to set aside arbitral awards by establishing an "application for verification"② system.

Arbitration institutions are making improvements to its Arbitration Rules to allow more efficient resolution of disputes that would satisfy the parties' need. Take CIETAC as an example, it has amended its Arbitration Rules 9 times over the years and gradually developed an efficient case management procedure. In its 2015 Arbitration Rules, CIETAC introduced the Emergency Arbitrator procedure, allowing the parties to apply for an emergency relief pursuant to the applicable law or agreement of the parties before the tribunal is formed.③ It also allowed the consolidation of two or more arbitration proceedings into one proceeding,④ and the

---

① *Notice on Some Issues Concerning the Centralized Handling of Cases Involving Judicial Review of Arbitration*: "centralized handling" means: (1) Tribunals (collegial panels) of courts hearing the foreign-related commercial cases at various levels shall act as specialized trial divisions to handle the cases involving judicial review of arbitration. (2) Cases in which any party concerned applies for ascertaining the effect of an arbitration agreement, revoking an arbitral award made by an arbitral authority in the mainland China, recognizing and enforcing an arbitral award made in Hong Kong Special Administrative Region (HKSAR), Macao Special Administrative Region (MSAR) and Taiwan Region (Taiwan), or a foreign arbitral award, shall be handled by the specialized trial divisions of courts at various levels. After a review, if a specialized trial division rules to recognize and enforce an arbitral award made in HKSAR, MSAR and Taiwan, or a foreign arbitral award, relevant cases shall be transferred to the corresponding department for enforcement. It should be noted that arbitral awards made by arbitral authorities in the mainland China shall be enforced by the enforcement departments of the competent courts, without being subject to the Centralized Handling Notice. (3) Cases that any party concerned is dissatisfied at the ruling on no acceptance, on dismissing the litigation or on objection to jurisdiction ruled by the court of first instance, which involve the validity of an arbitration agreement, and thus files an appeal, shall be handled by the specialized trial division of the people's court of second instance.

② *Relevant Provisions on Issues Concerning Applications for Verification of Arbitration Cases under Judicial Review.*

③ See Appendix Ⅲ of the 2015 CIETAC Arbitration Rules, available at: http://www.cietac.org.cn/index.php? m=Page&a=index&id=42&l=en, January 2, 2019.

④ See Article 19 of the 2015 CIETAC Arbitration Rules, available at: http://www.cietac.org.cn/index.php? m=Page&a=index&id=42&l=en, January 2, 2019.

joinder of additional parties into an existing proceeding when necessary.① By allowing the tribunal to render an award with a majority opinion, the CIETAC Arbitration Rules upheld the validity of its award with truncated tribunal, giving the parties fair and efficient resolution of disputes.

With CIETAC Hong Kong Arbitration Center's Guidelines for Third-Party Funding for Arbitration and CIETAC's Investment Arbitration Rules defining third-party funding for the first time in China, third-party funding was widely discussed at all levels. It will significantly encourage parties to pursue arbitration if used properly.

Another visionary innovation was made by CIETAC long before, which is the combination of arbitration and mediation. When settlement agreement could not be enforced without going through court procedures, CIETAC embedded a mediation option in its arbitrations rules to allow parties to reach a settlement in an arbitration proceeding. As a matter of fact, this practice was proven to be very successful in preserving the parties' business relations and resolving their disputes amicably.

(4) Mediation

China's mediation development parallels with the international trend. With its flexible nature, mediation is widely used by the courts to resolve disputes. According to the 2017 Work Report of the SPC, 23%-33% of the cases accepted by the peoples' courts were concluded by mediation in the years between 2013 and 2017. Whereas the data published by the Law Office of the State Council, from 2014 to 2016, as much as 41%-65% of the arbitration cases accepted by China's arbitration institutions were concluded by mediation.

CIETAC invented the combination of arbitration and mediation, a practice which is internationally known as the "Oriental Wisdom". It not only encourages

① See Article 18 of the 2015 CIETAC Arbitration Rules, available at: http://www.cietac.org.cn/index.php?m=Page&a=index&id=42&l=en, January 2, 2019.

dispute resolution but also helps to maintain friendship and cooperation between the parties. It is an example that more and more foreign arbitration institutions are following.

In order to jointly play an active role in the effective prevention and harmonious resolution of disputes and to promote the healthy development of the capital market, CIETAC established an independent Mediation Center and concluded a Memorandum of Cooperation with the National Equities Exchange and Quotations Limited Liability Company (NEEQ) in May 2018. The CIETAC Mediation Center's Mediation Rules incorporated a mechanism that bridges mediation with arbitration if the parties require so, providing full guarantee for the enforceability of the settlement agreement.

(5) Alternative Dispute Resolution Mechanism

CIETAC is also working on completing its Panel for Construction Projects Experts Review Mechanism to allow the experts to intervene at the early stage of a project.

Domestically, China's reform to delegate power, improve regulation and optimize services in the construction industry were carried out, resulting in significant changes on the domestic engineering, procurement and construction sectors. Among China's turnover of US $ 168. 59 billion in overseas contracted projects, over 50% were from "Belt and Road" projects. In satisfying the needs of the "Belt and Road" implementation and settling the emerging disputes related to overseas construction projects, China's domestic arbitration institutions play an important role. For example, CIETAC Silk Road Arbitration Center was officially established in Xi'an; Beijing Arbitration Center (BAC/BIAC), Asia International Arbitration Center (AIAC) and Cairo Regional Center for International Commercial Arbitration jointly proposed "Belt and Road Arbitration Initiative", etc.

3. Conclusion

International commercial dispute resolution mechanisms provide a full range of alternatives for parties to resolve cross-border disputes. It is driven by the diversified needs of the parties in cases arising out of closer economic exchanges. International litigation becomes more professional and provides enforceability by treaties and regional reciprocal arrangements. International arbitration builds on the existing New York Convention and shows the trend of becoming more cost-effective and efficient. These two paths to resolve international commercial disputes together contribute to a business friendly environment for global economy.

PPP项目困境破解:“烂尾”PPP项目投资方的退出路径

周月萍　樊晓丽*

摘要:本文从甘肃武威工业园区污水BOT项目社会资本方与政府方之诉中引发思考并提出疑问,进一步分析可能导致PPP项目出现“烂尾”的情形以及“烂尾”PPP项目投资方的退出路径,以期对读者有所裨益。

关键词:“烂尾”PPP项目　退出路径

一、引言:问题的提出

2015年正是全国各地贯彻国务院和各部委文件、如火如荼开展政府和社会资本合作(public-private partnership,PPP)项目的时候,而甘肃武威工业园区污水BOT(build-operate-transfer,建设—营运—转让)项目公司武威恒泰污水处理有限公司却于2015年正式起诉凉州区人民政府及甘肃武威工业园区管理委员会,主张因甘肃武威工业园区管理委员会无故单方解除合同,诉请确认《甘肃武威工业园区污水BOT项目特许经营权合同书》及《甘肃武威工业园区

* 周月萍,北京市中伦(上海)律师事务所合伙人,荣获《钱伯斯亚太指南2018》建筑工程领域推荐律师,上海国际仲裁中心等仲裁机构 仲裁员(主审工程和PPP争议解决)。

樊晓丽,北京市中伦(上海)律师事务所律师,业务方向:基础设施与建设工程、PPP再谈判与争议解决。

污水厂资产回购协议》解除,同时要求二被告支付项目投资款、建设期内产生的投资利息、出资资金的合理利润以及损失等共计近7000万元。

在该案中,政府方认为,施工进度影响了《甘肃省2011年污染物减排计划》对武威工业园区污水治理工程的要求,故而提出解除合同,并按未完工程原状接管项目实体工程;项目公司认为政府方侵害了其合法利益,为保全自身利益不得不采取诉讼的途径。那么,政府方和社会资本方缘何会走到对簿公堂的地步?

众所周知,由于PPP项目合作期较长、投资体量较大、法律关系较为复杂,故PPP项目推行全生命周期管理的理念,并要求合同各方有较强的契约精神。但是,在实际的合同履行过程中,因为这样或那样的原因,PPP项目发生纠纷导致PPP项目"烂尾"的概率确实不小。那么,碰到PPP项目"烂尾"的情况,社会资本方应通过什么途径退出?政府方或社会资本方又该如何应对?笔者试从以下几方面浅析其中要点,抛砖引玉,以期给拟参与或正在参与PPP项目的各方一些启示。

二、可能导致PPP项目出现"烂尾"的情形

PPP项目实践过程中,导致PPP项目"烂尾"的原因往往是多方面且互相影响的。如引言中提及的案例,政府方认为是由于施工进度影响《甘肃省2011年污染物减排计划》对武威工业园区污水治理工程的要求;而社会资本方则认为是政府方未按约定与社会资本和项目公司签订《特许经营权合同书》和《资产回购协议书》,也未按约定办妥承诺的文件(项目土地使用证、凉州区财政局出具的污水处理费列入财政预算内支付的承诺书,以及凉州区人大就同意财政承诺书所作出的决议文件等),项目建设期应依约顺延。总结下来,导致PPP项目"烂尾"往往是因为如下三个方面原因中的一种或多种。

(一)政府方原因

在PPP项目履行过程中,或由于政府方换届,或由于项目实施过程中出现影响公共利益的因素,抑或当地财政支付能力降低等原因,政府方提出单方解

除PPP合同。

(二)社会资本方内部原因

例如,因社会资本或项目公司未按期完成融资交割或者资金链断裂等,无能力继续履行协议约定,导致项目“烂尾”;又如,社会资本联合体投标,因分工等内部矛盾无法协调导致不能履行合同,政府方终止合作的。以上均是社会资本方的内部原因导致项目无法正常推进。

原则上,因社会资本原因导致的“烂尾”,政府方可通过重新招选社会资本的方式重启项目。PPP项目本身并不会产生“烂尾”,但是对于退出的社会资本而言,该PPP项目已终止。

(三)第三方原因

一般在PPP合同中会对不可抗力、法律变更造成的终止通过专款约定:如因任何不可抗力或法律变更阻止一方履行其义务且经过努力仍不可克服,自不可抗力或法律变更发生之日起连续超过90日,双方应协商决定继续履行本合同的条件或者同意按照PPP合同的约定终止合同。如果自不可抗力、法律变更发生之日起180日之内双方不能就继续履行的条件或终止合同达成一致意见,则任何一方有权根据合同约定向另一方发出终止意向通知。

在PPP项目中,也存在因不可抗力、法律变更等不可归责于双方的第三方原因导致的项目“烂尾”。在该种情况下,政府方与社会资本方可协商按照PPP合同约定的退出机制退出。

三、“烂尾”PPP项目投资方的退出路径分析

(一)可通过资产转让或股权转让方式实现退出

在PPP项目“烂尾”时,政府方与社会资本方可协商一致退出;协商不成时,通过诉讼或仲裁方式实现退出。社会资本方的退出路径主要包括资产退出和股权退出两种。

资产退出,即由项目公司将项目资产移交给实施机构或政府指定的其他接收机构;股权退出,即由社会资本方股东将项目公司股权移交给实施机构或政

府指定的其他机构。资产退出或股权退出的支付对价在后文中详述。

资产退出方案的优点在于,资产移交后,项目公司实现破产清算,无遗留债务,由政府方全盘接收无负债资产。但是,资产退出可能产生较重的税负(如印花税、土地增值税等)。

股权退出方案的优点在于,政府方通过接收项目公司股权而完全控股 PPP 项目公司,由 PPP 项目公司继续负责移交期间及之后的运营,保障项目提供公共服务的持续性。就政府方的支出而言,由于项目公司负债仍由项目公司继续承担,因此股权退出方案中政府对社会资本方的支付责任小于资产退出方案,且总体税负较低。缺点是,由于前期是由社会资本方控股,公司管理权交接风险增大、股权变更等手续烦琐。且股权退出,特别是涉及控股股东变更时,往往需要征得银行金融机构等债权人的同意。如社会资本方为国有企业,还将涉及国有股权转让的审批、进场程序等。因此股权退出的程序较为复杂,所需时间也较长。

需要说明的是,如无法协商一致而通过诉讼或仲裁等方式实现社会资本方的退出的,在循司法途径完成争议解决后,仍将回归到上述资产移交或股权移交的路径上来。

(二)“烂尾”PPP 项目的终止补偿及移交

1. 确定索赔主体

关于项目“烂尾”时终止的补偿,笔者认为首先应确定索赔主体。在 PPP 项目中,施工类的社会资本方往往具有双重属性——既是项目公司的社会资本方股东,又是与项目公司签订《施工/工程总承包合同》的总承包商。

笔者认为,根据合同相对性原理,总承包商应根据总承包合同向发包人项目公司进行索赔;而项目公司/社会资本方则应根据 PPP 合同向实施机构进行索赔。

2. 确定索赔金额

根据以上索赔主体,社会资本方应从总承包商与项目公司两个角度分别就索赔金额进行梳理。

总承包商梳理的索赔金额相对简单，应根据《施工/工程总承包合同》确定的计价规则对已完工程造价进行确定。

项目公司梳理的索赔金额则应包括：

(1)PPP合同签订前，社会资本方参与项目调查、合同谈判的投入，包括工作人员的交通住宿费用、聘请第三方的费用等；

(2)PPP合同签订后，社会资本方或项目公司实际已投入的损失，包括项目公司股东投入的资金占用成本、已支付政府方的前期费用、设计费用、施工造价、项目公司设立费用、与第三方签订合同需解约的损失等；

(3)预期利润。

四、研究"烂尾"PPP项目对其他PPP项目的启示

(一)建议完善PPP合同中的退出条款及终止补偿条款

明确、精准的合同约定在发生项目"烂尾"时，能给予双方协商解决问题的依据和基础。笔者建议在签订PPP合同时，明确约定违约条款、再谈判机制、合同解除条件、解除后的退出、终止补偿及相关赔偿条款。如对上述内容未做明确约定，则纠纷发生时仅能按照我国《合同法》中规定的法定解除条件解除合同，并主张损失赔偿。

1. 明确约定解除条件及违约责任

例如，可明确在严重违约的情形下守约方可单方解除合同的权利。

社会资本方可解除合同的情况一般包括：(1)政府方所做的任何声明和保证被证明有实质性不实，使政府方履行本合同的能力受到严重的不利影响；(2)政府方未按照合同的有关约定，向项目公司支付相应的财政补贴，在项目公司发出催告后的约定日期内仍未能支付的；(3)政府方未能按照约定履行征地拆迁、办理项目开工、投入运营应具备的各项前期审批手续等前置义务，造成工程无法按期建设、运营，单次或累计达到双方约定期限的。

政府方可解除合同的情况一般包括：(1)社会资本方未按照股东相关协议的约定履行出资义务；(2)项目公司所做的任何声明与保证被证明实质性不

实,使项目公司履行本合同的能力受到严重不利影响;(3)贷款人根据融资合同的约定,开始行使其融资文件下的担保权利;(4)未经政府方事先书面同意,对项目设施及有关财产以及项目公司在项目合同项下获得的权利设定任何抵押、质押或其他担保物权及第三方权益;(5)未经政府方同意无故关闭项目设施或中止项目运营,对公共利益造成严重损害等情形。

2. 建议明确约定“烂尾”PPP 项目的终止补偿条款

如可制定以下的终止补偿表(以资产移交退出为例,仅供参考),见表 1。

表 1 终止补偿表

终止事件	终止补偿金额
建设期内,项目公司严重违约事件导致的终止	移交资产的账面净值−建设期终止违约金
运营期内,因项目公司严重违约事件导致的终止	移交资产的账面净值−运营期终止违约金
建设期内,因甲方严重违约事件/政府部门征收、征用或中止或全部或部分收回特许经营权导致的终止	移交资产的账面净值+建设期终止违约金
运营期内,因甲方严重违约事件/政府部门征收、征用或中止或全部或部分收回特许经营权导致的终止	移交资产的账面净值+运营期终止违约金
不可抗力事件导致的终止	用重置成本法评估的移交资产的价值
法律变更事件对项目可行性产生严重不利影响导致的终止	移交资产的账面净值+合理的补偿

建设期终止违约金为:根据项目公司实际到位的注册资本金的时间、金额、约定利率计算的利息。约定利率等于中国人民银行公布的 5 年期贷款利率乘以一定比例。

运营期终止违约金=明确一定金额×(运营期终止时运营期的剩余年数/运营期总年限)

在“建设期内,项目公司严重违约事件导致的终止”及“运营期内,因项目公司严重违约事件导致的终止”情况下,如果移交资产为项目公司的全部资产,则相应的终止补偿金额应不低于融资文件项下的未偿还贷款本金及利息。

(二)建议加强项目管理和监督

其一,在出现政府方行使监督权、介入权或融资方行使介入权时,社会资本方/项目公司应积极提供应对方案,如补充提供担保、提供项目运行良好的记录或完成完善整改的承诺等,以推进项目的正常进行。

其二,在政府方出现违约导致合同解除的可能时,社会资本方/项目公司应及时发函督促政府方履约、与政府方共同协商处理方案等,避免后续严重后果出现时处于被动局面。

其三,需要提醒PPP项目的参与各方,在履行PPP合同或总承包商在履行施工合同时应提高项目管理水平,对于甲方要求、设计变更、工期顺延等做好完整的签证手续,并留存书面资料,以免在后续的诉讼、仲裁过程中因证据不足处于劣势地位。

(三)及时总结经验教训,在后续的项目实施过程中不断完善并改进

对于"烂尾"PPP项目,项目参与各方应总结其中的经验教训,避免类似情况再次发生。

对于一些缺乏合作意识、诚信观念的单位,可将其不良行为纳入地方PPP项目诚信系统,将一些"老赖"列入黑名单,避免再次合作。

同时,对于一些符合再启动条件的PPP项目,可以设立专门的项目库,重新组织政府和社会资本的合作,再次发挥PPP项目高效共赢的优势。同时应注意已完工的部分项目设施应以存量项目或在建工程等方式转化到再次启动的PPP项目中,实现原设施与后续实施的新/改建设施之间在资产权属、运营管理等方面的衔接,实现项目全生命周期效益最大化。

五、结语

在实践过程中,导致PPP项目"烂尾"的因素有很多,可能是政府方原因、社会资本方内部原因或第三方原因中的一种或多种。一旦发生PPP项目"烂

尾”,投资方可通过资产转让或股权转让实现退出,并在确定索赔主体和金额后取得 PPP 项目的终止补偿并完成项目移交。因此,笔者建议其他 PPP 项目的参与方可采取完善 PPP 合同中的退出条款及终止补偿条款,加强项目管理和监督,及时总结经验教训等措施,有效破解 PPP 项目出现“烂尾”的困境。

PPP项目合同争议特性与类型分析

孔繁琦*

摘要:PPP项目合同,于发生争议及其解决的特性上,有下列共通点:(1)PPP项目合同为非典型合同,较难直接适用《合同法》的规定解决争议;(2)PPP项目争议解决必须考虑政府与公共利益;(3)PPP项目争议的处理,倾向由社会资本方承担较多风险,且风险分配较难有一致标准;(4)PPP项目的争议解决,与财务条件的调整密切相关;(5)PPP项目的争议解决,常通过合同条款变更的方式处理,不以政府提供经济补偿为主;(6)PPP项目的争议解决具有高度个案性。

PPP项目合同的争议类型,可按筹办阶段、建设阶段、营运阶段及移转阶段加以归类,类型繁多。争议处理所适用之合同条款、法律规定及风险分配原则也会因应争议类型的不同而有所不同,或必须配合调整。有时财务计划的重新检讨、财务模组与假设参数的修正也是必要的。至于争议处理的方式,则需视争议发生阶段与类型的不同,选择诉讼、协调、调解或仲裁的方式解决。争议的处理要考虑如何使PPP项目合同具有生命性、延续性,并与时俱进,发挥灵活调整双方权利义务的功能。对此,除了必须有专业的财务评估作为依据外,亦须有充分了解PPP项目合同架构、风险分配与调整的合同管理或法律专业人才参与。

---

* 孔繁琦,台北环宇法律事务所主持合伙律师,中国国际经济贸易仲裁委员会仲裁员,中华仲裁委员会工程仲裁委员会主任委员。

关键词:PPP 项目　风险分配　自偿能力　筹办阶段争议　建设阶段争议　营运阶段争议　移转阶段争议

前言

国家基础设施的兴建以及公共服务的提供,考虑政府预算调配、解决财政负担、促进社会资本稳健发展及引进民间企业经营绩效与活力等因素,各国近年来有大幅采用政府与社会资本合作模式(public-private partnership,PPP)推动的趋势。

我国自 2013 年年底全面推进 PPP 改革以来,经过 6 年多的发展,PPP 工作在各方面都已取得显著进步。在推动的具体成效上,各级政府除陆续针对各类 PPP 项目进行评估及采购工作外,还纷纷与社会资本签订 PPP 项目合同,开始 PPP 项目合同的执行与履约。同时 PPP 项目合同的双方当事人,也通过资本市场和开发性、政策性金融等多元管道,取得相当额度的投、融资,可预见在接下来的十数年,PPP 项目的筹备、兴建及营运等活动,将进入高速蓬勃发展的阶段。

笔者自 1998 年起即担任我国台湾地区南北高速铁路 BOT(build-operate-transfer,建设—营运—转让)案的法律顾问,对于我国台湾地区高铁在兴建、营运阶段所面临的各类争议均有深入参与。在近 20 年的时间内,亦持续参与我国台湾地区许多 PPP 合同的争议处理,担任诉讼、仲裁的代理律师,协助合同双方当事人进行诚意协商,并曾担任多件 PPP 仲裁案件的仲裁员,以及协调案件的协调委员,对于 PPP 合同推动过程中遇到的争议类型、争议特性、争议处理途径,以及争议解决原则及趋势,特别是国人在政府与社会资本合作的架构下如何解决争议的态度,有一定程度的了解。深知 PPP 推动过程中遭遇履约争议的干扰,虽是不可避免的,但也是可以合理解决的。

鉴于 PPP 合同争议所涉层面既深又广,难以一次道尽,谨先就 PPP 合同的争议特性及争议类型,论析如下,以供各界参考。至于各类争议的处理途径、争议解决原则与实务趋势,日后有机会再逐一论述。

一、PPP项目合同争议的特性

PPP项目合同,其项目类型无论是公共交通项目、公用设施项目还是社会公共服务项目,其权源无论是特许权还是一般经营权,其付费机制无论是采政府付费、使用者付费还是可行性缺口补助的方式,在发生争议及其解决的特性上,均有下列共通点,有别于施工合同、DB(design-build,设计—建造)合同或EPC/Turnkey(engineering procurement construction/turnkey,工程总承包/交钥匙)合同的争议特性。

(一)PPP项目合同为非典型合同,较难直接适用我国《合同法》的规定解决争议

PPP项目合同规范的主要是项目建设、营运与移转此一项目生命周期的各阶段权利义务关系,其内容包括项目范围与期限、融资、用地交付、建设、营运、资产移转、付费机制、政府监督、保险、不可抗力与法律变更等各事项,且各条文彼此关联紧密,以维持合理分配风险的动态平衡为目标。在此条款架构下,无法将PPP项目合同归类为《合同法》所规定的某一合同类型,其性质应属非典型合同或混同合同。在发生争议而无法通过PPP项目合同条款解释予以解决时,未必能直接适用《合同法》建设工程合同,技术合同与供用电、水、气、热力合同等规定加以处理,而需以缔约真意、条款规范目的、风险合理分配等因素作为基础,检讨可否适用或类推适用《合同法》的某一条文。因此,PPP项目合同的争议,需要比传统建设工程合同更高的法律、工程与财务专业能力,方能有效及公平合理地解决。

(二)PPP项目争议解决必须考虑政府与公共利益

PPP项目虽然强调政府与社会资本合作的精神,也很重视合同订定及执行的公平性与稳定性,以增加社会资本投资诱因及融资单位融资意愿。但是,PPP项目毕竟与单纯的土地开发或商业经营有所不同,其核心价值仍在于公共服务的提供,以及基础设施的建设与营运,是政府提供人民服务的延伸,与政府和公共利益密切相关。因此,PPP项目的争议常常源自于社会资本无法如期如

质完成建设与提供服务,其争议解决的重点,是以满足政府行政目的与公共利益为目标,这也是为什么行政法院及公法学者力主应通过行政诉讼方式解决此类争议的原因。在必须考虑政府与公共利益的特性下,争议解决方式并非以单纯的违约责任承担与损害填补为主,而是以项目维持可行性,公共服务不中断为主,在政府财政可承受及社会资本应当承受相应损失的要求下,解决争议。

(三)PPP 项目争议的处理,倾向由社会资本方承担较多风险,且风险分配较难有一致标准

若 PPP 项目合同约定不明确,或未约定具体的法律效力,对于因此发生的争议,除适用或类推适用《合同法》的规定处理外,通常会从如何合理分配风险的角度考虑。

PPP 合同与传统建设工程合同的项目种类虽然都很广泛,但 PPP 项目除因面临建造风险而与传统建设工程合同风险处理原则相仿外,尚包括前期的投融资、建造完成后的营运,以及以营收摊还建造成本及资本化财务成本等重要阶段,其可能面临的风险类型及规模,会因项目种类的不同而有不同。例如,供电 PPP 项目的主要营运风险在于机组故障维修成本增加,不在于营收短少;而片区综合开发 PPP 项目的主要风险不在建筑设备的维护成本,而在招商失败与供给过剩等市场因素。且两者风险可能反映的潜在损失,亦与投资规模大小、社会资本经营效率,以及项目技术成熟与否密切相关。

因此,如何合理地分配风险,PPP 项目合同争议所涉及的因素,较传统建设工程合同更为复杂及多变;且风险分配的原则,也不同于传统建设工程合同,有类如国际咨询工程师联合会(International Federation of Consulting Engineers, FIDIC)、土木工程师协会(Institution of Civil Engineers, NCE)或其他国内外建设工程合同的范本可供依循,必须视 PPP 项目与规模的不同而有所不同,甚至必须待 PPP 项目开始推动后,再视实际的建设营运状况及实际遇到的具体情况,由双方协议或通过裁判的方式加以调整。

此外,PPP 项目合同与传统建设工程合同最大的不同在于,项目的建物与设施所有权于合同期限届满前原则上是归属于社会资本方,且营运收益主要部

分亦归属于社会资本方,而非政府方。基于民法所有权主义或占有主义,以及损失利益归属同一的法理,通常会由社会资本方承担较多的风险。在此原则下,如采用"可预见性风险分配理论"或"法律经济分析风险分配理论",对于PPP争议进行风险分配时,可能会对社会资本方控制风险的效率要求及成本要求采用较为严格的标准,使社会资本方获得的金钱或非金钱补偿,可能较传统建设工程合同的承包人要少。尤其是对于执照申请、建设、营运及资金成本等风险,此种情况更为明显。

(四)PPP项目的争议解决,与财务条件的调整密切相关

PPP项目能否顺利推动,除政府的支持,以及社会资本方的资质能力外,最重要的就是PPP项目在财务评估上是否可行,该项目是否具有相当的财务自偿性。简言之,就是社会资本方预估的项目本业及附属事业总收入,与预估建设、更换、维护资产设施的总支出,两者依公认合理的折现率换算至目标年度的现值总额,互为比较计算其自偿率(self-liquidating ratio, SLR)。如比率大于1,此PPP项目即具有自偿性,方有吸引社会资本投入的诱因,融资单位亦较愿意考虑以稳定的现金流入作为担保,提供计划性财务融资(project finance)。因此,PPP项目的财务评估,包括物有所值或自偿能力评估,以及净现值(net present value, NPV)与项目内部报酬率(internal rate of return, IRR)评估等,都是PPP案推动不可或缺的步骤。

PPP项目争议的发生,如对于合同双方影响较为轻微者,直接依合同条款约定处理,固然可以妥适解决。但是,如PPP项目的争议,发生延误建设期间、建设成本超支、延后营运、产生收费障碍、营运收入预期或非预期短少、增加贷款利息等额外支出,甚至是项目设施的毁损、效能丧失,或者发生须大额赔偿第三方损失等责任事由时,势必会造成实际的财务状况与PPP项目合同签订当时预估状况差异很大的结果,项目的财务可行性受到影响。此时,对于此类争议的解决,PPP项目合同双方或裁判者将无法单纯以合同违反或违约责任的方式处理,而必须依据不可抗力条款或其他条款的授权或解释,或适用"情事变更原则",通过合同条款的调整,改善项目的财务条件,恢复其财务可行性,使

PPP 项目可在社会资本方不能获得额外利益的前提下继续推动或移交政府。因此,PPP 项目高度的财务依附性,使 PPP 项目争议解决与财务条件调整密切相关。

(五)PPP 项目的争议解决,常通过合同条款变更的方式处理,不以政府提供经济补偿为主

承前所述,因为 PPP 项目的争议解决与财务条件的调整密切相关,所以常常通过合同条款变更的方式予以处理。在 PPP 项目合同履行过程中,因项目的资产所有权归属社会资本方,并由社会资本方通过该资产的营运获得收益,如政府对于项目建设与营运所生争议提出现金补偿,因政府并没有取得资产的所有权,也没有直接通过资产营运获得营收利益,无疑将使政府的经济补偿没有对价性,且会根本破坏应由社会资本方承担 PPP 项目建设营运风险的本质。因此,除非是可归责于政府的违约事由(如政府延迟付费,土地使用权延后提供),或政府行为造成的损失(如法律变更或执照迟发),或政府终局取得资产所有权的情形(如合同提前终止的资产移交与回购),才会以政府提出经济补偿或赔偿的方式解决争议,否则 PPP 争议的处理通常不会通过合同条款变更、豁免责任、延长建设或营运期、贷款援助、税费减免的方式解决。

不过,对于社会资本方违反 PPP 项目合同的责任,除社会资本方自己可能遭受的不利益(如延后营运使营运期相应缩短因此减少的营收)外,PPP 项目合同大多会约定社会资本方应负的违约金或损害赔偿责任,此种争议自然会以经济赔偿的方式解决,此应为 PPP 项目涉及政府与公共利益的原因使然。

(六)PPP 项目的争议解决具有高度个案性

因为 PPP 项目合同的争议通常通过协调、调解或仲裁方式解决,而协调委员、调解委员在处理争议时,通常会充分考虑合同双方的立场及需求,提出的解决方案弹性较大;再加上各委员的见解未必相同,因此,通过协调或调解解决争议的结果,各 PPP 项目个案差距颇大。至于采用仲裁方式解决的 PPP 项目争议,更因仲裁的保密性及仲裁判断个案原则的特征,亦难有一致的结果。一般争议交由法院审理,可能因判决先例或上级审的审查而就特定争议类型形成一定原则的解决方式,相比之下,PPP 项目的争议解决具有高度的个案性。

二、PPP项目合同的争议类型

根据笔者多年参与PPP争议处理的经验,可以将PPP项目合同的争议类型,按筹办阶段、建设阶段、营运阶段及移转阶段,分别归类如下。

(一)PPP项目筹办阶段的争议类型

自特定社会资本方中标后,至成立项目公司与政府签订PPP项目合同的期间,为PPP项目的筹办阶段。此阶段可能发生的争议,包括:社会资本方中标效力的争议,社会资本方资质不符合招标规定或违反招标文件规定可否撤销中标函的争议;社会资本方无法成立项目公司或拒绝签订PPP项目合同衍生的投标保函没收及损害赔偿争议;社会资本方在签订PPP合同时无法提供银行履约保函的争议等。

因为此等争议发生于PPP项目合同生效前,同政府与社会资本间尚无合同关系,故必须依据《政府采购法》及其相关法规,参考《行政许可法》或者《民法通则》等规定予以解决。且有相当数量的争议必须依照行政法的相关规定处理,无法通过协调、调解或仲裁方式处理。

(二)PPP项目建设阶段的争议类型

自PPP项目合同签订后,至项目开始部分或全部营运为止,大致上属于PPP项目的建设阶段。其间发生的争议,除与EPC或Turnkey合同的争议类似外,尚有政府是否完整履行义务的争议。常见的争议类型,包括项目融资取得额度不足及取得迟延的争议、政府协助事项与政府应办事项违反责任的争议、土地使用权瑕疵及交付争议、土地出让金或租金计算争议、项目公司股权变更争议、项目审批或证照许可迟延所生责任争议、设计审查标准争议、建设完工期限认定争议、工期展延争议、工期展延衍生时间关联成本补偿争议、逾期罚款争议、PPP项目合同建设期展延争议、完工认定标准争议、试运转通过与否争议、建造成本超支补贴争议、营建物价上涨补贴争议、不可抗力/除外情事认定及其责任争议、保险购买范围及违反责任争议、法律与政策变更补偿争议、特许权或工作范围变更争议、融资方介入权行使效力争议、履约保函到期更新争议,以及违约金争议等。

因为PPP项目建设阶段的争议,仍以建设成本、进度及质量的控制为主要关注事项,故其争议的处理,除适用PPP项目合同条款、适用或类推适用《合同法》规定外,工程风险分配原则亦被广泛地运用,争议性质应属民事争议。但是争议若与政府审批、特许权授权范围,或与政府的行政作为或不作为有关的,除可明确区隔为行政行为而可按行政争议处理外,产生于PPP项目合同履行的争议,是否亦可按行政争议确定管辖问题,仍有待法学界讨论厘清。

在我国台湾地区,"促进民间参与公共建设法"第12条规定,"主办机关与民间机构之权利义务,除本法另有规定外,依投资契约之约定,契约无约定者,适用民事法相关之规定","投资契约之订定,应以维护公共利益及公平合理为原则;其履行,应依诚实及信用之方法"。此规定已将PPP项目合同定性为民事契约,解决了过去究竟属于民事或行政争议的纷扰。当然,此民事合同的定性,只限于处理PPP项目合同的争议。至于政府在PPP项目合同履行过程中,另行基于行政主管机关地位,依据相关行政法规对于社会资本方所为的行政处分,若有争议,社会资本方仍应依行政程序法及行政诉讼法的相关规定,按照行政争讼程序解决争议。

(三)PPP项目营运阶段的争议类型

自PPP项目建设全部或部分完成,经政府有关单位验收同意后开始全部或部分营运,至项目合同开始进入移转阶段为止,属于营运期。在此期间发生的争议,主要围绕营运收入不如预期与营运服务质量不良所产生的影响。依据世界银行发布的《PPP参考指引2.0版》中所说明的PPP基本定义,社会资本方对于PPP项目必须承受主要的风险及管理责任,且其收益与营运表现相关。因此,如果PPP合同设计的权利义务无法满足前述定义的特性,或社会资本方没有能力提供符合质量要求的设施或服务以及承受相应的风险,或因不可抗力事由使风险超出社会资本方可承受的范围时,争议即会随之发生。

常见的PPP项目营运阶段争议,包括营运许可延后或无法取得的争议、营运期拟制起算的争议、营运不善的认定争议、设施维修更新不符规范争议、营运项目及营运方式违反合同争议、违反营运计划的认定争议、附属事业营运范围及收入使用限制争议、营运事故争议、政府付费(服务费或其他费用)计算与调整争议、可行性缺口补助金额计算与执行方式调整争议、政府保证收入或类似保证的有效性争议、项目收费定价与调价争议、权利金计算与调整争议、财务检查与资产处分违反规定争议、营收不如预期的补救争议、营运中断的补偿争议、贷款清偿及担保品处分争议、资产/不动产证券化与PPP项目合同规范冲突的争议、PPP项目合同营运期展延争议、不可抗力/除外情事认定及其效果争议、法律与政策变更补偿争议、营运绩效评估争议、优先续约权争议、特许权或营运许可范围变更的对价争议、政府接管营运争议、融资方介入权行使效力争议、履约保函到期更新争议,以及违约金争议等。

对于前述争议的解决,除依据合同条款请求或违反合同约定的争议(如服务费、权利金或违约金给付争议)可能直接以金钱补偿或赔偿外,有许多社会资本方实际营收与预估营收差异所衍生的争议,可能会以"不可抗力条款"或"公益变更条款"作为调控阀,通过这些条款的具体运作,以变更合同条款、减少权利金、调整服务费、豁免责任、变更社会资本方股权结构或延长营运期等方式解决。而此必须通过预测未来减少收入、重新检讨财务计划,甚至修正财务模组与假设参数的方式,才会获得较公平合理的调整数据。其中当然也必须将可归责于合同当事人的影响考虑在内,增减调整幅度。一般来说,"直接换算法"及"财务计划调整法"是较常采用的方法。而能使用此方法的,通常是采用仲裁、协调或调解等弹性较大的争议处理机制,向法院提起诉讼的方式则因受限于诉讼目标类型与诉讼法制,较难使用。

(四)PPP项目移转阶段的争议类型

如PPP项目最后必须将资产及设施移转给政府,于移转准备作业开始起至移转完成为止,即为移转阶段。而移转的原因,有合同期限届满及合同提前终止两种情况。因此,与合同提前终止有关的争议,也一并在此说明。

常见的PPP项目移转阶段争议,于合同期限届满的情形,主要集中在移转资产是否符合约定质量与维护条件的争议、有偿移转价格评估争议、移转资产存在权利瑕疵的争议、技术及知识产权转让范围争议、营运接管过渡期间权责划分争议、合同期限届满后继续委托营运范围及条件的争议。在合同提前终止的情形下,发生的争议类型则非常多,包括合同能否提前终止的争议、政府回购资产义务范围的争议、社会资本方应移交资产范围的争议、社会资本方拒绝移交资产及返还用地的争议、在建工程回购补偿金额的争议、营运资产回购补偿金额的争议、政府承受贷款债务及清偿范围的争议、资产/不动产证券化清算与权利归属争议、履约保函没收争议、违约金及损害赔偿争议等。而前述争议内容会因合同提前终止的原因是不可抗力、政府因素或社会资本方违约而有所不同。

由于 PPP 项目合同的移转阶段,距离双方签订合同时间点比较遥远,短则 15 年,长则 50 年、70 年,故合同双方常因难以预期未来情况而无法订定较周全的合同条款,有时还会认为移转争议短期不会发生而忽略商议完整条款的重要性,故移转阶段的争议,常会因合同条款的不完整而必须另外通过适用法律及风险分配原则、考虑公共利益等因素加以解决。至于合同提前终止的争议,则会因提前终止事由的不同而更为繁杂。但政府与社会资本方均希望尽速退场、终局解决争议的态度应比较一致,故对于此争议,双方通过协调、调解机制而和解的案例确实不少,其他无法解决的多为资产回购补偿价格多少而发生的争议,则留待诉讼或仲裁解决。

三、结论

PPP 项目合同的争议有其特殊性,且争议类型繁多,已如前述。但因 PPP 项目执行时间长,且事关国家及社会利益,其争议的解决,除已确定该项目确实无法以 PPP 模式推动外,大致上仍以维系 PPP 项目存续为考量方向。因此,争议的处理要考虑如何使 PPP 项目合同具有生命性、延续性,并与时俱进,发挥灵活调整双方权利义务的功能,实在是一门艺术。对此,除了必须有专业的财务评估作为依据外,亦须有充分了解 PPP 项目合同架构、风险分配与调整的合同管理或法律专业人才的参与,才能有效达成。而如何让合同双方在合同条款订定及协商时即预先合理规范各类争议的处理原则,并且在合同执行过程中,应对可能发生的争议并提前采取消弭争议的行为,更事关 PPP 模式推动的成败,值得各界关注。

国际投资争端仲裁的中国实践：投资仲裁规则与《ICSID公约》

王正志*

摘要：《投资仲裁规则》的制定符合国家“一带一路”建设的实际需要，有利于进一步完善国际投资仲裁制度。随着国际投资活动的快速发展，我国已经从投资规则的“旁观者”逐渐发展为投资规则重要的“参与者”。本文将对《投资仲裁规则》的一些主要特点及特殊规定与《ICSID公约》进行对比。

关键词：国际投资仲裁　投资仲裁规则　《ICSID公约》

中国国际贸易仲裁委员会（以下简称贸仲委）于2017年10月1日起施行《中国国际贸易仲裁委员会国际投资争端仲裁规则》（以下简称《投资仲裁规则》），自此，企业与投资所在国政府之间的争议可以在中国的仲裁机构进行仲裁。

近年来，仲裁案件数量的激增使企业及政府对独立、高效和公正的投资仲裁规则需求越发迫切，尤其是企业对仲裁规则人性化、本土化的需求愈加明显。自1900年常设仲裁法院（Permanent Court of Arbitration，PCA）在海牙成立，截至2019年1月1日，全球范围内的投资仲裁案件累计达到942件，其中约2/3

* 王正志，高文律师事务所高级合伙人，贸仲委仲裁员。

的案件系向位于华盛顿的国际投资争端解决中心(International Centre for Settlement of Investment Disputes,ICSID)提出,由ICSID根据《关于解决国家与他国国民之间投资争议公约》(ICSID Convention Rules and Regulations,以下简称《ICSID公约》)及其仲裁规则受理;其余1/3的案件,则基本由常设仲裁法院和瑞典斯德哥尔摩商会仲裁院(Arbitration Institute of the Stockholm Chamber of Commerce,AISCC)等仲裁机构受理或管理。[①]

《投资仲裁规则》的出台是保护投资者合法权益的需要。2019年9月12日,商务部、国家统计局和国家外汇管理局联合发布《2018年度中国对外直接投资统计公报》(以下简称《公报》),正式公布2018年中国对外直接投资统计数据。根据《公报》披露的数据,截至2018年年底,中国有超2.7万家境内投资者在全球188个国家(地区)设立对外直接投资企业4.3万家,全球80%以上的国家(地区)都有中国的投资。中国在“一带一路”沿线国家(地区)设立境外企业超过1万家,2018年当年直接投资流量178.9亿美元,年末存量1727.7亿美元,占比分别为12.5%和8.7%。中国对外直接投资地域分布高度集中,存量前20位的国家(地区)占总额的91.7%。在此背景下,由中国制定本土投资仲裁规则,并由中国境内的仲裁机构受理相关的投资争端,将为投资者寻求法律救济提供更多的选择,这不仅有助于维护中国投资者在境外投资的合法权益,也有助于维护外国投资者在中国投资的合法权益。当然,该规则也为想要采用有中国特色或大陆法系特色仲裁的非中国投资者或东道国提供一个新的选择。

除此之外,《投资仲裁规则》的出台还推动了“一带一路”倡议的需要。在“一带一路”倡议的实施过程中,相当一部分项目投资规模大、建设周期长,存在各类复杂情况,加上沿线不少国家政局不稳定、法制不完善,相关投资项目面临较高的政治风险和法律风险。制定中国本土的投资仲裁规则,有助于妥善解决我国企业与沿线国家之间的投资争端,更好地推动“一带一路”倡议的实施。

---

① 来源于联合国贸易和发展会议(United Nations Conference on Trade and Development,UNCTAD)关于投资者与国家争端解决的最新统计:World Investment Report 2019,p.103。

一、《投资仲裁规则》与《ICSID公约》的比较

《投资仲裁规则》由正文和附件组成。其中正文共6章58条,两个附件为《仲裁费用表》和《紧急仲裁员程序》。《投资仲裁规则》借鉴了ICSID等国际投资仲裁机构的仲裁规则,并根据国际投资规则的发展趋势,在透明度、第三方资助、紧急仲裁员程序等方面进行了探索,并具有仲裁与调解相结合等特色。

(一)管辖依据

1.《投资仲裁规则》第2条

当事人之间解决国际投资争端的仲裁协议可以置于合同、条约、法律法规或其他文件中。一方当事人通过合同、条约、法律法规或其他文件作出了提交仲裁委员会仲裁或按照本规则仲裁的意思表示,另一方当事人通过提起仲裁或以其他方式予以接受的,视为达成仲裁协议。

2.《ICSID公约》第25条

中心的管辖适用于缔约国(或缔约国向中心指定的该国的任何组成部分或机构)和另一缔约国国民之间直接因投资而产生并经双方书面同意提交给中心的任何法律争端。当双方表示同意后,任何一方不得单方面撤销其同意。

(二)仲裁地

1.《投资仲裁规则》第28条

当事人对仲裁地作出约定的,从其约定;当事人对仲裁地未作约定的,以管理案件的投资争端解决中心或香港仲裁中心所在地为仲裁地,仲裁庭也可视案件的具体情形确定其他地点,但该仲裁地通常应该位于《承认及执行外国仲裁裁决的公约》(the new York Convention on the Recognition and Enforcement of Foreign Arbitral Awards)的成员国境内。中国内地与中国香港特别行政区的不同法域为当事人提供了天然的选择空间,当然,仲裁庭在《承认及执行外国仲裁裁决的公约》的成员国内有权确定其他地点为仲裁地。

2.《ICSID公约》第54条

《ICSID公约》没有仲裁地的概念。《ICSID公约》第54条规定:每一缔约

国应承认依照本公约作出的裁决具有约束力,并在其领土内履行该裁决所加的财政义务,正如该裁决是该国法院的最后判决一样。

(三)三人仲裁庭组成

1.《投资仲裁规则》第12条

第12条第2款规定:第三名仲裁员由双方当事人在被申请人收到启动仲裁通知书之日起30日内共同选定或共同委托仲裁委员会主任指定。第三名仲裁员为首席仲裁员。

第12条第3款规定:当事人未在上述期限内选定或委托仲裁委员会主任指定首席仲裁员的,由仲裁委员会主任指定。

2.《ICSID公约》第2条、第38条

根据《ICSID公约》第2条的规定,双方可以商定仲裁庭的组成方式,如果无法达成一致,则适用《ICSID公约》第37条第2款:如双方对仲裁员的人数和任命的方法不能达成协议,仲裁庭应由3名仲裁员组成,由每一方各任命仲裁员1名,第三人由双方协议任命,并担任首席仲裁员。

第38条规定:如果在秘书长依照该公约第36条第3款发出关于请求已予以登记的通知后90日内,或在双方可能同意的其他期限内未能组成仲裁庭,主席经任何一方请求,并尽可能同双方磋商后,可任命尚未任命的仲裁员或数名仲裁员。主席根据本条任命的仲裁员不得为争端一方的缔约国的国民或其国民是争端一方的缔约国的国民。

(四)仲裁员的回避

1.《投资仲裁规则》第17条

当事人申请仲裁员回避,另一当事人同意的,或被申请回避的仲裁员主动提出不再担任仲裁员的,该仲裁员不再担任本案的仲裁员。上述情形并不表示当事人提出回避的理由成立。也就是说,即使当事人提出的回避理由不成立,只要是双方当事人同意的或被申请回避的仲裁员自己提出的,则仲裁员应当回避。

2.《ICSID公约》

相比而言,《ICSID公约》中并不存在双方当事人同意即可更换仲裁员的规定,《ICSID 公约》对申请回避的程序性要求非常复杂费时,并且 ICSID 的仲裁员回避申请在一般情况下由仲裁庭的其他“未受争议仲裁员”审核裁定。当然,仲裁规则制度的设立初衷就是为了保护当事方能够获得一个公正、独立的仲裁裁决,而 ICSID 回避机制的设立显然在公正性和效率方面易受质疑。

(五)仲裁语言

1.《投资仲裁规则》第 29 条

当事人对仲裁语言作出约定的,从其约定。当事人对仲裁语言没有约定的,由仲裁庭视案件的具体情形确定仲裁语言。

2.《ICSID 公约》第 22 条

可以同意当事人在仲裁程序中使用一种或两种官方语言(英国、法国、西班牙),如果他们在任何非官方语言上达成一致,则需仲裁庭在与秘书长磋商后才能予以批准。

(六)第三方资助信息披露

1.《投资仲裁规则》第 27 条

第 27 条第 2 款规定,获得第三方资助的当事人应在签署资助协议后,毫不迟延地将第三方资助安排的事实、性质、第三方的名称与住址,书面告知对方当事人、仲裁庭及管理案件的投资争端解决中心或香港仲裁中心。仲裁庭也有权命令获得第三方资助的当事人披露相关情况。

2.《ICSID 公约》

在投资仲裁案件中,仲裁庭为保障仲裁程序的公正性,会以程序令的形式要求当事人对其是否接受第三方资助,以及第三方资助人的身份进行披露。[①] 但是,《ICSID 公约》并没有明确该披露义务。因此披露内容的义务及程度取决于资助协议的具体约定,在实际案例中资助方通常会要求设立保密条款,不予披露资助信息。在这种情况下,如果仲裁庭通过程序令(或者明文规定)要求受资助方披露其受资助信息就会导致与协议约定的保密义务发生冲突。

① Muhammet Çap& Sehil In aat Endustri ve Ticaret Ltd. Sti. v. Turkmenistan(ICSID Case No. ARB/12/6).

(七)保密性

1.《投资仲裁规则》第 23 条

当部分或者全部程序需要保密时,双方当事人、仲裁庭和其他仲裁参与人均负有保密义务。

2.《ICSID 公约》

在 ICSID 仲裁机制中,随着《ICSID 公约》的修订和实施,对原来遵循的仲裁程序秘密性原则作了比较大的改革,在第三方加入程序、非争端方提交书面意见以及公布仲裁裁决方面,都朝着增加透明度的方向发展。但是,这些改革乃是以商事争端仲裁机制为框架进行的谨小慎微的改革,只是以尊重当事人合意为前提所进行的有限突破,一些新增加的透明度规定,也不过是秘密性原则的例外或补充而已。

(八)费用

《投资仲裁规则》采用了与贸仲委普通仲裁规则相当的收费模式。案件登记费为人民币 25000 元(约 3800 美元),机构管理费与仲裁员报酬以争议金额为基础按照特定比例进行计算。经当事人各方同意,仲裁员报酬可以高于规则中仲裁员报酬表的最高额,当事人也可以约定仲裁员报酬以小时费率为基础收取。当事人可以使用与人民币等值的外币缴纳仲裁费用。

相比之下,《 ICSID 公约》会在接收当事人的仲裁申请书时收取 25000 美元(一经收取,不予退还),在该仲裁申请书登记后,会另外收取 42000 美元。并且,仲裁庭成员每参加一天仲裁会议或工作满 8 小时的一天要收取 3000 美元。

二、《投资仲裁规则》的特殊规定(《ICSID 公约》中无类似规定)

(一)部分裁决

《投资仲裁规则》第 48 条第 1 款规定,仲裁庭认为必要或当事人提出请求并经仲裁庭同意的,仲裁庭可以在作出最终裁决之前,就当事人的某些请求事项先行作出部分裁决。部分裁决是终局的,对双方当事人均有约束力。第 2 款规定,当事人应履行部分裁决。一方当事人不履行部分裁决,不影响仲裁程序的继续进行,也不影响仲裁庭作出最终裁决。

同时,仲裁庭有权对裁决书进行更正、解释和作出补充裁决。此外,仲裁庭应将裁决书草案提交仲裁委员会核阅,在不影响仲裁庭独立裁决的情况下,仲裁委员会可以就裁决书的有关问题提请仲裁庭注意,这是《投资仲裁规则》的特色。

(二)仲裁与调解相结合

《投资仲裁规则》第43条规定,双方当事人有调解愿望的,或一方当事人有调解愿望并经仲裁庭征得另一方当事人同意的,仲裁庭可以在仲裁过程中对案件进行调解。

仲裁与调解相结合是贸仲委仲裁的显著特点。该做法将仲裁和调解各自的优点紧密结合起来,不仅有助于解决当事人之间的争议,而且有助于保持当事人的友好合作关系。实践证明,很多国际投资争端是经过调解最终得到了妥善解决并得到良好的执行。

(三)紧急仲裁员程序

紧急仲裁员制度,是指为了保障仲裁各方当事人的合法利益而在仲裁庭组庭之前依据当事人申请任命紧急仲裁员,以便对证据、财产作出保全措施的裁决或裁令,以保障当事人的合法财产在仲裁庭组庭之前不受非法侵犯的特别仲裁制度。[①]

贸仲规则规定当事人可依据《紧急仲裁员程序》向投资争端解决中心或香港仲裁中心申请紧急性临时救济,紧急仲裁员可以决定采取必要或适当的紧急性临时救济措施,紧急仲裁员的决定对双方当事人具有约束力。

(四)公开审理与透明度

根据《投资仲裁规则》第32条的规定,除非当事人另有约定或仲裁庭另有决定,开庭审理应公开进行。同时,该规则第55条规定,仲裁相关资料与信息

---

① 韩斯睿:《国际商事机构仲裁视角下的紧急仲裁员制度》,载《北京仲裁》2014年第4期。

（除机密信息和其他受保护信息外）可以由贸仲委公开。可以公开的资料与信息包括：仲裁申请书，仲裁答辩书，仲裁反请求申请书，当事人或第三方的书面意见。此规定积极回应了国际社会对投资仲裁制度的质疑，有助于《投资仲裁规则》被国际社会广泛接受。

第五届“中伦杯”获奖论文选登

编者按：

为进一步推进中国商事仲裁的发展，中国国际经济贸易仲裁委员会与中国人民大学法学院、中华全国律师协会、北京律师协会联合发起了“中国仲裁周”活动。“中国仲裁周”旨在打造一个全国性、国际性、开放性的仲裁宣传、交流和研讨的平台，每年举办一届。在2017年和2018年举办的“中国仲裁周”活动期间，“中国仲裁周”活动组委会分别举办了第五届和第六届“中伦杯”全国国际商事仲裁征文大赛活动，面向有志于研究国际商事仲裁理论与实践的教师、学生和实务工作者征文。

征文活动得到了广泛的欢迎和热烈的响应。“中国仲裁周”活动组委会邀请多位国内知名专家通过公开、公平、公正的程序进行评审，第五届最终评选出28篇获奖论文，第六届评选出30篇获奖论文。获奖论文对国际商事仲裁理论与实践中存在的问题进行了翔实的解读和深度的思考，提出的意见和建议对我国商事仲裁的未来发展不乏参考和借鉴价值。经“中国仲裁周”活动组委会推荐，本书将刊发部分获奖论文，以飨读者。

撤销仲裁调解书:现状与建言
——基于对司法实践的考察

元昱文*

摘要:当前法律和司法解释对能否申请撤销仲裁调解书规定得不明确,导致司法实践中在此及相关问题上存在不同认定。在仲裁和解协议并非当事人真实意思表示、仲裁调解书违背社会公共利益的情形下,径直否定仲裁调解书的可撤销性并不符合仲裁调解制度的预设。仲裁调解书的撤销事由至少应当包括无权代理签署仲裁和解协议和违背社会公共利益。

关键词:仲裁调解书　可撤销性　撤销事由

一、研究背景

中国的法律和实践坚定地鼓励仲裁和调解结合:①在法律层面,我国《仲裁法》第51条和第52条正式规定了仲裁调解制度;②在实践层面,除这项制度的

* 元昱文,中国政法大学国际法学院硕士研究生。

① 唐厚志:《正在扩展着的文化:仲裁与调解相结合或与解决争议替代方法(ADR)相结合》,载《中国对外贸易》2002年第2期。

② 我国《仲裁法》第51条规定:“仲裁庭在作出裁决前,可以先行调解。当事人自愿调解的,仲裁庭应当调解。调解不成的,应当及时作出裁决。调解达成协议的,仲裁庭应当制作调解书或者根据协议的结果制作裁决书。调解书与裁决书具有同等法律效力。”

第52条规定:“调解书应当写明仲裁请求和当事人协议的结果。调解书由仲裁员签名,加盖仲裁委员会印章,送达双方当事人。调解书经双方当事人签收后,即发生法律效力。在调解书签收前当事人反悔的,仲裁庭应当及时作出裁决。”

首倡者——中国国际经济贸易仲裁委员会外,《仲裁法》生效后新组建的仲裁机构纷纷将其纳入仲裁规则之中,并在实践中广泛应用。以能检索到的最新数据为参照:2016 年全国仲裁案件以调解和解方式结案共计 12 万件,占受案总数的 58%。[①]

根据我国《仲裁法》第 51 条的规定,若仲裁中的调解取得成功,则可能产生两种不同的结案方式:一是仲裁庭根据协议的结果作出裁决(合意仲裁裁决);二是仲裁庭制作调解书。当以合意仲裁裁决方式结案时,根据最高人民法院《关于适用〈中华人民共和国仲裁法〉若干问题的解释》(以下简称《仲裁法司法解释》)第 28 条[②]的规定,申请不予执行制度不适用于合意仲裁裁决。最高人民法院《关于人民法院办理仲裁裁决执行案件若干问题的规定》(以下简称《执行规定》)第 17 条[③]在延续这一原则性规定之后,增加了一种例外情形:可以对违背公共利益的合意仲裁裁决申请不予执行。至于能否申请撤销合意仲裁裁决,现行法律、司法解释并未明确规定,但由于合意仲裁裁决具备仲裁裁决的外观,应当认定可以撤销;[④]当以仲裁调解书结案时,根据前述《仲裁法司法解释》第 28 条和《执行规定》第 17 条的规定,同合意仲裁裁决一致,一般不能对仲裁调解书申请不予执行,除非其违背社会公共利益;至于能否申请撤销仲裁调解书,现行法律、司法解释均无明确规定。具体归纳见表 1。

表 1 《仲裁法司法解释》和《执行规定》的规定总结

类别	申请不予执行	申请撤销
合意仲裁裁决	不能申请,除非违背社会公共利益	具有裁决外观,推定可以申请
仲裁调解书	不能申请,除非违背社会公共利益	无明确规定

① 参见张维:《中国仲裁事业发展进入加速期,全国仲裁年受案量首次突破 20 万件》,载《法制日报》2017 年 5 月 5 日,第 6 版。

② 第 28 条规定:“当事人请求不予执行仲裁调解书或者根据当事人之间的和解协议作出的仲裁裁决书的,人民法院不予支持。”

③ 第 17 条规定:“被执行人申请不予执行仲裁调解书或者根据当事人之间的和解协议、调解协议作出的仲裁裁决,人民法院不予支持,但该仲裁调解书或者仲裁裁决违背社会公共利益的除外。”

④ 参见黄忠顺:《调解的共通效力》,载《国家检察官学院学报》2014 年第 3 期。

由此可见,在仲裁调解司法审查领域,关于仲裁调解书的可撤销性问题,无法从现行法律和司法解释中直接找到确切答案,成为该领域中缺失的一环。法律规定层面的无解,自然会带来学理上的争鸣。有学者认为,由于仲裁调解书与仲裁裁决书具有同等法律效力,有关仲裁裁决书的补正、补充裁决、撤销及执行的规定应延伸适用于仲裁调解书;①另有学者认为,法院作为行使国家司法权的主体,其诉讼活动必须依据法律进行,既然法律未授权法院行使撤销或不予执行仲裁调解书的权力,法院就不得超越法律规定行使权力。②

面对这一法律规定不明确、理论上存在争议的问题,在司法实践中,法院是如何认定的?对于申请撤销仲裁调解书的案件,法院作何裁判?笔者不揣浅陋,“从实践中来”:通过考察相关司法实践,旨在了解申请撤销仲裁调解书案件的“真实生存状态”;“到实践中去”:以考察结果为参照,提出建言,以期裨益于申请撤销仲裁调解书案件裁判的统一和规范。

二、司法实践

(一)分歧:撤销仲裁调解书“于法无据”还是“理所当然”?

笔者以“中国裁判文书网”、“北大法宝”法律数据库和“无讼”案例为检索工具,收集整理“申请撤销仲裁调解书”案例共计54个。③ 以裁判结果为分类依据,该54个案例存在撤销调解书、驳回起诉、驳回上诉、不予受理、驳回申请等不同情形,见表2。

---

① 参见宋连斌:《从仲裁与调解相结合到单独调解》,载《昆明理工大学学报》(社会科学版)2009年第11期;邵明:《论我国和谐社会中的民事调解》,载《学术界》2008年第2期。

② 参见王小莉:《仲裁调解书有关法律问题辨析》,载《仲裁研究》2008年第4期;廖永安、张庆霖:《论仲裁调解书撤销制度的确立》,载《烟台大学学报》(哲学社会科学版)2011年第2期。

③ 由于案例来源及检索方式的局限,笔者不能保证穷尽收集了所有相关案例,但结合裁判年度(2012~2017年)、法院地域分布(湖南、广东、吉林、河北、陕西、江苏、内蒙古、浙江、安徽、山东、山西、河南、上海、湖北)等因素综合考量,本次收集到的全部案例可以在一定程度上反映针对“申请撤销仲裁调解书”的司法实践现状。

表2 申请撤销仲裁调解书案例分类

<table>
<tr><th>类别</th><th>裁判结果</th><th colspan="2">频数(个)</th><th>频率(%)</th></tr>
<tr><td rowspan="2">肯定可撤销性</td><td>撤销仲裁调解书</td><td>12</td><td rowspan="2">22</td><td rowspan="2">41</td></tr>
<tr><td>驳回撤销申请</td><td>10</td></tr>
<tr><td rowspan="4">否定可撤销性</td><td>驳回起诉</td><td>4</td><td rowspan="4">32</td><td rowspan="4">59</td></tr>
<tr><td>驳回上诉</td><td>5</td></tr>
<tr><td>不予受理</td><td>3</td></tr>
<tr><td>驳回申请</td><td>20</td></tr>
<tr><td colspan="2">合计</td><td colspan="2">54</td><td>100</td></tr>
</table>

通过对54个案例的初步归类,可以直观地发现司法实践在“仲裁调解书是否具有可撤销性”这一基本问题上存在较大分歧:以“撤销调解书” 方式结案的案例反映了一部分法院对此问题持肯定态度,以“驳回起诉”“不予受理”方式结案的案例直接表明了一部分法院对此问题持否定态度。同样是裁定“驳回申请”的案例,其中20个案例是在否定仲裁调解书可撤销性的基础上驳回当事人的撤销申请,另有10个案例则以明示或默示[①]的方式肯定了仲裁调解书的可撤销性,继而以当事人的申请理由不符合法定撤销情形为由驳回当事人的撤销申请。以“驳回上诉”方式结案的5个案例均明示否定仲裁调解书的可撤销性。

这种分歧甚至体现在同一法院在同一年份的裁判之中。从主审法院和案号信息可以看出,陕西省汉中市中级人民法院(2017)陕07民特16号、陕西省汉中市中级人民法院(2017)陕07民特15号、陕西省汉中市中级人民法院(2017)陕07民特5号3个案例均由汉中中院于2017年裁判,但在仲裁调解书可撤销性问题上却存在不同认定。在前两个案例中,法院作出撤销裁定;在第三个案例中,法院以“裁定撤销仲裁调解书无法律授权”为由裁定驳回起诉。

① 默示方式表现为:不专门针对仲裁调解书可撤销性问题展开说理,直接援引我国《仲裁法》第58条裁判当事人的撤销申请是否成立。

上述54个案例中,有32个案例(占样本总量的59%)的法院否定了仲裁调解书的可撤销性(见图1)。通观这32个裁判文书,其共同意旨即"申请撤销仲裁调解书没有法律依据"。除此之外,还有法院提出其他理由进一步阐明其立场,这些理由大致可被分为三类:(1)从"减少对当事人意思自治的干预"出发,法院应坚持仲裁司法监督有限原则;①(2)根据《仲裁法司法解释》第28条的规定,"当事人请求不予执行仲裁调解书或者根据当事人之间的和解协议作出的仲裁裁决书的,人民法院不予支持",法院应严格限制当事人申请撤销仲裁调解书;②(3)诉讼程序方面的规定属于强制性规定,不可轻易对其进行扩张解释,法律未授权人民法院行使撤销仲裁调解书的权力,人民法院不得超越法律规定行使权力。③

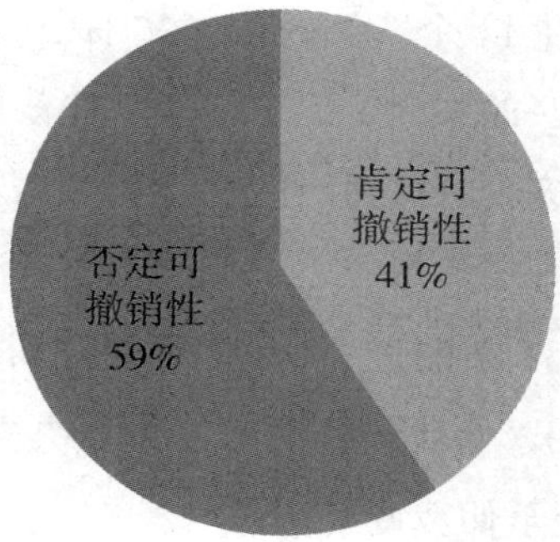

图1　肯定/否定可撤销性占比

在其余22个案例中(占样本总量的41%),法院肯定了仲裁调解书的可撤销性。以肯定的方式作为划分依据,该22起案件又可分为明示肯定和默示肯定两种模式,具体情况如表3所示。

---

① 参见陕西省汉中市中级人民法院(2017)陕07民特5号、安徽省淮北市中级人民法院(2016)皖06民特字12号、安徽省淮北市中级人民法院(2016)皖06民特3号、安徽省高级人民法院(2016)皖民特字第4号、湖北省宜昌市中级人民法院(2015)鄂宜昌中立民初字第00015号、安徽省淮北市中级人民法院(2017)皖06民特3号、山东省莱芜市中级人民法院(2016)鲁12民特3号。

② 参见陕西省汉中市中级人民法院(2017)陕07民特5号、湖北省宜昌市中级人民法院(2015)鄂宜昌中立民初字第00015号、山东省莱芜市中级人民法院(2016)鲁12民特3号。

③ 参见山西省高级人民法院民事裁定书(2016)晋民终438号。

表3 仲裁调解书的可撤销性的肯定方式

<table>
<tr><th>模式</th><th>具体情形</th><th colspan="2">频数(个)</th><th>频率(%)</th></tr>
<tr><td rowspan="2">默示</td><td>被申请人未提出异议,法院未作出说明</td><td>8</td><td rowspan="2">11</td><td rowspan="2">50</td></tr>
<tr><td>被申请人提出异议,法院未作出回应</td><td>3</td></tr>
<tr><td>明示</td><td>依据:仲裁调解书与仲裁裁决书具有同等效力</td><td colspan="2">11</td><td>50</td></tr>
<tr><td colspan="2">总计</td><td colspan="2">22</td><td>100</td></tr>
</table>

首先,值得注意的是,在法律和司法解释在仲裁调解书可撤销性问题上均没有明确规定的前提下,在11个案例的裁判文书中(尤其是其中3个"被申请人明确提出可撤销性异议"的案例),法院未对"仲裁调解书能否撤销"这一基础性问题作出回应,而直接适用我国《仲裁法》第58条。

其次,无论是在默示肯定情形下径直适用《仲裁法》第58条,还是明示肯定情形下对《仲裁法》第51条的援引,其背后的逻辑都是:即使并无撤销仲裁调解书的明文规定,但基于"仲裁调解书与仲裁裁决书具有同等效力",应将仲裁裁决书的撤销制度类推至仲裁调解书。

综上所述,在仲裁调解书可撤销性问题上,由于法律规定不明确,一如学理上的分歧,司法实践亦存在不同认定:一部分法院认为,申请撤销仲裁调解书于法无据,不予支持;另一部分法院认为,由于"仲裁调解书与仲裁裁决书具有同等效力",撤销制度当然类推适用于仲裁调解书。其中,59%的样本案例采纳前一种观点,41%的样本案例作出了后一种认定,表明司法实践在此问题上的分歧相对较大,统一裁判的需求较为迫切。

(二)差异:同样否定可撤销性,裁判结果却不一致

"驳回起诉"是指人民法院立案后,发现不符合我国《民事诉讼法》第119

条规定的4项起诉条件[①]或者属于《民事诉讼法》第124条所列7种情形[②]的，依照法定程序裁定予以驳回。根据我国《民事诉讼法》第154条的规定，[③]对驳回起诉裁定可以上诉；根据《诉讼费用交纳办法》第8条[④]的规定，裁定驳回起诉的案件不交纳案件受理费。相较于“驳回起诉”，首先，“驳回申请”被排除在《民事诉讼法》第124条规定的可以上诉的情形之外；其次，这不属于《诉讼费用交纳办法》第8条的统摄范围，被裁定“驳回申请”的，仍需交纳诉讼费用。因此，裁定结果的差异将导致当事人在上诉权利和诉讼费用上的不同境况。

在样本案例中，同样是基于“撤销申请没有法律依据”否定仲裁调解书的可撤销性，法院的裁判结果却不尽相同：在4个案例中，法院以“没有法律依据”为由裁定驳回起诉；在20个案例中，法院以“没有法律依据”为由裁定驳回申请。

后20个以“没有法律依据”为由裁定驳回申请的案例，对上诉权利和案件受理费的裁定也不一致，具体情况如表4所示。

---

① 《民事诉讼法》第119条规定：“起诉必须符合下列条件：(一)原告是与本案有直接利害关系的公民、法人和其他组织；(二)有明确的被告；(三)有具体的诉讼请求和事实、理由；(四)属于人民法院受理民事诉讼的范围和受诉人民法院管辖。”

② 《民事诉讼法》第124条规定：“人民法院对下列起诉，分别情形，予以处理：(一)依照行政诉讼法的规定，属于行政诉讼受案范围的，告知原告提起行政诉讼；(二)依照法律规定，双方当事人达成书面仲裁协议申请仲裁、不得向人民法院起诉的，告知原告向仲裁机构申请仲裁；(三)依照法律规定，应当由其他机关处理的争议，告知原告向有关机关申请解决；(四)对不属于本院管辖的案件，告知原告向有管辖权的人民法院起诉；(五)对判决、裁定、调解书已经发生法律效力的案件，当事人又起诉的，告知原告申请再审，但人民法院准许撤诉的裁定除外；(六)依照法律规定，在一定期限内不得起诉的案件，在不得起诉的期限内起诉的，不予受理；(七)判决不准离婚和调解和好的离婚案件，判决、调解维持收养关系的案件，没有新情况、新理由，原告在六个月内又起诉的，不予受理。”

③ 《民事诉讼法》第154条规定：“裁定适用于下列范围：(一)不予受理；(二)对管辖权有异议的；(三)驳回起诉；(四)保全和先予执行；(五)准许或者不准许撤诉；(六)中止或者终结诉讼；(七)补正判决书中的笔误；(八)中止或者终结执行；(九)撤销或者不予执行仲裁裁决；(十)不予执行公证机关赋予强制执行效力的债权文书；(十一)其他需要裁定解决的事项。对前款第一项至第三项裁定，可以上诉。裁定书应当写明裁定结果和作出该裁定的理由。裁定书由审判人员、书记员署名，加盖人民法院印章。口头裁定的，记入笔录。”

④ 《诉讼费用交纳办法》第8条规定：“下列案件不交纳案件受理费：(一)依照民事诉讼法规定的特别程序审理的案件；(二)裁定不予受理、驳回起诉、驳回上诉的案件；(三)对不予受理、驳回起诉和管辖权异议裁定不服，提起上诉的案件；(四)行政赔偿案件。”

表4 对上诉权利和案件受理费的裁定

序号	案号	能否上诉①	是否退费②
1	(2015)呼民仲字00023号	否	是
2	(2015)镇商仲审撤字第11号	否	
3	(2015)连商仲审撤字第00013号	否	
4	(2015)连商仲审撤字第00012号	否	
5	(2015)辽民他字第2号	否	否
6	(2015)安中民一初字第87号		是
7	(2015)并民再初字第6号	能	是
8	(2016)粤18民特41号		是
9	(2016)鲁12民特3号		否
10	(2017)沪01民特131号		
11	(2017)浙04民特3号		
12	(2017)浙04民特2号		
13	(2017)浙04民特9号		
14	(2017)浙04民特7号		
15	(2017)浙04民特6号		
16	(2017)浙04民特4号		
17	(2017)浙04民特8号		
18	(2017)浙11民特3号		
19	(2017)皖06民特3号		
20	(2017)沪01民特13号		

注:①表格中空白意为该裁判文书没有直接就裁判效力或上诉问题作出明确裁定,推定为不能上诉。

②表格中空白意为该裁判文书没有直接就案件受理费的交纳问题作出裁定,推定为不退免。

值得注意的是,在(2015)并民再初字第6号案件中,法院适用《民事诉讼法》第154条第1款第3项本应作出"驳回起诉"的裁定,最终却裁决"驳回申请",且裁定当事人可以上诉、获得退费,不知此系有意为之还是用词疏忽。本案申请人后又向山西省高级人民法院提起上诉,山西省高级人民法院在(2015)晋民终字第416号裁定书中却主张适用《民事诉讼法》第154条第1款第 11 项而非《民事诉讼法》第 154 条第 1 款第 3 项,明确否定了当事人的上诉权利。[①]

(三)错位:照搬仲裁裁决审查标准或"水土不服"

如前所述,在承认仲裁调解书可撤销性的案例中,法院的论证思路为:基于"仲裁调解书与仲裁裁决具有同等效力",撤销制度应类推适用于仲裁调解书。在肯定了仲裁调解书可撤销性的基础上,法院继而照搬仲裁裁决标准,适用我国《仲裁法》第 58 条[②]对仲裁调解书进行审查。有的法院甚至未作任何论证,径直将《仲裁法》第 58 条作为仲裁调解书的审查依据。理论上,仲裁调解书与仲裁裁决书的生成存在区别,仲裁中的调解不可能没有双方当事人的共同参与,[③]仲裁调解书的结果应当是双方当事人经由意思自治达成妥协的产物。并且根据《仲裁法》第 52 条的规定,当事人在签收之前可以反悔。基于这些因素,《仲裁法》第 58 条中规定的某些情形在撤销仲裁调解书案件中可能并没有适用空间。

司法实践中,一部分援引《仲裁法》第 58 条撤销仲裁调解书的案例确实印证了上述猜想。

在赤峰市中级人民法院审理的(2017)内 04 民特 19 号案中,经法院查明:双方当事人没有书面仲裁协议,虽然申请人对被申请人主张的双方口头协商同意申请仲裁这一事实并不认可,但申请人实际参加仲裁程序且未提出管辖权异

---

① 山西省高级人民法院在裁定中指出:"但一审法院依据《中华人民共和国民事诉讼法》第一百五十四条第一款第(三)项的规定赋予当事人上诉权不符合最高人民法院《关于人民法院裁定撤销仲裁裁决或驳回当事人申请后当事人能否上诉问题的批复》(法复〔1997〕5 号)'当事人无权上诉'的司法解释,应当依据《中华人民共和国民事诉讼法》第一百五十四条第一款第(十一)项的规定处理本案,对此,本院予以纠正,故上诉人孝义市金达煤焦有限公司提起上诉没有法律依据,本院不予支持。"

② 《仲裁法》第 58 条规定:"当事人提出证据证明裁决有下列情形之一的,可以向仲裁委员会所在地的中级人民法院申请撤销裁决:(一)没有仲裁协议的;(二)裁决的事项不属于仲裁协议的范围或者仲裁委员会无权仲裁的;(三)仲裁庭的组成或者仲裁的程序违反法定程序的;(四)仲裁裁决所依据的证据是伪造的;(五)对方当事人隐瞒了足以影响公正裁决的证据的;(六)仲裁员在仲裁该案时有索贿,徇私舞弊,枉法裁决行为的。人民法院经组成合议庭审查核实裁决有前款规定情形之一的,应当裁定撤销。人民法院认定该裁决违背社会公共利益的,应当裁定撤销。"

③ 参见王生长:《仲裁与调解相结合制度研究》,对外经济贸易大学法学院 2001 年博士学位论文,第 208 页。

议。法院最终适用《仲裁法》第 58 条第 1 款第 1 项,以“没有仲裁协议”为由裁决撤销仲裁调解书。笔者认为该裁判有值得商榷之处:考虑到调解的特殊性,虽然当事人之间没有书面仲裁协议,但从其全程参与仲裁程序且放弃提出管辖权异议的事实中可以认定其与被申请人具有仲裁的合意,法院嗣后以没有仲裁协议为由撤销该调解书,违背了当事人意思自治和诚实信用原则。

在广州市中级人民法院审理的(2017)粤 01 民特 792 号案中,法院认为,调解书中涉及的建筑物物权变动事项与案涉承包合同约定的工程承包不是同一法律关系,不属于案涉合同履行的范围,故可认定仲裁调解事项不属于仲裁协议的范围 。如果此案为仲裁裁决案件,法院依照上述裁判思路作出裁定并无不妥,但其是否可延伸至仲裁调解领域仍值得讨论。在本案中,仲裁调解书系依当事人之间的调解协议制成,即使双方当事人在调解协议中的约定事项超出了仲裁协议的范围,只要超出事项不属于仲裁机构无权仲裁的事项,就应当认定当事人在该事项上达成了新的仲裁合意,而不应径直以原先仲裁协议的范围为依据裁定撤销。

在衡阳市中级人民法院审理的(2016)湘 04 民特 4 号案中,法院认为,“仲裁委员会在接受仲裁申请后,仲裁员未实际参加仲裁活动,仅由书记员一人主持调解,违反仲裁程序”,故依据《仲裁法》第 58 条第 1 款第 3 项裁决撤销仲裁调解书。在赤峰市中级人民法院审理的(2017)内 04 民特 19 号案中,法院也以“未向当事人释明对管辖是否有异议”为由判定仲裁程序违法而撤销仲裁调解书。在这些案件中,虽然仲裁程序确有违法之处,但当事人在仲裁程序中并未对此提出异议,仍然参与调解并且最终达成和解协议,在此情形之下,若以程序违法为由径直撤销仲裁调解书,将有违诚实信用和“放弃异议”原则。

三、破局路径

(一)梳理:于法无据,但却“势在必行”

据笔者考证,最高人民法院在仲裁调解书可撤销性问题上也存在不同认定。

在此次分析样本中,两个案例援引最高人民法院《关于人民法院应否受理撤销仲裁调解书申请的复函》[(2013)民四他字第39号](以下简称《复函》)作为裁判依据。[①] 根据河北省沧州市中级人民法院(2015)沧民特字第1号裁定书,该《复函》的内容为:“根据《中华人民共和国仲裁法》第五十八条第一款的规定,当事人可以向人民法院申请撤销仲裁裁决,该法第五十一条第二款又规定,仲裁调解书与仲裁裁决书具有同等法律效力,这就意味着,仲裁调解书也应纳入司法审查的范围。因此,当事人依照中国仲裁法第五十八条的规定向人民法院申请撤销仲裁调解书的,人民法院应予受理。”

然而,在安徽省高级人民法院(2016)皖民特字第4号裁决书中,被上诉人援引最高人民法院研究室《关于人民法院应否受理当事人提起的申请撤销仲裁调解书之诉问题的研究意见》(以下简称《研究意见》)作为答辩依据。与上述《复函》中的观点截然对立,这份同样出自最高人民法院的《研究意见》否定了仲裁调解书的可撤销性:首先,人民法院受理当事人申请撤销仲裁调解书并无法律依据,法律未授予人民法院行使撤销仲裁调解书的权力,人民法院就不得超越法律规定行使;其次,从减少对当事人意思自治的职权干预,坚持仲裁司法监督有限原则而言,人民法院也不应受理当事人提起的申请撤销仲裁调解书之诉;最后,仲裁法规定了当事人在仲裁调解书签收前可以反悔,且在仲裁调解书的内容违反社会公共利益的情况下,人民法院可以依照《仲裁法》第58条第3款的规定对该仲裁调解书裁定予以撤销,或者依照《民事诉讼法》第258条(2017年修订后为第237条)第2款[②]的规定,对该仲裁调解书裁定不予执行,

① 参见河北省沧州市中级人民法院(2015)沧民特字第1号裁定书、江苏省淮安市中级人民法院(2016)苏08民特23号民事裁定书,但该《复函》原文在北大法宝数据库和《涉外海事商事审判指导》中都无法检索到。

② 第237条规定:“对依法设立的仲裁机构的裁决,一方当事人不履行的,对方当事人可以向有管辖权的人民法院申请执行。受申请的人民法院应当执行。被申请人提出证据证明仲裁裁决有下列情形之一的,经人民法院组成合议庭审查核实,裁定不予执行:(一)当事人在合同中没有订有仲裁条款或者事后没有达成书面仲裁协议的;(二)裁决的事项不属于仲裁协议的范围或者仲裁机构无权仲裁的;(三)仲裁庭的组成或者仲裁的程序违反法定程序的;(四)裁决所根据的证据是伪造的;(五)对方当事人向仲裁机构隐瞒了足以影响公正裁决的证据的;(六)仲裁员在仲裁该案时有贪污受贿,徇私舞弊,枉法裁决行为的。人民法院认定执行该裁决违背社会公共利益的,裁定不予执行。裁定书应当送达双方当事人和仲裁机构。仲裁裁决被人民法院裁定不予执行的,当事人可以根据双方达成的书面仲裁协议重新申请仲裁,也可以向人民法院起诉。”

制度设计上已经实现了充分救济当事人与维护仲裁效率性要求的平衡。[①]

笔者认同申请撤销仲裁调解书“于法无据”的认定,认为以《复函》为代表的“基于与仲裁裁决具有同等效力,推定仲裁调解书可以撤销”的观点值得商榷。首先,《仲裁法》第51条规定“仲裁调解书与仲裁裁决书具有同等法律效力”旨在强调生效的仲裁调解书的执行效力等同于裁决书,即二者在生效后都可以使仲裁程序终结,都可以确定当事人双方的权利义务关系,都对当事人产生拘束力,都可以作为申请法院强制执行的依据,但并不意味着两者就应适用同样的司法审查程序。正如民事诉讼程序中双方达成的民事调解书经当事人签收后具有与民事判决书同等的法律效力,但是却不能如判决书一样对其提出上诉。[②] 同样的道理也应适用于仲裁调解书。其次,法院作为行使国家司法权的主体,其诉讼活动必须依据法律进行,既然法律未授予法院行使撤销或不予执行仲裁调解书的权力,法院就不得超越法律规定行使。

然而,笔者对《研究意见》中提及的另两个理由,即“减少干预当事人意思自治、坚持司法监督有限原则”和“现有制度设计已经实现了充分救济当事人与维护仲裁效率性要求的平衡”,持保留意见。

首先,“减少干预当事人意思自治、坚持司法监督有限原则”的价值取向固然值得肯定,但其成立的前提是“存在当事人意思自治”,如若一方当事人实质上没有参与仲裁程序,仲裁庭组织该方当事人的无权代理人与另一方当事人进行调解,在此情形下生成的仲裁调解书并非当事人意思自治的产物,需要赋予当事人申请人撤销的权利进行救济。这种情形并非笔者臆造,确实存在于实践之中,见表5。

---

① 参见张军主编:《司法研究与指导》(2012年第2辑),人民法院出版社2012年版,第90页。

② 参见永安、张庆霖:《论仲裁调解书撤销制度的确立》,载《烟台大学学报》(哲学社会科学版)2011年第2期。

表 5　一方当事人实质上没有参与仲裁程序的情形

序号	案号及审理法院	法院查明事实
1	广东省深圳市中级人民法院(2015)深中法涉外仲字第 154 号	经审查,所有仲裁文书中陈××的签名均系伪造,不是陈××本人所签,陈××与曾××之间没有签订仲裁协议和调解协议
2	广东省深圳市中级人民法院(2015)深中法涉外仲字第 155 号	经审查,所有仲裁文书中陈××的签名均系伪造,不是陈××本人所签,陈××与朱××之间没有签订仲裁协议和调解协议
3	江苏省泰州市中级人民法院(2017)苏 12 民特 15 号	顾××与高××之间并无仲裁协议,其亦无同意参加仲裁的意思表示,施××在无权代理的情形下伪造了顾××授权的委托书,其以顾××的名义与高××达成的调解事后亦未得到顾××的追认

根据法院审理查明的结果,以上 3 个案例均符合一方当事人实质上没有参与仲裁程序的情形。另外,在济南市中级人民法院(2016)鲁 01 民特 98 号案、清远市中级人民法院(2016)粤 18 民特 41 号案中,原告均诉称"根本没有参与仲裁程序,对仲裁调解并不知情",最终均被法院以"撤销仲裁调解书没有法律依据"为由径直驳回。

其次,针对《研究意见》中提到的另一个理由,即"现有制度设计已经实现了充分救济当事人与维护仲裁效率性要求的平衡",笔者也有不同见解。第一,就《仲裁法》第 52 条规定的"仲裁调解书签收前可以反悔"的制度设计而言,在一般情形下当然可以发挥功效,但在前述全程无权代理、当事人根本没有参与仲裁程序的情形中却力有不逮,难以发挥作用。第二,《研究意见》还提出,《仲裁法》第 58 条第 3 款和《民事诉讼法》第 258 条(现为第 237 条)第 2 款中规定的法院可以基于"违反社会公共利益"主动裁定撤销或不予执行仲裁裁决,表明在仲裁调解书违背社会公共利益时,法院有裁定撤销的权力。笔者认为,《研究意见》在此处将关于仲裁裁决的规定类推至仲裁调解书并不合理,原因不再赘述。此外,即使法院可以"违反公共利益"为由撤销仲裁调解书,前述当事人未参与仲裁程序情形也很难被"违反公共利益"所统摄。

(二)建构:“另起炉灶”,尊重调解特性

笔者认为,有必要确立仲裁调解书撤销制度。如前所述,由于仲裁调解与仲裁裁决在运行机理和制度价值上的差异,照搬《仲裁法》第58条规定的仲裁裁决撤销事由,将其作为仲裁调解书的审查标准,可能会“水土不服”,前文中对相关司法实践的考察也可印证此点。因此,有必要“另起炉灶”,结合仲裁调解制度的特性,设定符合现实需要的仲裁调解书撤销情形。

首先,区别于仲裁裁决,仲裁调解程序基本上是由双方当事人的自由意志进行推进的,仲裁调解书也是基于当事人之间达成的和解协议作出,仲裁调解的这一特性对撤销情形的设定具有以下意义:第一,这意味着仲裁调解书无效而被撤销的事由主要针对违背当事人真实意思的情形。[①] 结合对司法实践的考察,笔者认为这类违背当事人意思自治的情形主要是仲裁调解中的无权代理行为。在这种情形中,和解协议的签署人没有事先获得当事人授权而参与仲裁调解程序并同对方当事人达成和解协议,事后也没有得到被代理人的追认,该和解协议理应视作无效。在此情形之下若还承认以该无效和解协议为依据作出的仲裁调解书的效力,则直接构成了对程序公正和实体公正的侵犯。[②] 第二,这同时意味着部分适用于仲裁裁决的撤销事由(如没有仲裁协议、超出仲裁协议范围、仲裁庭组成和仲裁程序违法、隐瞒证据、伪造证据等),基于诚实信用和“放弃异议”原则,不适宜作为仲裁调解书的撤销事由,从而减少法院对当事人意思自治的干预,坚持仲裁司法监督有限原则。

其次,在仲裁调解中,并非一切事项都能由当事人自由处分和妥协,争议事项的可仲裁性及仲裁机构的受案范围均系强制性规定。根据《仲裁法》第2

---

① 参见廖永安、张庆霖:《论仲裁调解书撤销制度的确立》,载《烟台大学学报》(哲学社会科学版)2011年第2期。

② 参见王生长:《仲裁与调解相结合制度研究》,对外经济贸易大学法学院2001年博士学位论文,第210页。

条、第 3 条的规定,[①]仲裁程序只能处理平等主体之间的合同纠纷和其他财产性纠纷,仲裁中的调解属于仲裁程序的一个部分,当然也不能突破仲裁法关于可仲裁性的规定。因此,"无权仲裁"应被设定为仲裁调解书撤销事由。

最后,"社会公共利益"也是仲裁调解不能损害的底线,法院可以不经当事人举证,依职权进行主动审查。但对"社会公共利益"应当进行从严解释,援引这一法律原则只能是特殊情况下,为维护国家、社会重大根本利益而不得已、例外地采取,不能滥用。[②]

综上所述,笔者建议,最高人民法院在作出司法解释时,可就仲裁调解书撤销事由作出如下规定:"当事人提出证据证明仲裁调解书有下列情形之一的,可以向仲裁委员会所在地的中级人民法院申请撤销裁决:(一)仲裁委员会无权仲裁;(二)签署和解协议未经当事人授权。人民法院经组成合议庭审查核实仲裁调解书有前款规定情形之一的,应当裁定撤销。人民法院认定该仲裁调解书违背社会公共利益的,应当裁定撤销。"

四、结语

素有"东方经验"之称的仲裁调解制度在实践中得到广泛运用,但是由于立法的不完善和调解结案本身的特性,仲裁调解制度在实务中同样遭遇了很多难题,仲裁调解书撤销问题即是其中一例。由于立法规定的不明确,这个问题在理论上存在较大争议,司法实践中的"同案不同判"情形更加值得关注。有鉴于此,确有必要对其展开研究。一如整个仲裁乃至全部法律制度,对效率与公平两大价值的权衡同样横亘在仲裁调解书撤销制度的建构问题上。在司法实践中,"无权代理"签署仲裁和解协议并非个例。为了维持最低限度的公

---

① 第 2 条规定:"平等主体的公民、法人和其他组织之间发生的合同纠纷和其他财产权益纠纷,可以仲裁。"

第 3 条规定:"下列纠纷不能仲裁:(一)婚姻、收养、监护、扶养、继承纠纷;(二)依法应当由行政机关处理的行政争议。"

② 参见沈德咏主编:《最高人民法院民事诉讼法司法解释理解与适用》(下),人民法院出版社 2015 年版,第 1277 页。

平,有必要设立仲裁调解书撤销制度,以便为此类情形中基本权利未受保障的当事人提供救济途径;同时,为了维护和尊重对仲裁调解制度的效率和固有属性,有必要做出有别于仲裁裁决的制度设计,将仲裁调解书的撤销事由限定在更为狭窄的空间内。

以国际投资仲裁对抗国际商事仲裁司法监督
——从个人权益在国际法层面上的保护谈起

黄鸿江*

摘要:投资者根据投资合同下的仲裁条款提起国际商事仲裁并获得有利裁决,但是由于东道国法院的司法监督行为,导致该裁决在东道国无法得到承认与执行;投资者继而又向国际投资仲裁庭提起仲裁申请,要求东道国承认与执行该商事仲裁裁决或作出赔偿。这种做法逐渐变成一种模式,并在多个投资仲裁庭中得到认可。在该模式下,投资合同下的争议事项并不因为经过国际商事仲裁程序而使国际投资仲裁庭失去管辖权,且后续进行的国际投资仲裁程序具有独立性,与先前的国际商事仲裁不构成平行程序。同样,国际投资仲裁庭也不因其对东道国法院不予承认执行国际商事仲裁裁决的行为进行审视,就认定其构成东道国法院的上诉机构。对于该模式应当持乐观的态度,因为其是个人权益在国际法层面上新的救济途径,具有合法性与合理性。同时,该模式在一定程度上反映出个人权益在国际法体系中日益受重视的趋势。

关键词:国际投资仲裁　国际商事仲裁　司法监督　个人权益

国际商事仲裁一直是解决跨境商业纠纷的重要手段。一般而言,各国都会在立法中确定本国法院对国际商事仲裁的司法监督权,由法院主动或根据申请

* 黄鸿江,中国政法大学国际法学院2018级国际法专业博士研究生。

介入到仲裁的各个环节中。实践中,外国投资者因投资合同争议提起国际商事仲裁,在获得有利裁决后向东道国法院申请承认与执行,东道国法院在对该国际商事仲裁裁决进行司法审查时,要么主动发布仲裁禁令、认定仲裁条款无效,要么过分拖延程序,使投资者获得的有利裁决无法被承认与执行。根据现代国际法中司法行为可归属于国家这一原则,①投资者将目光投向了投资条约规定的东道国对投资的保护义务,认为东道国法院的司法监督行为导致投资者无法实现有利裁决中的权益,进而损害了投资者的投资权益,并针对该司法监督行为提起了国际投资仲裁。从外在形式上来看,投资者将国际投资仲裁作为促进国际商事仲裁裁决执行的手段,通过提起国际投资仲裁来对抗东道国司法机关的司法监督行为。在这种救济途径下,国际仲裁庭需要对东道国司法机关的行为进行审查。

这种案件并不鲜见,而且日益增加。在这类案件中,国际投资仲裁庭对相关问题处理的不一致,进一步引发了对该模式的思考与顾虑。国际投资仲裁庭的管辖权来源于何处?东道国司法监督行为构成违反投资条约的判断标准是什么?该模式是否混淆了国际商事仲裁与国际投资仲裁两种争端解决机制,是否实质上构成东道国法院的上诉机制,从而侵犯了东道国的司法主权?这些问题是否会影响到《承认及执行外国仲裁裁决公约》(Convention on the Recognition and Enforcement of Foreign Arbitral Awards,以下简称《纽约公约》)所规定的对商事仲裁裁决承认与执行的机制?针对这些问题,本文主要从以下几个方面展开论述:首先,重点分析国际投资仲裁审查国际商事仲裁司法监督的实例,分析总结出案例中投资者提起的仲裁请求类型;对相似的几个案例按各个角度做归类,以提取公因式的方法总结出这种模式下几个案例的共性;其次,分析这种模式下的管辖权和其他程序问题,并针对这些问题提出笔者的意见与建议。

① Articles on Responsibility of States for Internationally Wrongful Act, Aticle4(1), available at http://legal.un.org/ilc/texts/instruments/english/draft_articles/9_6_2001.pdf, December 7,2018.

一、针对东道国司法监督提起国际投资仲裁的实践

(一)东道国司法监督构成间接征收

对于国际投资仲裁审查国际商事仲裁司法监督的实践,经常出现的一个问题是东道国司法监督是否构成间接征收。双边投资协定和自由贸易协定中,关于间接征收条款的规定一般不会做特别的说明,条约中仅仅会提及间接征收的形式及其后果,但对其具体要件和适用却不会规定得很明确。似乎缔约国假定一般的国际法原则已经足够对这个问题进行界定了。① 但也有例外的情况,如2004年的加拿大示范双边投资条约,就对间接征收的形式和要件作了具体的约定。② 不过整体的成文法还是处于非常不成熟的状态,而这也为间接征收在下述案件的适用留下了空间。

在此,首先应该提到的是"萨伊博姆公司诉孟加拉国"(Saipem S. p. A. v. Bengladesh)案(以下简称萨伊博姆公司案)。在本案中,萨伊博姆公司与孟加拉自然石油气公司(Petrobangla,以下简称孟加拉石油公司)在建筑合同中约定了仲裁条款,将达卡尔作为仲裁地,并约定以《国际商会仲裁规则》(ICC Rules of Arbitration)作为仲裁规则。在之后的合同履行中,双方产生纠纷,萨伊博姆公司依据仲裁条款向国际商会仲裁庭提起仲裁申请,孟加拉石油公司在仲裁过程中,因己方提起的程序性请求遭到仲裁庭的拒绝,于是向本地法院寻求帮助,要求法院依照1940年孟加拉仲裁法的规定,撤销该案中仲裁庭的权力。孟加拉法院支持了孟加拉石油公司的请求,认定仲裁庭的一些不当行为确实违反了仲裁法的相关规定,并发布撤销决定。国际商会仲裁庭没有理会法院的撤销决

---

① See Dolzer, Rudolf . "Indirect Expropriation of Alien Property." *ICSID Review-Foreign Investment Law Journal* 1.1, 1986, p. 56.

② 2004年加拿大示范双边投资条约规定:"缔约国确认以下共识:(a)间接征收源于缔约国一方具有相等于直接征收效果的措施或一系列措施,而无需权利的正式转移或彻底占有;(b)缔约国一方的措施或一系列措施是否构成间接征收须依个案事实具体分析,分析应考虑以下因素:(ⅰ)措施或一系列措施的经济影响,但仅缔约国一方措施或一系列措施对投资造成不利经济影响的事实不能构成间接征收;(ⅱ)措施或一系列措施对确切的合理投资回报期望的干预程度;(ⅲ)措施或一系列措施的性质。"

定，继续对案件进行审理并作出了有利于萨伊博姆公司的裁决。孟加拉石油公司在裁决作出之后又向孟加拉法院申请撤销该仲裁裁决，孟加拉的最高法院并没有支持孟加拉石油公司的观点，驳回了该撤销申请，但是认为该仲裁裁决因仲裁庭的权力在一开始已经被撤销，因此裁决本身也因为仲裁庭的无权而不存在，而“一个不存在的裁决既不能被撤销也不能被执行”。萨伊博姆公司在裁决无法得到承认执行的情形下，依据《孟加拉—意大利双边投资协定》向国际投资争端解决中心（International Centre for Settlement of Investment Disputes，ICSID）提起国际投资仲裁，认为孟加拉法院拒绝承认与执行国际商会仲裁庭裁决的行为构成征收。ICSID 仲裁庭最终裁定，基于投资产生的合同权利，在国际商会仲裁裁决过程中形成合同权利的“结晶”，该国际商会裁决依然属于条约所言的投资，因此，国际商会的裁决也能够被进行征收。① 在涉及是否成立征收时，仲裁庭主要从两个方面进行论证：一是仲裁裁决的可征收性。仲裁庭认为外国投资者根据合同争议所获得的仲裁裁决是一项宝贵的权利，这种权利对于合同的完成往往是非常重要的，而非物质权利可以作为被征收的对象是一种无须证明的共识。② 二是从东道国法院的行为进行分析。仲裁庭认为东道国法院的行为违反了执行仲裁裁决并尊重仲裁程序的义务，这种干预无疑违背了国际法，国家无权在其管辖范围内以任意的、侵权的和充公的行为来获取外来的财产或合同的权利。③ 在本案中，东道国法院的行为直接引起了投资者无法执行包含投资权益的仲裁裁决，实质上起到了没收投资者投资的效果。值得注意的是，在论证过程中仲裁庭还采用了一种非正面的论证方式，即认为双边投资协定条款中并没有限制法院的行为不能构成征收，东道国也没有引用任

---

① ICSID Case No. ARB/OS/07, Decision on Jurisdiction and Recommendation on Provisional Measures, 21 March 2007, para. 132.

② See, *e. g.*, Phillips Petroleum Iran v. Islamic Republic of Iran et National Iranian Oil Company, Iran-US Claims Tribunal, Case No. 39, Chamber Two, Award No. 425-39-2 of 29 June 1989, Yearbook of Commercial Arbitration, Vol. XVI (1991), pp. 298-321, para. 75. 34.

③ Saipem's letter of 24 March 2005 submitted at the hearing, with the agreement of Bangladesh [Tr. J. II 88:8-13], as Exh. C-10235, accept by tribunal, see the award, para. 131.

何判决来支持自己反对的立场,因此,东道国法院的行为能够构成征收。[①] 双边投资协定中的很多规定本身就是十分模糊的,国际投资仲裁庭以这种逻辑推导的方式,无疑表明了其具有明显的倾向性。

在之后的罗马克公司(Romak)案中,罗马克公司与乌兹别克斯坦国内一公司在小麦交易发生纠纷,罗马克公司按照合同的仲裁条款提起了商事仲裁,并获得有利裁决。但是当罗马克公司在乌兹别克斯坦法院申请执行该商事裁决时,法院认为罗马克公司未能提交相应的文书译本,且罗马克公司未能证明在商事仲裁程序中有告知被申请人任命仲裁员,并因此拒绝对该商事裁决的承认与执行。[②] 罗马克公司认为乌兹别克斯坦法院的行为构成征收,征收对象为其在合同中的权利。[③] 随后便按照《瑞士—乌兹别克斯坦双边投资协定》第 9 条的规定向联合国国际贸易法委员会提起国际投资仲裁。国际投资仲裁庭继承了萨伊博姆公司案的观点,认同该商事裁决是小麦交易合同中权利的体现。但本案仲裁庭最终认定,该小麦交易合同并不属于双边投资协定中的投资,因此驳回了原告的诉求。[④]

从上述两个案例可以看出,仲裁庭不否认国际商事仲裁裁决的可征收性。在分析东道国司法监督行为被认为构成间接征收的理由后会发现,仲裁庭主要从东道国司法监督行为的不法性进行分析的。对这种不法性的判断以国际法为依据(主要看东道国是否违反国际义务),而不是以国内法作为依据。[⑤] 例如,萨伊博姆公司案的仲裁庭认为,孟加拉法院撤销仲裁员权力的行为违背了《纽约公约》第 2 条所规定的义务。[⑥] 换个角度说,东道国司法监督行为的不法性,也是违背相应国际义务的一种体现,是对投资者合理期待的一种侵犯。国

---

① Saipem v. Bangladesh, Fianl Award, para. 132.

② *Romak S. A. v. the Republic of Uzbekistan*, Award of Nov. 26, 2009, para. 65, available at http://www.italaw.com/sites/default/files/case-documents/ita0716.pdf.

③ Ibid., para. 136.

④ Ibid., para. 211.

⑤ 参见宋连斌、梁师竹:《不予执行商事仲裁裁决构成间接征收的认定》,载《江西社会科学》2014 年第 6 期。

⑥ Saipem v. Bangladesh, Fianl Award, para. 167.

际仲裁庭认为,这种不法的司法监督行为构成间接征收。

(二)东道国司法监督未能提供有效司法途径

在国际投资仲裁审查国际商事仲裁司法监督的实践中,另一个值得关注的问题是东道国司法监督是否提供了"有效司法途径"(effective means of asserting claims and enforcing rights)。有效途径条款,是指东道国政府承诺,在其司法体系内向投资者提供有效途径,使投资者能够有效主张诉权和执行权利。该条款最早出现在美国政府签订的一系列双边投资协定中。[①] 有效途径条款相比于司法不公有着更低的门槛,只要东道国法院不能在司法系统内有效执行投资者诉求的行为就可能构成对该义务的违反。

在2010年"雪佛龙诉厄瓜多尔"(Chevron v. Ecuador)一案(以下简称雪佛龙案)的仲裁中,该条款首次被确认为独立于司法不公的一种单独标准,与司法不公并非从属关系,可以直接为投资者所适用。[②] 该仲裁庭也将这项标准同司法不公进行比较,认为投资者在适用该标准时,并不需要像适用司法不公一样,证明东道国司法体系内存在严重的缺陷,或者东道国法院存在极其恶劣的不当行为且严重违反司法公正,或者证明东道国政府有意干预司法。[③]

随后的"白色工业公司诉印度"(White Industries v. Republic of India)案(以下简称白色公司案)也涉及有效途径条款。在该案中,申请人白色公司与印度煤炭公司(Coal India)在1989年签订了一份煤矿开发和设备供应合同,由申请人向印度煤炭公司提供贷款。双方在合同履行中产生争议,申请人根据仲裁条款向国际商会仲裁院提起仲裁请求。2002年国际商会仲裁庭作出有利于白色公司的裁决。

白色公司向印度德里高等法院申请执行该国际商会裁决,印度煤炭公司则向印度加尔各答高等法院申请撤销该国际商会裁决,白色公司在撤裁程序中曾

---

① See US Model BIT 2004, available at https://ustr.gov/archive/assets/Trade_Sectors/Investment/Model_BIT/asset_upload_file847_6897.pdf, http://legal.un.org/ilc/texts/instruments/english/draft_articles/9_6_2001.pdf, December,7,2018.

② Chevron v. Ecuador, PCA Case No. 34877, Partial Award on the Merits, para. 242.

③ Ibid., paras. 244,248.

提出管辖权异议,被驳回后上诉至最高法院,德里高等法院的执行程序因此中止。截至 2010 年 7 月白色公司提起国际投资仲裁,印度国内法院撤裁程序和执行程序均未有裁决结果,白色公司在国际商会裁决书中的权益也迟迟得不到落实。对此,白色公司在本案中有多个主张,认为印度法院程序的过分拖延构成印度政府对白色公司投资的侵害,违反了印度所签双边投资条约中的征收、公平公正待遇、提供有效救济途径等多个规定。就有效途径的适用而言,白色公司案的仲裁庭沿用了雪佛龙案的标准,并且对印度国内法院的执行程序和撤裁程序分别进行了分析。

仲裁庭在分析过程中,并不是按照东道国法院行为的实质结果去做评判,而是紧密结合印度国内法院实践的现状来对东道国的行为进行评估。如在执行程序方面,仲裁庭认为案件立案至被中止执行的 3 年半时间里,虽然法院多次推迟庭审,也允许印度煤炭公司提交延期申请文件,但是考虑到印度法院本身的案件积压程度以及律师的有限时间,并不能认为该等拖延是异常的。对于撤裁程序方面,尽管印度法院的撤销程序进行了整整 9 年并且尚未得到结果,从实质情况来看已然是十分拖沓,但仲裁庭依然认为,在没有证据证明印度法院是恶意拖延程序的情况下,考虑到印度法院确实需要超负荷处理大量案件,不能认为白色公司对于案件能够得到快速处理享有合理期待。值得注意的是,仲裁庭在该案中虽然未认定东道国法院的行为构成征收或违反公平公正待遇原则,但通过东道国未提供"有效司法途径"的角度认定东道国构成对条约义务的违反。具体而言,仲裁庭认为,印度法院的拖延即便在主观上没有恶意,也确实有其客观因素的限制,但是考虑到对于投资者在撤裁程序中提出的上诉以及加快审理的申请,法院在 5 年时间内都未能进行处理,显然构成对有效途径条约义务的违反。

(三)东道国司法监督违反最惠国待遇

在国际投资仲裁审查国际商事仲裁司法监督的实践中,还涉及的一个问题是东道国司法监督是否违反最惠国待遇。

在 ATA 诉约旦(ATA v. Jordan)一案中, ATA 公司与约旦的国有公司

(APC)签订了一份国际咨询工程师联合会(FIDIC)合同,发生争议后ATA公司提交仲裁并获得有利裁决。APC公司随后向约旦法院申请确认裁决无效并得到约旦法院的支持,该法院同时认定合同中所含仲裁条款无效。在该案中,当事人根据《土耳其—约旦双边投资协定》第11条第2款所载最惠国待遇条款的规定,赋予申请人投资权益享受与东道国(本案中约旦)同其他国家缔结的双边投资协定所包含的实质性保证,认为《土耳其—约旦双边投资协定》中的最惠国条款使投资者有权依据约旦与其他国家签订的双边投资协定,并享受这些双边投资协定下有关的投资保护标准的待遇。[1]

关于违反最惠国待遇原则的申请,往往是一种包括性的诉求,在单一申请理由下,罗列各种基本的投资待遇原则。将东道国在其他双边投资协定中对投资保护的标准,都适用到对法院司法监督行为的评估系统中。这种方式直接使投资者享有挑选条约的权利,在提起具体的申请理由时,可以针对东道国签订的所有双边投资协定进行有目的的筛选,找寻对自己最为有利的条款,并要求投资仲裁庭按该条款对东道国法院的司法监督行为进行审查。

通过对实践的分析来看,投资者在申请国际投资仲裁时,往往不是以单一的理由提起仲裁,而是多种理由同时进行。在投资者获得有利的国际商事仲裁裁决无法在东道国得到承认与执行后,投资者即认为东道国政府在条约中所作的承诺无法实现,自身投资的合理期待落空,为了实现自身投资权益,投资者往往采取"广撒网"的方式,同时列明东道国违反了数个不同的投资待遇标准。这也在一定程度上表明,投资者对于请求能否成立本身也持怀疑的态度,继而将问题统统交由国际投资仲裁庭进行判断,只要任一理由成立,那么对于投资者来说就是胜利。

在分析了各个仲裁理由后,投资者往往首选以征收的名义提起仲裁申请,当投资者不确定能否达到征收的门槛时,则转而寻求其他的理由来寻求救济。

---

① *ATA Construction, Industrial and Trading Company v. the Hashemite Kingdom of Jordan*, Award of May 18, 2010, para. 114.

除了上述提到的几种理由外,还有诸如司法不公[①]、公平公正待遇[②]、有效的保护手段[③]、全面保护和安全条款[④]等。虽然从现行情况来看,这些理由往往作为间接征收以外的一种附带讨论,但是仍然有仲裁庭认为东道国的行为使投资者无法实现投资相应的合理期待,在构成间接征收的同时,也违反了公平公正待遇。[⑤] 甚至有仲裁庭认定东道国的行为尽管不构成间接征收,却未能提供有效的司法途径。[⑥] 间接征收和其他投资待遇的认定都含有违反投资者合理预期的要素。但是构成征收还有各种条件限制,例如,在有的案例中要证明构成征收,仲裁庭仍需证明投资者就投资所享有的合理期待的经济利益被完全剥夺,[⑦]或者要求穷尽救济。如在萨伊博姆公司案中,孟加拉政府就提出抗辩认为,对于是否构成征收,需要证明东道国法院的行为存在错误干预,而无论从拒绝司法还是间接征收的标准来看,穷尽本地的救济都应当作为一个实质前提。[⑧] 基于此,孟加拉政府认为投资者未对东道国法院的行为在合理的期限内就东道国国内的法律程序进行相应的上诉,作为前置要件的缺失,仲裁庭不能认定东道国法院的行为构成间接征收。虽然仲裁庭最终认为穷尽救济并非认定间接征收的实质要件,[⑨]但是在论证过程中设定了一个前提,即本案中的萨伊博姆公司已经在东道国法院的程序上花费了大量的时间和精力,即使在东道

---

① Desert Line, ICSID Case No. ARB/05/17; Romak, PCA Case No. AA280; ATA Construction, ICSID Case No. ARB/08/02.

② Desert Line, ICSID Case No. ARB/05/17; Romak, PCA Case No. AA280; ATA Construction, ICSID Case No. ARB/08/02; Frontier Petroleum, IIC 465 (2010); GEA Group Aktiengesellschaft, ICSID Case No. ARB/08/16; White Industries, Award of Nov. 30, 2011.

③ Effective means of protection; Frontier Petroleum, IIC 465 (2010); Chevron, IIC 505 (2011). White Industries, Award of Nov. 30, 2011.

④ Desert Line, ICSID Case No. ARB/05/17; Frontier Petroleum, IIC 465 (2010); GEA Group Aktiengesellschaft, ICSID Case No. ARB/08/16.

⑤ GEA Group Aktiengesellschaft, ICSID Case No. ARB/08/16.

⑥ White Industries, Award of Nov. 30, 2011.

⑦ 当然,这个并不是绝对的构成要件。例如,也有仲裁庭认为,受到起诉的行为对投资的经济价值造成严重的损害,也能构成间接征收。

⑧ Saipem v. Bangladesh, Fianl Award, para. 178.

⑨ Ibid., para. 181.

国国内的程序还未穷尽,也应当视作已穷尽可能的救济。[①] 从白色公司案开始,这种穷尽本地救济的前提限制也被尝试绕开。

从这几个案子来看,现在甚至存在一种倾向,即只要投资者的合理预期在东道国司法监督过程中受到损害,投资者就可以将该司法监督视为东道国政府针对投资的举措,并依据各种投资待遇来提出补偿请求。此外,这种请求在从最初的间接征收向其他投资待遇条款蔓延的同时,也使这种类型的案件纳入进国际投资仲裁体系的门槛逐渐下调。

二、国际投资仲裁的管辖权问题

国际投资仲裁与国际商事仲裁是两个完全独立的纠纷解决机制。投资者把不能实现商事仲裁裁决中的权益作为申请事由向国际投资仲裁庭提起仲裁,直接引发许多理论上的问题。国际投资仲裁庭是否具备对该类案件的管辖权?若答案是肯定的,那么其管辖权源于何处?默认这种模式的成立是否会造成两种纠纷解决机制的混淆,或者构成权利的滥用?针对这些问题,有必要结合条约规定、国际惯例,以及仲裁实践展开讨论。

(一)国际商事仲裁裁决能否构成投资

将东道国法院的司法监督行为纳入到国际投资仲裁机制内进行审查,首先需要解决的是管辖权问题。比如根据《关于解决国家与他国国民之间投资争端公约》(以下简称《ICSID 公约》)第 25 条第 1 款的规定,申请人提起申请应当符合条约关于管辖权的规定,须证明申请所涉的法律争议直接来源于一项投资。即便是提起非 ICSID 仲裁,仲裁庭往往也会要求申请人在提交的材料中证明所诉事由符合双边投资协定所要求的条件,即争议事项来源于条约所表述的"投资",毕竟条约下的纠纷解决机制设立的目的就在于保护投资者的投资。同样,国际投资仲裁机制能否对东道国法院的司法监督行为进行审查,前提条件是该司法监督行为所涉的事项为条约所言的"投资",因此有必要先对"投

① Saipem v. Bangladesh, Fianal Award, paras. 182-183.

资”的含义进行分析。

1. 国际投资仲裁庭的观点

对于该问题，各个仲裁庭的意见并不一致，综合来看，大概有以下三种观点：

第一，将提起商事仲裁的权利定性为双边投资协定文本中的投资。这种观点在萨伊博姆公司案以及ATA案中都有所体现。萨伊博姆公司案的仲裁庭认为，构成争议基础的各类事项以及相关的仲裁运作，都是《ICSID公约》下的投资。而仲裁裁决作为仲裁运作的结果，自然也是投资的构成部分。[①] ATA在该基础上进一步认为，仲裁条款是投资者在投资事项发生争议后，能够提起纠纷解决申请的基础，其本质上是针对投资以及相应法律行为的请求权，符合双边投资协定下对投资的定义，因此也能构成投资。[②] 在笔者看来，这类观点是将投资者在仲裁项下的所有权利，包括提起仲裁申请、参与仲裁程序、申请承认与执行仲裁裁决都归类于针对投资和包含经济价值的法律行为的请求权。在这类观点中，商事仲裁裁决本身不是一种投资，东道国法院对该裁决的司法监督对裁决自身形式完整不会产生实质影响，但是却直接影响到投资者在仲裁的一系列程序中所享有的权利。但是这种观点容易遭到质疑的地方在于，东道国很多时候并不会直接去阻止投资者提起商事仲裁，甚至当东道国认定仲裁庭没有权力的情况下，仲裁庭依然可以不管东道国的认定结果继续进行仲裁，在这种情况下就很难认定东道国侵犯了投资者“提起”商事仲裁的权利。

第二，认为国际商事仲裁裁决等同于投资，国际投资仲裁庭的管辖权来源于“权利结晶理论”，[③]即认为仲裁程序是权利结晶的过程，其本质上是将原有的合同权利的一部分通过商事仲裁这一过程，凝结在裁决中。这种“权利结晶理论”在白色公司案中也被仲裁庭所确认。该案仲裁庭认为，涉案的国际商事仲裁裁决中包含的权利是投资者初始投资中的一部分，因此也能享受双边投资

---

① *ATA Construction, Industrial and Trading Company v. the Hashemite Kingdom of Jordan*, Award of May 18, 2010, para. 114.

② Ibid., para. 117.

③ 原文为*crystallization of rights*。

协定下的投资保护。[①] 这种观点将商事仲裁作为一种权利转化的过程,即仲裁程序本身并不会改变原有权利的性质,即便在仲裁过程中有了其他主体的参与,且其请求权的基础发生了改变——由原先的合同请求权变成《纽约公约》下请求予以承认与执行的请求权,但是其权利仍来自于原始的投资,新的请求权无非是对原先合同请求权的一种凝练抑或者转化,但无损于其原先作为针对投资财产请求权的性质,因此仲裁裁决所赋予的请求权依然属于投资的范围。

第三,认为国际投资仲裁对该类事项没有管辖权,不适用双边投资协定项下的保护。在GEA集团股份公司诉乌克兰(GEA v. Ukraine)一案中,仲裁庭认为,无论是根据投资者和东道国之间签订的双边投资协定条款还是《ICSID公约》的内容,国际商会的仲裁裁决都无法构成投资,其充其量不过是一份法律文书,是对和解协议和还款协议中权利义务的再分配罢了(况且和解协议和还款协议本身也不能构成投资);即便裁决对因投资产生的权利和义务进行了重新分配,也不能使裁决自身成为投资。[②] 仲裁庭还直接对裁决书的特征进行概括,认为"裁决本身不会对东道国的经济有什么贡献作用,更不会有其他的投资特性,因为单从裁决书自身来看,不可能同乌克兰境内经济的发展有太大的关联"。[③] 这种分析角度太过割裂裁决与投资合同的权利,认为裁决将原先投资合同下的权利完全分离出来,并且形成了一个独立的请求权,忽略了该裁决的执行与否会直接影响到投资者的权益。诚然,商事仲裁裁决本身不会进行投资合同下的一些活动,但在这些投资活动产生争议时,正是仲裁裁决决定了投资者是继续还是终止这些投资活动。将裁决与投资合同的权利完全割裂,进行单独的分析显然忽略了投资运作一体化的特性。

应当明确的一点是,国际投资仲裁中所涉及的国际商事仲裁裁决,其仲裁

---

① *Saipem*, ICSID Case No. ARB/05/07, at f127, stated: "contract rights which are crystallized by the award constitute an investment ..." *White Industries*, Award of Nov. 30, 2011, at para. 7.6.10, stated: "the Tribunal concludes that the rights under the award constitute part of White's original investment, (i.e., being a crystallization of its rights under the Contract) and, as such, are subject to such protection as is afforded to investments by the BIT."

② *GEA Group Aktiengesellschaft*, ICSID Case No. ARB/08/16, paras. 161-162.

③ GEA v. Ukraine, para. 162.

条款所依附的原始合同为国际投资合同，如果该前提不成立的话，那么该商事仲裁裁决的事项便为纯粹的商业贸易争议，自然不能归属于双边投资协定的保护范围内，这一点在罗马克公司案中也已经被确认，仲裁庭认为仲裁裁决并不能使非投资项下的权利转化为投资。[①] 重点在于国际商事仲裁的过程是否会改变所涉争议的法律属性，仲裁庭作出的裁决，到底是自身形成了新的投资，还是仅仅构成原始投资的延续和转化，或者根本只是一纸文书。因此，有必要先对商事仲裁裁决的性质进行分析。

2. 国际商事仲裁的本质

从裁决自身实体内容的角度看，国际商事仲裁是一种当事人选择的，以不公开的、不诉诸法院的方式解决争议的有效方式。[②] 这种方式可能随着理论和实践的发展变得更加复杂，与一国司法系统有着越来越密切的联系，但是其本质仍然没有发生改变，即由当事人自行同意由第三方为他们解决争议，第三方根据案件事实作出决定，所作决定对当事人具有约束力，在当事人不愿意履行时可由法院强制要求履行该决定。可以说，仲裁是一种私力救济的程序，由于各国当局通过法律的支持，产生了公力的效力，形成一份有法律约束力的裁决。值得注意的是，仲裁的特殊性还在于，当终局裁决作出的那一刻起，仲裁庭的任务就已经完成，仲裁员的职责也即刻终止，仲裁庭不再对该争议拥有相关的管辖权。可以说在裁决作出之后，当事人和仲裁庭之间的特殊关系也就解除了。该裁决在得到承认与执行之前的这个时间段，裁决并不会对当事人之间的权利义务产生实质影响，更像是第三方对当事人之间争议事项的权利义务做了重新分配，当事人遵循这种分配方案，并认可该方案可以得到执行。传统的契约论也持类似的观点，认为仲裁裁决是当事人重新订立或完成的合同，[③]无非该“合

---

① *Romak S. A. v. the Republic of Uzbekistan*, Award of Nov. 26, 2009, para. 65.

② 参见［英］艾伦·雷德芬、马丁·亨特：《国际商事仲裁法律与实践》（第4版），宋连斌等译，北京大学出版社2005年版，第15页。

③ A. Samuel, *Jurisdictional Problems in International Commercial Arbitration: A Study of Belgian, Dutch, English, French, Swedish, U. S. and West German Law* 1989, p. 33. 转引自宋连斌：《国际商事仲裁管辖权研究》，法律出版社2000年版，第14页。

同”因被一国法律背书而比一般合同有更强的执行力。

无论该“合同”对当事人之间的关系如何分配，毫无疑问的是，这种分配是建立在原先争议事项的基础上的。这种再分配并不会在当事人之间设定超出原先事项的权利和义务。简单地说，仲裁裁决本身不会产生新的权利义务，无论再分配的方案同原先的权利义务有多大的区别，都只是类似零和游戏一般的配置，对于争议事项的本质属性并不会产生影响。同样，投资者在投资合同项下的权利义务，经过国际商事仲裁庭的裁决之后，裁决程序并不会改变当事人之间法律关系的属性，只要其原先的争议事项属于投资的范畴，那么该裁决无非是对投资权利的一种再配置方案，况且在裁决作出之后仲裁庭已经解散，裁决在一国法院介入进行承认与执行之前，依然是一种只存在于当事人之间的新的“合同”关系，类似于对原合同的再协商。而根据多数双边投资协定中常包含的“投资形式上的任何变化不影响其作为投资的性质”这一条款，应当认为裁决所涉事项依然保持了其投资的特性，商事仲裁裁决也因此构成投资。

从与诉讼进行比较的角度看，仲裁同诉讼是两种并行不悖的纠纷解决机制，但又具有一定的相似性，仲裁裁决往往被认为有与法院判决类似的效力。这一点从各国关于仲裁一裁终局制的规定中可以看出来。[①] 各国对于仲裁裁决的态度，特别是国际商事仲裁裁决，一般通过国内法进行有限制的支持与调整，不轻易否定裁决的效力，并以一种谦抑的态度，仅仅从程序上以及本国的公共秩序角度对该裁决进行监督。虽然各国对于商事仲裁裁决可以在一定范围内予以撤销，或者不予承认与执行，但是国际商事仲裁裁决在《纽约公约》的支持下，已经有类似于“国际性判决”的效力，为一国的法律所接受和认可。

原则上，东道国有义务在国内法律制度内为投资者建立一定的司法制度，来保证投资者的权益能够得到保护。这个司法制度包括了投资者就投资事项的纠纷有诉诸法院的权利，在诉讼程序中能够得到法院公正的审判等。这个司

---

① 如我国的《仲裁法》第9条规定：“仲裁实行一裁终局的制度。裁决作出后，当事人就同一纠纷再申请仲裁或者向人民法院起诉的，仲裁委员会或者人民法院不予受理……”《仲裁法》第62条规定：“当事人应当履行裁决。一方当事人不履行的，另一方当事人可以依照民事诉讼法的有关规定向人民法院申请执行。受申请的人民法院应当执行。”

法制度实质上是“国际法最低标准”的体现和保障。现实情况下东道国国内的诉讼程序并不会对投资的性质产生改变，相反，合法合理的诉讼程序本身是投资待遇的一种体现。投资合同下的权利在经过诉讼程序的转化或者“结晶”，也不会使相关事项失去投资的定义。同样地，作为与诉讼程序类似的仲裁程序，其在某些方面比诉讼程序更具备“自主性”和“民间性”，更不应该因为裁决的作出而认定其所涉的合同权利性质发生了改变。

此外，相关裁决与投资活动确实有着密切的联系，裁判结果一旦得到承认与执行，将对投资者的权益产生直接的影响，如果认定经过仲裁裁决的投资合同争议不能构成投资，那么就会产生一个荒谬的现象——当事人出于快速解决纠纷的意图，选择以国际商事仲裁的方式解决纠纷，却在后续程序中不得不放弃条约赋予的救济权利，这一点必然不在当事人的仲裁合意范围内。反过来说，当事人也可以私人行为的方式，改变条约所适用的范围，将部分投资权益的条约救济渠道从整体的国际保护机制中剥离出来，这显然是不可理解的。况且，当东道国法院的行为明显侵害到投资者的权益，并且违背其国际义务，条约仲裁已然是投资者最后的救济手段，在这个时候将其排除在管辖之外，无疑是对投资者权益的巨大伤害，也违背了投资条约签订的宗旨，因此商事仲裁裁决应当构成投资。

（二）国际商事仲裁司法监督能否作为国际投资仲裁的申请事由

在论证国际商事仲裁裁决构成投资之后，还需要解决的问题是，东道国法院的司法监督行为能否引起双边投资协定上的国家责任？在《纽约公约》未对司法监督的限度作具体规定的前提下，如果东道国严格按照内国法规定进行司法监督，能否成为国际投资仲裁的申请事由？下面对此进行分析。

1. 国家责任与司法机关行为的关系

早在19世纪的一些裁决中，就有当事人提出，根据西方国家“三权分立”的原则，法院具有独立性，出于相互制衡的需要，司法与其他政府部门之间各自对其行为负责，法院违法的行为因其独立性不能归责于整个国家，因此免除了国家对违法司法行为的责任。这种观点最终目的是想开脱国际责任，比较典型的有“湖广铁路债券案”中美国政府的观点以及“光华寮案”中日本政府的观点。[①] 当然,这种观点在现在看来是不可接受的,法国—意大利和解委员在1955年的一项裁决中,就对这种观点明确表示反对,认为“司法机关作出的判决就是一个国家机关的行为,就如同立法机关颁布法律或行政机关作出决定一样”。[②]

在国际社会的交往中,国家是以一个整体出现的,虽然在行使其权力的时候,需要由国内机关单位对外作出具体的措施,这些措施一旦产生国际义务,并不是归责于机关,而是由国家作为一个主体进行承担。不论这个机关的性质是什么样的,只要其行使权力时对外代表着国家,国家就没有理由在享受这种权力行使带来便利和利益的同时,不对该行为承担责任,这也是权利和义务对等的一种基本体现。况且从国际义务的角度来看,国际义务的约束并不能对国家的任何具体的机构或个别成员产生约束。[③]

这种归责原则在国际层面得到了广泛的认可,在国际法委员会的《国家对国际不法行为的责任条款草案》(以下简称《国家责任条款草案》)中即有所体现。[④] 对于国家机关的定义,《国家责任条款评注》进一步明确国家机关的级别、类型、属性、职能,都不影响其定性,在具体描述时采取了开放式的方法,认为其具有“最广泛的含义”,“国家机关对立法、行政和司法机关也不作区分”。[⑤]

---

① 在“湖广铁路债券案”中,美国政府以“其法院是依照《外国主权豁免法》行事,政府无权干涉法院的司法独立”为由来推卸责任。在“光华寮案”中,日本政府也是以日本宪法规定的“三权分立”“司法独立”为由企图推卸其违反国际条约的责任。

② 《国际常设法院刊物》A辑第7卷,第19页。转引自[奥]阿·菲德罗斯等:《国际法》(上册),李浩培译,商务印书馆1981年版,第144页。

③ 参见陈铁强:《国际法论文集》,法律出版社1985年版,第280页。转引自李寿平:《现代国际责任法律制度》,武汉大学出版社2003年版,第71页。

④ 国际法委员会的《国家责任条款草案》第4条规定:“任何国家机关,不论行使立法、行政、司法职能,还是任何其他职能,不论在国家机构中具有何种地位,也不论该中央政府机关或该领土单位机关具有何种职能,其行为应视为国际法所指的国家行为。”

⑤ 联合国《国家责任条款评注》规定:“因此第4条中的‘国家机关’具有最广泛的含义。它并不局限于中央政府的组成部门,也不局限于高级别的官员或就国家对外关系负有责任的个人。‘国家机关’的范围延伸至各个政府部门,不论类型或属性,不论行使何种职能,也不论在体系中的级别,省级甚至乡镇级别的国家机关都被包括在内。此种意义上的国家机关,对立法、行政和司法机关也不作区分。”

现有的国际投资仲裁实践也遵循这一观点，认为国家应当对其所有的国家机关的行为负责。在 CMS 天然气输送公司诉阿根廷（CMS Gas Transmission Company v. The Republic of Argentina）一案中，仲裁庭认为：“采取具体举措的行为人，其职权属于司法机关、立法机关还是行政机关，对于确认阿根廷在投资条约下的国际责任来说，并没有什么太大的意义。”[①]在国际实践中，国际社会成员都明示或暗示地承认国家的立法或司法机关的行为应归因于国家。[②] 在 1930 年的海牙国际法编纂会议上，起草委员会在征求各国对国家的行政机关、立法机关和司法机关的行为能否引起国家责任问题的意见时，各国政府的答复都是肯定的。[③]

因此，从理论上和实践上看，将东道国司法机关的司法监督行为产生的国际责任归于国家并没有什么太大的争议。

2. 国家责任与国内法之间的关系

仲裁的运作需要国家司法的支持，特别是在仲裁裁决的承认与执行上。仲裁程序及其裁决结果不仅决定了当事人之间利益的重新分配，也会对国家的社会公共利益产生影响，甚至会影响到一国法律适用的统一和完整。因此，法院对仲裁必须施以相应的审查和控制。考虑到《纽约公约》是关于仲裁承认与执行最为成功的公约，[④]在分析外国仲裁裁决的承认与执行以及相关的司法监督时，主要依据《纽约公约》的规定进行。根据《纽约公约》的规定，缔约国的主管机关对国际商事仲裁裁决关于承认与执行的审查主要有两个方面：第一是由当事人提起的，以穷尽式清单方式列明的事项；第二是由法院自主进行的，依本国

① CMS Gas Transmission Company v. The Republic of Argentina, Decision of the Tribunal on Objections to Jurisdiction(17 July, 2003), ICSID Case No. ARB/01/8, para. 108.

② 《1971 年国际法委员会年鉴》第 2 卷，第 247 页。转引自联合国第六十三届会议国际法委员会报告第 75 页，载 https://digitallibrary. un. org/record/712297/files/A_66_10-ZH. pdf? version=1，最后访问日期：2018 年 12 月 13 日。

③ 《1971 年国际法委员会年鉴》第 2 卷，第 248 页。转引自第六十三届会议国际法委员会报告第 75 页，载 https://digitallibrary. un. org/record/712297/files/A_66_10-ZH. pdf? version=1，最后访问日期：2018 年 12 月 13 日。

④ 安哥拉于 2017 年 3 月 6 日提交了其加入《纽约公约》的申请文件，生效日期为 2017 年 6 月 4 日。截至 2018 年 3 月，该公约共有 157 个成员国。

法律规定相关争议是否可用仲裁方式解决,或者承认执行该裁决是否会违背本国的公共政策等情况。

可以看出,公约下的司法监督,更多的是一种形式上的审查,不会涉及对裁决实质内容的干涉,即便是关于公共政策等方面的审查,也仅限制在承认与执行裁决可能产生的后果上,法院并不会对仲裁过程中认定的事实或相关的法律适用进行实质审查。这也是现代国际商事仲裁司法监督发展的趋势,并为各国所接受。

此外,《纽约公约》并非涵盖仲裁司法监督的所有事项,对于一些问题公约没有进行统一的规定,这部分由于未形成国际义务,因而属于各国的立法和司法的主权范围,由各国自行规定。这些问题具体包括仲裁协议的生效要件、[①]仲裁和诉讼平行程序的协调处理等。这一部分内容由于各国关于仲裁的规定不同,因此在干预程度上也呈现出差异来。例如,英国就是典型的对仲裁进行严格司法监督的国家,受"司法"至上思想的影响,英国认为法院的管辖权不容剥夺,而且还十分强调法院对仲裁的司法监督,特别是对仲裁实体问题的监督。[②] 这种严格司法监督体现在各个方面,如英国法院认为只要仲裁裁决书存在法律错误,法院就可以将其撤销。[③] 总而言之,对于司法监督的,各国的法律规定可能是矛盾的,在《纽约公约》有意留白的情形下,各国有充分的立法和司法主权对相关内容进行规定。

那么一国在完全符合国内法律规定的情形下所做的国家行为,是否会引起国家责任呢?首先应当明确的是,国内法与国际法分属两个不同的法律体系,一国的国内法规定只在国内发生效力,在国际法上并不具有普遍的法律效力。"认定国家行为是否构成国家责任,其法律依据也只能是国际法而不能是国内法。"[④]

---

① 关于仲裁协议的生效要件,《纽约公约》第2条第2款只规定有效仲裁协议的形式要件应为"书面协议"。

② 参见[英]施米托夫:《国际贸易法文选》,赵秀文译,中国大百科全书出版社1993年版,第606~608页。转引自史飚:《商事仲裁监督与制约机制研究》,知识产权出版社2011年版,第141页。

③ 参见杨良宜:《国际商务仲裁》,中国政法大学出版社1997年版,第14~15页。转引自史飚:《商事仲裁监督与制约机制研究》,知识产权出版社2011年版,第142页。

④ 参见《国家责任的条文:草案及其评注》第3条的规定。

在国内法的范围内,国家机关或个人根据国内法的授权所做出一定的行为,也可以被认定为国内法上的国家行为,但是这种国家行为应与国际法意义上的国家行为作出区分,国内法上国家行为的救济方式只能依托于国内法的规定。如国家赔偿,当国内法上的国家行为给公民带来人身或财产上的损害时,公民可以依托诉讼等方式获得赔偿。虽然赔偿主体都是国家,但这无非说明了国家在国内和国际上作为主体的双重性,两者具有完全不同的含义。如常设国际法院在 1926 年的“波属上西里西亚德国利益案”的裁决中就认为:“对国际法来说,国内法是单纯的实施,是国家的意志和活动的表现。”①也就是说,国家机关的行为违反国内法与否,与是否构成国际法意义上的国家责任并无必然联系,实质还在于国家机关的行为与国际法是否相抵触。这得到《国家责任条款草案》的印证,其第 4 条明确规定:“只有国际法可以认定一国的行为为国际不法行为。这种认定不因国内法认定同一行为合法而受影响。”《维也纳条约法公约》(Vienna Convention on the Law of Treaties)第 27 条也明确规定:“当事国不得援引其国内法规定为理由而不履行条约。”这种观点在一定意义上构成了普遍被接受的国际法原则。

因此,即便东道国法院完全按照国内立法规定实施针对国际商事仲裁的司法监督行为,依然可能引起国际法意义上的国家责任。但是,当法院声称适用《纽约公约》或“示范法”这样的国际规定的条款,却做出不合理的行为,是否也可以认定违反投资条约?这个问题十分有趣,实践中尚未出现这种案例,有待未来更多的实例来分析 ICSID 仲裁庭在审查类似理由时会采取什么样的观点。

三、国际投资仲裁对抗国际商事仲裁司法监督的程序问题

随着实践的发展,分属不同领域的国际商事仲裁和国际投资仲裁之间的差异越来越大。有观点认为,现行国际投资仲裁机制的一些主要问题在于,设立之初照搬了国际商事仲裁的商事化逻辑,其内在价值观和制度设计存在严重的

---

① 《国际常设法院刊物》A 辑第 7 卷,第 19 页。转引自[奥]阿·菲德罗斯等:《国际法》(上册),李浩培译,商务印书馆 1981 年版,第 144 页。

冲突。因此,国际投资仲裁的改革方向在于"去商事化",晚近国际投资仲裁改革的措施和方案也都蕴含了这一共同逻辑。[①] 在这个前提下,将两个机制之间的程序进行衔接,让国际商事仲裁处理的争议进入国际投资仲裁领域内,不得不让人担心这种程序衔接的合理性。为解除这些担忧,有必要从国际投资仲裁设立的初衷及其运行机制展开讨论。

(一)是否构成平行程序

在国际商事仲裁中,当事人之间因仲裁协议产生的商事仲裁管辖权虽然能够有效排除诉权,但是并不意味着就争议事项的各方面管辖都具有排他性。当事一方完全可以就同一个争端或两个紧密联系的争端的事项,向不同的争端解决机构提起申请。[②] 在国际投资仲裁中,同样会出现国际投资仲裁程序同其他程序相平行的情形。如"美加软木案",[③]针对相同的争议事项,可以同时在世界贸易组织(World Trade Organization,WTO)和国际投资仲裁机制中启动相应的程序。在WTO争端解决机制和国际投资仲裁两种程序中,核心争议点都是美国针对加拿大软木产业的反倾销与反补贴政策,投资仲裁中的当事一方为加拿大软木业者,其利益与WTO争端解决机制中当事一方的加拿大国家利益本身也存在一致性。投资者后续提起的投资仲裁增加了美国的诉讼负担,可被加拿大政府在WTO争端解决中用作磋商筹码来促使美国妥协。因此,两种程序本质上是基于类似法律事实提起的平行程序,但国际投资仲裁庭并不因在先的WTO争端解决程序而失去管辖权。两种程序的主体并不完全相同,且在侧重面向上也会存在区别。正如在针对东道国司法监督提起的国际投资仲裁中,被申请人转变为东道国政府,且在国际投资仲裁中,并不对在先的实体争议事项重新审理,而只是聚焦在东道国法院的行为上。这两种现象的本质都是管辖权

---

① 参见蔡从燕:《国际投资仲裁的商事化与"去商事化"》,载《现代法学》2011年第1期。

② See Bernardo M. Cremades, Ignacio Madalenaj, "Parallel Proceedings in International Arbitration", *Arb. Intl* 24, 2008, pp. 507-508.

③ 美加软木案中,美国的反倾销与反补贴政策在违反WTO规则的同时,也违反了国际投资法律规则下东道国应当给予投资者国民待遇的义务。因此,该案不仅涉及WTO法律规则体系下的相关规则,也涉及投资者权利受损及损害赔偿的问题,从而亦被纳入"投资者—东道国"仲裁机制所管辖的投资争端范围。

重叠的问题。平行程序的构成主要考量三个本质要素,即当事人的同质性、争议事项的同质性以及程序时间上的重叠性。当事人的同质性并不是指当事人完全相同,而是指两个程序的同一方当事人以同一身份行事,或者代表同一利益。[①] 争议事项的同质性在认定标准上与当事人的同质性相似,不要求争议事项的完全相同,只要事项来自同一法律关系或同一集合的法律关系,且诉求具有关联性,便同样可以认定其"实质相同"。时间上的重叠性则主要体现在不同程序同步进行,或者程序之间存在连续性。

从国际投资仲裁对国际商事仲裁司法监督进行审查的实践来看,投资仲裁程序中的主体发生了变更,投资仲裁庭也将争议限制在法院的干涉行为是否构成对投资条约的违背。[②] 国际投资仲裁的司法监督虽然可能会对原商事仲裁裁决的履行产生实质的影响,甚至会让东道国重新审核承认与执行的司法程序,但是这种影响并不是由于对原商事仲裁裁决下的法律事实和法律依据进行又一次审理而产生的,仅仅是从条约义务的角度来对东道国法院的行为进行定性和归责。无论是从事实上的争议事项,还是从诉求来看,都是完全不同的概念,应当认定后续的国际投资仲裁是一个全新的仲裁程序。

换个角度说,认定后续国际投资仲裁程序的独立性,也能对认为该程序构成东道国司法机关的上诉机制这一观点进行反驳。在确认国际投资仲裁庭参加仲裁的主体不同以及未对商事仲裁裁决的内容进行重新审理的基础上,还应当注意到,投资仲裁庭管辖权主要直接来自于条约,而不隶属于具体的管辖权体系,国际投资仲裁庭和地方法院不存在层级关系,国际投资仲裁庭仲裁的理由主要是因为东道国对双边投资协定的违背,而不包括商事主体对具体合同的违约,也与合同违约发生的背景没有相关性。

当然,在判定东道国法院是否构成违反条约时,还是有必要划清东道国法院普通错误和严重审判不公的界限。即便是程序事项,仲裁庭也不能决定法院在解释法律或者阐述法律观点时是否存在不当之处,也即仲裁庭不能对东道国

① 参见侯幼萍:《WTO 和 ICSID 管辖权冲突研究》,载《国际经济法学刊》2007 年第 2 期。

② Saipem v. Bangladesh, Fianl Award, para. 155.

国内法的问题进行调查或做出判断。[①] 但是,当正常立场的第三方都无法理解法官的裁判结果,或者有证据证明法官存在不良动机,认定法院的行为已经无法被认为是法治行为的情况下,该界限也是可以被打破的。

(二)是否构成滥诉

关于是否构成滥诉,一般是以个案的事实进行单独分析。这是因为滥诉的外在表现形式多样,无法详尽地列明滥诉可能存在的类型,理论上也尚未形成一个被普遍认可的概念,但是我们还是可以通过法理诠释的方法归纳一下滥诉的表征。一般认为,滥诉有两个普遍存在的构成要件:一是当事人行使诉权不具有必要性,属于非正当地利用程序;二是当事人是出于非法目的而利用诉讼程序。那么构成这两个要件的行为就可以被认定为滥诉,并要求当事人承担不利的法律后果。[②] 在判断是否构成滥诉时一般采用目的分析方法,即比较当事人提起程序的目的与程序设置的目的。国际投资仲裁机制本来设置的目的在于保护投资者的投资权益,但是如果投资者出于其他目的,将其他不相关的争议进行包装,使之符合双边投资协定的定义,并将东道国纳入国际投资仲裁程序中,以此来寻求巨额赔偿,在这种情况下就能将投资者的行为归入滥诉的范围。滥诉行为的外在形式可能是多样化的,可能是对投资定义的扭曲扩大,可能是挑选条约以获取有利的条约依据,可能是将投资仲裁作为其他程序的谈判筹码,也可能包括恶意回避东道国国内的司法程序,寻求国际投资仲裁以求避开东道国法院对国际商事仲裁的司法监督。滥诉行为的危害性不言而喻,东道国担心参加国际投资仲裁程序可能获得败诉的结果,甚至作为国际投资仲裁程序中的被申请方本身就会给东道国带来压力。为避免出现这种情形,东道国可能会在国家管理中有意地减少对投资的正当管制,进而可能降低对非投资利益的保护标准,投资者的滥诉行为会加深东道国这方面的顾虑。这种行为无疑是将国际投资仲裁变成谋取私利,或者挑战东道国主权的工具。

---

① E. g., Liman Caspian Oil v. Kazakhstan; TECO v. Guatemala; Jan de Nul v. Egypt.

② 参见徐树华:《国际投资仲裁中滥诉防范机制的构建》,载《法学》2017年第5期。

回归到现有的仲裁实践中,将典型的商事争议的裁决放置到投资者和东道国争端解决制度的平台上去执行这种行为是否构成滥诉,主要是从当事人在商事裁决不被承认与执行的情形下有无其他救济手段来进行判定。虽然救济手段的唯一性不能直接判定当事人不存在滥诉的行为,但是在一定程度上减少了当事人主观上存在恶性的可能性。东道国对国际商事仲裁司法监督的特殊性在于,其对国际商事仲裁裁决的利益有着十分巨大的影响。一旦当事人完成在一国法院系统内程序,并被东道国法院判定不予承认和执行相关裁决,基于仲裁一裁终局的特性,当事人很难再通过其他渠道进行救济。当然,随着非内国化理论的发展,即便仲裁裁决被撤销,当事人也可以在其他国家申请承认与执行,但不可否认的是,在一般情况下,这种损失都是严重且不可挽回的。

"破坏国际约定就产生以适当形式给予赔偿的义务,这是国际法的一个原则。"[①]虽然国际法在发展过程中,对于违反国际义务的制裁手段不断在丰富,但是这些手段往往是从国家层面上进行交涉。个人通过国际法进行维权的渠道并不多,当东道国对投资者权益造成影响时,除了通过双边投资协定和东道国国内法律寻求救济外,投资者并无太多选择的空间。

从国内法角度来说,当投资者自认已经在东道国司法程序内遭受非法的待遇后,便很难再要求投资者对该种救济途径抱有太多的信心。况且在提起国际投资仲裁时,无论是按间接征收还是按司法不公的投资待遇标准,其前置条件都要求投资者已经穷尽本地的救济。正如在萨伊博姆公司案中,孟加拉政府认为:"无论东道国法院的行为是被定性为征收还是司法不公,穷尽本地救济都应当成为请求成立的前提条件。"[②]即便仲裁庭得出了不同于以往主流意见的结论,认为穷尽救济并非认定间接征收的实质要件,[③]也是在认定萨伊博姆公司已经在东道国法院耗费大量的时间和精力,"被视作已经穷尽可能的救济"时其诉求才能得到支持。在这种情况下,国内法的救济选项要么已经被证明无

---

① [英]詹宁斯、瓦茨修订:《奥本海国际法》(第1卷第1分册),王铁崖等译,中国大百科全书出版社1995年版,第415页。

② Saipem v. Bangladesh, Fianl Award, para. 178.

③ Ibid., para. 181.

效,要么已经被穷尽,对于投资者放弃该选项也不能做过多的苛责。在这样的前提下,投资者出于正当目的,要求国际投资仲裁庭审查东道国法院的相关司法监督行为不应被认为构成滥诉。

四、国际法人本化背景下救济途径的发展

对以国际投资仲裁对抗国际商事仲裁司法监督的模式,应当持正面和乐观的态度。该模式是对国际商事仲裁裁决承认与执行渠道的开拓,甚至可以将其定性为国际商事仲裁裁决承认与执行的"工具"。这种模式的兴起和发展,一方面反映了国际投资仲裁这一救济途径的自我扩张和完善,另一方面也反映了国际法人本化的趋势。

(一)个人寻求国际法救济的新发展

以国际投资仲裁对抗国际商事仲裁司法监督这种模式的发展前提,是国际法人本化背景下个人在国际法地位的逐渐提高。随着经济全球化的发展,国际法不再是远离普通人的"高级政治"事物,而与公众的切身利益有着更为密切的关系。实际上,经济全球化下各国商贸的密切往来,使得经济全球化最终体现为个人在国际市场上进行的交易活动。①

这种救济模式是个人权利在国际法上的体现。根据国际常设法院的意见,个人可以享有国际法上的权利和义务。在"但泽法院管辖权问题"的咨询意见中,法院认为国际条约的缔约国可以为个人创设权利和义务,并且由缔约国国内的法院加以执行。②《国家责任条款草案》第33条第2款也规定,"本部分不妨碍任何人或国家以外的实体由于一国的国际责任可能直接取得的任何权利",明确了个人可以因为国家的不法行为取得国际法层面上

① 参见蔡从燕:《面对国家的个人与面对个人的国家——全球化背景下国际法发展的元动力问题》,载《法律科学:西北政法学院学校》2006年第6期。

② Tza Yap Shum v. Republic of Peru, ICSID Case No. ARB/07/06, Decisions on Jurisdiction and Competence (2009. 6. 19), paras. 67-77.

的求偿权利。[①] 国家司法机关在进行国际商事仲裁司法监督时的行为,如果违反了相关国际条约的约定,个人寻求多样的途径来救济自己的权益,是符合国际法规定的。

这种救济模式是对传统救济方式的扩充。实际上对这一途径的讨论,很大部分集中在是否存在滥用国际投资仲裁的问题上。国际投资仲裁的管辖有其独特性,是以缔约国在缔结过程中预先的让渡为前提,赋予投资者在纠纷产生时提起国际投资仲裁的权利。因此,在管辖认定中,明确缔约国的意思表示十分重要。这也是为什么仲裁庭必须对投资定义等问题一再强调,预防非投资事项进入到投资仲裁的程序中,使投资仲裁成为当事人谋求利益最大化的工具。但是,传统救济方式的限制十分明显,在行政和司法救济之外,当事人往往只能通过国家层面进行交涉。然而,在现行的国际经济秩序中,经济弱国往往难以进行公平、有效的交涉。突出的例子是,对于WTO《关于争端解决规则与程序谅解》第22条规定的报复权,弱国缺乏对贸易大国、强国实施报复的实力,难以为其国民提供有效的保护。该模式以个人为主体进行救济,在一定程度上弥补了原有救济途径的缺陷。

(二)国际法关注个人的本质回归

国际法的本质始终是对于个人的终极关注(ultimate concern)。[②] 过分严格地从"国家—国家"(state-state)间这种逻辑关系出发而否认、忽视个人在国际社会中的利益,在本质上是与国内法上承认和维护个人利益的愿望和要求是相矛盾的。[③]

在体系层面上来评价国际法,其最突出的特点就是整体上的"不成体系",或者说是"碎片化"(fragmentation of international law),体现的是世界各国在地

---

① 参见卜凌嘉:《从国际人权法看个人在国际法上的地位》,载《广东省社会主义学院学报》2011年第3期。

② See Malcolm N. Shaw, *International Law*, 4th edition, London, Cambridge University Press, 1997, p. 183.

③ 参见李伯军:《对个人作为国际法主体问题的重新认识》,载《河北法学》2004年第5期。

理、政治、经济等方面各自不同的力量、需求的结合。[①] 这种角力使国家主权不是"铁板一块",国家主权在国际组织里的频繁让渡成为这个时代国际法的一个主要现象。这样,个人直接在国际法上享受权利与承担义务或责任,即个人直接避开国家这个"中介"来寻求权利保护成为可能。实际上,除了国际投资仲裁外,在很多实践中,国际法已经赋予个人作为纠纷主体直接提起救济程序的权利。如《欧洲人权公约》中规定的个人诉权,赋予了个人"对抗本国的法律地位";1982年《联合国海洋法公约》规定,在处理某些海底争端时,个人与国家之间是平等的;《北美自由贸易协定》《世界能源宪章》甚至规定了个人可以直接选择争议的解决方式和途径,使个人有权以与有关缔约国平等的身份和地位参与争端的解决。

这种主权让渡有其必要性。国家的经济主权并不意味着对私人经济活动的完全控制,而且由于公权力本身具有内在扩张性,在国内还可以利用法治对权力进行约束,在国际法背景下,如果不以人为本,则主权国家由于缺乏更高位的制约,势必会影响国际法的实际运用。因此,国际法的人本化将推动国际法向更为完善的方向发展。当然,主权让渡下的个人救济途径,不意味着个人可以任意对抗国家。该模式下的救济途径,依然是国家认可之下的国际条约义务。国家愿意在何种程度、何种范围赋予个人这种救济途径,仍然可以由国家自行决定。

以萨伊博姆公司案为代表的数个案例,开创了通过提起国际投资仲裁来对抗国际商事仲裁司法监督的模式。投资者在摸索中,将请求的理由从最初的违背征收条款向其他投资待遇条款蔓延,这在一定程度上降低了这种救济模式的门槛。通过对相关理论问题的分析,可以确认在符合一定条件下,仲裁庭对该类型的案件确实有管辖权。其主要依据是,国际商事仲裁裁决只涉及对原先投资权利的重新配置,只是原先权利的重新表现,根据"投资形式上的任何变化不影响其作为投资的性质"这一条款,应当认为裁决所涉事项依然保持了其投

① 何志鹏、孙璐:《"科索沃独立不违法"咨询意见反思》,载《中国社会科学报》2010年12月14日,第9版。

资的特性。且国际投资仲裁是投资者最后的救济手段,在这个时候排除管辖权,无疑是对投资者权益的巨大伤害,也违背了投资条约签订的宗旨。

该模式的存在有其合法性与合理性,在一定程度上甚至可能促使一国法院变得更倾向于承认与执行国际商事仲裁裁决,也使个人权益在国际法层面多了另一保护途径。国际投资仲裁机制作为当今国际社会解决投资者与东道国之间投资争端的切实有效的工具,自当在国际法人本化的浪潮中,为各国投资者积极利用,使其在保护海外投资者合法权益上发挥出更大的作用。

案外人申请不予执行仲裁裁决之实证分析

——以 2018 年人民法院 41 份裁决为研究对象

袁杜娟　陈艳*

摘要：最高人民法院发布《关于人民法院办理仲裁裁决执行案件若干问题的规定》，创设了案外人申请不予执行仲裁裁决制度，标志着长期备受关注的虚假仲裁问题步入了制度化规范的新阶段。本文通过考察 2018 年人民法院审查此类案件的基本情况和分析中国现行相关法律规范，发现司法尊重并支持该制度，但同时可能存在以下问题：该制度可能会给现有的仲裁制度带来冲击；裁决执行内容不明确的认定标准不甚妥当；虚假仲裁的审查标准尚不明确；等等。鉴于此，本文认为，案外人应在准确理解申请条件的基础上，及时提出不予执行的申请，并提交合理有效的证据，做到有效打击虚假仲裁。同时，仲裁机构应完善案外人申请不予执行仲裁裁决的相关仲裁规则，建立虚假仲裁识别机制，杜绝虚假仲裁。此外，司法监督机构在发挥司法能动性、合理分配举证责任的同时，更应该准确把握司法监督的边界。

关键词：案外人　不予执行仲裁裁决　虚假仲裁　仲裁裁决执行规定

一、引言

商事仲裁的保密性、仲裁当事人的自治性、仲裁程序对案外第三人的封闭

---

* 袁杜娟，上海大学法学院副教授、ADR 与仲裁研究院秘书长。
陈艳，上海大学法学院 2016 级国际法学（ADR 方向）硕士研究生。

性、仲裁机构的中立性和证据判断上更大的裁量权以及仲裁的一裁终局性,使虚假仲裁更易泛滥,以致在实务中经常被恶意当事人用以损害案外人的合法权益。2018 年 2 月 22 日最高人民法院发布《关于人民法院办理仲裁裁决执行案件若干问题的规定》(以下简称《仲裁裁决执行规定》),创设案外人申请不予执行(non-enforcement)仲裁裁决制度,[①]填补了人民法院办理仲裁裁决执行案件在实践操作中的一些规则空白。同时,案外人申请不予执行仲裁裁决体现了人民法院对仲裁的司法监督与支持,突出了对仲裁当事人、案外人合法权益的保护,意在提高仲裁公信力和执行力,促进仲裁事业的健康有序发展。

鉴于《仲裁裁决执行规定》刚实施不久,对于案外人申请不予执行仲裁裁决制度的程序与内容规定得不够明确,可能导致法院在审查此类裁决的实践中存在诸多问题。本文以自《仲裁裁决执行规定》正式实施后法院审理结案的 41 份裁定为统计样本,旨在从实证层面客观地分析案外人申请不予执行仲裁裁决的案件中存在的问题,并提出合理的建议,拟帮助仲裁机构尽量避免裁决被不予执行的情况,同时也避免法院作出不当的不予执行仲裁裁决的裁定,从而完善案外人申请不予执行仲裁裁决制度。

二、样本分析:案外人申请不予执行仲裁裁决的基本情况

(一)样本选择

本文所选的调研样本,系 2018 年 3 月 1 日至 8 月 7 日我国人民法院审结的 41 例案外人申请不予执行仲裁裁决的案件(以裁判文书的落款时间进行统计)。样本的来源主要有两个渠道:中国裁判文书网[②]和 Openlaw 官方网站。[③]当然,由于客观原因(如法院无系统公布案例制度及未及时公布等),也许会存

① 最高人民法院《仲裁裁决执行规定》(2018 年 3 月 1 日实施)第 9 条规定:"案外人向人民法院申请不予执行仲裁裁决或者仲裁调解书的,应当提交申请书以及证明其请求成立的证据材料,并符合下列条件:(一)有证据证明仲裁案件当事人恶意申请仲裁或者虚假仲裁,损害其合法权益;(二)案外人主张的合法权益所涉及的执行标的尚未执行终结;(三)自知道或者应当知道人民法院对该标的采取执行措施之日起三十日内提出。"

② 载中国裁判文书网:http://wenshu.court.gov.cn/,最后访问日期:2018 年 8 月 7 日。

③ Openlaw:http://openlaw.cn/,最后访问日期:2018 年 8 月 7 日。

在数据上的遗漏,但笔者相信遗漏不多,且不会对统计产生实质上的影响。为了探究《仲裁裁决执行规定》的实施对于案外人申请不予执行仲裁裁决实践的现实意义,本文以2018年3月1日作为样本研究的起始时间,并且,上文所说的41份仲裁裁定书,均为无涉外因素的国内民商事裁决。

一般来说,对于申请不予执行仲裁裁决的案件,人民法院经审查之后,常见的处理结果有两种:裁定驳回不予执行的申请、裁定不予执行仲裁裁决。但在实践中,还有其他终结申请不予执行程序的情形,如申请人撤回申请、本次执行程序终结等。前述41份裁定书仅限裁定不予执行和驳回不予执行的申请,不涉及终结及中止不予执行程序的情形。

(二)案外人申请不予执行仲裁裁决司法监督案件的特点

1. 司法尊重并支持该制度

自2018年3月1日至8月7日,共统计我国人民法院审结案外人申请不予执行仲裁裁决的41起。如图1所示,上述案件中,裁定驳回不予执行的申请共38起,占样本案例总数92.68%,[①]裁定不予执行仲裁裁决共3起,占样本案例总数7.32%。从上述数据可以看出,法院仅在少数案件中否定仲裁裁决的法律效力。绝大多数情况下,法院尊重仲裁的独立性,肯定仲裁裁决的效力并对仲裁裁决的执行予以必要支持。

图1 案外人申请不予执行仲裁裁决结果比例

① 为保持数据的统一性,本文比例精度取保留小数点后两位数。

同时,法院裁定案外人申请不予执行仲裁裁决 3 起案件,其数量远超过法院裁定仲裁当事人不予执行和撤销仲裁裁决的年度案例总数。① 在这 3 起被裁定不予执行仲裁裁决的案件中,案外人通过向法院提出诉求,保障了自身的合法权益,同时有效地打击了虚假仲裁。这正体现了法院在虚假仲裁中案外人权利救济方面承担着重要的司法职责。

2. 案件分布呈现全国化趋势

从图 2 中可看出,目前审理案外人申请不予执行仲裁裁决的案件的人民法院主要是浙江省杭州市中级人民法院、广东省广州市中级人民法院、安徽省安庆市中级人民法院及辽宁省大连市中级人民法院。其中,浙江省杭州市中级人民法院共审结了 19 起案例,占调研样本总数的 46.34%;广东省广州市中级人民法院共审结 8 起案例,占调研样本总数的 19.51%;安徽省安庆市中级人民法院共审结了 4 起案件,占调研样本总数的 9.76%;辽宁省大连市中级人民法院共审结 3 起案例,占调研样本总数的 7.32%;北京市第二中级人民法院、湖南省长沙市中级人民法院、河南省南阳市中级人民法院等 7 个中级人民法院共审结 7 起案件,占调研样本总数 17.07%。

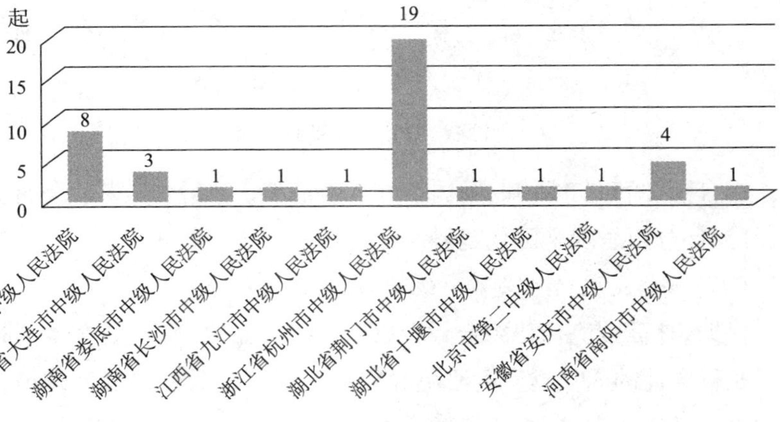

图 2　作出驳回裁决的法院

① 据上海国际仲裁中心统计,2014~2017 年仅有 3 起案件被裁定不予执行仲裁裁决,甚至在 2015 年、2016 年被裁定不予执行仲裁裁决的案件数为零;2013~2017 年的 5 年间仅有 1 起案件被裁定撤销仲裁裁决(此仲裁裁决指的是国内商事仲裁裁决,不包括劳动争议仲裁裁决)。以上数据由上海国际仲裁中心向笔者提供,而非通过公开渠道获取的资料。

从图 3 中可看出，案外人申请不予执行的仲裁裁决主要由深圳、杭州、广州、大连及安庆仲裁委员会所作出。深圳国际仲裁院、杭州仲裁委员会、中国广州仲裁委员会、大连仲裁委员会及安庆仲裁委员会所作仲裁裁决共 34 起，占调研样本总数的 82.93%。长沙仲裁委员会、九江仲裁委员会、荆门仲裁委员、北京仲裁委员会及南阳仲裁委员会等 7 个仲裁委员会共作出 7 起仲裁裁决，占调研样本总数的 17.07%。

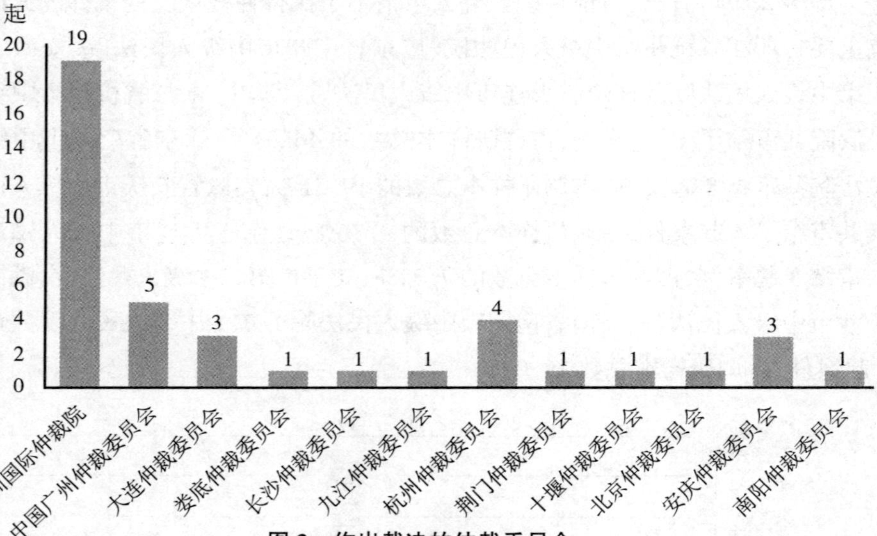

图 3　作出裁决的仲裁委员会

综合图 2 和图 3 可知，我国案外人申请不予执行仲裁裁决案件分布较为广泛，且案件分布呈现全国化趋势。

（三）被裁定驳回仲裁裁决统计与分析

根据《仲裁裁决执行规定》第 9 条和第 18 条之规定，结合本文被裁定驳回不予执行申请的 38 个样本，法院驳回的依据可分为法定驳回理由及非法定驳回理由。具体而言，这些依据可再被细分为以下 8 种理由（见图 4）："案外人未能证明仲裁案件当事人恶意申请仲裁或者虚假仲裁，损害其合法权益"（"理由 1"共 7 个，占总理由的 14.29%）；"案外人主张的合法权益所涉及的执行标的已执行终结"（"理由 2"有 2 个，占总理由的 4.08%）；"案外人未在自知道或者应当知道人民法院对该标的采取执行措施之日起三十日内提出"（"理由 3"无相关案例);"案外人未能证明系权利或者利益的主体"("理由4"有6个,占总理由的12.24%);"案外人未能证明其主张的权利或者利益合法、真实"("理由5"无相关案例);"案外人未能证明仲裁案件当事人之间存在虚构法律关系,捏造案件事实的情形"("理由6"有11个,占总理由的22.45%);"案外人未能证明仲裁裁决主文或者仲裁调解书处理当事人民事权利义务的结果部分或者全部错误,损害其合法权益"("理由7"无相关案例);"案外人申请不予执行仲裁裁决的理由为非法定理由"("理由8"共23个,占总理由的46.94%)。

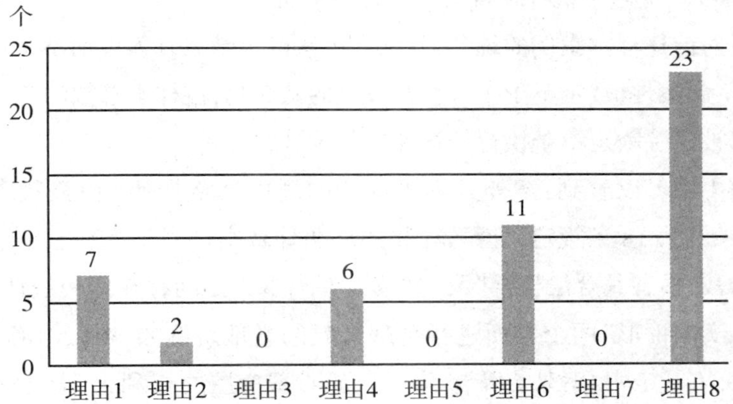

图4 被驳回的理由频数统计

注:在部分案件中,案外人申请不予执行仲裁裁决的理由不止一项,法院裁定的依据也不止其中一项,所以尽管此章节所分析的样本数量为38个,但事由统计理由为49个(法定理由与非法定理由之和)。

从图4数据中可以看出,在法定驳回理由中,"案外人未能证明仲裁案件当事人恶意申请仲裁或者虚假仲裁,损害其合法权益"(理由1)及"案外人未能证明仲裁案件当事人之间存在虚构法律关系,捏造案件事实的情形"(理由6)是法院裁定驳回申请的主要依据。由此可见,一定程度上可以说明,善意案外人如何证明仲裁案件的当事人虚假仲裁等是法院审理此类案件的关键点。

同时,除前述《仲裁裁决执行规定》的规定外,法院审理案外人申请不予执行仲裁裁决的理由还有"其他理由"(理由8)。本文认为,"其他理由"虽不在法院审理之列,但对我国案外人申请不予执行制度具有一定的促进作用,故将其纳入统计分析的范畴。在本文的研究样本中,法院以此为由驳回案外人的申请的总数为23个,占总样本的理由的46.94%,其中主要包括“隐瞒了重要证据,导致仲裁委作出错误的裁决”“损害公共利益”“仲裁程序违反法定程序”“当事人向人民法院申请撤销仲裁裁决被驳回后,又在执行程序中以相同事由提出不予执行申请的”等;此外,还包括但不限于“管辖权决定错误”等。

综上可知,案外人不得以“其他事由”(非法定事由)申请不予执行仲裁裁决。

(四)被裁定不予执行仲裁裁决统计与分析

通过对前述样本案例的统计,我国人民法院审结案外人申请不予执行仲裁裁决的41起案件,裁定不予执行仲裁裁决的共3起,占样本总数的7.32%。以下对3起被法院裁定不予执行的案件进行统计并分析。

从表1中可以看到,案外人提出申请的理由严格按照《仲裁裁决执行规定》第9条和第18条规定,且紧紧围绕“证明仲裁案件当事人恶意申请仲裁或者虚假仲裁,损害其合法权益”及“仲裁案件当事人之间存在虚构法律关系,捏造案件事实的情形”两个方面进行合理有效的举证。例如,在(2018)湘13执异32号民事裁定中,案外人华融公司为证明系房屋的权利人,向法院提供对(华剑首郡)6栋1808号房持有真实的抵押登记证明,证明该房屋现仍抵押登记在其名下的事实。

从这3起案例可知,案外人在向法院申请不予执行仲裁裁决时,应注意以下3点:第一,应准确理解申请理由,严格按照《仲裁裁决执行规定》的要求提出;第二,注意诉求提出的时限,在得知相关事实后应及时提出诉求;第三,为证明虚假仲裁,应提交合理的证据,以便有效打击虚假仲裁。

表1　被裁定不予执行仲裁裁决的申请与裁定理由对比

案号	案由	案外人提出申请的理由	法院裁定的判定理由
(2017)湘01执监3号	借款合同纠纷	仲裁裁决系虚假仲裁,损害了案外人的合法权益	借款本金及利息是虚假债务,仲裁当事人虚构债权并作出虚假的仲裁调解,损害了案外人的合法权益

续表

案号	案由	案外人提出申请的理由	法院裁定的判定理由
(2018)鄂08执异9号	建设工程施工合同纠纷	仲裁当事人签订了虚假的《工程竣工日期确定书》,恶意仲裁或虚假仲裁,损害了案外人的利益	仲裁当事人虚构法律关系、捏造案件事实的情形
(2018)湘13执异32号	商品房销售合同纠纷	仲裁当事人通过虚构债权债务合同,致裁决结果严重损害案外人对房屋的抵押权	根据案外人提供的房屋抵押权的证明,判定案外人系该房屋的权利主体,裁决损害了案外人的合法权益

三、问题审视:案外人申请不予执行仲裁裁决制度的突出问题及原因

通过对上述调研样本的分析可见,案外人申请不予执行仲裁裁决制度在一定程度上维护了案外人的合法权益,但该制度在执行过程中仍然存在若干问题。比如,如何界定案外人主体资格?如何明确虚假仲裁的认定标准和证明责任?如何在保障案外人合法权益的同时又能够防止滥用诉讼权利?下文综合上述仲裁裁决司法审查案件来分析案外人申请不予执行仲裁裁决存在的问题及原因。

(一)案外人申请不予执行仲裁裁决制度的突出问题

1. 仲裁案外人主体资格的界定及与案件的关联程度

据上文样本案例的分析可知,本文41起案例中有6起案例"因未能证明其为权利或者利益的主体"而被法院裁定驳回。例如,在(2018)粤01执异400号民事裁定书中,案外人倪某以其系涉案房屋权利人为由,主张涉案仲裁裁决损害了其利益。最后因倪某未能证明其对执行标的(涉案房屋)享有合法权益等,被法院最终驳回申请。从此起案例可引发出对以下问题的探讨,即该如何界定案外人的主体资格以及案外人与案件的关联程度。

(1)仲裁案外人的界定

《仲裁裁决执行规定》第18条第1项仅规定了"权利或者利益的主体",但未对"案外人"进行专门的定义。现有法律法规并无关于仲裁"案外人"的界

定,而仅有专家学者对其作出的学理上的界定。专家学者主要参考了民事诉讼领域的案外第三人制度,将仲裁中的"案外人"界定为:因法定或不可归责于自己的事实原因,未能参加民事仲裁程序,但是与该案件的仲裁结果有法律上利害关系的人。[①] 但本文认为,该种表述未能体现出仲裁的合意性,仲裁协议的签订直至仲裁程序的启动都是双方当事人合意协商的结果,这也在一定程度上排除了仲裁案外人参与仲裁程序的可能性。仲裁案外人的字面意思指的是仲裁程序以外的民事主体,其显著的形式特征为未参加特定案件的仲裁程序,但仅以此特征对仲裁案外人予以界定则过于宽泛。[②]

综上所述,仲裁的案外人系未参与正在进行或者已结束的仲裁程序,但又与该仲裁案件所涉的民商事纠纷有利害牵连关系的民商事主体。

(2)与案件关联性程度要求

《仲裁裁决执行规定》未明确案外人与仲裁裁决和/或执行标的需要满足何种关联性的要求,方可提起不予执行之请求或被认定为仲裁案外人。

在上文探讨的(2018)粤01执异400号民事裁定书中,案外人倪某以其系涉案房屋权利人为由提出不予执行仲裁裁决的申请,对于倪某主张的事实理由,因为广州市番禺区人民法院尚未作出判决(属于未决事项),所以受理不予执行申请的法院最终裁定,倪某在现阶段尚不能证明其对涉案房屋享有权利,应承担举证不能的法律后果。在此案件中,法院未说明倪某需提供何种证据方可证明其为对涉案房屋享有权利的案外人。为指导司法实践,相关法律应进一步明确案外人的认定标准。

2. 虚假仲裁的认定标准和证明责任

通过上文的样本案例分析可以发现,关于虚假仲裁的认定或证明存在许多值得思考之处。在(2018)鄂08执异9号案中,法院认定,虚假仲裁的关键在于"钟祥一建和生都公司存在虚构法律关系、捏造案件事实的情形,损害了案外

---

① 参见易晓东:《虚假仲裁中的案外第三人权益保护》,载《山西师大学报》(社会科学版)2018年第1期。

② 同上。

人彭某的合法权益”；在（2017）湘01执监3号案中，法院认定虚假仲裁的关键在于“湖南万博新材料有限公司与湖南盛世金融城置业有限公司虚构债权并作出虚假的仲裁调解，损害了案外人湖南众森联合投资有限公司的合法权益”。这两起案件引起笔者的思考：应如何界定是否构成虚假仲裁？由案外人承担举证责任是否存在不妥之处？

（1）难以就虚假仲裁的界定达成共识

由于我国理论界目前对于虚假仲裁研究的广度和深度不够，大家对虚假仲裁的界定一直未形成统一的认识和标准。虚假仲裁作为仲裁制度相关的法律概念，在理论界定上尚无统一的依据，专家和学者们对其理论认识各不相同。主流观点认为，虚假仲裁可以比照“虚假诉讼”的概念来界定。根据2008年浙江省高级人民法院出台的《关于在民事审判中防范和查处虚假诉讼案件的若干意见》，虚假诉讼是民事诉讼当事人互相串通并以欺诈的方式获得法院裁决或通过公证文书申请强制执行而获取非法利益的行为。① 此种观点以中国人民大学刑事法律科学研究中心谢望原教授为代表。谢教授主张，可以比照虚假诉讼对虚假仲裁进行界定，即虚假仲裁应当是虚构仲裁案件事实，且出于某一种非法或不正当的目的提起仲裁申请。② 另一种观点认为，虚假仲裁应当是仲裁当事人互相串通、虚构案件事实和法律关系，以虚假证据取得仲裁裁决，使仲裁当事人以外的第三人合法利益受到损害的行为。③

本文认为，对虚假仲裁的界定应该立足于仲裁的基本属性，并综合考量虚假仲裁的危害后果和规则目的。范围界定过窄不足以保护受侵害的案外人的权益，而范围界定过宽则不利于发挥仲裁独特的优势，且影响仲裁纠纷解决功能的有效发挥。综上可知，虚假仲裁应是主体在客观上实施了以伪造证据、恶

---

① 浙江省高级人民法院2008年制定的《关于在民事审判中防范和查处虚假诉讼案件的若干意见》（浙高法〔2008〕362号）第1条规定：“本意见所指的虚假诉讼是指民事诉讼各方当事人恶意串通，采取虚构法律关系、捏造案件事实方式提起民事诉讼，或者利用虚假仲裁裁决、公证文书申请执行，使法院作出错误裁判或执行，以获取非法利益的行为。”

② 参见张伯晋、程丁：《走出虚假仲裁司法救济的盲区》，载《检察日报》2013年9月26日，第3版。

③ 参见王晓伟、吴大华：《虚假仲裁之“何时休”与“以何休”》，载《凯里学院学报》2013年第2期。

意串通为手段的虚构法律事实和法律关系的行为，使仲裁员作出与事实不符的错误裁决或调解书。

(2)虚假仲裁的行为主体范围

从本文研究的样本中可知，在41起案外人申请不予执行仲裁裁决的案例中，有3起案例被人民法院裁定不予执行仲裁裁决。在这3起案例中，虚假仲裁的行为主体仅系仲裁程序中的双方当事人。但本文认为，应扩大解释虚假仲裁的行为主体范围。在特殊情况下，虚假仲裁的行为主体应该包括仲裁程序中的参加人，如仲裁当事人委托的代理人(包括自然人和法人)。适当的扩大解释，有利于对案外人的合法权益予以最大限度的保护。

(3)虚假仲裁的证明责任及取证

从以上案例可以得知，在目前案外人申请不予执行仲裁裁决的实践中，依然采取"谁主张、谁举证"的举证原则。由于仲裁具有私密性，仲裁裁决及其依据的调取存在困难，同时要证明虚假仲裁的存在于证据上要求很高，案外人取证十分不易；举证责任方面，举证责任的分配不公可能导致案外人不能提起申请不予执行之诉，虚假仲裁当事人既有恶意串通损害案外人的意图，一般会选择自行履行仲裁裁决或仲裁调解书，避免案件进入执行阶段以使案外人得以启动救济程序；此时，案外人由于无法提供充分的证据向法院申请不予执行，其可能会利用案外人的异议权来延缓执行期限，此行为有悖于法律打击虚假仲裁和支持仲裁科学发展的平衡初衷。

《仲裁裁决执行规定》第11条第2款规定："……人民法院审查时，认为必要的，可以要求仲裁机构作出说明，或者向仲裁机构调阅仲裁案卷。"该规定实际上为法院和仲裁机构协助案外人调查取证提供了依据，其设计有利于引导、鼓励当事人诚信仲裁、如实陈述，该规定除了能够协助仲裁机构在查明真相基础上作出裁决、实现实体公平外，也有利于推动诚信的仲裁文化。下文将进一步阐明关于具体分配举证责任的建议。

3. 滥用诉讼权利的问题

通过上文样本案例的分析，本文41起案例中有23起案例因申请事由不符合该案件受理的法定理由而被法院裁定驳回,驳回比例高达43.48%。由此可见,目前案外人申请不予执行制度已遇到与第三人撤销之诉相似的"滥诉"问题。此行为可能导致案外人滥用诉讼权利、浪费司法资源的不良后果。

案外人申请不予执行仲裁裁决制度是一种全新的制度,在立法和司法实践中难免会遇到很多问题。若任由案外人无限行使自身的诉权,最终可能使不予执行制度成为拖延执行时间的工具,最终损害仲裁的高效率。法律在设立一项权利时,既要设置该项权利的保护机制,又要考虑设置防止滥用该项权利的机制,保护权利和防止滥用权利在法律制度的设置上应当是平衡的。[①] 只有完善相应的制度和措施,才能保证案外人申请不予执行仲裁裁决制度合理有效地运行,防止出现仲裁案外人滥用诉权等情形。

4. 司法的有限审查权与仲裁私密性、独立性等原则之间的问题

司法的有限审查权与仲裁独立性的稳定关系对于案外人申请不予执行仲裁裁决制度的实施起着一定的保障作用。案外人申请不予执行仲裁裁决制度在本质上是对既判力的突破,是立法者在追求法律秩序的稳定性和追求实质正义之间的平衡。

仲裁司法审查权与仲裁私密性、独立性的关系,其实就是关于仲裁司法有限审查权与仲裁私密性、独立性等原则的关系,本文所指的法院对仲裁的司法审查权系仲裁司法有限审查权。依据我国《仲裁法》、《民事诉讼法》及《仲裁裁决执行规定》相关条款的规定,法律赋予法院有限的司法审查权,仅在《仲裁裁决执行规定》第9条、第18条规定的7个范围内对不予执行仲裁裁决申请进行审查。

在法院审理案外人申请不予执行仲裁裁决的案件中,法院的审理是否会破坏仲裁独立性原则,解决此问题的关键在于对虚假仲裁的判定。其一,虚假仲裁并非法律意义上的真正仲裁,其不受仲裁私密性、独立性的保护。从这个层面上看,法院对确实构成虚假仲裁案件进行的司法审查,并不会对仲裁体系的

---

① 参见孟庆吉、赵飞寒:《论恶意诉讼之成因与规制》,载《黑龙江省政法管理干部学院学报》2009年第1期。

确定性与稳定性产生负面影响。其二,若案外人申请不予执行的仲裁裁决并非虚假仲裁,法院对于此类案件的司法审查,有可能会突破仲裁的私密性。

综上所述,法院在充分行使自身有限司法审查权时,既要有效打击利用虚假仲裁进行侵害他人合法权益、损害仲裁制度公信力的行为,又要时刻保持对仲裁的有限审慎审查,即只在有限的法定范围内对仲裁进行司法审查,不破坏仲裁私密性、独立性等基本原则,在实施案外人申请不予执行仲裁裁决制度的同时,注意引导、鼓励、监督仲裁的健康有序的良性发展。

(二)案外人申请不予执行仲裁裁决所存在问题的初步分析

通过对上述41起案例的研究可以发现,我国案外人申请不予执行仲裁裁决制度中,存在法院审查范围和内容不够明确、举证责任分配不合理、虚假仲裁的认定标准不统一等诸多问题。问题的原因既有法律本身的缺位,也有在司法实践中的错误使用问题,以下从立法及实践层面对存在的问题进行初步分析。

1. 立法层面:过于原则、抽象且缺乏配套立法

案外人申请不予执行仲裁裁决制度在实践中存在的种种问题,主要归因于立法太过抽象,且缺乏配套的立法未对司法实践起到实质的指导作用。例如,《仲裁裁决执行规定》第11条第2款规定:“人民法院审查时,认为必要的,可以要求仲裁机构作出说明,或者向仲裁机构调阅仲裁案卷。”虽然此条款保障了仲裁的灵活性与效率,但对于法院的审理却不具有实际可操作性。如何准确判定“必要的”标准理由,此种情况无疑加大了法院的自由裁量权,进而可能扩大有限的司法审查权。因此,为使司法实践更易操作,配套立法和仲裁规则建设亟待加强。

2. 实践层面:人为因素和司法能力因素

除前述立法因素以外,法官及仲裁员的人为因素也不容小觑。从目前审查案外人申请不予执行仲裁裁决的实践中可以看出,我国司法审查人员欠缺完备的仲裁法知识体系。由于案外人申请不予执行仲裁裁决的新设,仲裁裁决的司法审查人员不仅起着救济案外人合法权益的作用,同时还肩负着引导、鼓励、监督仲裁发展的责任。然而,在一些司法实践中,由于办案司法人员缺乏虚假仲

裁的相关知识，或者不能准确理解司法对于仲裁既监督又支持的理念，在办案过程中无法准确识别虚假仲裁，未能起到防范虚假仲裁的作用。

本次调查虽未做到全面了解我国案外人申请不予执行仲裁裁决的情况，但是至少从某种程度上可以发现目前普遍存在的问题。《仲裁裁决执行规定》有关案外人申请不予执行仲裁裁决的规定较为原则化及简单化，这意味着其赋予了法官行使不予执行权的较大空间，在缺乏必要监督的情况下，该规定有可能带来法官滥用自由裁量权的结果。另外，仅就案外人申请不予执行仲裁裁决程序而言，此程序的主要参与者乃是法院和案外人，但是，仲裁机构及仲裁员应思考仲裁裁决被案外人向法院申请不予执行的诸多原因。

四、路径探究：完善案外人申请不予执行仲裁裁决制度的对策与建议

（一）对于案外人的建议

1. 准确理解申请条件，有效打击虚假仲裁

经对本文前述案例的分析，暂不讨论案外人是否提交证据以及其主张的情节，仅对申请不予执行仲裁裁决的条件进行分析。《仲裁裁决执行规定》第 9 条已明示列举了案外人向人民法院申请不予执行仲裁裁决应符合的具体条件。然而，在本文的研究样本中，41 起案例中仍有 23 起案例因提出申请的条件并非法定条件而被驳回申请。在其中的 19 起案件中，[①]案外人以仲裁当事人隐瞒了重要证据导致仲裁委员会作出错误的裁决提出申请，法院以其事由不符该案件受理的法定条件从而驳回。在 3 起案件中，[②]案外人以仲裁裁决违背公共

① 这 19 起案例参见（2018）浙 01 执异 36 号民事裁定书、（2018）浙 01 执异 41 号民事裁定书、（2018）浙 01 执异 43 号民事裁定书、（2018）浙 01 执异 50 号民事裁定书、（2018）浙 01 执异 53 号民事裁定书、（2018）浙 01 执异 60 号民事裁定书、（2018）浙 01 执异 68 号民事裁定书、（2018）浙 01 执异 69 号民事裁定书、（2018）浙 01 执异 70 号民事裁定书、（2018）浙 01 执异 71 号民事裁定书、（2018）浙 01 执异 82 号民事裁定书、（2018）浙 01 执异 86 民事裁定书、（2018）浙 01 执异 88 号民事裁定书、（2018）浙 01 执异 247 号民事裁定书、（2018）浙 01 执异 249 号民事裁定书、（2018）浙 01 执异 254 号民事裁定书、（2018）浙 01 执异 260 号民事裁定书、（2018）浙 01 执异 309 号民事裁定书、（2018）浙 01 执异 318 号民事裁定书。

② 这 3 起案例参见（2018）粤 01 执异 185 号民事裁定书、（2018）粤 01 执异 186 号民事裁定书、（2018）粤 01 执异 187 号民事裁定书。

利益而提出申请,法院依法作出不予审查的裁定;另外一起案例,[①]因仲裁程序是否违反法定程序不属于案外人申请不予执行仲裁裁决应予审查的法定范围,法院决定不予审查。

仲裁程序是否违反法定程序、仲裁裁决是否损害公共利益、仲裁程序中的当事人是否隐瞒了重要证据而导致仲裁员会作出错误的裁决等问题,实际上均不属于法院审查案外人申请不予执行仲裁裁决的法定范围,《仲裁裁决制定规定》对此已作出明确规定。这无疑体现出案外人对于申请不予执行仲裁裁决的条件认识不够。由此可知,准确理解申请条件,在向法院申请不予执行仲裁裁决的过程中,根据相应规定加以应对,才是案外人维护自身合法权益的必要前提。

2. 及时提出不予执行申请

在本文研究的样本案例中,因案外人未及时提出不予执行仲裁裁决的申请导致被法院裁定驳回申请的有2起案件。[②]《仲裁裁决执行规定》中关于案外人申请时限的规定有两个:其一,案外人主张的合法权益所涉及的执行标的尚未执行终结;其二,自知道或者应当知道人民法院对该标的采取执行措施之日起30日内提出。在一定程度上,此条款既是案外人申请不予执行的期限限制,同时也是司法对于仲裁支持的表现。在(2018)粤01执异185号案中,案外人冯某因仲裁机构未通知其作为第三人参加仲裁,认为仲裁程序严重违法,侵害了其合法权益,最终向法院提起不予执行仲裁裁决的申请。但笔者认为,在此起案件中,案外人冯某已知仲裁程序的进行,应及时向仲裁机构提出异议,而不是待仲裁裁决作出后,再采取申请不予执行仲裁裁决的事后救济措施。因此,当案外人遭遇仲裁裁决侵犯自身的合法权益时,最好能在仲裁程序中提出异议;若其不知晓仲裁程序的进行,在提交不予执行仲裁裁决的申请时,更应准确把握时限,及时提出诉求。

---

① 该案例参见(2018)粤01执异400号民事裁定书。

② 该2起案例参见(2018)鄂03执异93号民事裁定书、(2018)赣04执异10号裁定书。

3. 提交合理证据，证明虚假仲裁

《仲裁裁决执行规定》第 9 条已明确规定，案外人向人民法院申请不予执行仲裁裁决的，应当提交申请书以及证明其请求成立的证据材料。此证据材料指的是能够证明虚假仲裁的合理证据，而不是案外人所认为的有用证据。通过本文样本案例分析可知，多起案件中因案外人未能提供证据或未提供充分的、合理的证据证明仲裁案件当事人之间存在虚构法律关系、捏造案件事实的情形，从而导致虚假仲裁的诉求未被法院支持。

综上可知，在申请不予执行仲裁裁决的案件中，案外人应加强对其主张予以举证的意识，所提交的证据应有利于其诉求。

（二）关于仲裁机构及仲裁员的建议

虽然在案外人申请不予执行的仲裁裁决中，法院为彰显其对仲裁的监督与支持作用，对于案外人的申请多予以驳回，但此行为并不意味着仲裁机构及仲裁员对于其受理或审理的案件不存在任何错误。例如，在上文提及的（2018）粤 01 执异 185 号案中，仲裁机构在仲裁程序中是否违背《深圳国际仲裁院仲裁规则》（2016 年）第 18 条“追加当事人和加入仲裁程序”的规定，有待进一步探究。基于落实《仲裁裁决执行规定》的案外人申请不予执行仲裁裁决制度，作为仲裁案件审理的管理主体，仲裁机构应依法、合理行使权力，并完善相关仲裁规则，建立虚假仲裁识别机制，杜绝虚假仲裁。

1. 完善案外人申请不予执行仲裁裁决的相关仲裁规则

《仲裁裁决执行规定》关于案外人申请不予执行仲裁裁决制度的新设，对仲裁机构和仲裁员防范虚假仲裁提出了新的要求。目前，我国各大仲裁机构的仲裁规则尚无关于案外人申请不予执行仲裁裁决的规定。我国各仲裁机构应进一步修改完善案外人申请不予执行仲裁裁决的相关仲裁规则，对虚假仲裁裁决的处理作出程序规定。具体而言，仲裁机构可以采取以下措施：发挥仲裁机构的主观能动性，增加主动调查取证的规定；在保证仲裁程序合理化运行的前提下，增加案外人参与仲裁的规定；在保障仲裁机构独立办案的前提下，强化对仲裁裁决书的核阅;[①]对于缺席仲裁、仲裁涉及案外人等情形,应严格按法定程序最大限度地合理获取案件信息,减少不公平的裁决;在仲裁程序中,积极行使释明权,强化当事人的举证义务。

2. 建立虚假仲裁识别机制,杜绝虚假仲裁

建立虚假仲裁识别机制,从受理环节到审理案件全程防范虚假仲裁。首先,立案环节,如在立案、接待窗口的醒目位置设立禁止虚假仲裁的警示,印发打击虚假仲裁法律宣传手册,告知仲裁当事人虚假仲裁的后果,引导其诚信仲裁。其次,在审理仲裁案件时,仲裁庭应注意审查因当事人程序选择权的强化而可能带来的瑕疵和纰漏。再次,可以建立信息共享机制,在法院和仲裁机构之间实现案件信息共享,协调相关部门对仲裁机构信息查询方面予以配合和支持。复次,应定期举行仲裁员培训,提高仲裁员识别虚假仲裁的能力。最后,为防止仲裁员参与虚假仲裁,提醒仲裁员严格遵守自身的行为规范,可在现有法律制度之外,建立仲裁员的诚信档案记录制度,将故意进行违法仲裁或者屡次出现仲裁结果违法情形的仲裁员纳入诚信档案黑名单。

(三)对于司法监督机构的建议

在本文涉及的样本案例中,法院依据《仲裁裁决执行规定》的相关规定进行司法审查监督,立足案外人所提证据,综合案件整体情况作出驳回申请或者不予执行仲裁裁决的裁定。法院在合理行使裁判权的同时,也在虚假仲裁中对案外人的权利救济承担着重要的司法职责。鉴于目前《仲裁裁决执行规定》的内容过于原则化、抽象化,法院在案件的审理过程中应发挥司法能动性,合理分配举证责任,准确把握司法监督的边界。

1. 发挥司法能动性,合理分配举证责任

通过本文涉及的案例可知,鉴于虚假仲裁的隐蔽性、仲裁案件审理的不公开性,案外人很难获取仲裁案件当事人造假的核心证据。对于此种情况,法院应如何发挥司法能动性以保障善意案外人的合法权益?

---

① 目前,中国国际经济贸易仲裁委员会已具有非常完善的裁决书核阅制度,无此制度的仲裁机构,应建立并完善该制度。

首先,在举证责任分配上,举证责任的分配不公可能导致案外人不能提起申请不予执行仲裁裁决之诉,在审查案外人申请不予执行仲裁裁决时,司法监督机构可适当加重仲裁双方当事人的举证责任,合理分配案外人与仲裁当事人的举证责任。其次,受理法院应发挥司法能动性,在审查过程中要求仲裁机构作出说明,或者向仲裁机构调阅仲裁案卷。

2. 准确把握司法监督的边界

案外人申请不予执行仲裁裁决制度是执行程序中人民法院对仲裁活动进行司法监督的重要手段之一。法院在此类案件中,应准确把握司法监督的边界:一是法院坚持被动监督,进行被动审查,做到依申请审查;二是法院进行有限审查,遵守有限审查原则。法院对案外人申请不予执行仲裁裁决的司法审查,应遵循“有限审查”原则,限制对仲裁裁决的实体审查,避免审判权过分干预仲裁,即审查范围不宜过宽,严格按照《仲裁裁决执行规定》第 9 条和第 18 条的规定进行审查,不应随意扩大司法审查权的权限。法院在实践中应把握好审查尺度,做到既能保障善意案外人的权益,又能保障仲裁的独立性。这不仅需要司法实务界认真把握和斟酌,更需要通过立法进一步明确仲裁司法审查的内容、形式和依据。

五、结语

通过分析本文样本案例可见,案外人申请不予执行仲裁裁决制度有其存在的必要性。该制度在一定程度上保证了善意案外人的权利真正得以实现,能够有效遏制虚假仲裁。在司法实践中明确裁决执行内容的认定标准、虚假仲裁的审查标准以及裁决不予执行的救济措施等若干问题,有助于在实践中杜绝此类问题的产生。同时,在案件的执行过程中要注意司法监督与仲裁独立的合法边界,在实践中应根据具体案情具体把握审查尺度,而不应过分干预仲裁本身的独立性。但同时也应该注重保护案外人的合法权益,避免虚假仲裁损害案外人的合法权益。唯有如此,才能推动案外人申请不予执行仲裁裁决制度的完善。

虚假仲裁中案外人的法律救济

谢利锦　赵莹*

摘要：近年来，随着商事仲裁案件数量的增加，虚假仲裁也时有发生，成为当事人转移财产、逃避执行的非法工具。面对虚假仲裁，案外人难以找到及时有效的法律救济方法，因为仲裁程序的封闭性导致仲裁过程难以被外界知悉，立法层面上也缺乏对法院和检察院积极进行监督的授权，仲裁机构也未对如何纠正错误仲裁裁决进行规定。从当前案外人可以寻求的法律救济来讲，它们各自存在诸多弊端。例如：执行异议之诉所针对的法律文书并不包括仲裁裁决；由于法院对"违背社会公共利益"原则持审慎态度，案外人难以成功援引此条规定申请撤销生效仲裁裁决；虽然2018年最新的司法解释规定了案外人可以申请不予执行仲裁裁决，但此规定对于无须进入执行阶段的仲裁裁决也无能为力；虽然案外人可以提起侵权之诉，但按照规定法院需承认生效仲裁裁决确认的事实，因此案外人举证也成为一大难题。可以说，中国应对虚假仲裁的法律制度还有待完善。为了进一步应对虚假仲裁，笔者提出如下建议：首先，完善关于"违背社会公共利益"的司法解释；其次，将虚假仲裁入刑，加大惩罚力度；再次，进一步完善《仲裁法》的有关内容；最后，深化仲裁规则透明度改革。

关键词：虚假仲裁　执行异议　不予执行仲裁裁决　透明度改革

---

* 谢利锦，北京德恒律师事务所高级合伙人。
赵莹，北京德恒律师事务所实习律师。

一、背景介绍

仲裁作为一种重要的多元化纠纷解决机制，近年来发展迅速。中国国际经济贸易仲裁委员会发布的《中国国际商事仲裁年度报告(2016)》指出，2016 年中国 251 家仲裁委员会共受理案件 208545 件，比上一年增加 71621 件，增长率 52%；案件标的总额 4695 亿元，同比增长 14%。根据不完全统计，在 2017 年，中国所有仲裁机构受理案件的金额已经超出 6000 亿元。在 2017 年，主要仲裁机构受理案件数额与标的金额再创新高。例如，中国国际经济贸易仲裁委员会在 2017 年受理仲裁案件总计 2273 件，同比增长 7.67%，涉案标的额达人民币 719.88 亿元，同比增长 22.72%。北京仲裁委员会在 2017 年的受理案件数量为 3550 件，比上一年增加 538 件，同比增加 17.86%。这些统计数据显示，中国的仲裁以其公正、专业、高效、私密等特点，受到了商事主体的普遍欢迎，因而呈蓬勃发展之态势。

随着仲裁受理案件数量的大幅增加，虚假仲裁也同虚假诉讼案件一样，魅影显现。中国国内学者认为，虚假仲裁是指双方当事人恶意串通提起仲裁，通过虚构法律关系、提供虚假陈述或者伪造证据等手段，取得仲裁裁决。[①] 虚假仲裁案件不仅损害了仲裁机构的公信力，而且直接或者间接地侵害了案外人的合法权益。通过对已披露的案件进行分析，虚假仲裁的主要表现形式为被执行人通过虚假仲裁转移财产，逃避法院的强制执行；其他形式还包括通过虚假仲裁获取执行依据、获取诉讼中无须查证的证据或者直接完成所有权的变更等。[②] 例如，在一起民间借贷纠纷中，A 对于 B 有 3000 万元的债务，但是 A 与 B 签署了一个 6000 万元的借款合同，并让 A 作为大股东的 C 公司进行了保证。此后，B 作为申请人，要求 A、C 公司作为被申请人偿还债务。某仲裁委员会裁决 A 偿还债务，C 公司对于债务承担连带偿还责任。C 公司对于 A 的虚假债务的担保行为，未经过 C 公司的股东大会同意。该仲裁裁决实际上侵害

---

① 参见王晓伟、吴大华：《虚假仲裁之“何时休”与“以何休”》，载《凯里学院学报》2013 年第 2 期。

② 参见董暖、杨弘磊：《虚假仲裁案外人权利的司法救济研究》，载《法律适用》2017 年第 21 期。

了C公司的其他股东以及A的其他债权人的合法权益。在这种情况下,C公司的其他股东以及A的其他债权人如何维护自己的合法权益?

二、虚假仲裁的法律救济难在何方

仲裁具有保密、高效、一裁终局等特点。仲裁的自治性决定了仲裁活动应最大限度地尊重当事人的意愿,当事人依自己的理性进行判断,管理自己的事务。[①] 这意味着作为仲裁案件的案外人参与度极低,通常不知道或者很难知道有一个进行中的仲裁程序正在侵害其利益。即使在裁决作出之后,案外人也不会知道有这样一个裁决的存在。大部分的案外人是在执行环节才知道自己的利益受损了。例如,上述的民间借贷案件,C公司的其他股东是在法院要执行C公司的财产时,才知道公司的核心资产已经被查封了,而且马上就要被拍卖了。

仲裁程序的不公开性的另一层含义是仲裁的封闭性,这种封闭性很有可能会削弱仲裁的公正性。在某种意义上,仲裁程序的封闭性导致仲裁缺乏公众监督,造成信息的严重不对称,案外人无从得知这种情况下其权利可能遭受的侵害。[②] 仲裁案件的当事人向仲裁庭提交了什么样的证据,案外人无从得知,只能是想象和臆测。即使在知道自己的利益受损之后,案外人也面临举证难的问题。

从司法审查和监督的角度来看,我国现行《仲裁法》第58条、第59条规定的申请撤销仲裁裁决的主体是仲裁案件的当事人,案外人无权申请撤销仲裁裁决。该法第63条规定的不予执行申请主体是仲裁案件的被申请人,案外人无权根据《仲裁法》申请不予执行。对于案外人能否申请撤销仲裁裁决,在最高人民法院《关于对崇正国际联盟集团有限公司申请撤销仲裁裁决人民法院应否受理的复函》([2001]民立他字第36号)中,最高人民法院明确答复北京市高级人民法院:"《中华人民共和国仲裁法》第七十条规定的'当事人'是指仲裁案件的申请人或被申请人,崇正国际联盟集团有限公司并非V19990351号仲

① 参见汪祖兴:《试论仲裁的公正性与中国仲裁的监督机制》,载《现代法学》1998年第6期。
② 参见李昌超:《论仲裁案外人权利救济》,载《甘肃理论学刊》2013年第6期。

裁案件的申请人或被申请人,该公司不具备申请撤销该仲裁裁决的主体资格,故对该申请人民法院不予受理。"受司法审查程序启动的被动性与申请主体的限制,[①]仲裁案外人即使有证据证明仲裁当事人仲裁欺诈或错误仲裁裁决阻却其物权的行使,也因主体不适格而无法启动司法审查程序来保护其自身的合法权益。

那么,对于虚假仲裁,检察院能否抗诉?我国《民事诉讼法》第208~211条规定了最高人民检察院对各级人民法院已经发生法律效力的判决、裁定,上级人民检察院对下级人民法院已经发生法律效力的判决、裁定以及调解书可以进行抗诉,但对于仲裁裁决,则不能进行抗诉。在最高人民法院《关于人民检察院对撤销仲裁裁决的民事裁定提起抗诉,人民法院应如何处理问题的批复》(法释〔2000〕17号)中,最高人民法院也指出,"检察机关对发生法律效力的撤销仲裁裁决的民事裁定提起抗诉,没有法律依据,人民法院不予受理"。由此可知,检察院对于仲裁裁决无法抗诉。

仲裁机构自身能否纠正错误的仲裁裁决?目前的《仲裁法》显然没有赋予仲裁机构该项权力。浙江省人民政府法制办公室在其发布的《关于仲裁机构能否自行撤销仲裁裁决问题的指导意见的函》(浙府法发〔2010〕57号)中指出,《仲裁法》第7条规定仲裁应当根据事实,符合法律规定,公平合理地解决纠纷。仲裁机构应当遵守这一仲裁原则,对不符合事实和法律规定的仲裁裁决,依照仲裁规则予以纠正。鉴于《仲裁法》并未赋予仲裁机构该等权利,各地仲裁委员会的仲裁规则也没有对于仲裁委员会如何纠正其仲裁裁决作出规定。

综上所述,针对虚假仲裁,案外人可选择的救济措施均存在局限性。首先,仲裁程序的封闭性导致仲裁缺乏监督,案外人无法及时获得相关信息以便积极维权。其次,虽然法律规定了相关司法审查方式,但启动司法审查的主体都必须是仲裁当事人,单纯的案外人无法主动申请司法审查。再次,检察院对于虚假仲裁也无法积极抗诉。最后,《仲裁法》并没有赋予仲裁机构纠正虚假仲裁

---

① 参见于喜富:《被执行人虚假仲裁处罚与仲裁司法审查》,载《人民司法》2013年第13期。

裁决的权力,而仲裁机构本身也没有制定相关的仲裁规则。

三、案外人对于虚假仲裁的法律救济初探

就目前的法律体系而言,案外人对于仲裁案件当事人通过虚假仲裁或者恶意仲裁案件侵害自己合法权益的行为,可以选择如下四种方式来维护自己的合法权益:第一,提起执行异议之诉;第二,以"违背社会公共利益"为由申请司法监督;第三,案外人申请不予执行仲裁裁决;第四,提起侵权之诉。下面对这四种救济方式分别进行论述。

1. 执行异议之诉

在执行阶段,案外人围绕执行标的,可以提起执行异议之诉。《民事诉讼法》第227条规定:"执行过程中,案外人对执行标的提出书面异议的,人民法院应当自收到书面异议之日起十五日内审查,理由成立的,裁定中止对该标的的执行;理由不成立的,裁定驳回。案外人、当事人对裁定不服,认为原判决、裁定错误的,依照审判监督程序办理;与原判决、裁定无关的,可以自裁定送达之日起十五日内向人民法院提起诉讼。"根据最高人民法院《关于适用〈中华人民共和国民事诉讼法〉的解释》(法释〔2015〕5号)(以下简称《民诉法司法解释》),案外人提出执行异议之诉的时点应当是在有管辖权的执行法院对于案外人的执行异议申请驳回之后。提起这类诉讼时,案外人应当以申请执行人为被告,被申请执行人可以视情况被列为共同被告或者第三人。具体而言,在被执行人反对案外人异议的情况下,案外人应把被执行人列为共同被告;如被执行人不反对案外人异议的,案外人可以把被执行人列为第三人。

案外人提出执行异议之诉被有管辖权的执行法院受理后,在审理期间,执行法院不得对执行标的进行处分。《民诉法司法解释》第312条规定:"对案外人提起的执行异议之诉,人民法院经审理,按照下列情形分别处理:(一)案外人就执行标的享有足以排除强制执行的民事权益的,判决不得执行该执行标的;(二)案外人就执行标的不享有足以排除强制执行的民事权益的,判决驳回诉讼请求……"对于虚假仲裁案件,案外人选择执行异议之诉,尽管可以在某

种程度上维护自己的合法权益,但其提起的所谓异议之诉的法律文书并不包括仲裁裁决,即仍存在权力救济的真空地带。[①] 人民法院受限于该等具备法律效力的仲裁裁决,在缺乏明确法律规定以及司法解释的情况下,人民法院很难直接通过执行异议程序来保护案外人的合法权益。

2. 以“违背社会公共利益”为由申请司法监督

《仲裁法》第 58 条第 3 款规定:“人民法院认定该裁决违背社会公共利益的,应当裁定撤销。”《民事诉讼法》第 237 条第 3 款规定:“人民法院认定执行该裁决违背社会公共利益的,裁定不予执行。”这两款规定构建了法院依职权撤销仲裁裁决的法律依据。但对于什么是社会公共利益,法律没有明确的界定。通常认为,社会公共利益是以社会公众为利益主体的(其主体具有社会公众性),其内容具有普遍性。在目前的司法实践中,各地法院对于社会公共利益的理解各不相同,掌握标准不一。

珠海市中级人民法院(以下简称珠海中院)在处理一起不予执行仲裁裁决案件中,认为仲裁当事人存在恶意串通损害他人合法权益的行为,如果法院执行该仲裁裁决,将明显违背社会公共利益。该案件的基本情况是,2013 年 7 月 16 日周某、常某(系周某妻子)向珠海仲裁委员会提交仲裁申请书,请求裁决将金桦城市花园 2 栋 1 单元 360 号商铺和 17 栋银桦路 707 号商铺归其所有。理由是,2000 年 5 月 4 日周某和金富田公司签订了外墙涂料装饰工程承包合同。合同签订后,由于金富田公司擅自改变约定的涂料品牌致使周某损失 30 余万元。此后,金富田公司同意补偿周某、常某 30 万元,并用 360 号商铺和 707 号商铺抵付。2013 年 7 月珠海仲裁委员会受理该案,并裁决 360 号商铺和 707 号商铺归周某、常某所有。在执行阶段,珠海中院执行局作出执行裁定书,已将 707 号商铺登记至周某、常某名下,360 号商铺尚未登记至周某、常某名下。此时,边某、白某作为案外人向珠海中院提出执行异议申请。边某和白某提出,二人分别于 2001 年 3 月和 1999 年 2 月与金富田公司签订商铺认购合同。其中,

---

① 参见李昌超:《论仲裁案外人权利救济》,载《甘肃理论学刊》2013 年第 6 期。

边某购买707号商铺,已全额支付52万余元购房款;白某购买360号商铺,已支付总价款31万余元中的绝大部分款项,余款用于抵扣金富田公司逾期交房而应支付的违约金。二人称,由于金富田公司一直拖延,两个商铺至今未能办理房产证,但一直由边某和白某实际占有并对外出租使用至今。珠海中院经初步审查后认为,仲裁裁决确有可能存在错误,便依职权启动了仲裁司法审查程序,由民四庭以不予执行仲裁裁决案受理。珠海中院审查后指出,周某、常某的住所地为金桦城市花园,其为金富田公司施工的项目亦在该花园中。项目施工至今已有10余年,边某、白某接受涉案商铺之后一直占有并出租给他人实际使用至今。从常理推断,周某、常某应当知道涉案商铺的基本情况。在此情形下,周某、常某和金富田公司在仲裁中未向仲裁庭提交涉案商铺已存在房屋买卖合同关系的证据,却以和解协议的方式处分上述商铺,且价格明显低于市场价值和协商抵扣的真实价款。

珠海中院认定,通过上述一系列行为可以认定,周某、常某和金富田公司存在恶意串通损害他人合法权益的行为,如果法院执行该仲裁裁决,将明显违背社会公共利益。据此,裁定不予执行该仲裁裁决。

珠海中院在本案中适用的法律程序可以概括为如下三个步骤:(1)案外人边某、白某的执行异议,执行局经审查认为仲裁裁决可能存在错误,将执行异议案件提交审判委员会讨论;(2)审判委员会讨论后,认为仲裁裁决违反社会公共利益,有必要依职权启动审查机制,由立案庭以"不予执行仲裁裁决"为案由决定立案,交由民四庭负责审查;(3)民四庭审查后,认为仲裁裁决错误,裁定不予执行仲裁裁决。虽此案成功援引了"社会公共利益"条款,但由于"社会公共利益"条款概念模糊,难以界定其适用范围,司法实践中对于采用该条款一般采取极为审慎的态度,以防止概念的抽象性导致法律的不确定性。另外,案外人利益是否等同于社会公共利益,在司法实践中一直存有争议。①

① 参见董暖、杨弘磊:《虚假仲裁案外人权利的司法救济研究》,载《法律适用》2017年第21期。

3. 案外人申请不予执行仲裁裁决

2018年3月1日起实施的最高人民法院《关于人民法院办理仲裁裁决执行案件若干问题的规定》(以下简称《仲裁裁决执行规定》)就虚假仲裁与恶意仲裁案件中案外人的权益保护作出了较为系统的规定,赋予了案外人申请不予执行仲裁裁决的权利,使案外人能够比较直接地依法维护自己的合法权利。

《仲裁裁决执行规定》第9条规定,涉案标的尚在执行阶段的,案外人有证据证明仲裁案件当事人恶意申请仲裁或者虚假仲裁,损害其合法权益,可以向人民法院申请不予执行仲裁裁决或者仲裁调解书。此外,该法第9条还规定,案外人应当在知道或者应当知道人民法院对该标的采取执行措施之日起30日内提出申请。在上述珠海中院处理的商铺案件中,案外人边某是偶然知道自己的商铺已经被执行过户了。因此,在实践中如何界定第9条规定的30日的起算时点,对于案外人具有特别重要的意义;否则,案外人可能永久丧失向人民法院申请不予执行仲裁裁决的权利。《仲裁裁决执行规定》第19条第1款规定:“被执行人、案外人对仲裁裁决执行案件逾期申请不予执行的,人民法院应当裁定不予受理;已经受理的,应当裁定驳回不予执行申请。”

尽管在实践中存在无须进入执行程序的虚假仲裁裁决,如确权类的仲裁裁决以及证据类仲裁裁决。对此类虚假仲裁裁决,显然《仲裁裁决执行规定》也无能为力。但无论如何,2018年3月1日起施行的《仲裁裁决执行规定》对于虚假仲裁案件的案外人的权利保障第一次进行了系统性的、有针对性的规定,填补了此前的法律空白,具有积极的法律意义和社会意义。

4. 提起侵权之诉

虚假仲裁当事人通过虚假仲裁行为,给案外人的财产利益造成损害,而且虚假仲裁当事人主观上存在过错,因而形式上符合侵权的构成要件。依照法律规定,被侵权人可向虚假仲裁当事人提起侵权之诉。但值得注意的是,在仲裁裁决被撤销前,独立的侵权之诉存在诸多问题。首先,侵权之诉无力驳倒已生效仲裁裁决所确认的事实,最高人民法院《关于民事诉讼证据的若干规定》中明确规定,已为仲裁机构的生效裁决所确认的事实当事人无须举证证明。其次,即使案外人成功取得侵权之诉的胜诉判决,在执行时也会遇到判决与仲裁裁决相矛盾的情形。最后,我国《侵权责任法》保护的财产性权利仅限于物权,对于通过虚假仲裁逃避的债权是无力保护的。

由此可见,对于虚假仲裁给案外人造成的不利影响,虽然案外人可以通过提起执行异议之诉、以"违背社会公共利益"为由申请司法监督、申请不予执行仲裁裁决以及提起侵权之诉等方式进行救济,但这些救济措施都存在一定的局限性。

四、完善虚假仲裁应对制度的建议

根据前文所述,虚假仲裁极大地侵害了案外人的权利,案外人却无法找到及时有效的法律救济途径维护自身权益。包括执行异议之诉在内的几大法律救济途径都存在诸多不利之处,影响了案外人的积极维权。故笔者将在下文中对如何完善应对虚假仲裁的制度提出一些建议,期望为不断深化的司法改革提供一些借鉴。

1. 完善关于"违背社会公共利益"的司法解释

《仲裁法》第58条第3款以及《民事诉讼法》第237条第3款均规定了人民法院依照职权,以"违背社会公共利益"为由,可以裁定撤销或者不予执行仲裁裁决。

尽管有专家认为,最高人民法院应当作出司法解释,将虚假仲裁、恶意仲裁、违法仲裁等纳入"违背社会公共利益"范畴而进行治理。笔者认为,社会公共利益是指以社会公众为利益主体,涉及整个社会最根本的法律、最基础的道德规范和最重要的利益,其主体具有社会公众性,内容具有普遍性。因此,不能随意扩大解释,在法院依照职权以"违背社会公共利益"为由而裁定撤销或者不予执行仲裁裁决时,更应当非常谨慎,以避免司法过度干预仲裁。更应当看到,在每年20多万起的仲裁案件中,虚假仲裁案件是非常少见的。

2018年1月1日起施行的最高人民法院《关于仲裁司法审查案件报核问题的有关规定》明确规定,对于仲裁司法审查案件,各中级人民法院或者专门人民法院办理非涉外涉港澳台仲裁司法审查案件，经审查拟认定仲裁协议无效、不予执行或者撤销中国内地仲裁机构的仲裁裁决，应当向本辖区所属高级人民法院报核；待高级人民法院审核后，方可依高级人民法院的审核意见作出裁定。特别地，高级人民法院拟同意中级人民法院“以违背社会公共利益为由不予执行或者撤销我国内地仲裁机构的仲裁裁决”的，应向最高人民法院报核。笔者认为，最高人民法院上述司法解释的立法旨意在于保护和支持仲裁的发展，这个价值取向值得肯定。可以理解的是，最高人民法院倾向于对“社会公共利益”作出狭义的解释。因此，在新的司法解释下，前述珠海中院所审案件涉及的“一铺两卖”的做法能否被解释为“违背社会公共利益”是值得商榷的。

2. 虚假仲裁入刑

随着中国经济的高速发展，经济类的诉讼以及仲裁案件也得到了长足的发展。同时，通过虚假诉讼骗取法院裁判来实现非法目的的现象日益增多。为此，《刑法修正案（九）》专门增设了“虚假诉讼罪”，以加强对该类行为的打击力度。对于虚假仲裁，目前刑法体系未将其纳入犯罪范畴。在此情况下，部分怀有不良企图的当事人，利用捏造的事实或隐瞒重要事实，通过串通，利用仲裁非法占有他人财产或者逃避合法债务。在未将虚假仲裁纳入刑法打击范畴的情况下，虚假仲裁案件当事人的风险收益比很高。换言之，当事人进行一个虚假仲裁，最坏的结果是没有获得经济上的收益而已；但是如果成功，则收益巨大。但一个虚假仲裁，不仅侵害了他人的合法权益，同时也在很大程度上破坏了司法秩序，浪费了本就有限的司法资源，侵害了整个社会的法治环境。鉴于仲裁裁决与法院判决具有同等的法律效力，因此，增设“虚假仲裁罪”非常有必要。

具体而言，笔者建议对《刑法》第 307 条进行修正，增加一个罪名——“虚假仲裁罪”。在修改《刑法》前，对虚假仲裁行为可通过其他途径追究其刑事责任。一般情况下，案外人可就虚假仲裁提起侵权之诉，情节严重的可向公安机关提起刑事控告。[①]《民事诉讼法》第113条规定:"被执行人与他人恶意串通,通过诉讼、仲裁、调解等方式逃避履行法律文书确定的义务的,人民法院应当根据情节轻重予以罚款、拘留;构成犯罪的,依法追究刑事责任。"此外,由于被执行人的特定身份和义务,对实施了虚假仲裁行为的,如果认为需要追究刑事责任,可首先考虑是否构成拒不履行判决、裁定罪。[②]

3. 仲裁法的修订

我国《仲裁法》自1995年施行以来,立法机关仅在2009年以及2017年进行了文字性的修正工作,而未对其进行大的修改,其已经不能适应日新月异的仲裁事业的发展。相比《民事诉讼法》在2012年进行的全面的修改和2017年进行的完善,《仲裁法》就更无法与修改后的《民事诉讼法》进行衔接。为防范虚假仲裁和恶意仲裁,并保护案外人的合法权益,笔者认为,《仲裁法》的修改应当建立如下制度:

(1)案外人加入仲裁程序

具体而言,在依法保护仲裁私密性和效率的前提下,允许具有直接利益相关方的案外人通过合理方式加入进行中的仲裁程序。《中国国际经济贸易仲裁委员会仲裁规则》(2015年版)第18条规定了"追加当事人"的内容,但其适用有两个前提条件:一是被追加的第三方与仲裁案件的当事人一样,需要受到仲裁协议的管辖,而且为了与仲裁管辖权的相关规定保持一致,应被理解为受到同一仲裁委员会的管辖。二是追加第三方的申请只能由正在进行的仲裁案件的申请人或者被申请人启动,第三方即使与申请人与被申请人之间存在仲裁协议,并通过其他正当渠道(如上市公司的信息披露)了解到该案件的进行,也无法主动申请加入到该正在进行的仲裁程序中。

笔者此前处理过的一起上市公司收购的案例,就涉及公司股东(案外人)能否主动申请加入仲裁程序的问题。在该案中,上市公司H收购了K公司,并与K公司的若干自然人股东以及K公司签署了收购协议。后来,由于收购无

---

① 参见万学忠:《虚假仲裁受害人保护机制研讨会举行》,载《法制日报》2018年3月8日版。

② 参见江必新主编:《新民事诉讼法理解适用与实务指南》,法律出版社2012年版,第432页。

法按照计划进行，上市公司 H 终止了收购。为此，K 公司以及个别股东在某仲裁委员会提出仲裁申请，要求追究上市公司 H 的违约责任。问题在于，K 公司的其他股东在该程序开始时蒙在鼓里，后来从上市公司的公告中才得知仲裁事宜。尽管本案的各方最后以调解方式妥善解决了争议，但目前《仲裁法》对保障仲裁案外人合法权益的缺位，却由此可见一斑。

当前，随着社会经济生活的发展，不少国家的仲裁理论和实践逐步承认，在某些例外情况下，仲裁协议的内容对未签署此协议的主体具有法律约束力，即承认仲裁协议效力的扩张。仲裁协议效力扩张论意在突破仲裁协议本身的相对性，将非表面签字人纳入到仲裁协议的效力范围中来，推定为已有仲裁协议的当事人，从而开始一个仲裁程序。[①] 但是，仲裁协议效力的扩张必然造成仲裁效率与公正背反，以及“纠纷一次性解决”与“程序保障”的二律背反。因此，虽然案外人可试图突破仲裁协议的相对性成为当事人，但在仲裁庭谨慎态度的影响下，案外人的突破难度较大。

(2) 仲裁委员会完善内部监督制度

一裁终局是仲裁的基本制度之一，也是仲裁区别于诉讼制度的显著特征。一裁终局制度的好处是高效快捷，使当事人的争议很快能够得到法律意义上的决断，定分止争；但这一制度同样存在缺点，即当事人不能像在诉讼程序中那样对仲裁裁决进行上诉。如果仲裁案件的当事人之间串通，恶意仲裁，侵害案外人的合法权益，“一裁终局”将使案外人无法通过上诉程序来维护其合法权益。《仲裁法》将开庭与裁决的权力赋予仲裁庭，尽管仲裁员属于“三八两高”的专业人士，但需知在全国各地大大小小的仲裁机构中，仲裁员的数量多达 4 万余人，其中难免存在个别的“害群之马”。《仲裁法》第 54 条规定：“……裁决书由仲裁员签名，加盖仲裁委员会印章……”诚然，大家对于裁决书加盖仲裁委员会印章的法律效力存在不同的理解，主流观点基于仲裁是民间的纠纷解决机制，认为加盖印章只是从属性的，裁决的效力当以仲裁员的签名为准。但在中

① 参见萧凯、罗骁：《仲裁第三人的法理基础与规则制定》，载《法学评论》2006 年第 5 期。

国,公众以及司法实践对于印章具有独特的认知,印章在很大程度上代表着权威,代表着机构的信誉。在目前《仲裁法》规则下,即使仲裁委员会认为某仲裁裁决系当事人恶意串通,存在侵害案外人合法权益的情形,也不能进行有效的内部监督。笔者建议,在修改《仲裁法》时,明确仲裁机构在加盖印章之前,有权对仲裁裁决进行审核。仲裁庭在审理案件时应主动审视因当事人程序选择权的强化而可能带来的瑕疵和纰漏,如当事人选择同一仲裁员、明显证据自认的非对抗“手拉手打官司”现象、异常顺利接受调解现象等,这些都可能会暴露出虚假仲裁的“尾巴”。[①]

(3)完善案外人申请撤销、不予执行仲裁裁决与调解书制度

如前文分析,从司法审查和监督的角度来看,现行《仲裁法》第58条、第59条规定的申请撤销仲裁裁决的主体是仲裁案件的当事人,案外人无权申请撤销仲裁裁决。该法第63条规定的不予执行申请主体是仲裁案件的被申请人,案外人无权根据《仲裁法》申请不予执行。对于仲裁裁决或者仲裁调解书,即使考虑到《民事诉讼法》及相关司法解释为解决虚假仲裁而设置的案外人执行异议之诉制度、法院以“违反社会公共利益”为由的不予执行制度以及案外人申请不予执行仲裁裁决制度,仍无法充分保护案外人的合法权益。这是因为,上述制度的运行的结果也不能形成撤销仲裁裁决的法律效力,该等“问题仲裁裁决”仍然具备生效法律文书的法律效力(尽管不能被司法强制执行)。这不能不说是现行法律体系的无奈。因此,应修改《仲裁法》,赋予合法权益受到虚假仲裁侵害的案外人在合理的时间期限内向有管辖权的人民法院申请撤销、不予执行仲裁裁决或者仲裁调解书的权利。

(4)建立信息披露制度

如前所述,由于仲裁程序保密性的特点,当事人向仲裁庭提交的证据当然也不能披露给案外人。《仲裁裁决执行规定》第9条、第18条规定,案外人应当有证据证明仲裁案件的当事人恶意申请仲裁或者虚假仲裁,案外人也要就仲

---

① 参见王晓伟、吴大华:《虚假仲裁之“何时休”与“以何休”》,载《凯里学院学报》2013年第2期。

裁案件当事人之间存在虚构法律关系、捏造案件事实进行举证。如前分析，由于仲裁的保密性特点，要求案外人承担过高的举证责任，显然加大了案外人维护自身合法权益的难度。《仲裁裁决执行规定》以及其他相关司法解释没有就相关的案件档案移交以及信息的披露作出规定，法院在启动司法对于仲裁的监督程序之后，若要调阅相关案件的证据资料，仲裁委员会拒绝或延迟提供有关案卷资料，而案外人不掌握仲裁案件的资料，仲裁案件的当事人又拒绝提供。在此情况下，法院将无法查明事实。

因此，笔者建议，在《仲裁法》中明确，在案外人申请撤销或者不予执行仲裁裁决的情况下，法院与仲裁委员会应就案卷证据的交换和信息的披露建立合理的沟通机制，以便法院能够查明案情，保障案外人权益。

4. 仲裁规则透明化改革

近年来，国际仲裁程序透明度改革的趋势不断增强。联合国国际贸易法委员会（以下简称贸法会）通过的《毛里求斯透明度公约》于 2014 年生效。在论及前述公约中透明度规则的制定背景时，贸法会认为，目前绝大多数的投资人与国家的仲裁都是非公开的，但不可否认的是，此类仲裁常常涉及国家的公共利益，透明度规则的实施有助于公众对仲裁的监督，增强仲裁裁决的可预测性。贸法会认为，透明度规则将“大大有助于建立公平高效解决国际投资争议的协调法律框架，提高透明度，加强问责制，促进善治”。[①] 负责起草透明度规则的第二工作组认为，透明度规则可以增加公众对仲裁程序的理解和信任。[②] 值得注意的是，虽然工作组就案外人是否有权申请披露文件展开了讨论，但最终工作组认为，因国际投资争端仲裁涉及国家的可持续发展，涉及纳税人利益，故为保护公共利益，案外人有权提出申请。因此，贸法会透明度规则不仅可由当事人运用，也可由案外人运用，这有效保护了案外人的权益和国家的公共利益。此外，工作组还认为，透明度规则从保障知情权的角度保障了人权。但工作组

---

① 联合国国际贸易法委员会决议案（No. 68/109），载联合国贸易法委员会官网：https://undocs.org/zh/A/res/68/109，最后访问日期：2018 年 11 月 19 日。

② 联合国国际贸易法委员会第二工作组会议文件（No. A/CN. 9/646），载联合国贸易法委员会官网：https://undocs. org/en/A/CN. 9/646，最后访问日期：2018 年 11 月 19 日。

在制定透明度规则时强调,仲裁最大的特点在于意思自治,最明显的优点是高效性,因此在制定透明度规则时着重注意透明度规则与仲裁效率性和保密性的平衡。虽然贸法会制定的透明度规则目前仅适用于国际投资争端的仲裁,但是仲裁的透明化改革已势不可当。

当前透明化改革已扩展至商事仲裁领域。中国国际经济贸易仲裁委员会2012年发布的仲裁规则,对于仲裁员披露义务的修订也是对这一趋势的回应。国际商会发布《当事人与仲裁庭在国际商会仲裁规则下参与仲裁程序的指引》,认为仲裁院应尽力使仲裁程序更加透明,透明性不仅可以增加当事人的信息,更可以防止仲裁受到不准确和欠缺事实基础的批评。但国际商会也同样强调,应尽全力维护商事仲裁的保密性,因为与仲裁透明度增强相对应的,是商事仲裁保密性的弱化。[①] 例如,英国、法国的仲裁规则从默认保密原则改为"保密需要明示"。2009年发布的《美国仲裁协会仲裁规则》更是明确仲裁裁决可以公开。

在上述背景下,中国仲裁机构进行透明度改革、完善公众监督是顺应国际贸易仲裁发展趋势的必然要求。透明度改革不仅有利于仲裁机构"自证清白",仲裁当事人获得执行法院的支持,更有利于打击虚假仲裁的发生。因此,建议仲裁机构顺应国际商事仲裁改革潮流,在仲裁规则中增强仲裁透明度,如允许当事人或案外人申请仲裁庭就某决定说明理由、披露程序性事项,在最大限度上维护商事仲裁保密性的同时,保障案外人的知情权。

五、结语

实践中存在的当事人虚假仲裁问题犹如一颗毒瘤,既损害了案外人的合法权益,也损害了仲裁与司法的公信力。随着《仲裁裁决执行规定》的出台,中国虚假仲裁案外人维权之路有了重大进展。但值得注意的是,虽前途光明,但道路仍漫漫而崎岖。在仲裁"打假"之路上,法律法规、仲裁规则依然不够完善,

---

① 参见杨荣宽:《如何应对国际商事仲裁透明度增强与保密性弱化》,载《中国商报》2018年4月19日,A03版。

仲裁庭无法事前识别“假”仲裁,法院无法主动审查虚假仲裁,案外人知情权依旧难以保障,举证难度仍然难以克服。此类种种问题仍需仲裁机构、司法机关的共同努力。首先,在仲裁开始之前,仲裁庭需主动查明存在虚假仲裁的可能性,是否可以将可能受到仲裁结果“负影响”的相关人纳入仲裁当事人,保证仲裁的公正性。其次,案外人在经济生活中,应时刻保持警惕,关注与自己有关的纠纷动态,在仲裁开始前采取措施争取加入到仲裁程序中,并在仲裁后及时向法院提出司法审查的申请,或申请仲裁裁决的不予执行。法院在收到案外人的申诉后,应积极主动行使自身的司法监督职能,与仲裁机构建立有效的联动机制,及时有效地保护案外人的权益。

除各方主体积极作为外,中国仲裁体制仍存在不足,使当事人进行虚假仲裁的成本过低。因此,除不断完善仲裁法外,本文建议将虚假仲裁罪明确纳入刑法之中,给虚假仲裁之人以足够的震慑力。此外,对于受虚假仲裁不利影响的案外人,应给予他们向虚假仲裁当事人索赔的权利,提高虚假仲裁失败成本,进一步完善案外人的救济途径。

Set an Early Alarm

—The Natural Justice Concern over China's Arb-Med Process

Gu Huaning *

Abstract: This article sets out and comments on natural justice in China's commercial arbitration, and specifically on the design of and concern over the CIETAC arb-med process. Natural justice, though a common law concept, is reflected in the procedural requirements of China's commercial arbitration and courts' supervision over arbitration. The two basic rules of natural justice, i. e., the bias rule and the hearing rule, impose limits and boundaries on arbitrators and arbitration institutions. CIETAC has set high standards for its arbitrators to remain impartial and independent. Based on the changing arb-med design in various versions of the CIETAC Arbitration Rules, the article explores the ways and results of the CIETAC arb-med process. Based on relevant provisions and court cases involving the challenges to China's arb-med results, the author argues that natural justice is a concern for all of those involved in the arb-med process, including but not limited to parties, arbitrators and arbitration institutions. Due to the courts' attitude, it is essential for arb-med parties to set the natural justice

* Gu Huaning, CIETAC arbitrator.

alarm early in the process.

Keywords: natural justice, arb-med, bias, hearing, impartiality, independence, disclosure, public policy

International commercial arbitration, due to its consensual nature, must win trust from parties. The lack of parties' confidence will "lessen the potential utility" and "dilute its particular value". ① Injustice is unavoidable and threatens our shared values. ② In arbitration, the shared value is more than fairness. Parties expect to have impartial third parties to settle disputes efficiently. The tension between natural justice and efficiency has long been noticed. ③ Will parties of international commercial arbitration sacrifice certain flexibility and efficiency for natural justice? The answer is yes if an appropriate balance is kept between these values. Justice is so closely connected to our morality that justice can always arouse positive feelings such as contentment, gratitude and pride. ④ It is not only the call from parties, but also from arbitrators, arbitration institutions, legislative and judicial authorities. With more and more cross-border transactions and over-territorial commercial arbitration, we need to further explore the natural justice principles in the faster and wider globalization of both business and law.

Natural Justice in international commercial arbitration involves principles full of tension. Firstly, there is the tension between arbitrators' self-regarding and parties' regarding. Arbitrators, for their own interest, need to safeguard natural justice. Jan Paulsson regarded arbitrators, especially arbitrators in international

---

① A. S. Rau, "On Integrity in Private Judging", *Arbitration International* 14, 1998, p. 115.

② Tyler G. Okimoto, Michael Wenzel, "The symbolic meaning of transgressions: Towards a unifying framework of justice restoration", http://dx.doi.org/10.1016/S0882-6145(08)25004-6, May 15, 2017.

③ J. J. Bray, "Natural Justice", *Australian Journal of Public Administration* 29, 1970, p. 1.

④ Barry Markovsky et al., "Modularizing and integrating theories of justice", http://dx.doi.org/10.1016/S0882-6145(08)25008-3, May 15, 2017.

commercial arbitration, as elite corps[①] and proposed less limitation on these elites. However, no one can deny the necessity of imposing certain limitation on decision makers, no matter whether their power comes from parties' agreement or law.

Though Aristotle regarded natural justice as something intuitive and universal "as fire burns both here and in Persia", natural justice is more subjective than objective. Arbitrators' self-regarding may be different from parties' regarding. Unconscious bias is one of the results of such difference. To keep a balance in such tension, proper standards need to be set for international commercial arbitrators.

Secondly, the tension between private ordering and traditional ethics of adjudication[②] results in the hot debate over how much natural justice hurdle should be imposed on arbitrators. There are two contradicting views. One is to impose the same natural justice request on arbitrators as that of judges[③] due to the quasi-judicial nature of arbitration. Another is to set lower standards for arbitrators so that they can still conduct arbitration in an efficient and flexible way and leave the natural justice concern for a latter "appealing mechanism"[④]. As pointed out by John McMillan, "excess can be as damaging as a deficiency"[⑤]. A wise choice needs to be made for the further development of international commercial arbitration.

In addition to the balance between natural justice and flexibility, the balance within and beyond national level needs to be considered. Parties and arbitrators

① Jan Paulsson, "Ethics, elitism, eligibility", *Journal of International Arbitration* 14, 1997, p. 13.

② A. S. Rau, "On Integrity in Private Judging", *Arbitration International* 14, 1998, p. 115.

③ G. Eastwood, "A Real Danger of Confusion? The English Law Relating to Bias in Arbitrators", *Arbitration International* 17, 2001, p. 287.

④ Samantha Hepburn, "Natural justice and commercial arbitration", *Australian Business Law Review* 21, 1993, p. 43.

⑤ John McMillan, "Natural Justice: Too Much, Too Little or Just Right?", *AIAL forum* 58, 2008, p. 33.

may come from different social, cultural and legal background. The concept of justice may be interpreted differently under different social norms①. One arbitration procedure may involve various locations. The place where the dispute occurs may be different from the place of arbitration. The court for the recognition and enforcement of the award may be located in another country. Despite the tendency of international legal harmonization②, it is hard to coordinate among nations for a universal understanding and application of the natural justice principles in arbitration process. "A uniform and consistent interpretation of the principles of natural justice"③ is highly desirable but not practical. A more practical way is case-by-case analysis.

In the following parts, this article will focus on the natural justice in China's commercial arbitration (Part Ⅱ), examine the design of and concern over the practice of combining mediation with arbitration (the arb-med process) by China International Economic and Trade Arbitration Commission (CIETAC). Due to more recent natural justice concern over thisprocess, China is changing its practices and relevant regulations in the interest of natural justice (Part Ⅲ). The courts, considering the quasi-judicial nature of arbitration, prefer to leave relevant issues to arbitration institutions (Part Ⅳ). To conclude, this article recommends an early alarm for arb-med users if there is any natural justice concern (Part Ⅴ).

Ⅰ. Natural Justice in China's Commercial Arbitration

Natural justice covers two basic rules in international commercial

① Lawrence B. Solum, "Natural justice", *American Journal of Jurisprudence* 51, 2006, p. 65.

② Andrew Field, "The Bias Principle and Its Applicability to International Commercial Arbitrations in Australia", *Australian Dispute Resolution Journal* 10, 1999, p. 246.

③ Austin Pullé, "Securing Natural Justice in Arbitration Proceedings", *Asia Pacific Law Review* 20, 2012, p. 63.

arbitration. One is the bias rule and the other is the hearing rule.[①] Parties appoint arbitrators for their professional expertise and experience. Such party autonomy is highly respected and courts of most nations adopt the attitude of pro-arbitration and minimum intervention. However, pro-arbitration cannot be confused with pro-arbitrator.[②] From China's long tradition of mediation, we may find that natural justice or fairness has been sacrificed to a certain degree to realize social harmony. However, if the fair play rule cannot be ensured in China's commercial arbitration, the lack of trust and confidence will surely lead to the end of the system.

In the establishment and maintenance of the fair play rule in China's commercial arbitration, the Supreme People's Court (the SPC) plays a special role (section 1). China's commercial arbitration issplit into two systems, one is the domestic one, the other is the foreign-related one (section 2). Within the two systems, we may find the application of the bias rule (section 3) and that of the hearing rule (section 4). Since the SPC admitted arbitration rules as alternative criteria for procedural requirements, this article will combine the current CIETAC Arbitration Rules[③] with analysis. In practice, CIETAC adopts stricter standard for its arbitrators (section 5).

1. The SPC's Special Role

The SPC coordinates among Chinese courts in the supervision of arbitration. Such supervision is reflected in two processes. One is the revocation of arbitral

---

① Matthew Groves, "Exclusion of the rules of natural justice", *Monash University Law Review* 39, 2013, p. 285.

② Zhi Xuan Koo and Yong En Lim, "The intricacies involved in the pursuit of natural justice in arbitration-L W Infrastructure Pte Ltd. v. Lim Chin San Contractors Pte Ltd; [2013] 1 SLR 125", *Singapore Academy of Law Journal* 25, 2013, p. 595.

③ Revised and adopted by the China Council for the Promotion of International Trade/China Chamber of International Commerce on November 4, 2014. Effective as of January 1, 2015.

awards. The other is the enforcement of arbitral awards. Supposing one party applies for enforcement of an award while another party applies for revocation thereof in different courts, confusing or conflicting results may occur: the validity of the award is sustained by one court while the enforcement is denied by another. The SPC acts as the coordinator having the final say. The SPC's interpretation concerning the application of the PRC Arbitration Law (the 2006 SPC Interpretation)[①]is a compromise in the long-term uncoordinated ways and standards of setting aside or enforcing arbitral awards among different level courts. The SPC made it clear that revocation or non-enforcement of arbitral awards should be in strict accordance with the law.

The SPC acts more than a coordinator. From 1985 to 2015, the SPC issued 275 notices and replies regarding arbitration. With the rough PRC Arbitration Law, the SPC notices and replies can be put together to depict a better picture of arbitration provisions in China. Though not mentioning natural justice, the SPC made it clear in Article 20 of the 2006 SPC Interpretation that the "violation of arbitration procedure" stipulated in Article 58 of the PRC Arbitration Law refers to either the non-fulfilment of procedural requirements under the PRC Arbitration Law or the non-fulfilment of procedural requirements under the arbitration rules chosen by the parties. For the latter, a higher standard is set as "might affect the correct award of the case". It is quite a pity that the application of this standard has resulted in chaos since it is the courts' discretion to decide whether the violation of arbitration rules results in a

① Interpretation of the Supreme People's Court concerning Some Issues on Application of the Arbitration Law of the People's Republic of China (最高人民法院《关于适用〈中华人民共和国仲裁法〉若干问题的解释》), (People's Republic of China) Supreme People's Court, 23 August 2006.

wrong award. [①]

2. Different Procedural Requirements for Domestic and Foreign-related Arbitration

The PRC Arbitration Law learned much from China's long-developed foreign-related arbitration practices[②]. China started its commercial arbitration back in the 1950's. The first two arbitration institutions are CIETAC and China International Maritime Arbitration Commission (CMAC). Both were foreign-related and established within the China Council for the Promotion of International Trade. [③] China had promulgated no arbitration law till 1994 when the foreign-related arbitration practices were well-developed. Thus, the PRC Arbitration Law contains detailed provisions on domestic arbitration while sparing only one chapter among the eight chapters for brief provisions on foreign-related arbitration.

There is no definition of "foreign-related arbitration" in the PRC Arbitration Law. The answer lies in the SPC's interpretations. Though China is not a case law country and the SPC has no legislative power, the SPC's interpretations have played an important role in the understanding and implementation of the PRC Arbitration Law. There are over 30 SPC

---

① See, e. g., Second Intermediate People's Court of Beijing, People's Republic of China(北京市第二中级人民法院), (2005) ErZhong Min TeZi No. 06659 Civil Ruling [(2005)二中民特字第06659号民事裁定书].

② Yang Xiao, former SPC President, speech at the 17th ICCA Conference (16 May 2004), http://finance. sina. com. cn/roll/20040517/1348763658. shtml, June 12, 2017.

③ Decision of the Government Administration Council of the Central People's Government Concerning the Establishment of a Foreign Trade Arbitration Commission within the China Council for the Promotion of International Trade(中央人民政府政务院《关于在中国国际贸易促进委员会内设立对外贸易仲裁委员会的决定》), (People's Republic of China) Government Administration Council, 6 May 1954.

interpretations regarding arbitration.[①] Basically, there are three elements for the determination of "foreign-related". First, the nationalities, habitual residences or places of registration of parties. Second, the location of the subject matter. Third, the place where legal facts occur. The SPC also lists "other circumstances" in its interpretation which is left for further clarification in its case-by-case analysis and replies[②]. In practice, "foreign-related arbitration" has been extended to arbitration related to Hong Kong, Macau and Taiwan.

Foreign-related arbitral awards and foreign arbitral awards enjoy exemption from the judicial review over substantial matters involved in domestic arbitration under Article 58 of the PRC Arbitration Law. Chinese courts can only review procedural matters involved in foreign-related or foreign arbitral awards and are bound by an internal reporting system for revocation or non-enforcement of such awards[③]. The SPC's approval is necessary for the revocation or non-enforcement. It means all the courts must follow the same strict criteria for foreign-related awards under Article 274 of the PRC Civil Procedure Law or those for foreign awards under Article V of the New York Convention on the Recognition and Enforcement of Foreign Arbitral Awards (the New York Convention).

---

① Zhi Xuan Koo and Yong En Lim, "The intricacies involved in the pursuit of natural justice in arbitration-L W Infrastructure Pte Ltd. v. Lim Chin San Contractors Pte Ltd; [2013] 1 SLR 125", *Singapore Academy of Law Journal* 25, 2013, p. 595.

② The Interpretations of the SPC on Several Issues Concerning Application of Law of the People's Republic of China on Choice of Law for Foreign-Related Civil Relationships (I) [最高人民法院《关于适用〈中华人民共和国涉外民事关系法律适用法〉若干问题的解释(一)》], (People's Republic of China) the SPC, 7 January 2013.

③ Notice of the SPC on the People's Courts' Handling of Issues Relevant to Foreign-related or Foreign Arbitration Matters(最高人民法院《关于人民法院处理与涉外仲裁及外国仲裁事项有关问题的通知》), (People's Republic of China) the SPC, 28 August 1995.

3. The Bias Rule

Bias can taint an arbitrator, an arbitral award and international legal harmony.[①] Thus, arbitrators shall remain impartial and independent, and disclose any circumstances that may influence the impartiality or independence. It is hard to determine whether there is real bias. Even if there is no real bias by one arbitrator, parties may still doubt his or her impartiality or independence. In the international commercial arbitration, the "reasonableness" standard has been accepted for the test of bias[②] and certain boundaries have been set for the scope of disclosure[③].

The PRC Arbitration Law contains the impartiality requirement and the disclosure obligation of arbitrators in domestic arbitration. Under Article 13 of the PRC Arbitration Law, arbitrators shall be "righteous and upright". It further imposes disclosure obligation on arbitrators in Article 34, involving circumstances such as close relationship, personal interest or private meeting with parties. However, the independence requirement is not for arbitrators, but for arbitration process (Article 8) and arbitration institutions (Article 14). As to foreign arbitrators, it seems that the only requirement is "with special knowledge" (Article 67).

The CIETAC Arbitration Rules contains more detailed and specified provisions concerning the bias rule. These provisions are for both domestic and foreign arbitrators. The arbitrators shall be independent and impartial according to Article 24, 35 and 49 of the CIETAC Arbitration Rules. The disclosure

---

① John McMillan, "Natural Justice: Too Much, Too Little or Just Right?", *AIAL forum* 58, 2008, p. 33.

② Andrew Field, "The Bias Principle and Its Applicability to International Commercial Arbitrations in Australia", *Australian Dispute Resolution Journal* 10, 1990, p. 246.

③ James H. Carter, "Rights and Obligations of the arbitrator", *Dispute Resolution Journal* 52, 1997, p. 56.

obligation of arbitrators is limited to "justifiable doubts" and the disclosure shall be made "promptly" "in writing" (Article 31). However, it is not easy for parties to challenge arbitrators. Supporting evidence for the "justifiable doubts" is needed (Article 32). The time limit for parties to challenge arbitrators is either 10 days, if the challenge is based on the disclosure of arbitrators, or 15 days, if the challenge ground is alleged by parties.

It is noticeable that parties shall challenge within the time limit, otherwise they will lose the challenge right (Article 32 of the CIETAC Rules). However, in a 2016 ruling involving the revocation of a domestic arbitration award, the court determined that arbitrators should haveresigned when circumstances stated in Article 34 of the PRC Arbitration Law occurred with or without parties' challenge[①]. It is unclear whether such mandatory resignation is applicable to foreign arbitrators. Furthermore, there is no unified interpretation of "other relationships" stated in Item 3 of Article 34. Thus, it is the judges' discretion in the interpretation and determination while the test of "reasonableness" has not been adopted.

Chinese courts enjoy much discretionary power in the determination of bias. One extreme example is the revocation of a domestic arbitral award by the Beijing Second Intermediate People's Court in 2009 simply because there was no signature in an arbitrators' declaration of impartiality and independence.[②] If there is no unified interpretation of the bias rule, especially that of the "other relationships" which may result in bias, arbitrators may be

---

① Intermediate People's Court of Huainan City, People's Republic of China(淮南市中级人民法院), (2016) Wan 04 Min Te No. 314 Civil Ruling, 2 December 2016[(2016)皖民特字第314号民事裁定书].

② Second Intermediate People's Court of Beijing, People's Republic of China(北京市第二中级人民法院),[(2009) ErZhong Min TeZi No. 15518 Civil Ruling][(2009)二中民特字第15518号民事裁定书].

too scared to take their appointment which may result in revocation or non-enforcement of awards due to unexpected bias determination.

4. The Hearing Rule

The hearing rule involves two aspects. First, arbitrators need to conduct the proceeding fairly, which means parties shall be properly notified and have appropriate opportunities to make submissions or presentations. Second, awards must not contain any surprise, which means arbitrators shall deal with parties' arguments and explain why they support or reject the arguments. The notification requirement may be stricter in international arbitration due to the language barrier and delivery difficulties.

The PRC Arbitration Law and the CIETAC Arbitration Rules request parties be notified of arbitration proceedings in writing. The CIETAC Arbitration Rules further clarifies the time for notification and the way of delivery as "in person or sent by registered mail or express mail, fax, or by any other means considered proper by the Arbitration Court or the arbitral tribunal". The SPC admits "by email" as an acceptable way of delivery① and refers to arbitration rules for the determination of "proper notification"②.

The language barrier may result in the revocation or non-enforcement of

① The SPC's Reply on the Ruling for Refusal to Recognize and Enforce the Arbitral Award regarding the Lease Agreement of ABRA Ship dated 28 December 2004 Rendered in London, UK(最高人民法院《关于是否裁定不予承认和执行英国伦敦"ABRA 轮 2004 年 12 月 28 日租约"仲裁裁决的请示的复函》), (People's Republic of China) the SPC, 10 January 2007.

② The SPC's Reply on the Case regarding the Application of "AngfoHuapin" Joint Venture for the Recognition and Enforcement of the Award by the International Arbitration Court of the Belarusian Chamber of Commerce and Industry(最高人民法院《关于"昂佛化品"合资有限责任公司申请承认并执行白俄罗斯工商会国际仲裁院仲裁裁决一案的请示的复函》), (People's Republic of China) the SPC, 2 November 2012.

awards[①]. It is stated in Article 81 "language" of the CIETAC Arbitration Rules that the arbitration language shall be determined either according to the parties' agreement, be Chinese if there is no such agreement, or be designated by CIETAC "having regard to the circumstances of the case". The normal practice of CIETAC is to send a bilingual notice of arbitration before the arbitration language is determined.

As to the reasoning in awards, the requirement of the PRC Arbitration Law is "on the basis of facts" and "in compliance of law" (Article 7). The CIETAC requirement is similar but with addition of "with reference to international practices" (Article 49). Regarding evidence examination, the essential part of fact-finding, the PRC Arbitration Law requests all evidence be produced at oral hearings (Article 45) but fails to clarify the way of examining evidence. The CIETAC Rules limits producing of evidence to cases conducted with oral hearings and allows evidence to be examined either during oral hearing or after oral hearing in writing.

Chinese courts' attitude toward evidence examination in China's commercial arbitration is quite rigid. The standard in civil procedures is all evidence must be examined during oral hearing. [②] Chinese courts have followed the same standard in their supervision of arbitration. [③] It results in over burden of parties and arbitrators in fact-finding.

---

① CEEG (Shanghai) Solar Science & Technology Co., Ltd. v. LUMOS LLC, 2016 WL 3909579 (10th Cir. 2016); Qingdao Free Trade Zone Genius Int'l Trading Co., Ltd. v. P & S Intern., Inc., 2009 WL 2997184 (D. Oregon, 2009).

② Article 47 of The SPC's Provisions onEvidence in Civil Procedures(最高人民法院《关于民事诉讼证据的若干规定》), (People's Republic of China), 21 December 2001.

③ Second Intermediate People's Court of Beijing, People's Republic of China(北京市第二中级人民法院), (2011) ErZhong Min TeZi No. 09370 Civil Ruling[(2011)二中民特字第09370号民事裁定书], (2007) ErZhong Min TeZi No. 13159Civil Ruling[(2007)二中民特字第13159号民事裁定书] and (2006) ErZhong Min TeZi 10554 Civil Ruling[(2006)二中民特字第10554号民事裁定书].

5. CIETAC's Supervision over Arbitrators

CIETAC, to maintain its reputation and top-rank position in the more and more fierce competition among Chinese and foreign arbitration institutions, safeguards arbitration procedures conducted under its auspices. First and foremost, all the arbitrators shall abide by CIETAC's Rules for Evaluating the Behavior of Arbitrators coming into effect as from 1 March 2009.

The Rules for Evaluating the Behavior of Arbitrators adopts a much stricter rule of bias. First, the CIETAC staff shall not accept the parties' appointment (Article 6.6). Second, arbitrators shall sign written declaration of impartiality and independence when accepting appointment, disclosing all circumstances that may make it unsuitable for them to accept appointment (Article 7). The "unsuitableness" includes but is not limited to the circumstances of disclosure under the PRC Arbitration Law or the CIETAC Rules. For example, an arbitrator shall not accept appointment when he is too busy, unfit or lacks professional knowledge. The disclosing criteria is also above "justifiable doubts" or "reasonableness". The disclosure covers the working relationship, property interests or personal interests between an arbitrator, his relatives or his company and the parties, their agents or other tribunal members.

The Rules for Evaluating the Behavior of Arbitrators further clarifies "other relationships" stipulated in the PRC Arbitration Law as advising on the same case, working in the same organization as the parties or their agents in the last two years, working as legal counsel for the parties in the last two years, recommending legal counsels for the parties, getting involved inthe same case or related cases in different ways, or other circumstances which may influence the impartiality. CIETAC may warn, replace or disengage arbitrators with improper behaviours such as deferring the hearing, showing bias, being late for or distracted in hearing, or leaking information.

The CIETAC's strict application of the bias rule has resulted in over disclosure by arbitrators and frequent challenge by parties. One possible risk is too much emphasis on the bias rule will result in arbitrators' reluctance to accept appointments and interfere with parties' autonomy. Institution's tight control over arbitrators may also influence the independence of arbitrators. If parties use the challenge of arbitrators as a tactic to delay arbitration process, the flexibility and efficiency of the CIETAC arbitration will be damaged.

Ⅱ. The Changing Design of the CIETAC Arb-med Process

CIETAC has adopted the arb-med practice since its inception. Arb-med is named as "the combination of conciliation with arbitration"① in the CIETAC Arbitration Rules and the PRC Arbitration Law. It refers to a hybrid dispute resolution mechanism. Mediation has its long tradition in China. Under the influence of Chinese culture, Chinese people prefer shunning direct confrontation②. With higher social rank or respect from the parties, mediators tend to persuade or even push parties into a kind of compromise to settle disputes③. From the origin of the CIETAC Arb-med practice, we may find arb-med as disguised mediation (section 1). CIETAC is changing its arb-med process partly due to the natural justice concern (section 2). Tribunals and courts both adopt different attitudes toward arb-med results (section 3).

① "Conciliation" Is used in the CIETAC Rules and the PRC Arbitration Law. It is the same as "mediation". See Jianlong Yu, "Conciliation in Action in China and CIETAC's Practice", *Asia Pacific Law Review* 17, 2009.

② Tai-Heng Cheng and Anthony Kohtio, "Some Limits to Appy Chinese Med-Arb Internationally", *New York Dispute Resolution Lawyer* 2, 2009, p. 95.

③ Wm Theodore de Bary, *Sources of Chinese Tradition Volume* 2: *From* 1600 *Through the Twentieth Century*, New York, Columbia University Press, 2010.

CIETAC, being open to international practice, may further change its arb-med process to eliminate the cause of concern (section 4).

1. The Origin of the CIETAC Arb-med Practice

In the following, this article will explore the origin of the CIETAC arb-med practice through analysis of parties, arb-mediators and a typical case. It can show the background of CIETAC's adoption of the arb-med practice and the reason why arb-med was disguised mediation at the beginning.

First, parties. It is not surprising to find the arb-med cases involved a state-owned foreign trade company in China as one party and a foreign trade company as another. China's foreign trade was "a complete monopoly of the central government"[①] in the 1950s. The State Council made delicate plans for foreign trade to keep a balance between import and export. Only state-owned foreign trade companies authorized by the State Council could participate in the import and/or export. However, for these transactions, there was no Chinese law[②] and only a few bilateral treaties[③] to follow. Furthermore, the special identity of these state-owned companies made it difficult to settle disputes through litigation. Even today, the special identity of China's state-owned enterprises is still under debate.[④] Foreign parties would not have expected the same protection as their Chinese counterparts.

Second, arb-mediators. CIETAC adopted the panel of arbitrators from its inception and appointment of arbitrators from outside the panel had been

---

① Nicholas R. Lardy, *Foreign Trade and Economic Reform in China*, Cambridge, Cambridge University Press, 1992, p. 16.

② Xiangquan Qi, "Legislative History of the PRC's Law of the Application of Law for Foreign-Related Civil Relations", *Chinese Law & Government* 45, 2012, p. 3.

③ Douglas M. Johnston, *Agreements of the People's Republic of China*, 1949-1967: *a Calendar*, Harvard, Harvard university press, 1968, p. 5.

④ *TNB Fuel Service SDN BHD* v. *China National Coal Group Corporation* [2017] HKCFI 1016.

prohibited until CIETAC amended its rules in 2005. The 1956 CIETAC Rules stated that only committee members of the arbitration institution could be appointed as arbitrators. ① Nan Hanchen, the first president of the People's Bank of China, was chosen as the chairman and committee member of the arbitration commission, ② which was a typical example of the official background of the committee members. There was no foreign arbitrator in the panel. Foreign parties would have worried about the possible bias in the arb-med process.

Third, a case analysis. The above indicates that the imbalance of power may have been the biggest worry of those foreign parties participating in arb-med process. Through a case analysis, we may find the arb-med process involved more than the parties and the arb-mediators. With a vague boundary between the arbitration institution and the arb-mediators, and with the involvement of outsiders, such imbalance was broken.

The mediation was beyond the arb-med process. In January 1975, American Arbitration Association (the AAA) reached an agreement with China's Foreign Trade Arbitration Commission (the former name of CIETAC) to solve US-China trade disputes through "joint mediation". ③ In 1977, the two organizations successfully co-mediated a dispute involving the late delivery of cotton by an American company. The mediators were Mr. Strauss and Mr.

---

① Provisional Rules for the CCPIT Foreign Trade Arbitration Commission Arbitration Rules(《中国国际贸易促进委员会对外贸易仲裁委员会仲裁程序暂行规则》), (People's Republic of China) CCPIT Committee Meeting, 31 March 1956, art 4, 9-14.

② XieJianqun et al. (解建群等), *CCPIT History from* 1952 *to* 1994 (《贸促春秋:1952—1994》), China Finance and Politics Publishing House(中国财经政治出版社), 2013, pp. 32-39.

③ Zhou Xiaoyan(周晓燕), *Law and Practice in Settlement of Disputes Arising From Economic and Trade Transactions Involving Foreign Interests* (《涉外经济纠纷的法律与实务》), Zhongxin Publishing House(中信出版社), 1999, p. 80.

Holtzmann from the AAA, an American lawyer from the US-China Business Council and Mr. Xunyi Shao from CIETAC①. The case was settled by one arb-mediator with three outsiders. Both parties compromised to bear half of the loss.

No real arbitration or arb-med existed in the above case. There had been no provision on the practice of combining mediation with arbitration till the CIETAC amended its rules in 1988. We may find through the 1956 CIETAC Rules that arbitration was still a foreign concept mixedwith litigation at that time. For example, Article 21 requested public hearing and Article 30 urged tribunals to announce their awards at the end of oral hearing.

2. The Changing Design of the CIETAC Arb-med Process

The design of the CIETAC arb-med process is reflected in its rules. CIETAC amended its rules in 1988, 1994, 1995, 1998, 2000, 2005, 2012 and 2015. Among these versions, the 1988, 1994, 2000, 2005 and 2012 Rules contained major changes in the provisions on arb-med. Thus, this article will rely on the relevant provisions in the five versions to depict the changing design of the CIETAC arb-med process.

CIETAC amended its rules in 1988 to accommodate the increasing caseload and China's accession to the New York Convention. The Convention came into force in China on 22 April 1987. In August 1988, CIETAC handled over 250 cases② which was a sharp contrast to only 2 cases accepted by

① Wang Shengchang(王生长), *The Theory and Practice of Combining Arbitration with Conciliation* (《仲裁与调解相结合的理论与实务》), Law Press China(法律出版社), 2001, p. 309.

② Houzhi Tang, "International Commercial Arbitration in the Far East-the PRC Example", in Peter Sanders (ed.), *International Council for Commercial Arbitration-Arbitration in Settlement of International Commercial Disputes Involving the Far East and Arbitration in Combined Transportation* (Tokyo Conference, August 1988), p. 43.

CIETAC in 1956[①]. Article 37 of the 1998 CIETAC Arbitration Rules was the first stipulation on the CIETAC arb-med process. It allowed both CIETAC and tribunals to mediate cases. It is noticeable that under Article 51 of the PRC Arbitration Law, tribunals "shall conduct conciliation if both parties voluntarily seek conciliation". Thus, it is mandatory for tribunals to serve as mediators though the CIETAC Arbitration Rules stated tribunals "may" mediate. Tribunals should render consent awards when parties reached settlement agreements. There was still no clear boundary between the arbitration institution and tribunals. The CIETAC arb-med process adopted the simple arb-med-arb mode. Under such mode, arbitral tribunals, during the hearing of arbitration cases, serve as mediators and render consent awards if parties reach settlement.

The 1994 CIETAC Arbitration Rules corresponded to the PRC Arbitration Law. Parties' consent and tribunals' power of decision were respected in the Arbitration Rules. The mediation in arb-med went beyond the arbitration process. Parties could reach settlement by themselves (Article 44 of the Rules and Article 49 of the Arbitration Law). It differentiated the mediation process and the arbitration process. Parties or tribunals' opinion, view or statement, and any proposal or proposition shall not be invoked in the arbitration process or any other subsequent process (Article 51). It also allowed tribunals to mediate in manners they consider "appropriate" (Article 47). The normal manners of the CIETAC arb-mediators include "back to back", "face to face" and a mixture of both. "Back to back" means tribunals meet one party each time. "Face to face" means tribunals meet all the parties together. The most

---

① Xie. Jianqun et al. (解建群等), *CCPIT History from* 1952 *to* 1994(《贸促春秋:1952—1994》), *China Finance and Politics Publishing House*(中国财经政治出版社), 2013, p. 119.

popular one is a mixture of both and normally involves three rounds. In the first round, tribunals meet each party to find its position. In the second round, tribunals try to level parties' expectations. In the third round, tribunals help parties reach middle points.

The 2000 CIETAC Arbitration Rules put a new mode in the CIETAC arb-med process, i. e. med-arb. Parties may reach settlement agreements before arbitration and obtain consent awards by sole-member tribunals (Article 44).

The 2005 CIETAC Arbitration Rules highlighted the CIETAC arb-med process by categorizing all relevant provisions under Article 40 "Combination of Conciliation with Arbitration".

The 2012 CIETAC Arbitration Rules further clarified the CIETAC arb-med process in Article 45. With this clear provision, we may find the CIETAC arb-med modes as follows. First, med-arb. Sole-member tribunals render consent awards based on arbitration agreements reached by parties prior to arbitration. Second, arb-med. Parties reach settlement agreements during arbitration. CIETAC or tribunals make decisions on case withdrawal. Or tribunals make conciliation statements. Third, arb-med-arb. Tribunals mediate during arbitration and make consent awards when parties reach settlement agreements or render awards when mediation fails. Tribunals shall render awards based on facts and laws without being influenced by information obtained during mediation.

Considering the concern over double identities of arb-mediators, the 2012 CIETAC Arbitration Rules allowed parties to have separate mediation conducted by mediators other than arbitrators①. The arbitration process would

---

① Anthony Connerty, "The 2012 Revision of the CIETAC Arbitration Rules: A Look at the Most Significant Changes", *Dispute Resolution Journal* 67, 2012, p. 72.

be pending unless the mediation failed. However, it is still the CIETAC arbitrators' mandatory obligation to mediate cases if the parties consent to or request arb-med.

3. Different Attitudes toward Arb-med Results

There are four arb-med results under the current CIETAC Arbitration Rules. First, case withdrawal decisions. Normally parties will not re-initiate arbitration or initiate other proceedings after they reach settlement and withdraw cases. Second, consent awards based on settlement agreements reached prior to arbitration. Third, conciliation statements. Fourth, consent awards based on settlement agreements reached during arbitration. This section will discuss different attitudes toward conciliation statements and consent awards.

The CIETAC tribunals' attitudes toward conciliation statements and consent awards are different due to the contractual nature of arbitration and the limitation on tribunals' jurisdiction. Tribunals, under Article 51 of the PRC Arbitration Law, "shall make a written conciliation statement or make an arbitration award in accordance with the result of the settlement agreement".

Chinese Courts' attitude towards conciliation statements and consent awards are different as well. The SPC has shown its support to the arb-med practice by requesting Chinese courts to enforce arbitral tribunals' conciliation statements and awards (including consent awards)①. Chinese courts are ready to enforce a conciliation statement unless the settlement is against parties' will or law, or the enforcement is against national or public interest②. Consent awards are reviewed by Chinese courts under the same criteria as awards. The

① The SPC Provisions on Various Issues in the People's Courts' Enforcement(最高人民法院《关于人民法院执行工作若干问题的规定》), (People's Republic of China) the SPC, 8 July 1998.

② Civil Procedure Law of the People's Republic of China(《民事诉讼法》), (People's Republic of China) Standing Committee of the National People's Congress, 31 August 2012, art 201, 208.

SPC made it clear in Article 19 of the 2006 SPC Interpretation that awards beyond the scope of arbitration should be set aside partially or wholly.

Consent awards may be recognized and enforced as awards by a foreign court under the New York Convention. However, it is debatable whether consent awards based on settlement agreements reached prior to arbitration can be recognized and enforced under the Convention. Article Ⅱ. 1 of the Convention requires "all or any differences" be submitted to arbitration. Settlement before arbitration means no difference to be submitted[①].

Natural justice concern has aroused in the recognition and enforcement of consent awards based on settlement agreements reached during arbitration. The Russian Supreme Court refused to enforce a consent award rendered by the International Commercial Arbitration Court at the Russian Chamber of Commerce in late 2015. The party against whom the award was enforced had not been given the opportunity to present the case and comment on the tribunal's partial record of the settlement agreement in the consent award[②]. The common practice of arbitration institutions is to allow tribunals to limit the record of settlement agreements in consent awards within the scope of arbitration. However, consent awards with partial settlement agreements recorded may result in violation of the hearing rule since parties are not properly notified and have little chance to present their case.

---

① Huang Zhongshun(黄忠顺), "Discussion on the Nature and Force of Consent Awards"(《和解裁决的性质及其效力探微》), *Compilation of Thesis for the* 2015 *Annual Meeting of China Academy of Arbitration Law and the* 8*th Forum of China Arbitration and Justice*(载中国仲裁法学研究会2015年年会暨第八届中国仲裁与司法论坛论文集).

② Saba Sekulovic, Arbitrators Do (Not Always) Know Best: Consent Awards and Due Process, http://www.cisarbitration.com/2016/05/04/arbitrators-do-not-always-know-best-consent-awards-and-due-process/, May 15, 2017.

4. The Future of the CIETAC Arb-med Process

It is obvious that CIETAC follows international trend in designing its arb-med process. One example is the adoption of separate mediation in the 2012 Arbitration Rules. In the future, CIETAC may make a more flexible and practical design to accommodate to the flexibility and efficiency of arbitration process as well as eliminating natural justice concern over the arb-med process.

It is believed that a good dispute resolution process designed by probing into parties' underlying interests can not only solve disputes but also bring big value①. One good example is the IBM-Fujitsu arbitration case. The dispute was over Fujitsu Ltd. (Fujitsu)'s infringement of International Business Machines Corporation (IBM)'s copyright through developing and marketing IBM-compatible operating system software. The two parties signed settlement agreements through negotiation in 1983. In 1985, IBM initiated arbitration pursuant to the arbitration clause in the settlement agreements. The tribunal adopted a problem-solving method and designed a flexible dispute resolution process including mediation, rule-making proceedings, hearings, independent compliance monitoring and institutionalized mechanism for ongoing dispute resolution②.

In the IBM-Fujitsu arbitration case, the two co-arbitrators acted as arb-mediators and participated in the whole process of dispute resolution. Their success lay in the respect of natural justice. They maintained independent and impartial through the process, and gave both parties opportunities to not only present the case but also design the process.

Arb-mediators are required to build "a mental wall" to avoid being

---

① Robert Mnookin, "Creating Value Through Process Design: The IBM-Fujitsu Arbitration", *The Arbitration Journal* 47, 1992, p. 6.

② Ibid.

influenced by information acquired during mediation.[①] It is not easy. In practice, arb-mediators may try their best to avoid the prejudice of mediation information and render final awards based on facts supported by examined evidence in accordance with relevant laws. But it is almost unavoidable that parties' positions or proposals during mediation will have certain impact on arb-mediators' mind and influence their awards. Tribunals may follow the IBM-Fujitsu arbitration to let co-arbitrators mediate while presiding arbitrators can remain uninfluenced.

CIETAC needs to make a bolder design with more caution. The CIETAC tribunals' common practice is to shift from arbitration process to mediation process in the final stage of oral hearings. The way of combining mediation with arbitration can be diversified. For example, partial or interlocutory awards are allowed under the PRC Arbitration Law (Article 55) and the CIETAC Arbitration Rules. Tribunals may solve hard parts of parties' disputes in partial or interlocutory awards and urge parties to settle the rest. The combination of independent mediation with arbitration can be further explored. "Shadow' mediation"[②] through which mediators can sit with arbitrators with parties' consent may cut the time and cost for dual process.

Ⅲ. The Courts' Review of China's Arb-med Results

The courts' review of arb-med results involves two processes. One is revocation, another is recognition and enforcement of awards. The two processes may be carried out in different courts, or even in different nations.

---

① Harold I. Abramson, "Protocols for International Arbitrators Who Dare to Settle Cases", *The American Review of International Arbitration* 10, 1990, p. 1.

② Christian Bühring-Uhle, Arbitration and mediation in international business, London, Kluwer Law International, 2006, p. 258.

One court's determination may not necessarily influence the other's decision[①]. The New York Convention refers to the hearing rule explicitly while the rule against bias is a part of the public policy exception[②]. The public policy exception is the last resort for the bias rule. The following cases regarding the bias rule (section 1) and the hearing rule (section 2) show courts' caution in applying the public policy exception and reliance on arbitration rules in their decisions.

1. The Bias Rule

Gao Haiyan and Another v. Keeneye Holdings Ltd and Another (the Gao Haiyan case)[③] shows Hong Kong courts' application of the bias rule in enforcing mainland China's arb-med results and interpretation of public policy. Though Hong Kong courts recognize and enforce mainland China's arbitral awards according to the Arrangement Concerning Mutual Enforcement of Arbitral Awards between the mainland and the Hong Kong SAR[④], the grounds for refusal to recognize or enforce awards under the Hong Kong Arbitration Ordinance are almost the same as those under the New York Convention.

The Gao Haiyan case involves one arb-med process and four court procedures. The Xi'an Arbitration Commission (the XAC) rendered the No. [2009] 2232 arbitration award on 3 June 2010 after unsuccessful mediation at the Xian Shangri-la hotel without the respondents' participation on 27 March

---

① *Ye v. Zeng* [2015] FCA 1192, *Ye v. Zeng* (No. 2) [2015] FCA 1243, *Ye v. Zeng* (No. 3) [2015] FCA 1279, *Ye v. Zeng* (No. 4) [2016] FCA 386.

② Austin Pullé, "Securing Natural Justice in Arbitration Proceedings", *Asia Pacific Law Review* 20, 2012, p. 63.

③ [2010] HKCFI 980, [2010] HKCFI 240, [2011] HKCA 459.

④ The SPC's Arrangement on the Mutual Enforcement of Arbitral Awards between the Mainland and the Hong Kong SAR(最高人民法院《关于内地与香港特别行政区相互执行仲裁裁决的安排》), (People's Republic of China) 1 February 2000.

2010. The respondents applied for setting aside the award in the Xi'an City Intermediate People's Court (the Xi'an Court). The application was rejected. The applicants were granted leave by Judge Saunders of the Hong Kong First Instance Court to enforce the award on 2 August 2010. The Respondents applied to set aside the leave on 16 September 2010, complaining, inter alia, of collusion between the applicants, arbitrators and the General Secretary of the Xi'an Arbitration Commission. On 12 April 2011, Judge Reyes of the Hong Kong First Instance Court set aside the leave and refused to enforce the award "as a matter of public policy". On 2 December 2011, Judge Tang (with the agreement of Judge Fok and Judge Sakhrani) of the Hong Kong Court of Appeal allowed the appeal and set aside Judge Reyes' order.

Three issues regarding the bias rule are involved. First, the determination of bias. The Xi'an Court deemed no bias could be inferred from the Secretary General of the XAC acting as the co-mediator since he was authorized by the Chairman of the XAC as stipulated in the XAC Rules. Thus, the Xi'an Court relied on the arbitration rules in the determination of bias. The parties argued whether the test of "actual bias" or "apparent bias" should be relied upon. Judge Reyes stated in his order that "the minimalist version would cause a fair-minded observer to apprehend a real risk of bias" (para 53). He adopted the test of "apparent bias". Judge Tang deemed there was no conflict between the two ways of the test and found "no case of apparent bias" had been established. He said in para 86:

> *A court in Hong Kong is not in a position to express any view on the likelihood of Share Transfer Agreement and Supplemental Share Transfer Agreement being set aside under Article* 54 *of the PRC Contract Law. Also, much may depend on the view which the Arbitral Tribunal may form on the facts or the circumstances of the case.*

Second, waiver and estoppel. According to Article 5 of the XAC Rules which is similar with Article 10 “Waiver of Right to Object” of the CIETAC Arbitration Rules, parties in arbitral proceedings that did not objection to non-compliance with the rules shall be deemed to havewaived the right to object. Judge Reyes deemed that there had been no waiver. His main ground was the dilemma of the respondents since the Secretary General engaging in the mediation would have been the decision maker for the respondents' objection. He also found the respondents had not been estopped by the Xi'an Court ruling. Judge Tang regarded the respondents' continuance of arbitration as waiver and the Xi'an Court's refusal to set aside the award relevant to the enforcing court's decision. He quoted Judge Coleman's statement in *Minmetals Germany GmbH v. Ferco Steel Ltd*① at page 661.

> *In international commerce a party who contracts into an agreement to arbitrate in a foreign jurisdiction is bound not only by the local arbitration procedure but also by the supervisory jurisdiction of the courts of the seat of the arbitration. If the award is defective or the arbitration is defectively conducted the party who complains of the defect must in the first instance pursue such remedies as exist under that supervisory jurisdiction. That is because by his agreement to the place in question as the seat of the arbitration he has agreed not only to refer to all disputes to arbitration but that the conduct of the arbitration should be subject to that particular supervisory jurisdiction. Adherence to that part of the agreement must, in my judgment, be a cardinal policy consideration by an English court considering enforcement of a foreign award.*

① [1999] CLC 647.

Third, public policy. Judge Reyes refused to enforce the award "as a matter of public policy". The leading authority regarding public policy in Hong Kong is *Hebei Import & Export Corp v. Polytek Engineering Co Ltd*[①] in which Judge Chan of the Hong Kong Court of Appeal regarded public policy as "the most basic notions of morality and justice of the Hong Kong system" (page 20). Judge Tang pointed out that the result of a refusal to enforce the award "can be extremely unjust" when the court with the supervisory jurisdiction had refused to set it aside (para 65).

2. The Hearing Rule

The hearing rule is reflected in the Chinese case involving Tan Qiongfang's Application for setting aside a Chinese consent award[②].

The two main grounds for the setting aside application are no examination of key evidence and the violation of public interest. The Applicant Tan Qiongfang signed the House Purchase Contract with the Respondent Deli Company on 11 October 2012. On 15 October 2014, Tan submitted the dispute on late delivery of house to arbitration. Suining Arbitration Commission rendered the (2014) Sui Zhong Cai Zi No. 197 Award on 28 December 2015. In the award, the tribunal confirmed the validity of the settlement agreement signed by both parties during arbitration. The tribunal relied on the parties' settlement agreement to calculate the Respondent's compensation for late delivery as RMB 50 per square meter. Tan alleged that the settlement agreement had been submitted by neither party as evidence.

---

① [1999] HKCFA 40, [1999] 2 HKCFAR 111.

② The Case involving Tan Qiongfang's Application for Setting Aside Arbitral Award(《谭琼芳申请撤销仲裁裁决案》), Intermediate People's Court of Suining City, People's Republic of China(遂宁市中级人民法院), (2016) Chuan 09 Min Te No. 39 Civil Ruling, 21 June 2016[(2016) 川 09 民特 39 号民事裁定书].

The Intermediate People's Court of Suining City set aside the award based on the first ground. The court deemed that the arbitral tribunal had violated the PRC Arbitration Law and the fairness of the award had been influenced. According to Article 45 of the PRC Arbitration Law and Article 48 of the Arbitration Rules, all evidence shall be produced and examined during oral hearing. The arbitral tribunal had not requested either party to produce the settlement agreement as evidence. The parties had been deprived the opportunity to comment on or examine the agreement. Thus, the arbitration procedure "was not in conformity with the statutory procedure". The court decided to set aside the award as per Article 58. 3 of the PRC Arbitration Law.

3. Analysis

The bias rule is rooted in arbitration rules. The Gao Haiyan Case shows that it is hard to establish bias, no matter "apparent bias" or "actual bias", in courts' enforcement procedure. The enforcing court would respect the decision by the supervising court at the place of arbitration in the determination of bias. Chinese courts, under the pro-arbitration policy, normally refer to arbitration rules for such determination.

Courts are cautious with the public policy or public interest exception for enforcing awards. The ground for refusal to recognize or enforce awards is more than the uneasy feeling of parties or judges, but shall be the violation of fundamental principles of morality and justice with significant social influence.

The "statutory procedure" is the boundary for the hearing rule. Chinese courts are rigid in implementing the PRC Arbitration Law. Tribunals, when relying on settlement agreements, shall request parties present the agreements and give each party the opportunity to examine and comment.

Chinese courts' attitude toward "waiver" is very clear. Once parties fail to promptly and clearly raise objection to non-compliance of arbitration rules, they will be deemed having waived the right to object and cannot rely on such non-compliance in preceding procedures. As Judge Coleman stated, parties' choice to arbitrate in a foreign jurisdiction put them under the restraint of the local arbitration procedure and the supervisory jurisdiction of the courts at the seat of arbitration. Thus, parties, if having any natural justice concern over China's arb-med process, shall raise the concern with no hesitation.

Ⅳ. Conclusion: Set the Early Alarm

China's arb-med process is unique①. China has adopted and developed the arb-meb process since the 1950's. It is regarded as an "oriental experience"②. With over-60-year development, China's arb-med is getting more in line with the international practice. Emphasis has been laid on arb-mediators' impartiality and independence. Parties' procedural rights has been protected. The pro-arbitration attitude of courts both in and outside China has largely encouraged China's arb-med practice. However, it is noticeable that long and lasting life of both arbitration and arb-med lies in parties' confidence. Party autonomy is of utmost importance in arbitration and arb-med. If natural justice concern results in no confidence, either China's arbitration system or the arb-med practice will go into a dead end.

The elimination of natural justice concern over China's arb-med process involves parties (section 1), arb-mediators (section 2), Chinese arbitration institutions (section 3), Chinese courts (section 4) and Chinese legislators (section 5).

---

① Houzhi Tang, "People's China: No Stranger to International Arbitration", *The Arbitration Journal* 45, 1990, p. 27.

② Christine Kang, "Oriental Experience of Combining Arbitration with Conciliation: New Development of CIETAC and Chinese Judicial Practice", *Fordham International Law Journal* 40, 2017, p. 919.

1. Parties

Arbitration is flexible and the process design is up to the parties' consent. Parties may participate in the arb-med design as early as when they sign arbitration agreements. For example, parties can opt out of mediation in arbitration if they feel uncomfortable with the arb-med practice. Or parties can choose not to have any supervision over arb-mediators, agreeing arb-mediators will never be challenged or replaced. Such extreme examples may not eventuate, but they show how parties can take the initiative.

Parties shall be aware of "the statutory procedure" once they choose arb-med in China. There had been no ad hoc arbitration in China till the SPC made the breakthrough in 2016①. The majority of China's commercial arbitration is still institutional arbitration or institutional arb-med since arbitrators "shall" mediate cases under the PRC Arbitration Law. Parties, when selecting a Chinese arbitration institution to arb-med disputes, shall have a clear vision of the institution's arbitration rules. The non-fulfilment of procedural requirements under the arbitration rules may result in the revocation of arb-med results②.

Parties shall keep alert to procedural non-compliance. The stipulation on waiver is adopted in Chinese arbitration institutions' rules. If parties fail to object to any non-compliance with arbitration rules promptly and clearly, they may be deemed as waiving the right to object. The principle of estoppel may also obstruct complaints about any non-conformity in preceding procedures.

2. Arb-mediators

Arb-mediators are the real process designers. Most parties are not capable

---

① The Supreme People's Court Opinions on the Provision of Judicial Safeguards for the Construction of Pilot Free Trade Zones(最高人民法院《关于为自由贸易试验区建设提供司法保障的意见》),(People's Republic of China) Supreme People's Court, 30 December 2016.

② See Ⅱ. 1 above.

of designing arbitration or arb-med process by themselves. It is up to arb-mediators to tailor the process. The PRC Arbitration Law and Chinese arbitration institutions' rules allow arbitrators to mediate in a manner they deem appropriate.

Arb-mediators' process design shall be within the boundary of the PRC Arbitration Law and arbitration rules. They must maintain impartiality and independence in the arb-med process. Parties may challenge arbitrators or arb-med results on the ground of bias. Though there are stipulated circumstances of bias, Chinese courts have discretion in the determination of bias①.

Arb-mediators shall be cautious with rendering arb-med results. No matter whether parties reach settlement before or during arbitration, arb-mediators shall remind themselves of the scope of arbitration when recording settlement agreements in consent awards. Furthermore, arb-mediators shall always give parties reasonable opportunities to comment on or examine settlement agreements. If mediation fails, arb-mediators shall try not to be influenced by information acquired during mediation. The final awards could only be based on facts and law'②. A secure way of examining evidence and/or settlement agreements is to have them produced and examined during oral hearing.

3. Chinese Arbitration Institutions

Chinese arbitration institutions have enjoyed more power than their foreign counterparts. The PRC Arbitration Law does not follow the competence-competence doctrine. Instead, it entitles arbitration institutions to rule on jurisdiction of tribunals (Article 20). Though some institutions, such as CIETAC, authorize tribunals to make jurisdiction decisions, there is still no

① See Ⅱ.3 above.

② See Ⅱ.4 above.

clear boundary between the power of arbitration institutions and that of tribunals.

Chinese arbitration institutions may act as mediators in arb-med process. According to the XAC Rules, the Secretary General may mediate with the authorization from the Chairman. In practice, institution staff may step in arb-med process even if there is no such stipulation in arbitration rules. Arb-med process, in its nature, is more of arbitration than mediation. Arb-mediators' power, no matter in arbitration or arb-med, originates from parties' consent. Thus, it is necessary to set a clear boundary between the power of arbitrators or arb-mediators and that of arbitration institutions.

Chinese arbitration institutions shall maintain the impartiality and independence of both arbitrators and institutions. The PRC Arbitration Law sets standards for arbitrators and requests arbitration institutions to have their panels of arbitrators under the standards (Article 13). Some institutions, such as CIETAC, allow parties to appoint arbitrators from outside the panel under the same standards and with the approval of institutions. CIETAC started engaging arbitrators through training and examination in 2010 to ensure the quality of its panel of arbitrators①. However, the quality of arbitrators goes far beyond professional knowledge, experience or skills. It is for the benefits of parties and arbitration institutions to have trustworthy arbitrators who can help parties find better solutions and defend the reputation of institutions and themselves.

Chinese arbitration institutions shall formalize the arb-med practice, especially in foreign-related cases. The PRC Arbitration Law allows the setting up of arbitration institutionsin Chinese cities (Article 10), but specifically

① Successful Completion of the CIETAC's Open Selection of Arbitrators(中国国际经济贸易仲裁委员会《贸仲公开选聘仲裁员初选工作顺利完成》), http://www.cietac.org/index.php? a = show&id = 1793&m = Article.

stipulates that the China Chamber of International Commerce (the CCOIC) may establish foreign-related arbitration institutions (Article 66). It seems that only arbitration institutions established by the CCOIC can handle foreign-related cases. However, the State Council encouraged offices of legal affairs in various levels to set up arbitration institutions handling both domestic and foreign-related cases[①]. That means arb-med results of over 250 Chinese arbitration institutions may be reviewed by foreign courts. Some institutions are inexperienced in handling foreign-related cases and have little concept of natural justice. It is urgent for Chinese arbitration institutions to formalize the arb-med practice and avoid procedural defects which may result in revocation or non-enforcement of arb-med results.

Chinese arbitration institutions shall have follow-up services for the arb-med process and get in line with international trends. The purposes of offering follow-up services are getting feedback for improvement of arb-med design, encouraging parties to settle disputes unsolved in arb-med process and avoiding procedural non-conformity. Along with the economic globalization, global legal standards have been increasingly unified[②]. Chinese arbitration institutions need to be aware of international trends and adjust their practices accordingly.

4. Chinese Courts

Chinese courts have their dual roles in supporting and supervising China's arbitration and arb-med. The SPC has been actively supporting China's arbitration and arb-med through its interpretations, notices and replies to lower

① Circular of the General Office of the State Council on Making Good Arrangements for the Reorganization of Arbitration Institutions and the Establishment of the China Arbitration Association(国务院办公厅《关于做好重新组建仲裁机构和筹建中国仲裁协会筹备工作的通知》),(People's Republic of China) State Council, 13 November 1994.

② Shahla Ali, "Approaching the Global Arbitration Table: Comparing the Advantages of Arbitration as Seen by Practitioners in East Asia and the West", *The Review of Litigation* 28, 2009, p. 791.

level courts regarding specific cases. Chinese courts shall limit their intervention in arbitration. Conciliation statements and consent awards shall be recognized and enforced. However, rigid standards have been adopted in the judicial review over China's arb-med process.

Chinese courts shall show more respect to party autonomy and the contractual nature of arb-med. No arbitration or arb-med practice could prosper without courts' support. Chinese courts shall be more flexible under the pro-arbitration policy. The SPC sets a higher standard for noncompliance of arbitration rules①. Thus, Chinese courts, when reviewing procedural defects in arb-med process, shall consider whether the defects are substantial enough to result in revocation or non-enforcement of arb-med results.

Chinese courts shall keep balance in the dual roles of supporting and supervising China's arbitration and arb-med. Foreign courts, when recognizing or enforcing Chinese arb-med results, may refer to Chinese courts' determination regarding the bias rule or the hearing rule. Chinese courts, with the guidance of the statutory requirements, shall bear in mind the natural justice requirements and the in-born yearning for efficiency and flexibility of arbitration and arb-med.

5. Chinese Legislators

The PRC Arbitration Law is in urgent need of amendments. Chinese arbitration institutions are facing fierce competition in the domestic and international markets. It is impossible for China to rank among the most preferred international commercial arbitration destinations without a modernized and internationalized arbitration law.

Chinese legislators shall follow the call for natural justice in international

---

① See Ⅱ. 1 above.

commercial arbitration when amending the PRC Arbitration Law. A clear division should be made between arb-mediators and arbitration institutions. Thus, the independence of arb-mediators can be ensured. Chinese arb-mediators shall get their remuneration from parties instead of from arbitration institutions as partial arbitration fees[①]. Chinese arbitration institutions shall refrain from interfering with arb-med process.

Meanwhile, arb-med, as a unique practice in China, shall enjoy more flexibility under the amended PRC Arbitration Law. Arb-med should be an opt-in process instead of a mandatory one. Parties shall be allowed to design or empower arb-mediators to tailor an arb-med process to realize their best interests and achieve the biggest value.

China's arb-med process has gained its reputation by helping parties to reach settlement and maintain long-term relationships. Arb-med users may set the early alarm for natural justice concern to enjoy the advantages better. Active involvement of parties, diligence of arb-mediators and sufficient support from courts and legislators will surely keep the worries away.

---

① Circular of the General Office of the State Council on Distributing the Plan for Restructuring Arbitration Commissions, the Provisional Regulation on the Registration of Arbitration Commissions and the Regulation on Fee Schedules of Arbitration Commissions(国务院办公厅《关于印发〈重新组建仲裁机构方案〉、〈仲裁委员会登记暂行办法〉、〈仲裁委员会仲裁收费办法〉的通知》), (People's Republic of China) State Council, 28 July 1995.

论中国内地的临时仲裁机构化：关于构建多层次审查机制的提议

黄泽宇*

摘要：在国际商事仲裁领域，越来越多的国际仲裁机构提供适用临时仲裁规则的仲裁服务。与一般的机构仲裁业务不同，国际仲裁机构在此类仲裁服务中仅仅担任指定机构或者提供秘书、技术性质的管理服务。这种可称为“临时仲裁机构化”的全球趋势已经迫使机构仲裁与临时仲裁之间原本清晰的分界线变得模糊不清，依靠传统的识别方法已经无法轻易判断此类混合式仲裁是机构仲裁抑或临时仲裁。由于中国现行仲裁法律不允许在内地开展临时仲裁，且自由贸易试验区皆位于中国内地，因而能否有效应对“临时仲裁机构化”所带来的法理挑战，关系到在中国自由贸易试验区引进临时仲裁。本文将着重探讨在我国内地“临时仲裁机构化”潮流中出现的混合式仲裁所引发的法律问题。

关键词：自由贸易试验区　临时仲裁机构化　混合式仲裁　司法审查

一、引言

在现代商事领域，仲裁已经成为解决当事人之间商事纠纷最常用的替代性

---

* 黄泽宇，澳门大学法学院2016级博士研究生，澳门大学法学院国际商法法学硕士，中国人民大学法学院法学学士。

争议解决机制之一。随着商事仲裁在世界各个独立法域自发性地兴起与发展，仲裁在学理上可分为泾渭分明的两种类型，即临时仲裁和机构仲裁。[①] 一般而言，机构仲裁会牵涉“与国家司法体系并行不悖且能组成‘虚拟法庭’的常设机构”，而临时仲裁却没有此类常设机构的参与。[②] 鉴于临时仲裁具有文件不公开性和程序保密性等特点，并且没有统一的常设机构或者国际组织对临时仲裁的案件量进行统计，因此当前尚且不能借助任何权威数据来判断上述两类仲裁中的哪一种更受当事人欢迎。尽管如此，大多数学者均认为，机构仲裁与临时仲裁之间存在清晰明辨的分界线。传统意义上的机构仲裁与临时仲裁存在很多不同之处，其中最显著的差别在于，机构仲裁通常会适用由仲裁机构起草的一套完整的仲裁规则，而在临时仲裁中双方当事人一般通过协议约定仲裁程序或者指定适用现存的仲裁规则，[③]如《联合国国际贸易法委员会仲裁规则》（以下简称《贸法会仲裁规则》）。[④]

机构仲裁与临时仲裁之间原本清晰的分界线在“国际商事仲裁机构化”[⑤]（包括“临时仲裁机构化”）的浪潮中开始变得模棱两可。[⑥] 常设仲裁机构在国

① See Michael John Mustill, "Arbitration: History and Background", 6 *Journal of International Arbitration* 43, 1989, p. 44.

② Ibid., p. 44. 至少就普通法而言，直至临时仲裁走出私人房间、出现在17世纪的判例汇编和法令之后，人们才渐渐知晓除了纠纷发生后临时安排人手和选定仲裁员解决单个纠纷之外的内容。

③ See I. J. Bouchez, "The Prospects for International Arbitration: Disputes Between States and Private Enterprises", in A. H. A. Soons (eds.), *International Arbitration: Past and Prospects: A Symposium To Commemorate The Centenary Of The Birth Of Professor J. H. W. Verzijl* (1888-1987), Martinus Nijhoff Publishers, 1990, p. 125.

④ 《联合国国际贸易法委员会仲裁规则》(*Arbitration Rules of the United Nations Commission on International Trade Law*)，1976年通过(U. N. G. A. Res. 31/98)，于2010年修订(U. N. G. A. Res. 65/22)，2013年《贸法会仲裁规则》吸纳了 *UNCITRAL Rules on Transparency for Treaty-Based Investor-State Arbitration* (U. N. G. A. Res. 68/109)。

⑤ See Emmanuel Gaillard, John Savage (eds.), *Fouchard, Gaillard, Goldman On International Commercial Arbitration*, Kluwer Law International, 1999, pp. 33-35.

⑥ 参见本文第二部分“揭开‘临时仲裁机构化’的面纱”。

际仲裁的发展历程中所扮演的重要角色已经在国际公约[①]和各国的仲裁立法实践[②]中得到了认可。尽管仲裁机构可以提供更高效的专业服务，但当事人选择机构仲裁解决纠纷并不总是最明智的选择，因为他们可能会失去临时仲裁本身具备的比较优势。例如，在临时仲裁中，当事人在挑选仲裁员方面享有较多的意思自治空间、在仲裁程序设计上拥有更大的灵活性以及更少的机构管理费用支出。[③] 随着当前机构仲裁的兴起，逐渐壮大的仲裁机构开始尝试拓展临时仲裁业务。众多的常设仲裁机构可以在适用《贸法会仲裁规则》的临时仲裁中，扮演指定机构的角色或者提供案件管理服务。随着仲裁机构积极参与临时仲裁，混合式仲裁大量出现在国际仲裁实践中。在这种混合式仲裁中，由仲裁机构参与并担任指定机构或者提供一定行政管理服务，同时适用《贸法会仲裁规则》或者其他临时仲裁规则。[④] 然而，混合式仲裁的大量出现不可避免地给机构仲裁和临时仲裁的传统划分带来了不小的挑战。此外，法院在对仲裁协议的效力进行司法审查的过程中也需要解决一个定性问题，即指定仲裁机构又约定适用《贸法会仲裁规则》的仲裁协议约定的是机构仲裁还是临时仲裁？这个定性问题在对临时仲裁持有怀疑态度的国家或者地区(如中国)显得尤为突出，对该问题的解决在一定程度上决定了处于司法审查中的仲裁协议是否有效。

因此，我们有必要对“临时仲裁机构化”趋势及其带来的相关问题进行探讨。为此，本文按照以下思路进行阐述：首先，揭示在世界范围内逐步兴起的以混合式仲裁的形式出现的“临时仲裁机构化”趋势。其次，鉴于中国仲裁法对

---

① 参见联合国《承认和执行外国仲裁裁决公约》(《纽约公约》，1958 年，纽约)第 1 条第 2 款，1959 年 6 月 7 日生效，330 U. N. T. S. 38；《欧洲国际商事仲裁公约》(1961 年，日内瓦)第 1 条第 2 款第 b 项，1964 年 1 月 7 日生效，484 U. N. T. S. 349；《关于解决国家与他国国民之间投资争议公约》(1965 年《华盛顿公约》)第 1 条，1966 年 10 月 14 日生效，575 U. N. T. S. 159。

② 如《联合国国际贸易法委员会国际商事仲裁示范法》第 2 条(a)项，U. N. G. A. Res. 61/33, U. N. Doc. A/61/453，2006 年 7 月 7 日修订；法国《民事诉讼法》第 1451 条、第 1455 条、第 1493 条、第 1495 条（法兰西共和国)；英国《1996 年仲裁法》(第 23 章，适用于英格兰、威尔士和北爱尔兰)第 3 条。

③ See Emmanuel Gaillard, John Savage (eds.), *Fouchard, Gaillard, Goldman On International Commercial Arbitration*, Kluwer Law International, 1999, p. 33; Harry L. Arkin, "International Ad Hoc Arbitration: A Practical Alternative", 15 *International Business Lawyer* 5, 1987, p. 5.

④ See Thomas H. Webster, *Handbook of UNCITRAL Arbitration*, Sweet & Maxwell, 2010, p. 12.

临时仲裁所持的否定态度,本文将探究临时仲裁机构化趋势蔓延到中国内地后在中国内地现行法律框架下会产生的法律问题。通过对2014年中国法院针对混合式仲裁作出的一个典型裁定进行分析,本文将深入探讨人民法院在对混合式仲裁进行司法审查时遇到的难题。最后,笔者提议,构建一个分三步走的多层次审查机制来帮助中国法院判断混合式仲裁的性质,即判断一个兼具机构仲裁和临时仲裁色彩的混合式仲裁是否为临时仲裁。

二、揭开"临时仲裁机构化"的面纱

1.《贸法会仲裁规则》与临时仲裁

《贸法会仲裁规则》最初在1976年通过的时候,是当时世界上唯一一套专门可适用于国际临时仲裁的程序规则。[①] 通过《贸法会仲裁规则》的联合国大会决议指明,这套全面的仲裁程序规则是专门为临时仲裁制度设计的。[②] 同时,这套程序规则是在与国际商事仲裁领域知名的国际仲裁机构进行广泛磋商后制定的。[③] 为了不断满足商业需求,联合国国际贸易法委员会(以下简称贸法会)在2010年对《贸法会仲裁规则》进行了一次大规模的修订。[④] 此外,贸法会规则有力促进了仲裁程序规则的高度趋同,许多仲裁机构全盘采纳了《贸法会仲裁规则》作为常用的程序规则,或者以这套规则为模板拟定自己的仲裁规则。[⑤]

---

① See Gary B. Born, *International Arbitration: Cases and Materials*, Wolters Kluwer, 2nd edn., 2015, p. 73.

② See U. N. G. A. Res. 31/98, 1976.

③ See U. N. G. A. Res. 31/98, 1976.

④ 《贸法会仲裁规则》(*Arbitration Rules of the United Nations Commission on International Trade Law*),1976年通过(U. N. G. A. Res. 31/98),于2010年修订(U. N. G. A. Res. 65/22),2013年《贸法会仲裁规则》吸纳了 *UNCITRAL Rules on Transparency for Treaty-Based Investor—State Arbitration* (U. N. G. A. Res. 68/109)。

⑤ See Gary B. Born, *International Arbitration: Cases and Materials*, Wolters Kluwer, 2nd edn., 2015, pp. 73-74. 例如,美国仲裁协会其及国际争议解决中心(American Arbitration Association and its International Centre for Dispute Resolution, AAA & ICDR),新加坡国际仲裁中心(Singapore International Arbitration Centre, SIAC),香港国际仲裁中心(Hong Kong International Arbitration Centre, HKIAC)和美洲商事仲裁委员会(Inter-American Commercial Arbitration Commission)。

《贸法会仲裁规则》被广泛认为是国际临时仲裁领域最主要的一套仲裁规则。[①] 但是，这并不意味着这套程序规则不能被仲裁机构援引适用于在其管理下的机构仲裁或者临时仲裁。事实上，《贸法会仲裁规则》从通过之日起一直被仲裁机构和其他有关机构(如商会和行会组织)以特定的方式援引适用。[②] 除了能够帮助仲裁机构以《贸法会仲裁规则》为模板拟定自己的仲裁规则外，《贸法会仲裁规则》还能被仲裁机构援用适用于由其参与并充当指定机构或者提供秘书、技术性管理服务的临时仲裁。[③] 但在这里必须明确区分仲裁机构在适用《贸法会仲裁规则》时担任指定机构和提供秘书、技术性管理服务所实现的不同功能。[④] 具体而言，仲裁机构担任指定机构所能实现的功能包括：[⑤]指定仲裁员、[⑥]关于对仲裁员的异议的决定或者更换仲裁员、[⑦]协助确定仲裁员的收费、[⑧]提出对费用交存问题的咨询意见。[⑨] 1982 年《贸法会建议》还提供了一个仲裁机构可以提供的秘书、技术性管理服务的清单，包括但不限于：转递当事一方和仲裁员的来往函电、协助仲裁庭安排庭审、安排仲裁庭庭审或者审议会议室、提供有关庭审的速记记录，以及其他方面的秘书或者文书助理工作。[⑩]

为提高仲裁效率，贸法会在 2012 年参照 2010 年修订的《贸法会仲裁规则》对 1982 年《贸法会建议》进行了相应修订。2012 年版的《贸法会建议》开篇就

---

① See Thomas H. Webster, *Handbook of UNCITRAL Arbitration*, Sweet & Maxwell, 2010, p. 11.

② 《根据〈联合国国际贸易法委员会仲裁规则〉在仲裁方面帮助仲裁机构和其他有关机构的建议》(1976 年)，于 1982 年通过，Supplement No. 17 (A/37/17)，以下简称 1982 年《贸法会建议》；《关于协助仲裁机构和其他有关机构根据〈贸易法委员会仲裁规则〉进行仲裁的建议》(2010 年修订本)，2012 年通过，U. N. G. A. Res. 67/90，以下简称 2012 年《贸法会建议》。下文对这两个文件的引用均以英文版本为准，包括页码的注明。

③ 1982 年《贸法会建议》，第 421~424 页(以《贸法会仲裁规则》为程序规则进行的临时仲裁可以有充当指定机构或者提供秘书、技术性质管理服务的仲裁机构参与和推动)。

④ 1982 年《贸法会建议》，第 17 段，第 422 页；值得注意的是 2012 年《贸法会建议》在第 15 页增加了一项仲裁机构可以提供的功能，即“对如何确定开支和收费的提议进行审查”。

⑤ 1982 年《贸法会建议》，第 422~423 页。

⑥ 《贸法会仲裁规则》(1976)，第 6 条，第 7 条第 2 款。

⑦ 《贸法会仲裁规则》(1976)，第 12 条第 1 款，第 13 条。

⑧ 《贸法会仲裁规则》(1976)，第 39 条。

⑨ 《贸法会仲裁规则》(1976)，第 41 条第(3)项。

⑩ 1982 年《贸法会建议》，第 423 页。

确定了仲裁机构或者其他有关机构使用《贸法会仲裁规则》的三种不同方式。首先,《贸法会仲裁规则》可以作为模板指导这些机构拟定自己的仲裁规则。[①] 其次,仲裁机构和其他有关机构可以根据《贸法会仲裁规则》对争议进行仲裁或者提供特定的行政服务。[②] 最后,仲裁机构能够按照《贸法会仲裁规则》的规定接受指派担任指定机构。[③] 上述三种仲裁机构使用《贸法会仲裁规则》的方式展现出《贸法会仲裁规则》在适用范围上的广泛性,即该套仲裁规则不仅可以适用于没有仲裁机构参与的临时仲裁,也可以适用于有仲裁机构参与的临时仲裁或者机构仲裁。

本文所关注的重点问题是与有仲裁机构参与并且提供秘书、技术性管理服务或者担任指定机构的"混合式仲裁"相关的定性问题。具体而言,在对仲裁进行司法审查的过程中,法院应当判断该"混合式仲裁"究竟是机构仲裁还是临时仲裁。

2. 关于担任指定机构或者提供管理服务的仲裁机构适用《贸法会仲裁规则》的程序指引

由常设仲裁机构或者贸法会制定的仲裁规则是国际商事仲裁程序法方面重要的法律渊源。仲裁规则本身具有契约性质,阐明了国际商事仲裁领域的程序惯例和基本原则。[④] 作为统一仲裁程序法领域最成功的一套仲裁规则,《贸法会仲裁规则》和相关的法律文件是在深入探究"临时仲裁机构化"这一趋势时需要参考的重要资料。在前述部分探讨的《贸法会建议》的启发和鼓励下,越来越多的仲裁机构已经修改了它们的仲裁程序规则,增订了与仲裁机构可以在临时仲裁中担任指定机构或者提供行政服务的内容相关的规定。例如,国际商会仲裁院(International Chamber of Commerce International Court of Arbitration)制定的《国际商会在联合国国际贸易法委员会仲裁或者其他临时仲裁中担任指

① 2012年《贸法会建议》,第4页,B节第5~9页。

② 2012年《贸法会建议》,第4页,C节第9~14页。

③ 2012年《贸法会建议》,第4页,D节第15~24页。

④ See Emmanuel Gaillard, John Savage (eds.), *Fouchard, Gaillard, Goldman On International Commercial Arbitration*, Kluwer Law International, 1999, p. 179.

定机构的相关规定》,[①]以及斯德哥尔摩商会单独制定的《斯德哥尔摩商会仲裁院在2010年〈贸法会仲裁规则〉下管理案件的程序规定》和《斯德哥尔摩商会仲裁院在2010年〈联合国国际贸易法委员会仲裁规则〉下担任指定机构的程序规定》。[②] 为适应"临时仲裁机构化"这一全球性的发展潮流,许多国家或者地区的商事仲裁机构已经单独制定了适用《贸法会仲裁规则》进行的贸法会仲裁的程序规则。[③] 最近,深圳国际仲裁院(SCIA)制定了《深圳国际仲裁院关于适用〈联合国国际贸易法委员会仲裁规则〉的程序指引》。[④] 通过这些专门为适用《贸法会仲裁规则》制定的程序规定,仲裁机构一般会指明它们是否会提供担任指定机构的服务,抑或提供秘书、技术性管理服务。一般而言,这些程序规则规定了仲裁机构可以提供的三种服务组合:(1)仅担任指定机构;(2)提供秘书、技术性管理服务而不担任指定机构;(3)同时担任指定机构和提供一般性质的行政管理服务。[⑤]

3. 临时仲裁机构化

在"临时仲裁机构化"潮流的推动下,有相当数量的仲裁机构常常会按照

---

① International Chamber of Commerce (ICC) International Court of Arbitration: *Rules of ICC as Appointing Authority in UNCITRAL or Other Ad Hoc Arbitration Proceedings*,自2004年1月1日起生效。

② The Arbitration Institute of Stockholm Chamber of Commerce (SCC): *SCC Procedures for the Administration of Cases under the* 2010 *UNCITRAL Arbitration Rules & SCC Procedures as Appointing Authority under the* 2010 *UNCITRAL Arbitration Rules.*

③ American Arbitration Association (AAA) International Centre of Dispute Resolution (ICDR)(美国仲裁协会其及国际争议解决中心): *Procedures for Cases under the UNCITRAL Arbitration Rules*; Singapore International Arbitration Centre (SIAC)(新加坡国际仲裁中心): *Practice Note on Case Administration of Arbitrators & Financial Management for Cases under the UNCITRAL Rules* 2010; Hong Kong International Arbitration Centre (HKIAC)(香港国际仲裁中心): *the* 2015 *HKIAC Procedures for the Administration of Arbitration under the UNCITRAL Arbitration Rules*, effective as of 1 January 2015; Swiss Chambers' Arbitration Institution (SCAI)(瑞士商会仲裁院): *Rules of the Swiss Chambers' Arbitration Institution as Appointing Authority in UNCITRAL or other Ad Hoc Arbitration Proceedings*; Deutsche Institution für Schiedsgerichtswesen (DIS)(德国仲裁院): *UNCITRAL-Arbitration Rules Administered by the DIS*, entered into force on 1 May 2012。

④ 深圳国际仲裁院,又称"华南国际经济贸易仲裁委员会":《深圳国际仲裁院关于适用〈联合国国际贸易法委员会仲裁规则〉的程序指引》,自2016年12月1日起施行。关于该《程序指引》的讨论,参见本文第三部分中2标题(3)的相关内容。

⑤ 2012年《贸法会建议》,第14页。

《贸法会仲裁规则》、《贸法会建议》或者仲裁机构程序规则的有关规定参与临时仲裁,不是通过担任指定机构的方式,就是通过提供一定行政管理服务的方式,或者两者皆有。于是,有仲裁机构积极参与的混合式临时仲裁应运而生,给“临时仲裁程序没有仲裁机构参与”这一传统观念带来了冲击。从本质上讲,有仲裁机构积极参与的混合式临时仲裁在法律性质上仍旧是为满足当事人的特殊需要而适用一套临时仲裁规则的临时仲裁。但是,仲裁机构的积极参与使这类混合式临时仲裁与严格意义上没有仲裁机构参与的临时仲裁有明显区别。此外,一些仲裁机构甚至独立起草了一套与机构仲裁规则并行适用的临时仲裁规则。① 因此,当事人可以将他们之间的纠纷提交至这些仲裁机构,通过适用机构仲裁规则或者适用临时仲裁规则组成仲裁庭来解决纠纷。这种兼具机构仲裁与临时仲裁色彩的混合式临时仲裁就是本文所主要讨论的“临时仲裁机构化”的具体表现。

正如仲裁界学者评论的那样,首先,“临时仲裁机构化”会使临时仲裁程序本身给当事人带来的灵活性和便宜性等利益或者好处大打折扣。② 其次,“临时仲裁机构化”会让临时仲裁与机构仲裁之间的分界线模糊不清,仅凭仲裁程序是否有仲裁机构参与已经无法准确判断该仲裁程序是机构仲裁还是临时仲裁。③ 最后,在临时仲裁与机构仲裁之间的分界线日益模糊的情况下,法院在司法审查中需要采用多层次审查机制来判断“混合式临时仲裁”的性质,即判断这种仲裁是机构仲裁还是临时仲裁。④

---

① 保加利亚工商会(Bulgarian Chamber of Commerce and Industry):Rules Concerning Ad Hoc Arbitration Assisted by the Court of Arbitration at the Bulgarian Chamber of Commerce and Industry, adopted on 17 January 1989;珠海仲裁委员会:《横琴自由贸易试验区临时仲裁规则》,自2017年4月15日施行;广州仲裁委员会:《中国互联网仲裁联盟临时仲裁与机构仲裁对接规则》,自2017年9月19日通过并生效。

② See Emmanuel Gaillard, John Savage (eds.), *Fouchard, Gaillard, Goldman On International Commercial Arbitration*, Kluwer Law International, 1999, p. 33.

③ 在2014年浙江逸盛案中,人民法院在对涉案仲裁协议进行司法审查的过程中要解决的一个有关定性的问题就是既指定中国国际经济贸易仲裁委员会对涉案纠纷进行仲裁又约定适用《贸法会仲裁规则》的仲裁协议约定的是机构仲裁,抑或临时仲裁。

④ 参见本文第五部分。

三、中国仲裁法律下的“临时仲裁机构化”之审查

1. 中国仲裁法律关于临时仲裁的规定

中国《仲裁法》[①]和相关司法解释(如最高人民法院《关于适用〈中华人民共和国仲裁法〉若干问题的解释》,以下简称《2006年司法解释》[②])并未对临时仲裁进行界定。尽管如此,从严格意义上讲,中国法律不允许在中国内地范围内进行临时仲裁,即仲裁地为中国内地的临时仲裁缺乏合法性基础。[③] 这一观点源于对《仲裁法》第16条和第18条的严格解释。《仲裁法》第16条规定了有效的仲裁协议在中国法律框架下必须具备的三个要件,其中一个要件就是明确选定解决纠纷的仲裁机构。[④] 从另一个角度来看,《仲裁法》第18条则对没有明确约定仲裁机构时仲裁协议的效力作出了规定:“仲裁协议对仲裁事项或者仲裁委员会没有约定或者约定不明确的,当事人可以补充协议;达不成补充协议的,仲裁协议无效。”最高人民法院对《仲裁法》第16条和第18条采取了严格解释的方法,认为仲裁地位于中国内地的仲裁应当是机构仲裁,[⑤]因而仲裁地在中国内地的临时仲裁是被禁止的。[⑥]

---

① 中国《仲裁法》,1994年8月31日第八届全国人民代表大会常务委员会第九次会议通过,自1995年9月1日起施行,2009年8月27日进行第一次修正,2017年9月进行第二次修正。

② 最高人民法院《关于适用〈中华人民共和国仲裁法〉若干问题的解释》,法释〔2006〕7号,2005年12月26日由最高人民法院审判委员会第1375次会议通过,自2006年9月8日起施行。

③ See, e. g., Tietie Zhang, “Enforceability of Ad Hoc Arbitration Agreements in China: China's Incomplete Ad Hoc Arbitration System”, 46 *Cornell International Law Journal* 361, 2013, p. 367; Wang Wenying, “Distinct Features of Arbitration in China: An Historical Perspective”, 23 *Journal of International Arbitration* 49, 2006, p. 49.

④ 《仲裁法》第16条规定:“……仲裁协议应当具有下列内容:(一)请求仲裁的意思表示;(二)仲裁事项;(三)选定的仲裁委员会。”

⑤ 《2006年司法解释》第16条是关于判断涉外仲裁协议效力的法律适用问题的冲突法规范。该条规定:“对涉外仲裁协议的效力审查,适用当事人约定的法律;当事人没有约定适用的法律但约定了仲裁地的,适用仲裁地法律;没有约定适用的法律也没有约定仲裁地或者仲裁地约定不明的,适用法院地法律。”因此,如果当事人约定了判断涉外仲裁协议效力的准据法以认可临时仲裁协议的效力,如中国香港特别行政区法律,或者明确约定允许临时仲裁的仲裁地,如中国香港特别行政区,那么在中国内地法律下无效的临时仲裁协议可以在中国香港特别行政区法律下被认定为有效。

⑥ 《2006年司法解释》第4~6条。

关于有效的仲裁协议必须明确选定仲裁机构的规定,造成了大量临时仲裁裁决被人民法院拒绝承认和执行。[①] 不仅如此,基于临时仲裁协议作出的仲裁裁决也会被人民法院以违反我国《仲裁法》第16条和第18条及相关司法解释为由撤销。其中,关于判断没有选定仲裁机构的涉外仲裁协议效力的司法审查案件,最著名的莫过于2003年"旭普林"案。[②] 该案的双方当事人在仲裁协议中约定:"Arbitration: ICC Rules, Shanghai shall apply."最高人民法院在回复中认为,根据确认仲裁条款效力准据法的一般原则,应当按照仲裁地的法律,即中国法律,认定所涉仲裁条款的效力。[③] 在给江苏省高级人民法院的回复中,最高人民法院以该案所涉仲裁条款没有明确指出仲裁机构为由,认定该仲裁条款无效。最高人民法院在"旭普林"案中予以明确的仲裁协议须指明仲裁机构的立场,在《2006年司法解释》第4条中以司法解释的形式予以确定。[④] 由此看来,虽然《仲裁法》并未明文规定排除以中国内地为仲裁地进行临时仲裁的可能性,但是从中国的立法和相关司法实践可以推出以下结论:如果当事人约定的仲裁地在中国内地,那么他们只能通过机构仲裁的方式来解决争端,而临时仲裁则是不被允许的。[⑤] 该结论不仅仅是对《仲裁法》第16条和第18条进行严格解释的结果,在司法实践中也曾被最高人民法院在"中国人民保险公司广

---

① See, e.g., Tietie Zhang, "Enforceability of Ad Hoc Arbitration Agreements in China: China's Incomplete Ad Hoc Arbitration System", 46 *Cornell International Law Journal* 361, 2013, p. 367; Wang Wenying, "Distinct Features of Arbitration in China: An Historical Perspective", 23 *Journal of International Arbitration* 49, 2006, pp. 367-368.

② 最高人民法院《关于德国旭普林国际有限责任公司与无锡沃可通用工程橡胶有限公司申请确认仲裁协议效力一案的请示的复函》,〔2003〕民四他字第23号,2004年7月8日颁布。

③ 最高人民法院《关于德国旭普林国际有限责任公司与无锡沃可通用工程橡胶有限公司申请确认仲裁协议效力一案的请示的复函》,〔2003〕民四他字第23号,2004年7月8日颁布。关于中国法院确认仲裁条款效力的准据法一般原则,参见《2006年司法解释》第16条。

④ 《2006年司法解释》第4条规定:"仲裁协议仅约定纠纷适用的仲裁规则的,视为未约定仲裁机构,但当事人达成补充协议或者按照约定的仲裁规则能够确定仲裁机构的除外。"

⑤ See Weixia Gu, "Arbitration in China", in Tom Ginsburg & Shahla Ali (eds.), *International Commercial Arbitration In Asia*, Juris Publishing LLC, 2013, p. 88; See, e.g.; Tietie Zhang, "Enforceability of Ad Hoc Arbitration Agreements in China: China's Incomplete Ad Hoc Arbitration System", 46 *Cornell International Law Journal* 361, 2013, p. 367; Wang Wenying, "Distinct Features of Arbitration in China: An Historical Perspective", 23 *Journal of International Arbitration* 49, 2006, p. 377.

东省分公司与广东广合电力有限公司等保险合同纠纷案”中采纳作为民事裁定书的裁决理由。[①] 该案所涉仲裁协议约定：“仲裁：有关本保险单的一切争议应提交给争议双方书面指定的一位仲裁人裁决，或如果双方就聘请一位单独的仲裁人不能取得一致意见，则从任何一方提出书面要求之日起，争议双方在一个日历月份内以书面各自指定一位仲裁人；如果双方仲裁人仍不能取得一致意见，则由双方仲裁人书面指定一位裁决人。裁决人将与仲裁人一起主持仲裁会议，其所作的裁判决定将是本公司承担赔偿责任的先决条件。”在该案中，最高人民法院认为，该仲裁协议违反了《仲裁法》第 16 条第 2 款的规定，并且没有根据《仲裁法》第 18 条达成关于选定仲裁机构的补充协议，因而认定本案所涉仲裁协议无效。

2. 中国内地有限度地引进临时仲裁与中国内地的“临时仲裁机构化”

(1) 中国内地法律有限度地认可临时仲裁的域内合法性

一般而言，临时仲裁协议和基于临时仲裁协议作出的仲裁裁决在中国现行法律下是无效的，临时仲裁裁决是可以被人民法院以没有指明仲裁机构为由撤销的。尽管如此，在中国内地以外的地方作出的临时仲裁裁决在中国内地是可以被人民法院承认和执行的。这要归功于《承认及执行外国仲裁裁决公约》[②]（以下简称《纽约公约》）和一系列区际双边安排。[③] 临时仲裁裁决在《纽约公约》第 1 条第 2 款规定的“仲裁裁决”所包含的范围之内，并且中国在批准加入《纽约公约》时并没有作出排除公约适用于临时仲裁裁决的保留。[④] 对于通过区际

---

① 中国人民保险公司广东省分公司与广东广合电力有限公司等保险合同纠纷案，中华人民共和国最高人民法院民事裁定书，(2002)民四终字第 29 号，判决日期：2002 年 10 月 31 日。

② 参见联合国《承认和执行外国仲裁裁决公约》(《纽约公约》，1958 年，纽约)，第 1 条第 2 款，1959 年 6 月 7 日生效，330 U. N. T. S. 38；最高人民法院《关于执行我国加入的〈承认与执行外国仲裁裁决公约〉的通知》[法(经)发〔1987〕5 号，1987 年 4 月 10 日发布]。

③ 最高人民法院《关于认可和执行台湾地区仲裁裁决的规定》(法释〔2015〕14 号)，2015 年 7 月 1 日生效；最高人民法院《关于内地与澳门特别行政区相互认可和执行仲裁裁决的安排》(法释〔2007〕17 号)，2008 年 1 月 1 日实施；最高人民法院《关于内地与香港特别行政区相互执行仲裁裁决的安排》(法释〔2000〕3 号)，2000 年 2 月 1 日实施。

④ 《纽约公约》第 1 条第 2 款规定：“仲裁裁决一词不仅指专案选派之仲裁员所作裁决，亦指当事人提请裁断之常设仲裁机构所作裁决。”这条关于仲裁裁决的定义的规定中的“专案选派之仲裁员所作裁决”被广泛解释为临时仲裁裁决。

双边安排承认和执行临时仲裁裁决,最高人民法院在2009年发布了一则关于在中国内地执行于我国香港特别行政区作出的临时仲裁裁决的通知。[①] 该通知旨在指导人民法院在审查于香港特别行政区作出的临时仲裁裁决,认为只要不存在最高人民法院《关于内地与香港特别行政区相互执行仲裁裁决的安排》第7条规定的情形,在香港特别行政区作出的临时仲裁裁决可以在内地得到执行。换言之,在香港特别行政区作出的临时仲裁裁决原则上在内地是可以被承认和执行的。正是基于最高人民法院对在香港特别行政区作出的临时仲裁裁决在承认和执行方面的友好态度,深圳国际仲裁院在其制定的《深圳国际仲裁院关于适用〈联合国国际贸易法委员会仲裁规则〉的程序指引》第3条中推定仲裁地为香港特别行政区,除非当事人另有约定或者仲裁庭另有决定。[②] 在程序指引中加入该项对仲裁地的推定,是为了降低已经作出的临时仲裁裁决在中国内地法院被拒绝承认和执行的风险。在当前中国内地法律对临时仲裁仍持有排斥和怀疑态度的情况下,此种规定甚为必要。同理,在我国澳门特别行政区作出的临时仲裁裁决,原则上在中国内地也可以得到执行。[③]

如上所述,在符合一定条件的情况下,在仲裁地位于中国内地以外的地方作出的临时仲裁裁决可以在中国内地得到承认和执行。然而,在中国内地作出的临时仲裁裁决被人民法院承认和执行的案例则十分少见。据笔者所知,目前只有一个公众可知的在中国内地作出的仲裁裁决由当事人自愿履行。[④] 总而

---

① 最高人民法院《关于香港仲裁裁决在内地执行的有关问题的通知》(法〔2009〕415号,2009年12月30日实施)。

② 《深圳国际仲裁院关于适用〈联合国国际贸易法委员会仲裁规则〉的程序指引》第3条规定:"当事人对仲裁地有约定的,从其约定。当事人没有约定的,仲裁地为香港,除非仲裁庭另有决定。"深圳国际仲裁员案件管理处的办案秘书告诉笔者,该条规定是SCIA在草拟该程序指引的过程中与最高人民法院法官和香港律师界从事仲裁业务的人士进行广泛商谈的智慧结晶。

③ 最高人民法院《关于印发〈全国法院涉港澳商事审判工作座谈会纪要〉的通知》(法发〔2008〕8号,2008年1月21日颁布)第25条。

④ 该案为1999年中国外运北京公司大连分公司与海南东大海洋运输公司的租船合同纠纷案。胡正良教授在此案中接受双方指定担任独任仲裁员,对双方当事人之间的争议以"调解意见书"的形式予以解决。但是,时任中国国际经济贸易仲裁委员会副秘书长康明先生认为,该"调解意见书"实质上是一份临时仲裁裁决,仲裁程序是以临时仲裁的方式进行的。参见康明:《临时仲裁的成功实践以及相应的思考》,载《国际商法论丛》2003年第1期。

言之,仲裁地位于中国内地的临时仲裁在中国现行法律下原则上是不被允许的,因此在中国内地作出的临时仲裁裁决面临着被人民法院拒绝承认和执行或者被依法撤销的风险。但是,禁止在中国内地进行临时仲裁的原则性规定在一定情形下出现了松动的迹象,在中国内地有限度地承认临时仲裁的域内合法性已成为大势所趋,尤其考虑到临时仲裁本身具备的优势和当前“临时仲裁机构化”这一全球趋势。

(2)在中国内地自由贸易试验区有限度地引进临时仲裁

中国内地对临时仲裁所长期持有的否定态度根源于人们对政府机构或者公共部门的过度依赖以及对替代性争议解决方式(ADRs)的不信任。然而,“临时仲裁机构化”这一潮流吸引仲裁机构积极参与临时仲裁并扮演辅助性角色,降低了中国内地仲裁届人士和商业人士对没有仲裁机构参与的临时仲裁的排斥态度。为顺应这一潮流,最高人民法院于 2016 年在中国内地有限度地放宽对临时仲裁的限制,允许临时仲裁成为可供当事人选择的替代性争议解决机制之一。中国内地对临时仲裁态度的转变,要归功于最高人民法院发布的为自由贸易试验区的发展提供司法保障的工作文件。① 最高人民法院《关于为自由贸易试验区建设提供司法保障的意见》(以下简称《自贸区保障意见》)第 9 条第 3 款规定:“在自贸试验区内注册的企业相互之间约定在内地特定地点、按照特定仲裁规则、由特定人员对有关争议进行仲裁的,可以认定该仲裁协议有效。人民法院认为该仲裁协议无效的,应报请上一级法院进行审查。上级法院同意下级法院意见的,应将其审查意见层报最高人民法院,待最高人民法院答复后作出裁定。”尽管可能不包含涉外因素,但是适用于涉外仲裁案件或者国际仲裁案件的层报审查制度可被参照适用于在自贸区注册的企业提起的临时仲裁

① 参见最高人民法院《关于为自由贸易试验区建设提供司法保障的意见》(法发〔2016〕34 号,2016 年 12 月 30 日颁布实施)第 9 条。

(又称为“三特定仲裁”)。①

《自贸区保障意见》关于在中国内地自由贸易试验区有限度地引进临时仲裁的规定引发了中国仲裁法学界和实务届人士的热议,他们对该意见第9条第3款与《仲裁法》第16条和第18条的不协调颇有异议。此外,最高人民法院发布的工作文件仅许可在自由贸易试验区有限度地开展临时仲裁,这是否意味着在这些试验区开辟“法外之地”? 这也是一个有待论证的命题。尽管面临着许多质疑和挑战,但是将临时仲裁引入中国内地是不可逆转的趋势,并且已经得到了最高人民法院的大力支持。在这一背景下,珠海仲裁委员会在2017年颁布并通过了《横琴自由贸易试验区临时仲裁规则》(以下简称《横琴临时仲裁规则》)。《横琴临时仲裁规则》仅适用于在自由贸易试验区内注册的企业之间的临时仲裁,并且是依托《自贸区保障意见》制定的。② 该套规则明确规定,在当事人没有约定指定仲裁员或者其他指定仲裁员机构不能完成仲裁员指定的情况下,珠海仲裁委员为指定仲裁员机构。③ 通过该套规则的实施,珠海仲裁委员会在将临时仲裁制度引入横琴自由贸易试验区的过程中扮演了主导角色,并且仲裁机构的积极参与使得自由贸易试验区的临时仲裁制度附带强烈的混合式仲裁的特征,这也是中国临时仲裁制度的一大特色。

(3)《深圳国际仲裁院关于适用〈联合国国际贸易法委员会仲裁规则〉的程序指引》

为了在深圳前海自由贸易试验区开展临时仲裁业务,深圳国际仲裁院结合《贸法会建议》的相关规定,并参照其他仲裁机构制定的适用《贸法会仲裁规则》的特定程序规则,制定了《深圳国际仲裁院关于适用〈联合国国际贸易法委员会仲裁规则〉的程序指引》。深圳国际仲裁院制定的程序指引自2016年12

---

① 关于中国法院在处理涉外仲裁案件或者国际仲裁案件时需要适用的层报审查制度,参见最高人民法院发布的两个工作文件:最高人民法院《关于人民法院处理与涉外仲裁及外国仲裁事项有关问题的通知》(法发〔1995〕18号,1995年8月28日实施),第1条;最高人民法院《关于人民法院撤销涉外仲裁裁决有关事项的通知》(法〔1998〕40号,1998年4月23日实施)。

② 《横琴临时仲裁规则》第1条。

③ 《横琴临时仲裁规则》第3条。

月1日起实施,旨在为在深圳前海自由贸易试验区注册的企业提供临时仲裁服务,并为基于多边或者双边投资条约发起的投资仲裁提供平台。[①] 这是目前已知的第一个由中国仲裁机构专门制定的可以适用《贸法会仲裁规则》并担任仲裁员指定机构的程序规则。该适用《贸法会仲裁规则》的程序指引规定了深圳国际仲裁院能够进行的管理事项和提供的服务,包括指定仲裁员、就仲裁员回避作出决定、仲裁案件财务管理等管理事项和协助仲裁庭与当事人之间、当事人互相之间的通信联系、协助转递当事人的财产保全等申请、提供庭审服务、推荐调解机构或者谈判促进机构等服务项目。[②] 依照该程序指引,当事人可以将争议提交至深圳国际仲裁院,但是可以选择适用2013年版《贸法会仲裁规则》进行机构仲裁,或仅请求深圳国际仲裁院在临时仲裁程序中担任指定机构或者提供管理服务。[③] 在制定适用《贸法会仲裁规则》的程序指引时,深圳国际仲裁院考虑到中国内地法律不许在域内通过临时仲裁解决纠纷,因而在该程序指引的第3条特别规定除非仲裁庭另有规定,在当事人对仲裁地没有约定的情况下推定仲裁地为对临时仲裁持欢迎态度的香港特别行政区。

四、“临时仲裁机构化”在中国内地仲裁法语境下可能面临的法律问题

在中国法律语境下,“临时仲裁机构化”面临的主要法律问题即混合式仲裁协议的定性。“2014年浙江逸盛案”触及该问题,下面对该案的相关情况和法律问题进行分析。

1. 中国内地关于混合式仲裁的标志性案例:“2014年浙江逸盛案”

“2014年浙江逸盛案”是中国法院首次承认混合式仲裁协议法律效力的标志性案例,法院在该案中明确允许当事人基于合意将双方争议提交至中国的仲

---

① 《深圳国际仲裁院关于适用〈联合国国际贸易法委员会仲裁规则〉的程序指引》。笔者曾就该程序指引的起草动机采访了深圳国际仲裁院秘书迟文卉。据她了解,该程序指引的制定只是深圳国际仲裁院吸引国际客户前来中国寻求利用临时仲裁制度或者投资仲裁制度解决商事或者投资纠纷的第一步。

② 《深圳国际仲裁院关于适用〈联合国国际贸易法委员会仲裁规则〉的程序指引》第4条。

③ 《深圳国际仲裁院关于适用〈联合国国际贸易法委员会仲裁规则〉的程序指引》第4条、第12条。

裁机构加以解决,但是可以约定仲裁庭适用《贸法会仲裁规则》,而不适用受理案件的仲裁机构本身制定的机构仲裁规则。[①] 申请人浙江逸盛石化有限公司(以下简称逸盛)与被申请人英威达技术有限公司(卢森堡)(以下简称英威达)之间达成的仲裁协议约定:"仲裁应在中国北京中国国际经济贸易中心(CIETAC)进行,并适用现行有效的联合国国际贸易法委员会仲裁规则。"[②]申请人逸盛向宁波市中级人民法院(以下简称宁波中院)申请确认该仲裁条款无效,因为双方达成的仲裁条款属于典型的关于临时仲裁的约定,为中国法律所禁止。但是,被申请人英威达答辩称本案仲裁条款明确约定贸仲委(CIETAC)为仲裁机构,属于典型的关于机构仲裁的约定,在中国内地法律下应为有效。在通过层报审查制度得到最高人民法院关于本案仲裁协议效力认定的复函意见后,宁波中院作出裁定,认为双方当事人虽然对所选定的仲裁机构名称表述有误但能够确定具体的仲裁机构,应当认定选定了仲裁机构,该仲裁协议并不违反中国《仲裁法》的规定,应属有效。[③] 但无论是最高人民法院关于此案的复函,还是宁波中院在民事裁定书中的说理部分,均仅局限于对本案仲裁条款是否明确选定仲裁机构这一问题进行认定,并未正面回应当事人的答辩意见所关注的焦点问题,即当事人在本案仲裁条款中约定的是机构仲裁还是临时仲裁。作为关于中国法院如何认定混合式仲裁协议效力问题的典型个案,"2014年浙江逸盛案"被列入最高人民法院为"一带一路"建设提供司法服务和保障的典型案例。[④] 在对该典型案例的评述部分,最高人民法院阐明,在"2014年浙江逸盛案"中,中国法院首次认可当事人约定由中国的常设仲裁机构依据《贸法会

① 浙江逸盛石化有限公司诉英威达技术有限公司(卢森堡)申请确认仲裁协议效力纠纷案,(2012)浙涌仲字确第4号民事裁定书,审结日期:2014年3月21日。

② 浙江逸盛石化有限公司诉英威达技术有限公司(卢森堡)申请确认仲裁协议效力纠纷案,(2012)浙涌仲字确第4号民事裁定书,审结日期:2014年3月21日。见涉案双方签订的《技术许可协议》第11.2条。

③ 参见最高人民法院《关于浙江逸盛石化有限公司申请确认仲裁条款效力一案请示的复函》,〔2013〕民四他字第60号,2013年12月18日;(2012)浙涌仲字确第4号民事裁定书。

④ 典型案例之六,依据最高人民法院《关于人民法院为"一带一路"建设提供司法服务和保障的若干意见》,法发〔2015〕9号,2015年6月16日发布。

仲裁规则》管理仲裁程序的仲裁条款的效力,并明确该条款约定的是机构仲裁,而非临时仲裁。鉴于该案例树立的典型示范意义,人民法院以后在认定当事人既约定中国的常设仲裁机构又约定适用《贸法会仲裁规则》的仲裁条款效力时,应当参照最高人民法院在"2014 年浙江逸盛案"中的"一刀切"做法,认定其有效且是关于机构仲裁的约定。

在"2014 年浙江逸盛案"中,虽然双方当事人花费了大量篇幅争论本案中的仲裁条款约定的是机构仲裁抑或临时仲裁,但是最高人民法院和宁波中院并未直接回应该焦点问题,错过了利用本案对中国内地仲裁法语境下的临时仲裁进行定义和定性的良机。尽管如此,本案为讨论在中国法律下区分机构仲裁和临时仲裁提供了重要素材,本案当事人双方在辩论环节围绕临时仲裁定性问题提出的论点、一审承办法官在结案后发表的文章都是可供参考的材料。[①]

2. 逸盛认为双方约定的是临时仲裁的论据

逸盛向宁波中院申请确认仲裁条款无效的理由主要有三个:首先,双方争议的仲裁条款没有明确选定中国《仲裁法》第 16 条所定义的"仲裁委员会";其次,该条款属于典型的临时仲裁条款,因为双方约定适用的是通常用于临时仲裁的《贸法会仲裁规则》;最后,已经开始的仲裁程序是按照临时仲裁方式进行的。逸盛在选择辩论策略时注意到了中国《仲裁法》第 16 条关于"选定的仲裁委员会"这一效力要件的规定,即如果该仲裁条款被认定为临时仲裁条款,该协议在中国内地现行法律下是无效的。

3. 英威达认为双方约定的是机构仲裁的论据

同样,首先,考虑到中国内地现行法律不认可临时仲裁,英威达极力主张本案仲裁条款已经明确选定贸仲委(CIETAC)为仲裁机构,因此该仲裁条款是在中国现行法律下有效的机构仲裁条款。从另一个角度讲,英威达认为,如果双方当事人意图进行临时仲裁,就完全没有必要在仲裁条款中列出该仲裁机构的名称。其次,《贸法会仲裁规则》并非临时仲裁专用规则,而可以广泛适用于世

① 参见胡曙炜、赵江涛:《常设仲裁机构亦可适用 UNCITRAL 仲裁规则》,载《人民司法(案例)》2014 年第 18 期。

界各地的机构仲裁。最后,本案已经进行的仲裁程序是按照机构仲裁的方式进行的,而非按照逸盛所主张的临时仲裁程序进行。因此,英威达认为,法院应当尊重当事人的意思自治,贯彻支持仲裁的精神,认可该案约定机构仲裁的仲裁条款的效力。

4. 宁波中院裁定书未决的法律问题之刍议

虽然宁波中院的庭审法官在民事裁定书中没有直接回应双方当事人在辩论环节提出的争议问题(本案所涉仲裁条款约定的是机构仲裁抑或临时仲裁),但是该案的一位承办法官在一篇文章中表达了自己对这个问题的看法。首先,他对临时仲裁的含义及其与机构仲裁的区别进行了解读,认为:"临时仲裁是相对于机构仲裁的概念。机构仲裁是指由常设仲裁机构进行管理,一般依据该家仲裁机构自己的仲裁规则进行的仲裁。相对机构仲裁而言,临时仲裁可以概括为无需任何仲裁机构进行程序上的管理或控制,根据当事人之间签订的仲裁协议或事后协商的程序规则,产生仲裁员组成仲裁庭负责审理争议,并在作出裁决后自行解散的仲裁。"其次,他重申了在中国《仲裁法》第16条和第18条的规定下临时仲裁协议无效这一立场,同时他也强调双方约定适用《贸法会仲裁规则》并不足以证明该仲裁条款约定的是临时仲裁。[①] 为了佐证这一观点,他也援引了许多国际仲裁机构可以适用《贸法会仲裁规则》来管理仲裁程序的国际实践,并且指出,贸仲委(CIETAC)在其制定的仲裁规则中为适用《贸法会仲裁规则》管理仲裁程序已经作出了相关规定。[②]

相较宁波中院在民事裁定书中没有对双方的争议点进行回应,这位庭审法官在文章中分享了他的论证逻辑和法律推理,其中有两点尤其值得关注。首先,虽然中国《仲裁法》对临时仲裁未曾有定义,但该法官表达了自己对临时仲裁这个概念的理解,并且总结临时仲裁区别于机构仲裁的三个显著特征。其次,该法官注意到了在国际层面兴起的"临时仲裁机构化"潮流,越来越多的国

① 参见胡曙炜、赵江涛:《常设仲裁机构亦可适用 UNCITRAL 仲裁规则》,载《人民司法(案例)》2014年第18期。

② 参见《中国国际经济贸易委员会仲裁规则》(2012年版)第4条第3款。现行的《中国国际经济贸易委员会仲裁规则》(2015年版)保留了该条款,没有对此作出实质更改。

际仲裁机构开始选择适用《贸法会仲裁规则》管理仲裁程序。但在他看来，即使仲裁机构适用《贸法会仲裁规则》进行仲裁，这些仲裁仍然属于机构仲裁而非临时仲裁。然而，在作出此种定性时，该法官并没有深入考察仲裁机构在仲裁程序中扮演的角色以及其他事实因素。在仲裁机构仅为适用《贸法会仲裁规则》的临时仲裁提供秘书、技术性管理服务的情形下，这种"一刀切"定性的做法显得有些武断。

五、结论

尽管机构仲裁与临时仲裁之间存在许多区别，但是在实务中仍然很难仅凭仲裁机构是否参与仲裁程序这一简单事实来判断混合式仲裁是临时仲裁还是机构仲裁。尤其在"临时仲裁机构化"这一趋势下，由于仲裁机构通过适用《贸法会仲裁规则》或其他临时仲裁规则积极参与临时仲裁业务，临时仲裁与机构仲裁之间的分界线变得更加模糊。区分临时仲裁与机构仲裁的传统标准是仲裁程序是否在形式上由一个常设仲裁机构进行管理。[①] 另外，正如加里·B. 博恩(Gary B. Born)教授评论的那样，机构仲裁一般是适用机构仲裁规则，并且几乎都是由一个指定机构来协助组成仲裁庭并且确定仲裁员收费或者其他支出。[②] 但对于以"2014 年浙江逸盛案"为代表的案件，这些学者提出的判断方法仍然略显粗简。

在中国外运北京公司大连分公司与海南东大海洋运输公司租船合同纠纷案中，即使最后的裁决是以"调解意见书"的形式作出的，但仍被视为临时仲裁裁决的原因主要有三个：首先，当事人将纠纷提交仲裁解决的意图在合同条款以及他们与胡正良教授的通信往来中表达得清晰明确，而且没有仲裁机构被选定。其次，双方都坚持己见，互不相让，同时请求胡正良教授作为公正中立的第三方依据与航运和货物运输相关的规则或者惯例对双方纠纷作出裁决。最后，

---

① See e. g., Gerald Aksen, "Ad Hoc Versus Institutional Versus Institutional Arbitration", 1 *ICC International Court Arbitration Bulletin* 2, 1991, p. 8.

② See Gary B. Born, *International Arbitration*: *Cases and Materials*, Wolters Kluwer, 2nd edn., 2015, p. 69.

根据相关参与人士的观察,该案程序是按照临时仲裁的程序开展的,并且胡正良教授最后选择以"调解意见书"的形式作出裁决,正是因为考虑到中国法律不认可在中国内地开展临时仲裁。这些背后的考量和观察能够给法官和其他仲裁实务者就如何通过多层次审查的方式判断混合式仲裁是否临时仲裁提供一定的借鉴。

这个多层次审查机制包含了三个渐进式的具体步骤,需要审查若干区分临时仲裁与机构仲裁的相关因素。第一步是对仲裁协议进行合理解释以充分尊重当事人意思自治。在解释的过程中,应当基于支持仲裁的精神探究当事人的意图,到底是要通过机构仲裁还是临时仲裁的方式解决纠纷。如果仲裁协议没有指明仲裁机构或者没有选择适用机构仲裁规则,那么应当推论当事人意图通过临时仲裁的方式解决纠纷。反之,如果仲裁协议明确选定了一个仲裁机构参与仲裁程序,但是选择适用《贸法会仲裁规则》或者其他临时仲裁规则,那就需要通过第二步来做具体的判断。第二步是对被选定的仲裁机构在仲裁程序中扮演的角色或者实现的功能进行考察。即使当事人双方约定适用《贸法会仲裁规则》或者其他临时仲裁规则,如果被选定的仲裁机构从一开始的指定仲裁员到最终的确定仲裁费用或者审查裁决全程参与并进行管理,那么该仲裁程序应当被认定为机构仲裁。但是如果仲裁机构只负责帮助指定首席仲裁员或者提供秘书性质的行政服务,如速记或者同声传译等服务,不参与其他程序的管理或者控制,那么应当推定该仲裁程序为临时仲裁。第三步,审查者应当检查已经进行的程序的特征和在指定仲裁员环节当事人与仲裁员之间的通信记录,以便最终确认该仲裁程序是机构仲裁还是临时仲裁。这一套分三步走的多层次审查机制旨在为人民法院在仲裁司法审查中区分机构仲裁和临时仲裁提供参考,尤其是在遇到类似于"2014年浙江逸盛案"中的混合式仲裁的情况时能够明确判断是否临时仲裁。与最高人民法院和宁波中院采取的"一刀切"的做法相比,这套多层次审查机制更具合理性。

热点 时评

准确解读《若干意见》 合力提高仲裁公信力

姜丽丽*

摘要:《关于完善仲裁制度 提高仲裁公信力的若干意见》(以下简称《若干意见》)是指导当前中国仲裁制度改革与完善的顶层设计,关乎当前深化仲裁改革的进路以及《仲裁法》未来修改方向。《若干意见》是在全面推进依法治国和对外开放背景下,以贯彻落实《仲裁法》精神为主线,对仲裁实践中不符合《仲裁法》精神与立法目的的体制机制、制度环境进行完善和优化,对仲裁未来发展方向、创新目标和重要定位进行指导的纲领性文件。其将仲裁委员会治理改革作为完善仲裁制度的核心,首次正面、权威地回应了仲裁机构作为公益性非营利法人的法律定位,指明其"去官方化"的改革目标,并明确了专业化、智能化、社会化的创新提升方向;要求通过改革创新真正发挥仲裁的特殊制度优势,不断增强中国商事法律制度的国际竞争力和公信力。

关键词:仲裁公信力 《仲裁法》修改 仲裁机构性质 公益性非营利法人 仲裁机构改革

2018年12月31日中共中央办公厅和国务院办公厅(以下简称"两办")正

---

* 姜丽丽,法学博士,中国政法大学仲裁研究院研究员,副院长。本文原型是作者为司法部举办的全国司法行政领导干部仲裁专题培训课专门撰写的解读中央"两办"意见的授课资料。

式下发了《关于完善仲裁制度 提高仲裁公信力的若干意见》，这是对党的十八届四中全会提出的“完善仲裁制度，提高仲裁公信力”深化改革任务的具体落实，也是对党的十九大提出的加强预防和化解社会矛盾机制建设的积极响应。《若干意见》的发布，是在纪念改革开放40周年之际，在仲裁事业面临深化改革、开放发展的关键时刻，对中国仲裁发展方向、改革道路和目标宗旨的整体回应，它是指引中国仲裁法制建设的重要规范性文件。对《若干意见》的理解与贯彻，应当结合全面推进依法治国的总目标以及中国仲裁法律制度的现状与发展趋势，深入思考，正确解读。只有深入理解《若干意见》的内涵，才能够凝聚共识，促进发展，共同提高仲裁公信力。

我国1994年颁布的《仲裁法》是中国仲裁法律制度的基石。此后，国务院为贯彻实施《仲裁法》，连续以办公厅名义配套下发四个文件，分别是国办发〔1994〕99号文、〔1995〕38号文、〔1995〕44号文和〔1996〕22号文。“《仲裁法》+国办发四文件”奠定了中国仲裁法律制度的“基本底色”，共同保障了仲裁法律制度初建阶段的顺利实施。此后二十多年，随着社会主义市场经济和改革开放的蓬勃发展，中国仲裁事业也取得了长足进步。为解决仲裁发展与规范的问题，《仲裁法》司法解释也多有出台，在不同层面起到了完善仲裁制度的重要作用，但缺乏针对仲裁行业整体发展和制度完善，统筹社会各方面的综合性指导意见。《若干意见》此次以“两办”文件形式下发，权威性高、影响力大、涉及面广，可谓“久旱甘霖”，必将对中国仲裁长远发展发挥重大作用。现就《若干意见》整体思路、重点内容，结合仲裁学理与出台背景等进行解读。

一、整体思路解读：继往开来、内外衔接

《若干意见》共分五大主题总计23条，五个主题分别是：(1)认真贯彻落实仲裁法律制度；(2)改革完善仲裁委员会内部治理结构；(3)加快推进仲裁制度改革创新；(4)提高仲裁服务国家全面开放和发展战略的能力；(5)加大对仲裁工作的支持与监督力度。结合主题及其具体内容分析，指导意见总的思路可谓继往开来、内外衔接。

"继往开来"首先是"继往"——贯彻落实《仲裁法》及相关仲裁法律制度，深入理解其基本原则和内在精神，是完善仲裁制度的前提与根本。改革绝非否定历史和现实，切实"贯彻落实"《仲裁法》的立法精神本身就是改革的方向，改革与之不符、不相适应的现有实施机制是进一步完善仲裁制度的基本路径。确定这一前提后，《若干意见》第二部分至第四部分则针对改革的重点内容和目标要求展开。其一，是改革的对象。众所周知，"仲裁委员会"是仲裁法律制度实施的核心机构，因此，改革完善其治理结构就是完善整体仲裁制度的"内在动因"。其二，是改革的内容。第三部分从仲裁服务社会的角度，具体指出了"加快仲裁制度改革创新"的几大方面，并提出了要求。其三，在提出了改革要求基础上，还要立足长远，高瞻远瞩回应改革创新的战略目标，也就是"开来"——"提高仲裁服务国家全面开放和发展战略的能力"。如此前呼后应，"继往开来"的整体架构已然清晰。

作为权威性的中央文件，也是专业领域的指导性文件，在内外关系处理方面，抓住了任何领域的改革都是"牵一发而动全身"，需要内呼外应、相互衔接的要义。虽然前面四部分都是"围绕"仲裁制度来讲，但任何一项改革意见实施都绝非仲裁一己之力可以推动，而需要社会各方面配套措施的支持。因此，第五部分专门提出要"加大对仲裁工作的支持与监督力度"，提出要努力形成"党委领导、政府组建、机构独立、司法监督、社会监督的仲裁工作新格局"。最后这一部分作为总结与强调，与前面改革完善仲裁制度的内容要求可谓"内外衔接"——这既是对仲裁行业和相关部门的指导，也是对外部环境、社会各方"协同配合"完善仲裁制度的要求。如此，《若干意见》在整体上既有指导性、前瞻性，又有现实性、可行性。

二、重点内容概述

作为影响全局的指导性文件，发挥作用的关键在于能否实事求是、直面问题，只有找准问题"对症下药"，才会真正具有"指导"意义。据了解，《若干意见》出台历经原国务院法制办到重新组建的司法部两个阶段，通过全国调研、委托课题,征集各地各行业意见建议,收集国际同业信息等方式广开言路,全面调研,多次论证。在此基础上,《若干意见》前言指出:"仲裁工作面临着仲裁委员会内部治理结构不完善、仲裁发展秩序不规范、仲裁国际竞争力不强、监督制约机制不健全、支持保障不到位等新情况新问题,影响了仲裁公信力,制约了仲裁事业的健康快速发展。"这段话总结精练,对仲裁当前面临之重要问题切中肯綮。

从学界研究、行业关注和媒体报道综合分析,近十年来,关于民商事仲裁制度的讨论,主要集中于三大领域:其一,针对仲裁机构体制和管理方面的问题,包括仲裁机构能否不受干预独立运作,仲裁机构内部治理机制如何完善,仲裁案件办理水平参差不齐、损害仲裁公信力,个别仲裁机构"偏离"乃至违反仲裁的非营利性、公益性,搞不正当竞争等。其二,针对仲裁法律制度改革创新方面的讨论,包括《仲裁法》的修改建议,仲裁规则和相关规范的完善与创新意见,中国仲裁如何国际化、增强国际竞争力的各种建议和尝试,区域仲裁、行业仲裁乃至新兴领域仲裁如何发展的探讨,以及仲裁如何适应互联网与新技术的发展等。其三,围绕仲裁配套制度完善进行的讨论,包括对仲裁的司法支持与监督,国家相关领域制度改革对仲裁的影响问题等。其中,仲裁与司法的关系近些年逐步理顺,"支持仲裁"的司法政策相对稳定。而相关领域改革对仲裁的影响则一直相对难以理顺,其中比较突出的有:仲裁的收费制度由行政事业性收费向经营服务性收费转变的改革与配套问题;以自贸区建设、"一带一路"倡议为代表的扩大对外开放背景下,对仲裁高需求带来的仲裁国际化与"临时仲裁"改革问题;从事业单位分类改革到政府机构整体深化改革的大框架大背景下,"倒逼"仲裁机构改革的基础制度建设问题等。

总结上述三方面的问题,可以看出,《若干意见》通过"五大主题"整体进行了回应,而且是立足现实、结合国情,给出了方向性的指导。下面对《若干意见》的重点内容分别进行解读。

三、主线突出:以仲裁机构治理和改革为主线贯穿始终

任何事业的改革都如同"望山"——"横看成岭侧成峰,远近高低各不同",

主体、视角、发展阶段不同,则观点诉求各异,仲裁改革尤其如此。因此,作为事关全局的指导性文件,要真正推动深化仲裁制度改革,必须要有一个核心“抓手”来拎出改革的“主线”——也就是从哪里下手改革能够革弊鼎新、激活仲裁发展活力。

理论上认为,民商事仲裁服务于市场经济纠纷解决需求,经济越发达、发展速度越快的地方则经济纠纷越会频发,仲裁事业应当发展得更好更快;从仲裁与诉讼同为解决民商事争议的重要途径角度,仲裁与民商事诉讼的发展趋势应当大致相同。毋庸置疑,近些年因中国经济改革发展带来的纠纷解决社会需求是巨量的,这从民商事诉讼连年暴涨给法院带来的改革“压力”就可窥斑见豹。但实证研究发现,仲裁的实际发展情况与理论上的发展趋势并不完全吻合。例如,位于“中部地区”的武汉,其经济发展、司法水平等综合实力远远比不上某些沿海经济发达城市或中心城市,但武汉仲裁的整体发展情况却被业内认为超过不少经济发达地区的仲裁水平,成为中国仲裁具有代表性的较好发展区域。全国范围内,还有不少经济发展相对较好的省会城市、副省级城市,其仲裁发展水平却远不如某个经济相对落后的地级市。以诉讼为参照系,对比最高人民法院发布的民商事争议诉讼数据和司法部发布的仲裁统计数据可知,整体比较,近些年仲裁处理的民商事争议的总量大约是诉讼的2%~3%;局部观察可见,相较于法院诉讼案件连年增长难以应付的普遍情况,不少地方的仲裁却“门前冷落车马稀”;而个别发展较好的地区的仲裁业务量则可与诉讼相提并论或各有千秋,影响力大。

放眼中国仲裁的现实情况,其发展整体是仲裁机构为主导、以城市行政区域划分为业务覆盖范围的基本模式。前述仲裁理论与实践的发展差异表明:一是仲裁整体上没能完全反映、满足经济社会发展的客观需求,相当多地区的仲裁发展水平与社会需求不相匹配;二是仲裁作为诉讼外独立的纠纷解决机制的社会功能没能得到充分发挥,认知度低、业务能力弱;三是仲裁发展不平衡的原因,有客观条件差异的因素,但更重要的是不同仲裁机构的体制机制等内在问题的制约,即在经济社会发展带来的争议解决客观需求等外部条件不变的情况下,仲裁机构的发展能力和水平成为仲裁事业发展的关键变量。实地调研也证明,仲裁机构发展相对落后的原因,多是仲裁机构自身治理结构不完善、体制机制僵化,因而缺乏发展动力所导致。因此,要改革完善仲裁制度,激发仲裁活力,就要从如何发挥仲裁机构的主观能动性入手,其核心就是仲裁机构的自身治理和改革问题。

对此,《若干意见》第一、第二部分分别从宏观到微观两个层面,对仲裁机构的治理和机制改革问题进行了全面指导。第一部分重点从宏观上规范仲裁委员会从产生到运行的基本制度,强调要在设立换届、机构独立、公平诚信、有序竞争等几大方面"认真贯彻落实"仲裁法律制度。第二部分则是从仲裁委员会的运行机制、管理方式等方面提出了具体指导意见。首先,是要求仲裁机构按照决策权、执行权、监督权分立制衡原则建立治理机制。其次,是要健全机构"内控机制",强化案件质量管理和内部监督制约。再次,对仲裁的"两支核心队伍建设"提出了指导意见,一是改进仲裁员选聘管理工作,二是推进仲裁秘书职业化专业化建设。最后,重点落实在"积极稳妥推进仲裁委员会内部管理机制改革"这一核心问题上。《若干意见》提出,政府要以"适应仲裁工作特点,有利于提高仲裁公信力和增进仲裁工作活力"为改革目标,以"赋予仲裁委员会在人事、财务、薪酬制度等方面相应自主权"为改革进路,鼓励仲裁机构积极稳妥推进改革。同时,《若干意见》在资产管理方面,一方面,提出要建立"仲裁事业发展基金",保障仲裁机构可持续发展;另一方面,则强调了严防国有资产流失的措施,避免仲裁机构沦为某些个人或组织的营利工具。

《若干意见》宏观和具体指导意见的结合,传递出的信息是:第一,当前的仲裁法律制度整体上是能够支持保障仲裁事业发展的,问题在于欠缺"认真贯彻落实";第二,仲裁机构管理体制改革的目标、道路和指导思想是与仲裁法律制度一脉相承的,改革的内容是顺应《仲裁法》精神,是对仲裁法律制度的"贯彻落实+完善提升"。

《若干意见》通过开篇近一半的篇幅"抓主线"谈改革后,接着第三、第四部分就是进一步提出要求:"加快推进仲裁制度改革创新"+"提高仲裁服务国家全面开放和发展战略的能力”。显然,若仲裁机构怠于改革,活力不足,后面这两项要求就难以实现。最后,为保障改革到位,在“加大对仲裁工作的支持与监督力度”部分,《若干意见》从加强党的领导、依法全面履行政府职责角度,再次给各方“加压”,提出要“把仲裁事业发展纳入当地经济社会发展规划和法治政府建设考核评价体系”,以及加强仲裁行业信用体系建设,建立仲裁委员会第三方评估制度等相关社会监督措施。

对《若干意见》五个主题前后对照解读可知,虽然指导意见对仲裁机构改革没有提出明确的“进度表”,但实际上已经把仲裁委员会的改革发展提升到了前所未有的高度和紧迫程度:不改革,意味着当地政府和仲裁机构历经 20 余年而没能认真贯彻仲裁法律制度,难辞其咎且要承担责任;不改革,仲裁机构就难以实现其服务社会需求和国家战略的存在价值,面临被淘汰的命运;不改革,将直接影响中央“全面推进依法治国”的总目标,背离法治。对怠于改革发展的机构,《若干意见》也有相关措施,其中第 13 条明确提出“推进行业协作和仲裁区域化发展”,鼓励仲裁机构之间开展良性竞争与合作。结合仲裁“协议管辖”不受地域限制的特点,如果当地政府和仲裁机构还意识不到改革的紧迫性和重要性,不积极推进,那下场可能就是沦为其他中心仲裁机构的一部分乃至被解散,大浪淘沙,不进则退。

四、直面争论:权威回应仲裁机构“定性”,指明改革方向

要从仲裁机构入手“深化改革”,首先要面对的就是多年来各界一直争论的仲裁机构的定性问题。近些年,仲裁机构“民间化”还是“行政化”之争演化为一种“标签”话语,批判仲裁“行政化”的言论盛行,但争论与批判并未让仲裁界明晰仲裁委员会到底是什么、怎么做的问题。很多仲裁人自嘲多年困惑的一个“终极问题”是:知道仲裁是什么,但不知道仲裁机构到底是什么。业内人士可能更理解这句话背后的真实含义——这一方面是对仲裁机构在国家治理体系中的定位、在政府改革中的去向,以及对仲裁事业自身发展方向的不确定,另一方面也是对当前仲裁机构治理结构不完善、体制机制理不顺现状的真实写照。

据调研统计,在中国当前总计250余家仲裁机构中,80%以上的仲裁机构被归类于"事业单位",其他还有社会团体、中介组织等多种情形。而"事业单位"是个"筐",本身形态各异,已经处于分类改革逐步缩减的历史进程当中,被归类其中的这"八成多"仲裁机构也因此在改革中面临选择,各家机构的改革取向和进度差异较大。关键在于,仲裁机构无法在现有事业单位改革分类中找到完全适合的模式。因此,仲裁机构改革纠结的问题是:能否跳出传统"事业单位"这个"筐"?以及若跳出"事业单位"后,自己到底是什么性质的单位呢?对此,在作为民法典总纲的《民法总则》出台前,也有过很多争论,希望《民法总则》能够对此给予明确。2017年《民法总则》颁布实施,对法人定义及分类重新予以划分,但业界对仲裁机构的"定性"和"归类"依然困惑,这成为仲裁机构改革观念上和实践中难以逾越的"门槛"。

鉴于此,《若干意见》依据法律、凝聚共识,首次回应了仲裁委员会"定性"问题。其在第二部分对仲裁委员会的改革意见中开宗明义地指出,"仲裁委员会是政府依据仲裁法组织有关部门和商会组建,为解决合同纠纷和其他财产权益纠纷提供公益性服务的非营利法人"。

全面解读这一说法,可以看出,这是整合了《仲裁法》和相关法律的规定,对俗称的仲裁机构,即《仲裁法》上的"仲裁委员会",所作出的权威概括性界定。为彰显其重大意义,特从以下几个层次深入解读:

1. 仲裁机构是"独立法人"组织,这是其基本法律属性

仲裁机构作为"法人",应当具有独立的法律人格,能够独立地享有民事权利,承担民事义务,适用关于法人的一般法律规定。明确仲裁机构的法人地位,意味着明确其法律人格的独立性,明确它应当具有独立的财产,独立的"事权"。实践中很多人因为仲裁机构由政府牵头组建,往往忽略或否认其独立地位,《仲裁法》立法时对此也有关注。为了明确政府"组建"之后仲裁机构与政府的关系,《仲裁法》特别在第14条强调了仲裁机构的"独立性",明确规定仲裁委员会独立于行政机关,与行政机关没有隶属关系。这是完善仲裁机构治理

结构，改革相关制度的基本前提。

对于仲裁机构“法人”定位，也即其独立性的理解，涉及当前应如何处理仲裁机构与社会各方的“内外关系”。首先，“对外”强调的是其“独立法人地位”，是处理仲裁机构与其他相关部门、单位之间关系的法理基础。2018 年以来开展的政府机构改革中，笔者关注到个别地区的政府改革方案把仲裁机构纳入政府组成部门，甚至把仲裁机构与其他承担一定行政管理职能的部门合并为一个部门，这显然属于违法行为，应当及时纠正。其次，“对内”是处理仲裁机构与其分支机构或派出机构之间关系的法理基础，在对仲裁机构能否设立、如何设立分支机构，以及如何规范总分机构行为等类问题上，如无特殊规定的，则应当遵循法律关于法人在该类问题上的一般规定。

对“独立法人”的理解，还涉及对实务中认为仲裁机构有“两张皮”的观念的厘清。“两张皮”是指仲裁机构对外有两个面目——“仲裁委员会”与仲裁委员会的“办事机构”。例如，不少仲裁机构登记的事业单位法人名称为“××仲裁委员会办公室”，而非“××仲裁委员会”。仲裁机构从事仲裁法律行为，出具仲裁文书时对外依法都是“仲裁委员会”，但日常管理和从事其他民事活动时，可能是以登记的办事机构的名义，导致外部对其认识不清，主体混淆。从学理上说，“团体的法律人格的赋予，是民法理论最富想象力和技术性的创造”，法人本是社会上具备一定组织机构、为一定的利益或目标实现而实际存在的，被法律赋予了民事主体地位的组织体。作为一个组织体而非自然人，法人必然要有自己的组织机构，才能够产生并通过一定的方式实现自己的意思，从而具有一定的民事权利能力和民事行为能力。拥有自己的名称、组织机构、住所和财产/经费也是法人成立的必要条件；而“主要办事机构”在法律上的意义主要在于确定法人的“住所”，即《民法总则》第 63 条规定之“法人以其主要办事机构所在地为住所”。关于仲裁委员会办事机构的规定，最早出现在国办发〔1995〕44 号文的《重新组建仲裁机构方案》中，其中“关于仲裁委员会”部分的第 5 项规定：“仲裁委员会下设办事机构，负责办理仲裁案件受理、仲裁文书送达、档案管理、仲裁费用的收取与管理等事务……”这也体现在其后的《仲裁委员会章程示范文本》中。因此,“办事机构”是为了实现仲裁委员会这一法人组织体的主体功能而必然要有的组织机构设置,其代表的只能是法人本身,享有法人主体地位的应当是仲裁委员会而非其办事机构,办事机构不能独立存在。正所谓“皮之不存毛将焉附”,如果“两张皮”之间出现了问题,那是法人内部治理的问题,如常见的办事机构过分强势而仲裁委员会过分弱化的问题,但若割裂二者关系来谈问题显然是荒谬的。正因如此,“改革完善仲裁委员会内部治理结构”才成为《若干意见》专门强调的主题。

2. 仲裁机构是“非营利法人”

“非营利法人”是《民法总则》对法人的基本分类之一,与之相对的是“营利性法人”。除设立目的是否公益或营利外,二者的根本区别在于是否向出资人、设立人或者成员分配所得利润。仲裁机构作为非营利法人,意味着对当前一些所谓“创新改革”仲裁机构的行为和做法的明确规范:第一,任何参与机构设立的出资方均不可获得利润分配。这是仲裁机构不可逾越的底线,也是仲裁机构改革的“红线”。目前个别对仲裁机构进行“股份制改革”以分配利润之类的所谓“创新”方案涉嫌违法,可以休矣。第二,“非营利法人”并不是说仲裁机构不可以“盈利”,不盈利则机构没发展,长期不盈利可能就要难以为继而被撤销或解散;恰恰相反,仲裁机构明确自己的非营利法人定位,就是要据此制定合理的非营利法人治理结构和适合其发展的体制机制,依法取得收入积累法人财产,才能实现可持续发展。

“非营利法人”的定位还意味着对仲裁机构面对事业单位分类改革选择的指导。《民法总则》第87条第2款规定“非营利法人包括事业单位、社会团体、基金会、社会服务机构等”,这是一个开放性规定。《若干意见》并未明确规定仲裁机构属于现有四个“有名”类型中的哪一类非营利法人。现根据立法背景、条文释义来具体分析在非营利法人类型中,仲裁机构的定位问题。

(1)事业单位法人

该类法人的规定在立法上曾有“存废”之争。建议不规定的原因是根据2011年中共中央、国务院《关于分类推进事业单位改革的指导意见》,结合事业单位分类改革的三个方向,改革后的事业单位完全可以拆分对应三类法人:承担行政职能的可以划归机关法人,从事生产经营活动的可以划归营利法人,从事公益服务的可以划归非营利法人。既然改革后可以各得其所,事业单位也就没有单独规定的必要。最后立法部门考虑到事业单位改革还在进行中,法律要适应改革需要并应保持稳定性,对社会上大量存在的事业单位类型仍然需要作出规定。[①] 但与之前的《民法通则》不同,《民法总则》尊重事业单位改革的要求和方向,规定的事业单位法人仅指"从事公益服务的事业单位",对此,第 88 条表述为:"具备法人条件,为适应经济社会发展需要,提供公益服务设立的事业单位……"结合国家对事业单位改革的要求,允许保留的主要是国家举办的必要的公益机构,所以对该规定的理解逻辑上应为:事业单位应当是公益性组织,提供公益服务;当前从事公益服务的事业单位在分类改革中可以保留公益性事业单位身份;但从事公益服务的组织不一定都是事业单位。

此外,国务院《关于修改〈事业单位登记管理暂行条例〉的决定》第 3 条规定:"事业单位经县级以上各级人民政府及其有关主管部门批准成立后,应当依照本条例的规定登记或者备案。"第 5 条规定:"县级以上各级人民政府机构编制管理机关所属的事业单位登记管理机构负责实施事业单位的登记管理工作……"结合法律与行政法规规定来看,事业单位的典型特征是"国办公益",由国家机关举办并隶属于某个"行政主管部门",采取编制管理,实行国家干部人事制度。从事业单位的改革方向来看,判断公益类事业单位的尺度主要有两个:一是公益服务的社会需求层次,是否全民性的、必要性的"刚需";二是公益服务的社会资源配置程度,是否市场可以解决的,以及市场可以解决的程度。举例而言,义务教育、公立高等教育、民办教育都具有公益性,但显然义务教育是全民性必要的基层社会需求、公益属性最强,高等教育次之,民办教育再次之。公益属性越强的机构,国家给予的支持(如财政拨款)和监督力度也会更强,这是权利义务相一致的必然结果。事业单位改革的导向是保留公益属性最

① 参见李适时主编:《中华人民共和国民法总则释义》,法律出版社 2017 年版。

强、最重要的少量机构并强化对它们的支持和监督,而不是要保留所有具有公益属性的机构。仲裁机构具有公益属性,但在社会需求层次方面不属于全民性的刚性需求;在资源配置方面,整体上仲裁服务可以由市场配置和调节,作为个体的机构服务具有较强的可替代性。因此,整体上仲裁机构不宜被划分为公益性事业单位。

另外,虽然当前事业单位也在改革过程中,但这种长期形成的行政色彩浓厚的管理体制,让仲裁机构短期内难以实现《仲裁法》明确规定的"独立于行政机关"的法定要求;而实践中部分已经改革为公益一类或公益二类事业单位[①]的仲裁机构,在治理结构和管理体制上并未有、也难以有根本变化。可以说,对于仲裁机构而言,向"事业单位"这一类型的改革,实践已经证明是不成功的。

(2)社会团体法人

该类法人的特点是"会员制",从设立目的上可分为"公益性"和"互益性"两种。《民法总则》第90条表述为:"具备法人条件,基于会员共同意愿,为公益目的或者会员共同利益等非营利目的设立的社会团体……"显然,中国当前的仲裁机构不是"基于会员共同意愿"、为"会员共同利益"而设立,可以不予考虑。

(3)捐助法人

《民法总则》第92条规定"具备法人条件,为公益目的以捐助财产设立的基金会、社会服务机构等,经依法登记成立,取得捐助法人资格……"该条是关于基金会、社会服务机构、宗教活动场所等捐助法人资格取得的规定。学理上,捐助法人主要对应的是大陆法系法人分类中的"财团法人",即以捐助财产为成立基础的法人。其中的"社会服务机构",主要指的是在民政系统登记的"民办非企业",顾名思义,其特点是"民间而非国有资产"所办。另一特点是以捐助财产为基础成立,故而法律赋予捐助人对捐助法人有特别的监督权,包括可

① 即根据前述《关于分类推进事业单位改革的指导意见》提出的事业单位分类改革方案,承担公益服务的少量公益性事业单位按照市场能否配置资源为标准,划分为公益一类和公益二类事业单位:承担基本公益服务不能或不宜由市场配置资源的,划入公益一类;可部分由市场配置资源的,划入公益二类。

以申请法院撤销其决定等。因此,就该类法人以捐助财产为基础,强调民间资产兴办及捐助人的监督权而言,与仲裁机构的设立基础和特征也不吻合。

(4)为公益目的成立的非营利法人

这不是一种而是一类非营利法人的规定,也是《民法总则》第三章"法人"之第三节"非营利法人"最后一条(第95条)的规定,该规定涉及非营利法人的一大分类标准——是否为公益目的成立。该条是从法人终止时剩余财产处置角度的规定,但明确给出的信息是,非营利法人因设立目的不同而被区别开来。《民法总则》第95条规定:"为公益目的成立的非营利法人终止时,不得向出资人、设立人或者会员分配剩余财产……"这是因为公益性法人会享有国家给予的公益事业的优惠政策乃至政府经费资助,并因其公益性而容易获得社会各界的支持或捐赠,其剩余财产具有相当程度的"公共性",而非限于设立出资。故公益性非营利法人剩余财产处置原则是,仍要用于公益目的并尽可能用于相同或近似目的。换句话说,如果以公益目的成立的仲裁机构终止,其剩余财产原则上将仍然要用于公益性的仲裁事业。因此,看似《民法总则》对非营利法人只是列举了四种常见法人种类,实际它还明确了非营利法人因设立目的是否"公益性"而区分的两类,即公益性非营利法人与其他非营利法人。对于以公益目的而设立的仲裁机构而言,公益性非营利法人可以成为其跳出事业单位法人之外的适合选择。因为,这既可以保留其公益性,享受国家对公益性法人的支持和优惠,又可以摆脱行政管制和编制限制,建设符合自身发展的非营利法人治理结构,独立运行,改革发展的空间相对充足。

综上,结合法律解释原则,对仲裁机构的"非营利法人"定位可以进一步理解为:①仲裁机构在事业单位改革中,应当首先尊重机构的"独立性",最好选择跳出事业单位的分类,成为法律规定的其他非营利法人;②仲裁机构在现有法律框架内,更符合公益性非营利法人的特征与要求;③仲裁机构可以根据法律对公益性非营利法人的要求,选择适合自身特点的法人治理机制,进行仲裁机构自我发展道路的改革探索;④国务院办公厅发布的《关于建立和完善事业单位法人治理结构的意见》等其他公益性非营利法人在治理结构方面的改革意见,以及法律对其他非营利法人的规范与监督,可以作为仲裁机构改革的借鉴。《若干意见》的规定,也是遵循《民法总则》的立法精神,为仲裁机构等非营利法人的改革预留了空间。

3. 仲裁机构是提供“公益性”服务的组织

这是在中央文件层面首次正式提出仲裁委员会的“公益性”特征,强调仲裁委员会提供的是“公益性服务”,与《民法总则》关于公益性非营利法人的规定相契合,也符合中国仲裁法律制度精神和现实国情。

从前述对非营利法人的法律分析可知,非营利性与“公益性”的内涵与外延都有差异,非营利法人也区分其设立是否基于公益目的而有不同法律规定。故对“公益性”的理解,应认为它同时涵盖“非营利性”和“社会公益”两个层面:“非营利性”强调的是对出资人不得分配利润的限制;而“公益性”更多的是强调该组织的存在具有社会公益价值,也就是对其“社会效益”的评价权重要高于经济效益权重。这反映在仲裁委员会自身发展定位,以及社会对其的考察、评估机制中,不能“唯经济效益马首是瞻”,内部办理仲裁业务不能过分或单一考虑成本收益,外部对其考核评估需更要注重其社会效益。

从社会治理角度来看,“公益性组织”意味着既需要相应的社会支持与政策引导,也需要相应的社会性管制。仲裁活动要“依法独立进行”,仲裁机构享有“独立法人”的法律地位,并不意味着其完全不受国家机关和社会的监管。对仲裁“独立性”的保障,关键是强调无论是行政机关、司法机关及其他相关部门,无论是支持还是监督仲裁,都要通过法治方式进行,要合法支持、依法监督。

鉴于仲裁机构是由政府牵头组建的,因此在处理政府与仲裁机构的支持与监督关系方面,尤其要注意方式方法。例如,政府若要支持仲裁,可以通过购买服务形式引导仲裁服务基层社会治理或特定领域的纠纷化解项目,而不是通过行政命令;政府可以为仲裁机构提供必要的办公场所或租金优惠支持,而不是财政拨款;国家还可以制定减免仲裁机构及仲裁员所得税的税收优惠立法或政策来支持该行业的国际化发展等。这些方式也是国内外常见的支持公益事业的有效途径。对公益机构的监督管制方面,常见的有行业准入或特许制度、信息公开制度、价格管制(政府指导价)制度、财务审计制度、第三方评估制度等常用的监督制度,这些在《若干意见》中也有提及。

"公益性"的提出,对支持与监督仲裁的目标和宗旨也有相应要求,即"要以最大限度实现仲裁的社会效益"为主导目标,政府与社会各界要据此来制定或落实对仲裁的支持与监督的配套制度。

4. 仲裁机构必须严格依法设立

《若干意见》提出"仲裁委员会是政府依据仲裁法组织有关部门和商会组建",这是依据《仲裁法》的规定,强调其组建的"法定"要求;同时强调"新组建仲裁委员会必须严格依法设立,不符合规定条件的不得设立"。重申《仲裁法》关于组建仲裁机构的法定要求,既是对《仲裁法》的贯彻落实,也是对仲裁机构设立不规范的法律后果的强调与警示:"凡未按规定设立……一律不得开展仲裁活动。未经设立登记的,仲裁裁决不具有法律效力。"

综合解读仲裁机构的"法定性"内涵,包括:(1)设立主体法定,非《仲裁法》明确授权组织不能随意组建仲裁机构,当前有可能成为新设仲裁机构主体的只能是《仲裁法》规定的市人民政府;(2)设立条件和程序法定,"设立"是一个具体的过程,应依法进行,不能随意突破《仲裁法》的规定,未经设立过程而宣布"成立"一家仲裁机构;(3)违法后果法定,一旦组建设立违法,则其仲裁行为无效。由此可见,仲裁机构这种法人要从事仲裁活动,其设立必须具有"合法性"前提;若其本身创设的合法性存疑,将直接影响其仲裁法律行为的效力,造成严重的社会后果。

"法定+公益+非营利"共同构成仲裁机构这种"法人"的基本特性,其相互之间又关联呼应。仲裁机构创设的"法定性",是对应其"公益性"而必然会带有的典型的社会管制特征,体现了对仲裁机构的"行业准入制度",实际上是仲裁监督保障体系的"前期控制"部分。这种合法性要求,对于仲裁机构接受社会监督而言,则要求其应当向社会公示自己设立的合法性依据,包括依法成立的相关文件与登记证书,这是仲裁机构信息公开的必要内容。"法定"还意味着,当前中国仲裁法律制度对仲裁机构这种特殊的非营利法人采取的是"依法准入”制度,以此来控制该行业机构的数量、分布,并彰显其公益特性。“公益+非营利”则构成了仲裁机构改革方向的基本定位,在此基础上改革其作为“公益性非营利法人”的治理结构,是未来仲裁机构发展的必由之路,对此,《若干意见》第二部分进行了具体的方向性指导。

五、面向未来:瞄准“三个方向”

《若干意见》既然是立足历史节点“继往开来”,在抓住改革主线、直面核心问题后,必然要回答“承前启后”的仲裁改革方向与发展要求,这集中体现在第四部分及相关条款。关于《若干意见》对仲裁未来发展提出的要求,笔者总结为:瞄准“三个方向”,提升国际竞争力。现详述如下。

“三个方向”是指在下一步深化改革中,加快推进仲裁制度改革创新的方向可归纳为“三化”:社会化、智能化与专业化。

1.“社会化”是从仲裁融入社会治理体系,提升国家治理能力角度提出的改革方向

《若干意见》提出,要“充分发挥仲裁在国家治理体系中的作用,把仲裁融入经济社会发展的各个领域”。在专项中央文件层面,再次强调要充分发挥仲裁在“国家治理体系”中的作用,这是将仲裁的社会价值提到了前所未有的“新高度”,也是对仲裁在新时期发展提出的新要求。

笔者也了解到对此质疑的意见:强调仲裁“社会化”,是否意味着是让仲裁机构脱离追求解决复杂专业民商事纠纷的“高大上”方向,转而走化解基层民间纠纷的“低俗化”路线?笔者认为,这过分“低估”或“狭隘”了仲裁社会化的深远意义。现代社会发展在经历了前工业化时期强调社会分工的阶段后,已经进入了后工业化时代的“分工+融合”阶段。现代社会更细化的社会分工,同时意味着需要更畅通的沟通与融合能力,5G、互联网、物联网、数字化、“人机一体”都是社会发展走向“融合”时代的显著特征。因此,从争议解决到国家治理,乃至“全球治理观”的出现,都更注重各种传统模式的创新融合发展。体现在科研领域,跨学科、跨专业、体系化的研究也成为针对社会急需而兴起的前沿

务实的方向。中国的仲裁制度是基于传统民商事仲裁传统、吸纳国际商事仲裁惯例而创设,时间虽短,但经历着中国社会及国际环境前所未有之剧烈变革,也必然要适应现代社会,尤其是中国社会急速改革发展带来的社会治理的客观需求。

因此,对"社会化"方向的理解,笔者认为当前应主要把握两个层面:第一,仲裁要积极适应更广泛的社会纠纷解决领域的需求,这是仲裁存在发展的社会基础。相对于《仲裁法》对"可仲裁性"的范围的宽泛界定,当前仲裁的实践覆盖面还相对较窄。第二,仲裁要与国内外其他纠纷解决方式、纠纷解决组织建立起融合衔接的机制,既要"多元"又要"融合",既要国内通行又要对接国际,是纠纷解决与社会治理发展的必然趋势。仲裁只有建立起与各种纠纷解决方式和相关组织的互通衔接机制,才能够发展为更具影响力的社会纠纷解决"枢纽"。这两方面是仲裁面向未来发展的坚实基础。

总之,"社会化"是仲裁发展的长期战略,仲裁人需以更广阔的视野理解并贯彻这一思路。

2. "智能化"是面向未来最重要的人类社会发展特征

《若干意见》提出的"积极发展互联网仲裁",实际上是提出了仲裁未来必然要走"智能化"的发展方向。智能化发展的现实状态是,智能化技术及其相关的高科技领域走在前端,而其他社会应用领域则是逐步接受、迅速扩展。整体而言,仲裁属于提供专业社会服务的产业端,必然要与服务对象的智能化程度和进展相匹配,才能够顺利发展不被淘汰。

当前,无论是传统的商事领域,还是更广泛的社会治理领域,仲裁服务对象的智能化程度、速度和广度都在不断提升。尤其是引领时代发展的商事领域,受商业利润和市场经济的驱动,必然是敏感而快速进行智能化提升的前沿领域,若仲裁停滞不前,则无法与之匹配,必将陷于发展危机。其中特别有代表性的是金融领域的发展。金融领域的交易模式已经从制式化、格式化到票证化、标准化,并在新技术支持下逐步实现了在线化和智能化,金融的互联网化和互联网金融越来越成为金融的普适形式,而大量在线产生的纠纷却无法通过在线配套机制解决,这已经成为制约金融资本效率的重大“瓶颈”之一。仲裁作为典型商事纠纷解决机制,本身应当具备与商事活动对接的能力,但目前仲裁的智能化水平整体发育落后,显然还不能承担起这一重任。

3.“专业化”是仲裁的本质特征之一,也是当前中国仲裁发展尚不充分的方面之一

仲裁相对诉讼等其他纠纷解决方式,最重要、最显著的特性之一就是“专业化”。与诉讼逐步形成的民事、刑事、行政等以法律关系性质来划分的业务领域的专业化分工不同,仲裁的专业化更多地体现为不同裁判者在不同领域的专业经验及其对于专业问题的内行判断,以及与之配套发展的仲裁作为纠纷解决机制的专项服务能力的社会化与专业化。这既是仲裁服务商业的传统决定的其敏于适应商业变迁的结果,也是仲裁在工业化时代适应社会分工和商品贸易的国际流通需求而快速发展为国际通行纠纷解决机制的内在原因。

具体而言,仲裁的“专业化”发展方向包括:(1)要提升仲裁机构服务能力的专业化;(2)要提高仲裁员仲裁业务能力的专业化;(3)要促进社会支持仲裁制度和资源的专业化。

在仲裁机构的专业化方面,《若干意见》首先强调了要从改进决策机制“优化委员会的人员构成”入手,再次重申《仲裁法》关于“委员会成员中,法律、经济贸易专家不得少于三分之二”的规定。为落实该项规定,保障委员会的专业性与自主决策权,上海市首先“亮出”自己的改革措施——2019年2月27日公开发布的中共上海市委办公厅、上海市人民政府办公厅《印发〈关于完善仲裁管理机制提高仲裁公信力　加快打造面向全球的亚太仲裁中心的实施意见〉的通知》(以下简称《上海意见》)第3条第3款“推进仲裁机构体制机制改革”中直接规定:“仲裁机构的决策机构组成人员由设立人按照章程产生,不得由公务员担任或兼任。原由政府机关组建的仲裁机构在三年内完成脱钩改制工作;公务员担任或兼任仲裁机构的决策机构组成人员的,三年内全部退出。仲裁机构依法享有决策和管理自由权。”决策专业化,必然要求执行组织的专业化,因此仲裁机构内部治理结构的完善,以及具体到《若干意见》第8条的“推

进仲裁秘书职业化和专业化建设”都是仲裁机构服务专业化改革的必然要求。《若干意见》在第 7 条“改进仲裁员选聘和管理工作”中，也指出仲裁委员会“可以对聘任的仲裁员按照不同专业设立仲裁员名册，鼓励根据各自实际探索仲裁员推荐名册”。《若干意见》第 13 条和第 14 条关于推进行业协作和完善仲裁规则的指导意见，更是具体要求推动仲裁的“专业化”建设。其第 13 条连续用了几个“专业”来强调要“研究建立专业仲裁工作平台，培养专业仲裁人员，制定专业仲裁规范，促进仲裁的专业化发展”，其第 14 条提出“鼓励……探索制定专门、专业领域的特别仲裁规则，提升仲裁的专业化服务水平”。

“专业化”改革方向意味着仲裁机构在改革中，首先要正确定位自身的“专业机构”特性，从内部治理、人员选聘、业务开展等各方面都要进行专业化改革。这也是仲裁行业未来发展的一个“专业分工”的方向——发展到一定程度的仲裁机构，可以及时根据发展需求和自身条件定位自己的“专业化发展方向”，发展出自身的品牌特色，而不一定都要做“大而全”的仲裁服务。

“专业化”改革还意味着要有支持仲裁的专业化社会机制与资源。《若干意见》提出的专业化的仲裁人才培养、职业化的仲裁教育培训、社会第三方对仲裁的中立评估与监督等，都需要社会资源来支持。仲裁委员会不可能承担起仲裁发展的全部责任，支持仲裁发展需要对全社会资源的动员，而其中教育科研的支持最为直接和紧迫。对此，上海市有着明确认识，《上海意见》第 3 条第 5 款“加强仲裁专业人才队伍建设”中明确提出了包括“加大仲裁专业人才培养力度”、“加强仲裁专业人才培养的国际合作”和“加大仲裁专业人才的国际交流力度”三方面措施，具体包括“鼓励我市高等院校开设仲裁专业课程，为上海仲裁专业人才队伍体系化发展提供支持……支持上海仲裁协会、市律师协会、高等院校与境内外知名法学院校及国际组织通过建立联合培养、专项培养等学位项目的方式，培养国际化仲裁专业人才。鼓励和引导我市青年律师、学者及在校大学生赴境外知名法学院校、国际组织、国际仲裁机构以及律师事务所参加国际仲裁学习和实务培训”等。上海市这一具有宣示性和引领性举动，充分体现出人才培养与教育科研之于仲裁专业化发展的重要性。

六、坚定目标:提高仲裁的国际竞争力

在提出“社会化+智能化+专业化”三个面向未来的改革方向后,《若干意见》继而指向未来的发展目标,也是深化改革的要求——提高仲裁的国际竞争力。笔者认为,这一要求是仲裁“适应国家全面开放新格局和重大战略发展需要”的必然结果。理解并贯彻提高仲裁国际竞争力的目标要求,对深化仲裁改革有积极意义和战略价值。

首先,以提高仲裁的国际竞争力为目标,有助于对仲裁“国际性”的深入理解与思考。国际性是仲裁真正具有特色和优势的现代属性,是仲裁在所有纠纷解决机制中最重要的战略价值,也是仲裁之所以能够跻身于服务国家战略、构成“国家治理体系”重要内容的根本原因。如果意识不到仲裁国际化特征及其重要性,仲裁的存在价值就大打折扣。在这个意义上,如果想把仲裁彻底划分为国际仲裁与国内仲裁,“分而治之”的思路可能也走不通。因为若局限于国内视角,相对于诉讼乃至调解,仲裁在纠纷解决数量上有数十倍差距,可能不如地方一个基层法庭的功能;在社会认知度和影响力上,仲裁过于小众而不被了解,可能显得无足轻重;从社会资源的支持看,至今国内都没有将仲裁列为一个学科,仲裁法在法学教育中都尚未普及。总体而言,如果仲裁只是限于“国内”的话,其可替代性很强,缺乏独立价值。仲裁之所以能够越来越显示其重要性和地位,更多是基于其自身具备的“国际通行、国际执行、国际认可”的“跨国”(transnational)特征。国际仲裁是人类社会发展到全球经济一体化时代、逐步走向“人类命运共同体”过程中融合发展的共同选择,也是中国在深化改革、扩大开放过程中适应国际规则的必然结果。中国仲裁虽立足中国实践,但国际性是它不可或缺的内在属性。随着中国经济的全面升级与对外开放的纵深发展,中国开始引领“一带一路”,已经成为国际化的主角,中国化与国际化不再是相对而是相融的概念,仲裁更不可能再局限于国际国内的划分,只有从这个高度理解仲裁,中国仲裁才能够有深化改革的动力和服务国家战略的能力。

其次,理解仲裁的国际性特征,也有助于深入理解仲裁没有地域管辖与级

别管辖的制度设计，以及《若干意见》提出的要建设“区域仲裁中心”、鼓励仲裁机构进行良性竞争与合作的构想。《仲裁法》实施20余年后，仲裁机构组织体系在地域化的基础上，已经发展出了“跨地域”仲裁服务实践，除中国国际经济贸易仲裁委员会、中国海事仲裁委员会外，其他一些发展较好的仲裁机构，受理跨地域当事人、甚至双方当事人都是“非本地”的案件都逐渐增加，体现出仲裁非地域管辖的特色。从仲裁服务社会需求的角度，在市场经济和依法治国背景下，地域和行政区划早已经不能成为“壁垒”。在商贸交往、人员流动、科技进步等各方面作用下，社会纠纷的产生基础早已经突破了地域，而更多地进入行业领域，甚至出现在无法确认地域管辖的虚拟世界。因此，仲裁的国际性，与仲裁跨地域发展的本质都是资本与商业突破地缘政治而谋求自由发展的本性使然，开放、包容与制衡应当是仲裁的外在表现。因此，指望以地方行政力量来管控仲裁或限制仲裁的跨地域、国际化发展，既不理性，也不现实。仲裁的这一特性决定了仲裁机构与行政机关的又一本质区别：既然仲裁服务的对象和提供服务的主体都不受地域限制，那就意味着它必须是独立自治的法人，而不能是某地政府部门。这也决定了仲裁机构之间必然具有一定程度的竞争关系，但竞争的关键应当在于谁更具有仲裁公信力，而对其社会控制的关键在于对竞争行为合法性的规范。

最后，提高仲裁的国际竞争力，有助于尽快完善仲裁制度，倒逼中国仲裁公信力的提升。在未来全面对外开放的大趋势下，仲裁作为服务业必然要逐步放开，直面国际竞争。而且，国际仲裁在实践中早已经“登堂入室”，在自贸区政策鼓励下正逐步适应中国市场需求，中国仲裁如不尽快适应国际需求、提高国际竞争能力，后果可想而知。对此，上海市作为首家引入国际仲裁机构的中心城市，在其深化仲裁改革文件中高瞻远瞩提出要“推进仲裁行业有序开放”，明确提出：允许境外知名仲裁机构在上海设立代表机构；鼓励本市仲裁机构与境外知名仲裁机构开展业务合作；鼓励和引导本市仲裁机构、仲裁员积极参与国际性商事仲裁活动，积极参与国际投资仲裁争议解决机制建设，不断提升本市仲裁机构服务国家对外开放战略和参与国际竞争的能力和水平；在上海打造国际争议解决平台。这种开放与积极参与竞争的气魄值得赞许。

对于中国仲裁行业而言,上海市“推进仲裁行业有序开放”的举措,实际上代表了下一步仲裁发展的方向和《仲裁法》修改应考虑的重点内容。众所周知,本届全国人大常委会已经将《仲裁法》修改纳入立法规划第二类项目,可以预见,《仲裁法》的修改意见和方案将成为未来一段时期内的研究讨论热点。既然此次上海市经征求司法部意见,在《若干意见》出台后率先发布改革措施,必然具有引领效果,可以认为是得到了一定程度的认可与鼓励。对此,有人可能简单认为上海只是代表“一线城市”的仲裁改革意见,笔者认为绝非如此。上海地位特殊,肩负改革开放重任,在仲裁领域的这次积极呼应,应当理解为,它是在“两办”文件立足全国、不宜过于具体的意见平衡基础上,基于自身受中央支持的特殊开放地位而作出的更为明确的改革示范,它引领的将是下一步仲裁法制发展和仲裁实务改革的方向。

提高仲裁的国际竞争力,并非要求所有仲裁机构都具备国际化的水平与能力,但这是对中国仲裁整体制度完善的必然要求。既然国际化是仲裁的本质特征之一,就要求中国仲裁也必须适应国际仲裁的发展要求,乃至积极参与国际仲裁规则、制度的制定与完善。中国仲裁的对外形象必然要以完善的中国仲裁制度及其相关法治建设作为背书,而不能仅凭一家或数家仲裁机构自身发展情况作为中国仲裁公信力基础。因此,提高中国仲裁国际竞争力的过程,与完善中国仲裁制度的内在进程互为表里。只有中国仲裁制度整体得以完善,中国仲裁对外对内的公信力才能真正得以提升。

中国仲裁的国际化,绝不意味着中国仲裁简单复制某些国际仲裁的做法,而是应当将国际仲裁的优秀理念与制度与中国的纠纷解决文化、现实国情进行融合适应,找出适合中国仲裁发展的国际化之路。这也是将前述仲裁面向未来改革发展的“三个方向”与提高国际竞争力的目标相结合理解的重点所在。

七、结语

《若干意见》是在中央文件层面首次对中国仲裁深化改革、开放发展作出的权威性指导性规范，是《仲裁法》颁布实施后最重要的行业发展指导意见。它承前启后、继往开来，在仲裁事业发展的关键时刻，从国家治理与发展的高度，对仲裁进行了总结与梳理，必将对未来中国仲裁法治建设、制度完善起到至关重要的作用。因此，认真贯彻实施《若干意见》将成为未来一段时期以仲裁行业为中心的社会各界的重要任务，希望笔者此篇解读文章能够为此贡献绵薄之力。

非洲商法协调组织新的非诉争议解决制度述评

朱伟东[*]

摘要：非洲商法协调组织是非洲大陆一个重要的地区性商法协调组织。该组织新的非诉争议解决制度包括仲裁和调解。它修订后的仲裁制度吸收了国际上仲裁发展的最新内容，扩大了受案范围，明确了具体期限，增加了新的程序，提高了仲裁效率。它新引进的调解制度主要是以联合国国际贸易法委员会2002年《调解示范法》为版本制定的，同时考虑到本地区的法律传统和实际情况。新的调解制度也适用于外国投资者与投资东道国政府之间的投资争议。考虑到中国与该组织成员国现有的多边和双边法律框架，该组织的非诉争议解决制度，为中国投资者解决在当地发生的投资和商事争议提供了非常便利的途径。

关键词：非洲商法协调组织　仲裁　调解　商事　投资

一、引言

非洲商法协调组织是非洲大陆上一个致力于商法协调化和统一化的重要地区性组织，它的法语名称是 Organization pour l' harmonisation du Droit des

---

* 朱伟东，法学博士，中国社科院西亚非洲研究所研究员、教授。

Affairs en Afrique(简称 OHADA),英文名称是 Organization for the Harmonization of Business Law in Africa(简称 OHBLA)。人们一般用 OHADA 作为该组织的通用简称。非洲商法协调组织主要是由一些非洲法郎区国家,在1993 年根据《非洲商法协调条约》成立的。该组织目前共有 17 个成员国,分别是贝宁、喀麦隆、科特迪瓦、加蓬、乍得、塞内加尔、尼日尔、马里、赤道几内亚、几内亚、几内亚比绍、布基纳法索、中非共和国、多哥、科摩罗、刚果(布)和刚果(金)。[①] 这些国家成立非洲商法协调组织的目的是统一本地区的商法,改善投资环境,吸引外资,促进经济发展,从而推动地区一体化的实现。

非洲商法协调组织制定的商法被称为"统一法"(uniform law)。目前,该组织通过的统一法分别涉及一般商法、公司法、破产法、会计法、担保法、合作社法、执行法、仲裁法等。为确保统一法在成员国内得到统一适用和解释,解决该地区出现的各类商事纠纷,该组织还成立了司法与仲裁共同法院(the Common Court of Justice and Arbitration)。司法与仲裁共同法院兼有诉讼和仲裁职能。非洲商法协调组织的仲裁有两类:一类是根据《非洲商法协调条约》和《司法与仲裁法院仲裁规则》(Arbitration Rules of the Common Court of Justice and Arbitration,以下简称《仲裁规则》)[②]的规定在司法与仲裁共同法院管理下进行的仲裁程序;另一类是根据《仲裁统一法》(Uniform Act on Arbitration)[③]的规定,在非洲商法协调组织成员国内进行的仲裁。非洲商法协调组织早在 1999 年 3 月 11 日就通过了《仲裁统一法》和《仲裁规则》。经过近 20 年的发展,该法及规则暴露出许多问题和缺陷,为此,非洲商法协调组织自 2015 年起就开始着手准备修订工作。2017 年 11 月 23 日该组织通过了《仲裁统一法》和《仲裁规则》修订版,同时通过了第十部统一法——《调解统一法》(Uniform Act on

① "History of OHADA", http://www.ohada.org/index.php/en/, December 18, 2018.

② Full text is available at the website of OHBLA: http://www.ohada.org/attachments/article/2490/Reglement-Arbitrage_CCJA-English.pdf, December 18, 2018.

③ Full text is available at the website of OHBLA: http://www.ohada.org/attachments/article/2490/Acte-uniforme-Arbitrage-English.pdf, December 18, 2018.

Mediation)。[①] 这些新的法律和规则已在 2018 年 3 月 15 日生效。修订后的《仲裁统一法》和《仲裁规则》对该地区存在的仲裁制度进行了多方面改革，而《调解统一法》则开创性地在该地区引进了调解制度。这些改革和创新举措会对该地区的投资、商事争议解决带来重要影响。在该地区投资的中国企业和商人，必须关注这些改革和创新，以便在出现投资、商事争议时，可以做到有的放矢，选择合适的争议解决途径，有效维护自己的合法权益。

二、在司法与仲裁共同法院内进行的仲裁程序

根据《非洲商法协调条约》的规定，司法与仲裁共同法院的职能有两种，即司法职能和仲裁职能。在仲裁职能方面，司法与仲裁共同法院仅充当仲裁机构的角色，它自己并不解决当事人提交的争议，只是指定或确认仲裁员、听取仲裁程序进展情况，以及对仲裁裁决进行审查等。它作出的决定仅具有行政性质，不具有司法判决的性质。在仲裁程序过程中，司法与仲裁共同法院的书记官长(或首席书记官，Chief Registrar)将作为仲裁机构的秘书长行事。《非洲商法协调条约》对司法与仲裁共同法院的仲裁程序有具体的规定，同时，新修订的《仲裁规则》对仲裁程序作了补充规定。

只有在争议与成员国具有某种联系时，才可利用司法与仲裁共同法院的仲裁程序。根据《非洲商法协调条约》第 21 条以及《仲裁规则》第 2 条第 1 款的规定，只有在下列情况下才可将合同争议提交司法与仲裁共同法院通过仲裁方式解决：当事人一方在某一成员国内有住所或惯常居所，或合同的一部分或全部已在或将在某一成员国内或多个成员国内履行。如果当事人已在合同中约定或在争议发生后双方同意将争议提交给司法与仲裁共同法院通过仲裁解决，则此类仲裁程序就必须遵守《非洲商法协调条约》及《仲裁规则》的规定。修订后的《仲裁规则》还规定，司法与仲裁共同法院还可管理依据投资法律文件(特别是投资法、双边投资保护条约或多边投资条约)提起的仲裁程序。这就扩大

① Full text is available at the website of OHBLA: http://www.ohada.org/attachments/article/2490/Acte-uniforme-Mediation-English.pdf, December 18, 2018.

了司法与仲裁共同法院受理案件的范围,也方便外国投资者利用该机构解决投资争议。

(一)仲裁协议

仲裁协议是仲裁大厦的基石,在整个仲裁程序中发挥着重要作用。《非洲商法协调条约》和《仲裁规则》均没有规定仲裁协议必须以书面形式作成,但对于当事人而言,最好采用书面仲裁协议,以避免日后出现争议。《非洲商法协调条约》和《仲裁规则》没有单独就仲裁协议的形式作出规定,但对仲裁协议不存在以及仲裁协议的效力进行了规定。如果表面上在当事人之间不存在采用《仲裁规则》的仲裁协议,在被申请人反对司法与仲裁共同法院的仲裁,或被申请人在 30 日内没有对进行仲裁申请作出回应的情况下,司法与仲裁共同法院可以根据秘书长的建议,在 30 日内决定是否受理仲裁请求。① 如果司法与仲裁共同法院认为存在提交给它进行仲裁的表面协议,即便另一方当事人随后拒绝参与仲裁程序,仲裁程序仍可继续进行。②

《仲裁规则》也采用了仲裁条款独立原则和仲裁庭自裁管辖权原则(competence-competence)。当一方当事人提出有关仲裁协议的存在、有效性及范围的异议时,如果仲裁庭认为存在表面的仲裁协议,它就可决定仲裁程序继续进行。在这种情况下,仲裁庭会决定自己对争议有无管辖权。③ 在没有相反约定的情况下,如果仲裁庭认为仲裁协议有效,即使合同无效,仲裁庭仍可对争议作出裁决。④

(二)仲裁庭的组成

根据《仲裁规则》第 3 条的规定,仲裁庭可由独任仲裁员或 3 名仲裁员组成。如果当事人没有对仲裁员人数作出约定,则司法与仲裁共同法院会指定独任仲裁员审理案件,除非案情表明需要指定 3 名仲裁员。如果当事人约定由独任仲裁员审理争议,他们可协议指定 1 名仲裁员,并由司法与仲裁共同法院对

① 《仲裁规则》第 9 条。

② 《仲裁规则》第 10 条第 2 款。

③ 《仲裁规则》第 10 条第 3 款。

④ 《仲裁规则》第 10 条第 4 款。

此予以确认。如果在收到一方当事人仲裁请求后的30日内,双方未能就独任仲裁员的指定达成协议,则由司法与仲裁共同法院作出指定。如果双方约定由3名仲裁员审理争议,则他们可在仲裁申请或仲裁答辩状中指定各自的仲裁员。若一方当事人放弃作出指定,则由司法与仲裁共同法院替该方当事人作出指定。如果双方当事人没有约定第三名仲裁员由他们各自指定的仲裁员进行指定,则该仲裁员由司法与仲裁共同法院指定。如果双方当事人约定由他们各自指定的仲裁员指定第三名仲裁员,在这两名仲裁员无法就第三名仲裁员的指定达成一致意见时,仍由司法与仲裁共同法院指定第三名仲裁员。

《仲裁规则》还对多方当事人仲裁的可能性作出了规定。该规则第3条第1款规定,当要求多方申请人或被申请人就仲裁员的指定作出共同建议,而他们不能在规定时间内就仲裁员的指定达成一致意见时,司法与仲裁共同法院应指定仲裁庭的所有成员。这样,就可避免在指定仲裁员时对当事人的不平等待遇。

仲裁员应从司法与仲裁共同法院拟定(每年更新)的仲裁员名单中进行选择。当司法与仲裁共同法院指定仲裁员时,它必须考虑到当事人的国籍、居所地、仲裁员和代理人的居所地、当事人所使用的语言、需要解决的争议的类型,以及争议所适用的法律。

在当事人之间没有约定而由司法与仲裁共同法院指定仲裁员时,为尽快完成指定,司法与仲裁共同法院应根据下列程序作出指定:司法与仲裁共同法院秘书长会给双方当事人各提供一份至少含有3名候选人的相同名单,每一方当事人可在秘书长规定的期限内标出他们优先选择的仲裁员次序,或删掉他们反对的仲裁员。随后,司法与仲裁共同法院会根据双方当事人选择的仲裁员的优先次序确定仲裁员。如果按照这种途径仍不能确定仲裁员,司法与仲裁共同法院就可根据自己的自由裁量权确定仲裁员。①

《仲裁规则》要求所有仲裁员应独立于当事人,并且应向司法与仲裁共同

① 《仲裁规则》第3条第3款。

法院秘书长报告任何可能使当事人怀疑其独立性的情形。在这种情况下,秘书长应向当事人书面说明情况并要求他们在规定期限内作出评论。司法与仲裁共同法院受理对仲裁员提出的异议。对仲裁员的异议必须由当事人在其收到仲裁员任命通知后30日内提出,或发现使异议成立的事实后的30日内提出。在秘书长通知相关仲裁员、当事人以及仲裁庭的其他成员在规定期限内提出书面意见后,司法与仲裁共同法院应决定是否受理异议请求,并在适当情况下对异议请求的实体问题作出处理。①

根据《仲裁规则》的规定,仲裁员原则上不能辞职,必须参与仲裁程序直到结束。② 不过,如果存在充分理由,司法与仲裁共同法院可以接受仲裁员的辞职。如果当事人对仲裁员提出的异议成立、仲裁员死亡或其辞职已被接受,则该仲裁员必须被更换。如果独任仲裁员或仲裁庭主席提出辞职,但其辞职未被接受并且他拒绝继续参与仲裁,那么该仲裁员必须被更换。如果他是3人仲裁庭的普通成员,司法与仲裁共同法院在考虑仲裁程序的进程及两名留任仲裁员的意见后将决定是否更换他。如果司法与仲裁共同法院决定他不应该被更换,仲裁程序就会继续进行,并在他不参与的情况下作出仲裁裁决。③

如果仲裁员在法律上或事实上不能履行仲裁员的职责,或不能适当地履行职责,也可对其予以更换。在此情况下,当事人和仲裁员(包括将被更换的仲裁员)都被要求作出自己的评价。当予以更换的仲裁员是当事人指定的仲裁员时,作出该指定的当事人可以对新仲裁员的指定发表意见,但司法与仲裁共同法院并不受该意见的约束。在上述情况下,仲裁庭重新组成时,仲裁庭在和当事人商议后应自行决定是否应重复以前的仲裁程序。④

仲裁庭组成后,在某些情况下其可以决定仲裁的听审地点、仲裁的程序规则、争议的法律适用,以及决定自己是否具有管辖权。例如,根据《仲裁规则》第13条的规定,如果当事人在仲裁协议及随后的协议中没有约定仲裁地点,则

① 《仲裁规则》第4条第1款、第2款。
② 《仲裁规则》第4条第1款。
③ 《仲裁规则》第4条第3款。
④ 《仲裁规则》第4条第4款、第5款。

司法与仲裁共同法院在将仲裁文件转给仲裁庭之前会对仲裁地点作出决定。仲裁庭在与当事人协商后,可以在它认为适当的地点举行听审和审议。如果相关情况导致仲裁无法在之前决定的地点进行,则司法与仲裁共同法院可应当事人或仲裁员的请求选择另一仲裁地点。仲裁程序的进行应适用《仲裁规则》;如该仲裁规则没有相应规定,可适用当事人约定的规则;在当事人无约定时,仲裁庭可决定是否适用某一程序法。① 对于争议实体问题的法律适用,在当事人没有对争议所适用的法律作出约定时,仲裁庭可以适用它认为最适当的法律,但无论如何,仲裁庭应考虑合同的条款以及国际商事惯例。此外,在当事人明确同意的情况下,仲裁庭还可作为友好调解人解决争议。②《仲裁规则》第21条规定,如果当事人对仲裁庭审理全部或部分争议的管辖权提出异议,仲裁庭可在仲裁程序的任何时间对自己是否具有管辖权作出临时、部分或最终裁决。

(三)仲裁程序

仲裁申请人向秘书长提出仲裁申请后,仲裁程序启动。仲裁申请必须包含一些《仲裁规则》第5条所明确规定的信息,包括:当事人的姓名、职业、商号、通信和电子地址,以及为进行仲裁而选择的住所;当事人之间的仲裁协议或仲裁请求据以提起的其他法律文件;争议的摘要、申请人的请求以及相关证据;有关仲裁员人数及指定的建议;当事人之间有关仲裁地点、仲裁语言、适用于仲裁协议、仲裁程序以及仲裁实体问题的法律的约定;在无此类约定时,仲裁申请人对这些问题的有关建议。仲裁申请人在提交仲裁请求时,还应根据规定支付一定的费用。秘书长在收到仲裁请求后,会立即通知被申请人。秘书长收到仲裁申请的日期被认为是仲裁开始之日。③

被申请人必须自收到秘书长有关仲裁程序开始的通知之日起30日内,对仲裁申请提出答辩。根据《仲裁规则》的规定,答辩书除简要陈述对仲裁请求的立场外,被申请人还必须表明,他是否承认当事人之间存在将争议提交司法

---

① 《仲裁规则》第16条。
② 《仲裁规则》第17条。
③ 《仲裁规则》第5条。

与仲裁共同法院进行仲裁的仲裁协议书。[①] 同时，被申请人也可提出反请求，申请人可在30日内对此进行答辩。[②] 一旦这些答辩完成后，或超过提交答辩的日期后，司法与仲裁共同法院就会决定预交的仲裁费用、在当事人没有约定仲裁地的情况下决定仲裁的所在地并启动仲裁程序。[③]

仲裁庭在收到相互交换的请求书后，应最迟在45日内举行一次仲裁庭和当事人的见面会，并起草备忘录以决定仲裁的目的以及某些程序事项。[④] 这些备忘录必须含有各方当事人简要的仲裁请求，当事人之间作出的有关仲裁地点、仲裁语言、所适用的程序规则和实体法以及仲裁协议准据法的任何约定。若当事人没有约定仲裁所使用的语言，仲裁庭与当事人协商后，应迅速对该问题作出决定。在该会议上，仲裁庭还必须询问当事人是否希望仲裁庭充当友好调解人的角色，并根据公平原则作出裁决。

仲裁庭还会采取一些适当措施以有利于仲裁程序的顺利进行。它会确定一个临时的日程表，包括听审日期等。除非当事人另有约定，听审日期应确定在见面会后的6个月内。[⑤] 不过，如有必要，仲裁庭可以主动或应当事人的请求对临时日程表作出修正。在此情况下，修改后的日程表应提交给司法与仲裁共同法院。仲裁裁决必须在仲裁程序结束之日起90日内签署，司法与仲裁共同法院应仲裁庭的请求可延长该期限。[⑥]

仲裁庭所适用的程序规则就是《仲裁规则》中所规定的规则。在《仲裁规则》无相应规定时，应适用当事人所约定的规则；若当事人无此约定，则由仲裁庭决定所适用的规则。仲裁庭可参考某一国内的程序法，但这不是强制性的。[⑦] 仲裁庭必须适用当事人所选择的实体法；若当事人无此选择，则仲裁庭

---

① 《仲裁规则》第6条。
② 《仲裁规则》第7条。
③ 《仲裁规则》第7条、第8条。
④ 《仲裁规则》第15条。
⑤ 《仲裁规则》第15条第1款(f)。
⑥ 《仲裁规则》第15条第3款、第4款。
⑦ 《仲裁规则》第16条。

在考虑合同条款和任何相关的国际商事惯例后,适用它认为最适当的法律。[①]

如果有一方当事人对仲裁庭的管辖权提出异议,他必须最迟在第一次见面会上提出。如果存在公共政策方面的原因,仲裁庭也可主动在仲裁程序的任何阶段对其管辖权进行调查。在此情况下,它要听取当事人的意见。在仲裁庭的管辖权受到质疑时,它可在临时裁决中,或在对当事人有关实体问题的答辩听审后作出的最终或部分裁决中,对管辖权问题作出决定。[②]

除非当事人另有约定,仲裁庭在仲裁程序中有权下令采取临时或保全措施。如果需要凭执行令来实施此类措施,那么当事人可马上向司法与仲裁共同法院院长或特别指定的司法与仲裁共同法院法官提出申请。若案件还未由仲裁庭审理,或在紧急情况下需要采取临时或保全措施,相关当事人可向成员国国内法院提出采取此类措施的申请,但司法与仲裁共同法院必须获得有关此类申请以及成员国国内法院下令采取的任何措施的通知,并且司法与仲裁共同法院必须随后将此情况通报给仲裁庭。[③]

(四)追加当事人、多方当事人和多方合同

根据国际上仲裁的发展趋势,修订后的《仲裁规则》增加了有关追加当事人、多方当事人和多方合同的规定,这些规定与国际商会仲裁院 2017 年 3 月通过的仲裁规则十分相似。

《仲裁规则》将追加当事人的情况分为两种,即被动追加(intervention forcée)和主动追加(intervention volontaire)。《仲裁规则》第 8-1 条规定了被动追加情况。根据该条规定,如果仲裁程序中的一方当事人希望追加受仲裁协议约束但未参与仲裁程序的人员,他可以向秘书长提出追加申请。在仲裁庭组成前,司法与仲裁共同法院决定提交此类追加申请的期限。如果在提交追加申请时,仲裁庭已经组成或仲裁员已被指定或已得到确认,追加申请将不会被受理,除非仲裁程序的当事人以及被追加人员都同意而且仲裁庭在考虑仲裁程序的

① 《仲裁规则》第 17 条。

② 《仲裁规则》第 21 条。

③ 《仲裁规则》第 10.1 条。

进展后同意接受该申请。如果受仲裁协议约束但没有参与仲裁程序的人员希望加入仲裁程序（主动追加），他必须在仲裁庭组成前提出此类请求。在仲裁庭组成后，主动追加当事人的情况必须得到仲裁庭和所有当事人的事先同意。①

如果一项争议存在多方当事人，只要他们同意按照《仲裁规则》进行仲裁，司法与仲裁共同法院就可启动仲裁程序。在此类多方当事人的仲裁中，所有当事人都可针对其他当事人提出请求。提出仲裁请求的多方当事人应按照《仲裁规则》第5条的规定提交相应的材料。仲裁庭在收到秘书长转交的所有仲裁文书后，它会决定提交新的请求的程序。②

根据《仲裁规则》第8-4条的规定，对于产生于多项合同或与多项合同有关的请求，可以在单独一项仲裁中提出。如果此类请求是基于多个仲裁协议提出的，仲裁庭必须确信：所有当事人都同意按照本规则进行仲裁，而且这些仲裁协议之间存在一致性，以及所有当事人都同意在一个仲裁程序中解决这些请求。虽然该条规定借鉴了国际商会仲裁院2017年《仲裁规则》第9条和第10条有关多方合同和仲裁合并的规定，但二者存在一些不同。例如，根据国际商会仲裁院2017年的仲裁规则，对于根据多项仲裁协议提出的请求可以合并在一个仲裁程序中，但除要求这些仲裁协议存在一致性外，还要求仲裁是发生在相同当事人之间，且争议产生于相同的法律关系。从结构和具体规定来看，国际商会仲裁院的仲裁规则有关多方合同和合并仲裁的规定更为明确、科学、严谨。

（五）仲裁程序的结束

在旧的《仲裁规则》中，没有关于仲裁程序结束的规定。修订后的《仲裁规则》第19-1条规定，在下列情况下，仲裁庭可结束仲裁程序：在当事人根据程序日程安排提交最后一次有关实体问题的陈述后；或在仲裁申请人撤回仲裁请求后，除非被申请人提出反对而且仲裁庭认为它对于彻底解决争议具有合法利益；或仲裁庭确信仲裁程序的继续进行已无必要或已无可能。

---

① 《仲裁规则》第10.2条。

② 《仲裁规则》第8-3条。

在仲裁程序结束后,除非得到仲裁庭书面的明示同意,当事人不得提交新的请求和材料,也不得提出新的意见或证据。

(六)仲裁裁决

1. 裁决的内容和形式

旧的《仲裁规则》只是规定仲裁裁决必须说明理由,但没有规定裁决必须包含的其他内容。修订后的《仲裁规则》第22条第1款明确规定,除当事人有其他约定外,仲裁裁决应含有下列内容:作出裁决的仲裁员的姓名;作出裁决的日期;仲裁庭所在地;当事人的姓名、住所或商号;必要时,代理人或其他协助人员的姓名;有关各方当事人的要求、理由及仲裁阶段的说明。新的《仲裁规则》同样要求仲裁裁决必须说明理由。如果仲裁庭是根据当事人授权作为友好调解人解决争议的,则裁决中必须对此作出说明。仲裁裁决的作出地点就是仲裁地点,裁决的日期是经司法与仲裁共同法院审核后的签署日期。

仲裁裁决可根据当事人约定的程序和形式作出;如果当事人没有此种约定,在仲裁庭是由3名仲裁员组成的情况下,裁决应根据多数意见作出。仲裁员应在裁决上签名。如果1名或2名仲裁员拒绝签名,应在裁决书中注明,这并不影响仲裁裁决的效力。①

裁决签署前,有关仲裁庭管辖权的裁决草案、结束仲裁程序的部分裁决草案以及最终裁决草案必须提交秘书长供司法与仲裁共同法院进行审核。其他裁决无须事先审核,但要呈交司法与仲裁共同法院备案。司法与仲裁共同法院对裁决进行审核时,仅就形式方面的修正提出建议。如果裁决是最终裁决,司法与仲裁共同法院会就仲裁费用的最终数额向仲裁庭提出建议,并决定仲裁员的费用。最终裁决必须指明仲裁费用,并决定各方当事人所承担的比例。司法与仲裁共同法院应自收到裁决书草案后的1个月内完成审核。② 当事人付清仲裁费用后,秘书长会将签署后的仲裁裁决交给当事人。③

---

① 《仲裁规则》第22条第3款。

② 《仲裁规则》第23条、第24条。

③ 《仲裁规则》第25条。

2. 裁决的修改、解释和补充

任何有关修改裁决中非实体性错误的请求、对裁决进行解释的请求，或对仲裁员没有审理的事项作出补充裁决的请求，必须在裁决交给当事人后的30日内向秘书长提出。秘书长在收到此类请求后马上转交给仲裁庭及对方当事人，并给予他们30日的期限提出自己的意见。如果不能重新组成仲裁庭，而且当事人无法就新仲裁庭的组成达成一致意见，司法与仲裁共同法院可以指定1名独任仲裁员对仲裁裁决的解释、修改或补充作出处理。该独任仲裁员应自受理请求后的45日内作出新的裁决，该裁决仍应根据上述规定进行复核。

在复核程序中，如果任命了新的仲裁员，当事人必须向其支付费用；如果没有任命新的仲裁员，当事人则无须再向仲裁员支付费用。在当事人提出修改、解释或补充仲裁裁决的申请并且仲裁庭进行了审理的情况下，如有新的仲裁费用，在当事人提出的申请被仲裁庭完全驳回时，此类新的费用应由提出申请的当事人承担；否则，这些费用将根据裁决中确定的比例由各方承担。①

根据《仲裁规则》签发的仲裁裁决在各成员国领域内具有最终既判力，和成员国国内法院作出的判决具有同等效力，可在任一成员国领域内得到执行。② 但此类裁决要在成员国内得到执行，首先必须获得一个执行令。③

3. 裁决的撤销和执行

(1)裁决的撤销

在旧的《仲裁规则》中，没有规定裁决的撤销程序，但规定当事人可对仲裁裁决的有效性和既判力向司法与仲裁共同法院提出异议。如果司法与仲裁共同法院认为仲裁裁决无效，也不具有既判力，它就可撤销仲裁裁决。旧的《仲裁规则》没有明确规定当事人可以就仲裁裁决的有效性和既判力提出异议的理由，而且它还规定，此类异议不得依据反对执行令的理由提出，这就会给当事人在实践中提出此类异议带来极大麻烦。修订后的《仲裁规则》没有再采用此

---

① 《仲裁规则》第26条。

② 《仲裁规则》第27条。

③ 《仲裁规则》第30条。

类异议程序,而是明确规定了仲裁裁决的撤销程序。根据新的规则,只要仲裁裁决不会因为违反国际公共政策而被撤销,当事人便可以约定放弃利用撤销裁决这一程序。如果当事人没有作出此类约定,他们就可利用这一程序寻求撤销一项仲裁裁决。当事人必须在收到仲裁裁决通知后的2个月内向司法与仲裁共同法院提出申请,并通知对方当事人。否则,司法与仲裁共同法院将不会受理该申请。撤销仲裁裁决的申请应依据下列理由提出:仲裁庭在没有仲裁协议或在仲裁协议无效或失效的情况下作出仲裁裁决;仲裁庭组成不当或独任仲裁员指定不当;仲裁庭越权裁决;仲裁庭没有遵守对抗制原则;仲裁裁决违反国际公共政策;仲裁裁决没有说明理由。①

司法与仲裁共同法院应在收到撤销裁决申请后的6个月内作出决定。如果司法与仲裁共同法院认为对裁决效力提出的异议理由充分,它就会宣布裁决无效。如果当事人提出请求,它可就案件实体问题进行听审并作出新的判决。如果当事人没有要求司法与仲裁共同法院对实体问题进行审理,应仲裁程序中最审慎一方当事人的请求,仲裁程序可自被司法与仲裁共同法院认可有效的最后一次行为时重新开始。②

(2)裁决的司法审查与第三人异议程序

除可对裁决的效力提出异议外,当事人也可根据《司法与仲裁共同法院程序规则》第49条请求对裁决进行修正,或请求司法与仲裁共同法院在裁决撤销后就案件实体问题作出的判决进行修正。根据《司法与仲裁共同法院程序规则》第49条,此类请求在以下情况发生时才被接受:发现了对裁决具有决定性影响的事实,而在签发裁决时仲裁庭、司法与仲裁共同法院以及提出此类请求的当事人都未发现该事实。修改裁决的请求必须自发现新的事实后的3个月内向司法与仲裁共同法院提出,如果在裁决或判决作出之日起10年后提出此类请求,则此类请求不会被接受。

在仲裁裁决对第三人的权利造成损害时,第三人可根据《司法与仲裁共同

① 《仲裁规则》第29条第2款。

② 《仲裁规则》第29条第5款。

法院程序规则》第47条规定的条件,提出第三人对仲裁裁决的异议申请。①

(3)裁决的执行

如果当事人希望执行司法与仲裁共同法院的仲裁裁决,他必须向司法与仲裁共同法院院长申请执行令(exequatur)。执行令由司法与仲裁共同法院院长或由他特别指定的法官签发。他们如果同意签发执行令,还必须向被申请人作出执行令通知。被申请人自收到执行令通知后的15日内可以提出反对执行令的意见。在此情况下,司法与仲裁共同法院应根据《司法与仲裁共同法院程序规则》的有关规定,召集双方当事人进行听审。② 只有在下列情况下,司法与仲裁共同法院才会拒绝签发执行令:仲裁庭在没有仲裁协议、仲裁协议无效或失效的情况下作出裁决;仲裁庭越权作出裁决;仲裁庭没有遵守对抗制程序原则;仲裁裁决违反国际公共政策。③ 如果执行令被法院拒绝,提出申请的当事人可在收到拒绝其申请的通知后的15日内,向司法与仲裁共同法院提出异议。如果司法与仲裁共同法院院长在对被申请人的异议进行审理后,决定作出执行令,则当事人不得提起任何程序。④

三、根据《仲裁统一法》进行的仲裁

非洲商法协调组织在2017年11月23日通过的新《仲裁统一法》,对旧法中存在的一些过时和含糊的规定进行了修改,明确了一些具体期限,并根据国际上最新的仲裁立法趋势增加了许多新内容。但新法并非完全推翻旧法的规定,而是在旧法的基础上作出了相应的修正和澄清。与旧法相比,新《仲裁统一法》更有利于争议的解决。本部分将根据新《仲裁统一法》的规定,对其仲裁程序进行简单的介绍。

(一)《仲裁统一法》的适用范围

《仲裁统一法》第1条规定,该法适用于仲裁地位于非洲商法协调组织某

① 《仲裁规则》第33条。
② 《仲裁规则》第30条第1款、第2款。
③ 《仲裁规则》第30条第5款。
④ 《仲裁规则》第30条第3款、第4款。

一成员国内的所有仲裁。该法没有对国内仲裁和国际仲裁进行区分。因此,在成员国内进行的无论是国际仲裁还是国内仲裁,均应受该法的调整。如果当事人选择在某一仲裁机构进行仲裁并且选定了仲裁规则,但仲裁地在某一成员国内,则《仲裁统一法》仍可适用。

根据《仲裁统一法》第2条的规定,能够通过仲裁方式解决的事项不限于商事事项,任何涉及可以自由处置的权利的事项均可提交仲裁。这表明,对于任何不涉及需要公共机构干预的权利的争议都可进行仲裁。该法第2条还规定,个人和法人实体都可将争议提交仲裁。它还特别规定,国家或其他地区公共机构以及公共公司也可将争议提交仲裁,此类实体不能以本国国内法的规定、自身缺乏订立仲裁协议的能力或仲裁协议无效来主张所涉争议不能提交仲裁。

(二)仲裁协议

最常见的仲裁协议是当事人在合同中订立的仲裁条款。不过,在争议发生后当事人可签订仲裁议定书将争议提交仲裁。[①] 此外,根据《仲裁统一法》第3条的规定,当事人提交仲裁的意思表示也包含在有关投资的法律文件(特别是投资法、双边投资保护条约或多边投资保护条约)中。这就明确把投资争议纳入《仲裁统一法》的调整范围内,外国投资者可利用该条规定把相关投资争议提交到非洲商法协调组织某一成员国内的仲裁机构。

当事人的仲裁协议须以书面形式或可证明其存在的任何其他方式作成。[②] 一般认为,"可证明其存在的其他方式"应包括当事人来往函电中提到的含有仲裁协议的某一文件。例如,许多国家(如法国)都认可当事人所提及的某一文件中仲裁条款的效力,这体现了国际上支持仲裁的趋势,当然这也是合同当事人特别应当注意的一个问题。

《仲裁统一法》明确规定了仲裁协议的独立原则。根据该法的规定,首先,该原则意味着仲裁协议独立于主合同,主合同是否有效不影响仲裁协议的效

① 《仲裁统一法》第3-1条第1~3款。

② 《仲裁统一法》第3-1条第4款。

力;其次,仲裁协议并不必然受主合同准据法或某一特定国内法的支配,它要根据当事人的共同意图进行解释。[①] 这一规定与法国《仲裁法》的规定十分相似,它非常有助于维护仲裁协议的有效性,有利于实现当事人通过仲裁解决争议的期望。但这种直接按照当事人的共同意图来判断仲裁协议效力的规定与一些重要仲裁公约(如 1958 年《纽约公约》)的规定不符,在仲裁裁决的承认和执行方面可能会带来问题。[②]

(三)仲裁庭的组成

《仲裁统一法》第 5 条规定,仲裁庭必须由独任仲裁员或 3 名仲裁员组成。在当事人之间没有约定时,仲裁庭应由独任仲裁员组成。此外,仲裁员只能由自然人担任。这是一条强制性规定,如果当事人约定由 2 名仲裁员组成仲裁庭,该仲裁庭就可能会被认为组成不当,它作出的裁决就可能因此被撤销。因此,在当事人只约定指定 2 名仲裁员时,仲裁庭必须由双方当事人同意指定的第三名仲裁员一起才能组建。如果当事人不能就第三名仲裁员的指定达成一致意见,则第三名仲裁员应由已经指定的 2 名仲裁员指定。如这 2 名仲裁员仍不能就第三名仲裁员的指定达成一致意见,则该第三名仲裁员应由成员国内有管辖权的法院指定。

当事人可自由约定指定、解除或更换仲裁员的规则。[③] 若无此种约定,或该约定不能充分包括所有事项,则应适用《仲裁统一法》中的相应规定。如果当事人选择 3 人仲裁庭,则每方当事人应指定 1 名仲裁员,再由这 2 名仲裁员指定第三名仲裁员。如果一方当事人在收到另一方当事人指定仲裁员请求后的 30 日内没有作出指定,或如果已指定的 2 名仲裁员在他们被指定后的 30 日内没有指定第三名仲裁员,则成员国内有管辖权的法院可根据一方当事人的请求作出上述指定。如果仲裁庭由独任仲裁员组成,而双方当事人不能就该仲裁员的指定协商一致,则成员国内有管辖权的法院可根据一方当事人的请求作出

---

① 《仲裁统一法》第 4 条。

② 参见朱伟东:《中国涉外仲裁协议效力的认定:困境与出路》,载《仲裁与法律》2010 年第 116 辑。

③ 《仲裁统一法》第 6 条第 1 款。

指定。[①] 旧的《仲裁统一法》没有对国内法院指定仲裁员的时间作出规定，实践中可能造成有些法院故意拖延仲裁员的指定。为了防止出现这种情况，新的《仲裁统一法》明确规定，成员国内有管辖权的法院在收到指定仲裁员的请求后，必须在15日内作出指定，除非该成员国国内立法规定了更短的时间，而且当事人不得对法院作出的有关指定仲裁员的决定提起上诉。[②] 该法明确要求，所有仲裁员应保持独立、公正，如果仲裁员认为存在当事人可对其公正和独立提出异议的理由，他应提请当事人注意。他只有在获得当事人的一致书面同意后，才能接受当事人对他的指定。[③]

如果当事人对仲裁员的指定发生争议，而且他们没有就仲裁员的异议程序作出约定，此类异议就应由成员国内有管辖权的法院受理。希望对仲裁员提出异议的当事人应在发现引起异议的事实或理由后的30日内提出异议。该法院应在收到仲裁员异议请求后的30日内作出处理。如果该法院在30日内未能对该异议请求作出处理，当事人可请求司法与仲裁共同法院就此异议作出处理。针对成员国国内有管辖权的法院作出的驳回异议请求的决定，当事人只能向司法与仲裁共同法院提起上诉。[④] 而在旧的《仲裁统一法》中，当事人不得对成员国法院就仲裁员异议请求作出的决定提起上诉。新的规定显然是考虑到了《非洲商法协调条约》中有关司法与仲裁共同法院可以受理来自成员国的、涉及统一法适用上诉的规定。

（四）仲裁程序

新的《仲裁统一法》专门增加了一条有关仲裁前程序的规定。根据该规定，如果当事人之间存在协议要求他们在诉诸仲裁前采用其他方式解决争议，在一方当事人要求通过此类方式解决争议时，仲裁庭应对此问题进行分析，必要时协助完成仲裁前程序。如果仲裁前程序没有启动，仲裁庭可以在它认为合适的时间内中止自己的程序，以让当事人提起仲裁前的相关程序。如果仲裁前

---

① 《仲裁统一法》第6条第4款。

② 《仲裁统一法》第6条第5款。

③ 《仲裁统一法》第7条。

④ 《仲裁统一法》第8条。

程序已有效提起,仲裁庭可决定是否中断自己的程序。[①] 这一规定显然是考虑到当事人在仲裁协议中约定有协商或调解解决争议的情况。例如,许多当事人通常在仲裁协议中约定,若发生争议,先通过协商或调解程序解决;如果协商或调解不成,再通过仲裁方式解决。考虑到协商和调解方式在非洲的广泛使用,增加这样的规定十分必要。

《仲裁统一法》第 9 条规定,仲裁程序中的当事人必须得到平等对待,且有陈述案情的机会。此外,根据该法第 10 条的规定,当事人有权将争议提交仲裁机构进行仲裁,但在这种情况下,当事人应受他们所选择的仲裁机构的规则约束,除非他们明确约定不适用其中的某些规则。仲裁程序自一方当事人提起组建仲裁庭的请求后开始。

《仲裁统一法》中规定了如下一些基本的正当程序规则,这些规则可确保当事人可获得平等和公正对待:

1. 当事人有责任证明各自的请求,不过,仲裁庭可指导他们提供必要的解释和证据;

2. 仲裁庭在其裁决中不得采信当事人在仲裁程序中没有适当机会陈述案情的某些理由或文件;

3. 当事人获知仲裁程序中存在某些不公正情形时,必须立即提出,否则他就会被认为已放弃了此种权利。[②]

除上述基本的程序规则外,仲裁庭必须使用当事人所选择的某一仲裁机构的规则或某一国家程序法中的规则。如果当事人没有约定所适用的规则,仲裁庭可自己决定所适用的适当规则。[③]

仲裁庭必须根据当事人选择的实体法就案件的实体问题作出裁决。如果当事人没有选择所适用的法律,仲裁庭就应选择它认为是最适当的法律,必要时应考虑国际商事惯例。如果当事人允许,仲裁庭也可根据公平原则作出

① 《仲裁统一法》第 8-1 条。

② 《仲裁统一法》第 14 条。

③ 同上。

裁决。[①]

《仲裁统一法》还确认了当代仲裁实践确立的仲裁庭自裁管辖权原则，如仲裁庭有权就自己的管辖权(包括有关仲裁协议的存在或效力的问题)作出裁决的原则。对仲裁庭管辖权的异议必须在对案件实体问题进行答辩前提出，除非它是根据随后发现的事实而提出的。在仲裁庭的管辖权受到质疑的情况下，仲裁庭可就其管辖权作出单独裁决，或在一个裁决中就管辖权问题和案件实体问题作出处理。如果仲裁庭单独就管辖权问题作出了裁决，而且其继续进行仲裁程序以对案件实体问题作出处理，那么有关管辖权的裁决可以立即进入撤销程序，而无须等到仲裁庭就案件实体问题作出最终裁决。[②]

和其他当代仲裁法一样，《仲裁统一法》规定，在当事人之间存在仲裁协议的情况下，仲裁程序优先于任何法院程序。这样，如果仲裁程序开始前或开始后一方当事人将争议提交某一国内法院解决，另一方当事人依据仲裁协议对法院的管辖权提出异议，法院就必须放弃管辖，除非仲裁条款显然无效并且仲裁程序尚未开始。在这种情况下，法院必须在15日内就自己的管辖权作出决定。当事人可将该决定向司法与仲裁共同法院提起上诉。[③]

即使存在仲裁条款，法院仍有可能在所认可的紧急情况下，下令采取临时措施或保全措施，或者此类措施将在成员国之外的某一国家采取，但条件是下令采取的此类措施不涉及对争议实体问题的审查。[④] 此外，在获取证据时，如果有必要得到法院的协助，仲裁庭可以根据自己的动议或应当事人的请求向有关成员国的法院寻求协助。[⑤]

除非当事人另有约定，裁决应在最后一个仲裁员接受任命之日起的6个月内作出。[⑥] 该期限可根据当事人的协议予以延长，或由仲裁庭或当地法院根据

---

① 《仲裁统一法》第15条。

② 《仲裁统一法》第11条。

③ 《仲裁统一法》第13条。如果仲裁程序已开始，仲裁庭自己有权根据第11条的规定就仲裁协议的存在或效力作出裁决。

④ 《仲裁统一法》第13条。

⑤ 《仲裁统一法》第14条。

⑥ 《仲裁统一法》第12条。

当事人的请求予以延长。

《仲裁统一法》第 14 条还规定,当事人在仲裁程序过程中应审慎、迅速,不得采取拖延措施。如果申请人没有合法理由不陈述自己的请求,仲裁庭就可结束仲裁程序;如果被申请人不提出自己的答辩,仲裁庭就可继续仲裁程序,不能认为被申请人缺席的事实等同于已接受申请人的所有请求;如果一方当事人没有出庭或提交相应证据,仲裁庭可继续仲裁程序并根据它拥有的证据材料作出处理。

仲裁程序可因作出最终裁决或因作出终结令而结束。仲裁庭可在下列情况下作出终结仲裁程序的命令:仲裁申请人撤回请求,而被申请人和仲裁庭没有提出反对;所有当事人都同意终结程序;仲裁庭认为继续进行仲裁程序已无必要或已不可能;仲裁最初的或延长的期限已过;存在对请求、弃权或交易的承认。[①]

(五)仲裁裁决

1. 仲裁裁决的形式和内容

《仲裁统一法》规定,仲裁裁决可根据当事人约定的程序和形式作出。在当事人没有作出约定时,如果仲裁庭是由 3 名仲裁员组成,则仲裁裁决应根据仲裁员的多数意见作出。如果在仲裁程序进行中,当事人达成和解,他们就可请求仲裁庭根据他们约定的形式作出仲裁裁决。[②]

除仲裁裁决主文外,仲裁裁决必须包含下列内容:作出仲裁裁决的仲裁员的姓名;作出仲裁裁决的日期;仲裁庭所在地;当事人的姓名、商号以及他们的住所;必要时,代理人或律师的姓名;有关当事人各自的请求、证据及仲裁进程的简要说明。此外,仲裁裁决一定要附上理由。如果仲裁庭是根据当事人的授权作为友好调解人(amiable compositeur)解决争议的,也必须在裁决中说明。[③]仲裁裁决必须由仲裁员签署。如果少数仲裁员拒绝签名,必须在裁决中予以说

---

① 《仲裁统一法》第 16 条第 3 款。

② 《仲裁统一法》第 19 条。

③ 《仲裁统一法》第 20 条。

明。少数仲裁员不签署裁决的行为并不影响裁决的效力。①

裁决一旦签署后,仲裁庭对争议就不再具有管辖权。不过,它仍可对裁决作出解释,或对裁决中的错误或疏漏作出修正。另外,如果仲裁庭没有对某一请求作出裁决,它可以作出补充裁决。在上述情况下,当事人应在收到裁决通知后的30日内向仲裁庭提出申请,仲裁庭必须在45日内作出解释或对裁决作出补充或修正。如果仲裁庭不能重新组成,当事人可请求成员国有管辖权的法院对上述问题作出处理。② 仲裁裁决一经作出,就对所涉争议具有既判力(res judicata)。③ 仲裁庭可根据当事人的请求,允许临时执行仲裁裁决,或驳回当事人的请求,但要说明理由。④

2. 仲裁裁决的撤销

针对仲裁裁决,当事人并不具有普通的上诉权利。⑤ 但在有限情况下,当事人可提起撤销程序以撤销一项裁决。当事人也可约定放弃申请撤销仲裁裁决的权利,除非仲裁裁决违反了国际公共政策。⑥ 如果当事人申请撤销一项仲裁裁决,他必须在收到仲裁裁决通知后的1个月内向成员国有管辖权的法院提出。成员国国内法院应在受理该请求后的3个月内作出处理。如果成员国国内法院没有在此期限内作出处理,当事人可在该期限届满后的15日内向司法与仲裁共同法院提出撤销仲裁裁决的请求。司法与仲裁共同法院应在收到请求后的6个月内作出处理。⑦ 如果成员国国内有管辖权的法院对撤销仲裁裁决的请求作出了裁定,当事人还可就该裁定向司法与仲裁共同法院提起上诉。⑧

根据《仲裁统一法》第28条的规定,如果仲裁庭已下令临时执行仲裁裁

① 《仲裁统一法》第21条。
② 《仲裁统一法》第22条。
③ 《仲裁统一法》第23条。
④ 《仲裁统一法》第24条。
⑤ 《仲裁统一法》第25条。
⑥ 《仲裁统一法》第25条第1~3款。
⑦ 《仲裁统一法》第27条。
⑧ 《仲裁统一法》第25条第4款。

决,当事人提出撤销仲裁裁决的请求可以终止裁决的执行,直至成员国有管辖权的法院对该请求作出处理。该法院还有权处理因临时执行仲裁裁决而产生的争议。

《仲裁统一法》第 26 条规定了当事人可以提出撤销仲裁裁决的理由。这些理由包括:不存在仲裁协议、仲裁协议无效或仲裁庭作出裁决时仲裁协议已过期;仲裁庭组成不当;仲裁庭没有遵守授权条款的规定;仲裁庭没有遵守对抗制原则;仲裁裁决违反国际公共政策;仲裁裁决没有说明理由。如果仲裁裁决不是因不存在仲裁协议、仲裁协议无效或失效而被撤销的,在仲裁程序中勤勉审慎行事的一方当事人就可请求根据《仲裁统一法》启动新的仲裁程序。[①]

《仲裁统一法》还规定了仲裁裁决的第三人异议程序以及裁决的复查程序。根据规定,没有参与仲裁程序的第三人如果认为仲裁裁决侵害了其权利,他可向仲裁庭提出异议。[②] 在裁决作出后,如果发现了可能会对裁决结果产生决定性影响的新事实,而且在裁决作出前仲裁庭和相关当事人都不知悉该事实,则当事人可请求仲裁庭对裁决进行复审。如果仲裁庭已无法再重新组成,当事人也可向成员国有管辖权的法院提出对裁决进行复审的请求。[③]

3. 仲裁裁决的承认与执行

只有获得成员国国内有管辖权的法院发布的执行令后,仲裁裁决才能得到执行。[④] 为获得裁决的承认和执行,裁决胜诉方当事人应向法院提供裁决书正本以及仲裁协议的副本,或其他符合要求的文件副本。[⑤] 如果上述文件不是根据被请求签发执行令的那个成员国的国内官方语言作出的,则请求签发执行令的当事人必须提交由该国官方语言作成的上述文件的译本,此类译本须经当地法院注册的翻译人员证实为真。[⑥] 在旧的《仲裁统一法》中,要求上述文件须以

---

① 《仲裁统一法》第 29 条。
② 《仲裁统一法》第 25 条第 5 款。
③ 《仲裁统一法》第 25 条第 6 款。
④ 《仲裁统一法》第 30 条。
⑤ 《仲裁统一法》第 31 条第 1 款、第 2 款。
⑥ 《仲裁统一法》第 31 条第 3 款。

法语作出,因为当时的《非洲商法协调条约》规定的非洲商法协调组织的工作语言只有法语。这样的规定引起很多人士的批评,因为这样的规定会带来许多不便。如果仲裁裁决需要在喀麦隆执行,仲裁裁决和仲裁协议都是以英语作出,按照旧的规定,还要将仲裁裁决和仲裁协议等相关文件翻译成法语,这显然十分不便。新的《仲裁统一法》考虑到了这一点,及时对此作出了修正。

《仲裁统一法》规定的拒绝签发执行令的理由只有一条,即仲裁裁决明显违反了国际公共政策规范。① 这样的规定显然非常有利于仲裁裁决在成员国国内得到承认与执行。与其他许多仲裁法不同,该法明确采纳了"国际公共政策"这一概念,显示出相当大的勇气和魄力。如果允许成员国按照本国公共政策标准来决定是否应当执行仲裁裁决,就会造成仲裁裁决在不同国家会受到不同对待,从而影响仲裁裁决的执行。但遗憾的是,《仲裁统一法》并没有明确规定何为"国际公共政策",考虑到涉及统一法解释和适用的问题应由司法与仲裁共同法院作出最终处理,这就可避免对这一概念在不同成员国出现不同的解释。

新的《仲裁统一法》明确规定了成员国国内法院签发执行令的期限,这样可以避免延误仲裁裁决的执行。根据规定,成员国国内有管辖权的法院应自收到当事人签发执行令请求后的15日内作出裁定。如果该法院没有在上述期限内作出裁定,则视为该法院已同意签发执行令。如果国内法院同意签发执行令或已被视为同意签发执行令,裁决胜诉当事人就可请求该法院的书记官长对根据仲裁裁决作出的执行令进行盖章,随后仲裁裁决就可得到执行。②

如果成员国国内法院作出拒绝签发执行令的裁定,当事人可向司法与仲裁共同法院提起上诉。相反,若成员国国内法院作出同意签发执行令的裁定,则当事人不得对此提起上诉,不过当事人可以提出撤销裁决的请求。③ 如果撤销裁决的请求被驳回,则仲裁裁决和执行令立即生效。④

---

① 《仲裁统一法》第31条。

② 《仲裁统一法》第31条第5款、第6款。

③ 《仲裁统一法》第32条。

④ 《仲裁统一法》第33条。

《仲裁统一法》第34条规定,对于不是根据本法的规定作出的仲裁裁决,它们在成员国内的承认和执行要根据可适用的国际公约的规定进行。例如,对于根据埃及法老在埃及作出的仲裁裁决,如果要在喀麦隆申请承认与执行,则可根据双方都加入的《纽约公约》的规定进行。如果两国之间不存在相关国际公约,则仲裁裁决的承认与执行可根据《仲裁统一法》的规定进行。例如,如果在马拉维根据马拉维法律作出的仲裁裁决要在几内亚比绍申请承认与执行,由于双方都不是《纽约公约》的成员国,就可根据《仲裁统一法》的规定进行相关程序。考虑到《仲裁统一法》对仲裁裁决的承认和执行规定了更为宽松的条件,利用该法的规定更容易使仲裁裁决得到承认与执行。

从上面的分析可以看出,《仲裁统一法》与《仲裁规则》的制定吸收了国际上有关国际商事仲裁法律文件的优点,体现了较强的时代性与先进性。同时,它们又不拘泥于现有国际商事仲裁法律文件的规定,作出了许多前瞻性的规定,特别是在裁决的撤销和执行等方面,例如,它们在裁决的撤销和执行程序中明确采用了国际公共政策的概念。虽然非洲商法协调组织的仲裁法律制度还存在某些不足,但非洲商法协调组织的立法者为推动地区一体化而表现出来的勇气和胆魄值得其他地区一体化组织学习。

四、非洲商法协调组织内的调解程序

仲裁、调解、调停、协商等争议解决方式在非洲历史悠久,它们并非西方的舶来品。在非洲传统社会中一直存在通过调解、调停等友好解决争议的做法,以恢复团体的和平,维持社会的和谐。在殖民统治时期,殖民者在非洲引进了西方的争议解决方式,传统的争议解决方式只在当地部族团体内适用。非洲国家独立后,一些国家为了实现法律的统一化,对传统争议解决方式并未给予应有的重视。实际上,传统争议解决方式在非洲的冲突管理和争议解决方面发挥着重要作用,它们反映了非洲人处理争议的智慧。随着传统的友好争议解决方式的价值被人们逐渐认可,非洲国家和地区也开始通过立法认可友好争议解决方式,一些非洲国家和地区还设立了许多国内和地区性友好争议解决机构。

非洲商法协调组织就十分重视这些友好争议解决方式，它在1999年就通过了《仲裁统一法》，而且在《非洲商法协调条约》中明确鼓励当事人通过仲裁方式解决合同争议。2017年11月23日非洲商法协调组织通过了《调解统一法》，为该地区通过调解方式解决争议提供了统一而明确的法律依据。从《调解统一法》的规定来看，它主要是以联合国国际贸易法委员会2002年《调解示范法》为版本制定的，同时又考虑到本地区的法律传统和实际情况。

(一)调解的相关定义及适用范围

根据《调解统一法》第1条的规定，"调解"(médiation)是指由当事人请求第三人协助友好解决因某一法律关系、合同关系或其他类似关系而产生的争议、冲突或不和关系的一种过程，无论其名称如何。和《仲裁统一法》一样，本法中的当事人包括自然人、法人、公共机构或国家。这表明外国投资者可以利用该法的规定，通过调解方式解决投资者与东道国政府之间的投资争议。"调解员"(médiateur)是指经当事人请求而调解解决争议的第三人，无论他们在成员国中的职业或名称如何。

根据《调解统一法》第1条第2款的规定，调解可由当事人提起(称为协议调解，médiation conventionnelle)，也可经成员国国内法院(médiation judiciaire)、仲裁机构或有权的公共机构的要求或请求而提起。从调解的形式来看，调解可以是临时调解，也可以是机构调解。①

《调解统一法》第2条规定，本法的规定适用于调解，但它不适用于法官或仲裁员在司法或仲裁程序中试图促成当事人直接友好解决争议的情况。从这条规定来看，它只是规定了该法所适用的调解的类型，但它并没有规定该法的地域适用范围。不过，根据《非洲商法协调条约》有关统一法的规定，该法显然适用于在非洲商法协调组织成员国内进行的调解，无论是临时调解还是机构调解。如果当事人选择通过成员国国内的调解机构解决争议，当事人就要遵守该机构的调解规则。② 对于调解规则没有规定的情况，仍需适用《调解统一法》的

① 《调解统一法》第1条第3款。

② 《调解统一法》第3条。

规定。

(二)调解程序的启动

《调解统一法》第4条规定了两种启动调解程序的方式:在当事人之间存在书面的或其他形式的调解协议时,调解程序自一方当事人实施该调解协议之日开始。若不存在调解协议,一方当事人可邀请另一方当事人通过调解解决争议。如果对方当事人在收到书面邀请后的15日内,没有接受该邀请,或者书面邀请中确定的期限到期后,对方当事人没有接受该邀请,这可以视为对方当事人拒绝该调解邀请。

成员国有管辖权的法院或仲裁机构可在与当事人协商后,中止其程序,让当事人调解解决争议。在此情况下,成员国国内法院或仲裁机构应确定其程序中止的期限。除当事人另有约定外,调解程序的开始会中断时效。如果调解程序未达成和解协议而结束,时效自调解程序结束之日重新计算。[①]

《调解统一法》第15条还特别规定,在当事人同意调解并明确承诺在一段特定时期内或在某一特定事件发生以前,不就现有或未来的争议提起仲裁或司法程序时,仲裁庭或法院应当确认这种承诺的效力,直至所承诺的条件实现为止。但上述规定不适用于一方当事人为维护其权利而提起临时或保全程序的情况。此类程序的提起不能被视为对调解协议的放弃或调解程序的终止。

(三)调解员的指定

《调解统一法》没有规定调解员的人数,当事人可协商选择1名或数名调解员。在选择调解员时,当事人可授权自然人或法人(特别是提供调解服务的机构或中心)协助指定调解员。当事人可要求上述指定人员或机构推荐有资格或能力提供调解服务的人员,也可由他们直接指定调解员。[②]

在推荐或指定调解员时,指定人员或机构应进行全面考虑,以确保指定的人员独立、公正并能履行职责。在必要时,还应考虑指定的调解员和当事人具有不同的国籍,特别是在当事人具有不同国籍的情况下。

---

① 《调解统一法》第4条第4款。

② 《调解统一法》第5条第1~4款。

在指定前,可能被指定为调解员的人员应披露所有可能对其公正性或独立性引起合理怀疑的情形。在被指定为调解员时,调解员应通过书面声明确认他的独立性和公正性以及他履职的保证。自其被指定之日起以及在整个调解程序期间,调解员应毫不迟延地向所有当事人披露可能对其公正性或独立性引起合理怀疑的新情况。

在调解员向当事人披露上述新情况后,他应告知当事人有权反对他继续履行职责。如果一方当事人随后拒绝其继续进行调解,则调解员的职务结束。[①]

为防止出现利益冲突的情况,《调解统一法》第14条就调解员能否担任仲裁员、专家证人或律师的情形作了明确规定。根据该规定,除非当事人另有约定,调解员不得在曾经是或目前是调解程序标的事项的争议或者因相同法律关系而产生的或与其有关的另一争议中,担任仲裁员、专家证人或律师。[②]

(四)调解程序的进行

当事人可以通过提及某一调解规则,自由约定调解程序进行的方式。在当事人没有作出此种约定时,调解员应在考虑案件的所有情况、当事人的期望以及快速解决争议的必要性后,采取他认为适当的方式进行调解。在所有情况下,调解员都应审慎履行职责,并在调解程序中平等对待所有当事人,同时应考虑案件的所有情况。[③]

调解员不应把争议解决方案强加给当事人。他可在调解程序的所有阶段,根据当事人的要求以及他认为最适当的方式,提出争议解决建议。此外,为了解决专业方面的问题,调解员在与当事人协商后,可以建议他们指定一个专家证人,以获得相关专业方面的意见。[④]

与许多调解法不同的是,《调解统一法》还专门规定了调解程序中调解员和成员国国内提供调解服务的机构应遵循的指导原则。这些原则包括尊重当事人意思自治原则,调解员道德正派、独立公正原则,调解程序保密、高效原则。

① 《调解统一法》第6条第2款。

② 《调解统一法》第14条。

③ 《调解统一法》第7条第1~3款。

④ 《调解统一法》第7条第4款、第5款。

《调解统一法》第9条和第10条具体阐明了上述原则。根据该法第9条的规定,调解员可与当事人进行单独或集体会面或联系。如果调解员希望单独与一方当事人和/或其代理人进行会面或联系,他应在此前或在单独联系或会面后告知另一方当事人和/或其代理人。如果调解员收到一方当事人有关争议的信息,他就应向调解程序中其他方当事人披露这一信息。但是,如果一方当事人在向调解员提交有关信息时明确要求保密,则调解员不应将此信息披露给其他当事人。《调解统一法》第10条则规定了调解信息对外保密的原则。根据该规定,除非当事人另有约定,与调解程序有关的一切信息均应保密,但按照法律要求或者为了履行或执行和解协议而披露信息的除外。

《调解统一法》第11条规定了调解程序中的证据在其他程序中的可采性问题。该条第1款规定,调解程序的一方当事人或任何第三人,包括参与调解程序行政工作的人在内,不得在仲裁、司法或类似的程序中以下列事项作为依据、将之作为证据提出或提供证言或证据:

1. 一方当事人关于参与调解程序的邀请,或者一方当事人曾经愿意参与调解程序的事实;

2. 一方当事人在调解中对可能解决争议的办法所表示的意见或提出的建议;

3. 一方当事人在调解程序过程中作出的陈述或承认;

4. 调解人或一方当事人提出的建议;

5. 一方当事人曾表示愿意接受调解人提出的和解建议的事实;

6. 完全为了调解程序而准备的文件。①

无论上述信息或证据的形式如何,本条第1款均适用。仲裁庭、法院或政府其他主管当局不得下令披露本条第1款所述的信息。违反本条第1款规定提供此类信息作为证据的,该证据应不予采纳。但按照法律要求或者为了履行或执行和解协议的,可以披露或者作为证据采纳此类信息的除外。② 无论仲

① 《调解统一法》第11条第1款。
② 《调解统一法》第11条第3款。

裁、司法或类似的程序与目前是或曾经是调解程序的标的事项的争议是否有关,本条上述规定均适用。但上述保密义务并不适用于调解程序启动前就已存在的证据或者在调解程序关系之外所产生的证据。[①]

《调解统一法》第11条基本上完全照搬了国际贸易法委员会《调解示范法》第10条的规定。只是该法第11条第5款的规定与《调解示范法》第10条的规定稍微有所不同。《调解示范法》第10条第5款规定:"以本条第(1)款的限制为限,在仲裁或司法或类似程序中可予采纳的证据并不因其曾用于调解中而变成不可采纳。"显然,《调解统一法》第11条第5款规定的可接受的证据的范围更为广泛,不但包括调解程序启动前就存在的证据,也包括在调解程序外部关系中所产生的证据。

(五)调解程序的终止

《调解统一法》第12条规定了调解程序终止的情形。根据该规定,调解程序在下列情形下终止:

1. 各方当事人和调解员签署了书面和解协议的,于协议签署之日终止。

2. 调解员在同各方当事人协商后发布书面声明,宣布继续进行调解已无意义的,于声明发表之日终止;或者调解员重启调解程序后,一方当事人不再参加新的调解程序的。

3. 各方当事人向调解员发出书面声明,宣布终止调解程序的,于声明发表之日终止。

4. 一方当事人向对方或其他各方当事人和已指定的调解员书面声明,宣布终止调解程序的,于声明发表之日终止。

5. 调解期限到期,除非当事人在与调解员协商后共同决定延长该期限。

如果由法院或仲裁员下令进行的调解程序终止时,当事人没有达成和解协议,司法程序或仲裁程序就恢复正常;如果同样的调解程序是因当事人达成友好和解协议而终止,法院或仲裁员可以对和解协议进行确认。

---

① 《调解统一法》第11条第4款、第5款。

（六）和解协议的执行

如果当事人达成了书面和解协议，该协议就是强制性的并具有约束力，并可获得执行。当事人可共同向公证员提出请求，对和解协议进行公证并予以签署。公证员应相关当事人的请求，可以发给他们执行令的副本。[①]

成员国国内有管辖权的法院也可应当事人的共同请求或应一方当事人的请求，对和解协议给予承认和执行。法院不得修改和解协议的条款，它只应审核和解协议的真实性，并在收到当事人请求后的15日内作出是否承认和执行和解协议的裁定。根据《调解统一法》的规定，只有当和解协议违反公共政策时，法院才能拒绝承认与执行。[②]

如果法院在15日内没有作出裁定，和解协议就可自动得到承认与执行。寻求执行和解协议的一方当事人就可向法院书记官或其他主管机构签署执行令状。反对执行该和解协议的当事人，可在收到附有执行令状的和解协议通知后的15日内，向司法与仲裁共同法院提出反对执行和解协议的请求。司法与仲裁共同法院会在6个月内对该请求作出处理。[③]

当事人不得对成员国国内法院作出的同意承认和执行和解协议的裁决提出上诉。对于成员国国内法院作出的拒绝承认与执行和解协议的裁定，当事人只能向司法与仲裁的共同法院提起上诉，司法与仲裁的共同法院会在6个月内作出处理。[④]

五、结论：非洲商法协调组织非诉争议解决制度的创新及意义

通过上面对非洲商法协调组织仲裁和调解法律制度的介绍可以看出，该组织不但改革、完善了旧的仲裁制度，而且引进了调解制度，丰富了该组织内非诉争议解决制度的内容，扩大了当事人选择非诉争议解决方式的范围。具体而言，修订后的《仲裁统一法》与《仲裁规则》主要针对以下方面进行了改革：

---

① 《调解统一法》第16条第1款、第2款。

② 《调解统一法》第16条第3~5款。

③ 《调解统一法》第16条第6款。

④ 《调解统一法》第16条第7款。

1. 扩大了受理案件的范围。修订后的《仲裁统一法》和《仲裁规则》明确规定,争议的当事方除可根据合同中的仲裁条款或事后达成的仲裁议定书提起仲裁程序外,还可根据投资法、双边投资保护条约或多边投资条约的规定提起仲裁程序。与原有规定相比,这显然扩大了可受理的仲裁案件的范围。

2. 明确了相关期限。原来的《仲裁统一法》和《仲裁规则》对很多仲裁程序没有作出明确的期限规定,这就容易造成程序久拖不决。例如,原来的《仲裁统一法》没有明确规定成员国法院指定仲裁员的期限、当事人对仲裁员提出异议以及成员国法院对此类异议进行处理的期限,也没有明确规定成员国法院裁定仲裁协议有效或无效以及是否存在的期限,更为重要的是,甚至没有明确规定仲裁裁决的撤销期限以及有关仲裁裁决执行令的期限,这种情况在过去的仲裁实践中给当事人、仲裁庭、成员国法院以及司法与仲裁共同法院带来很多困惑和不便。修订后的《仲裁统一法》和《仲裁规则》对上述期限作了明确规定,有利于仲裁程序的顺利进行。

3. 缩短了部分程序期限。《仲裁统一法》和《仲裁规则》中原有的许多期限规定过长,影响了仲裁程序的效率。为此,修订后的《仲裁统一法》和《仲裁规则》缩短了相应的期限,有利于仲裁程序的高效进行。例如,《仲裁规则》将被申请人提出答辩的期限、司法与仲裁共同法院裁定是否存在仲裁协议的期限,以及当事人提出修订或补正仲裁裁决的申请期限,分别从45日缩短至30日,同时将仲裁庭召集当事人召开首次会议的期限以及将仲裁裁决草案提交仲裁员进行审查的期限,从60日缩短至45日。这些期限的缩短可以大大减少仲裁程序的时间,提高了仲裁程序的效率。

4. 增加了部分程序。针对原来《仲裁统一法》和《仲裁规则》中存在的程序缺陷,修订后的《仲裁统一法》和《仲裁规则》都增加了仲裁前置程序以及仲裁的终结程序。仲裁的前置程序为协商、调解等程序的进行提供了便利条件,而仲裁的终结程序则明确规定了仲裁程序可以终结的具体情形,使仲裁程序更加完整、流畅。《仲裁规则》还针对国际上仲裁发展的最新趋势,增加了第三人介入程序、多方当事人和多方合同的合并仲裁程序,使司法与仲裁共同法院的仲裁程序更能符合仲裁时代发展的要求。

在调解制度方面，新的《调解统一法》在非洲商法协调组织内开创性地引进了调解程序。调解程序的引进既兼顾了非洲社会的传统，又能顺应国际上争议解决的潮流。非洲商法协调组织的《调解统一法》为该地区通过调解方式解决争议提供了统一而明确的法律依据。从《调解统一法》的规定来看，它主要是以联合国国际贸易法委员会2002年《调解示范法》为版本制定的，同时又考虑到本地区的法律传统和实际情况。根据《调解统一法》的规定，外国投资者也可以通过调解方式解决与投资东道国政府之间的投资争议。根据《非洲商法协调条约》有关统一法的规定，该法适用于在非洲商法协调组织成员国内进行的调解，无论是临时调解还是机构调解。从《调解统一法》的规定来看，调解作为非洲商法协调组织内的一种新的非诉争议解决程序，具有相当的灵活性和高效性。对于那些希望和投资东道国保持长期合作关系的外国投资者来说，调解不失为一种解决争议的优先选择。

非洲商法协调组织的成员国主要位于非洲西部和中部，拥有丰富的自然资源和矿产资源丰富，与中国的经济互补性强。此外，这些国家在交通、能源、电信、环保等基础设施建设和产业升级换代方面，具有巨大的投资空间。长期以来，这些国家在立法和司法上的不确定性影响了包括中国在内的一些国家在该地区的投资和贸易。非洲商法协调组织成立以来，该地的立法和司法环境得到极大改善。因此，该组织会成为中国企业和商人投资非洲市场时解决争议的一个重要平台。

在争端解决方式方面，非洲商法协调组织非常重视通过仲裁解决商事争端。中国商人和投资者也乐于通过仲裁解决商事争端，而且非洲商法协调组织的仲裁规则与中国国际经济贸易仲裁委员会的仲裁规则有许多相似之处，这无疑是吸引中国商人和投资者在该地区进行贸易和投资的又一有利因素。另外，《调解统一法》的通过也为中国投资者解决投资争议提供了另一种友好解决方式。

如果考虑到中国和非洲商法协调组织成员国之间现有的多边和双边法律

框架,该组织的争议解决制度的作用就更加凸显。在非洲商法协调组织的17个成员国中,刚果(布)、几内亚比绍、赤道几内亚和多哥还没有加入《纽约公约》;贝宁、布基纳法索、中非共和国、科摩罗、几内亚比绍、尼日尔还没有同中国签订双边贸易协定;中非共和国、科摩罗、几内亚比绍、尼日尔、塞内加尔、多哥还没有同中国签署双边投资保护协定,贝宁、喀麦隆、乍得、刚果(金)、几内亚5个国家虽然同中国签署了双边投资保护协定,但这些协定迄今尚未生效。这种情况非常不利于中国商人和投资者解决在当地发生的贸易和投资争议。非洲商法协调组织上述争议解决法律制度很好地解决了这一问题。因此,在目前情况下,非洲商法协调组织的上述争议解决法律制度为中国在该地区的投资与贸易提供了一种有效的法律保障。

国际投资仲裁上诉机制再审视

覃华平*

摘要:近几十年来,投资者与东道国投资仲裁机制一方面被广泛运用,另一方面也暴露出一些问题,包括仲裁裁决缺乏一致性、仲裁费用高昂、仲裁程序冗长,以及仲裁员缺乏多元性和公正独立性等。国际社会提出了诸多解决方案,包括设立仲裁上诉机制和建立国际投资法庭等。就设立仲裁上诉机制而言,其可行性值得怀疑,不应作为对国际投资仲裁改革的方向。可以通过制定国际统一投资协定范本、组织专家委员会对国际投资条约主要内容进行重述,以及提高仲裁员多样性和专业能力方面,对国际投资仲裁机制予以完善。

关键词:投资仲裁　上诉机制　投资法庭

一、引言

根据联合国贸易和发展会议(United Nations Conference on Trade and Development,UNCTAD)公布的数据,截至2019年2月,各国签订了大约2970个双边投资条约,其中2367个处于生效状态;另外,还有383个其他条约中包

* 覃华平,法学博士,中国政法大学国际法学院副教授,国际私法研究所副所长。研究方向为国际私法、国际航空法、国际仲裁。本论文得到国家留学基金委员会的资助。

含有投资条款,生效的有312个。[①] 此外,1987年到2017年,共有855起投资者与国家之间的投资争议案件得到解决,其中超过半数以上的案件是在国际投资争端解决中心(International Centre for Settlement of Investment Disputes, ICSID)解决的。[②] 从这些统计数据可以看出,一方面,各国对国际投资高度重视,积极签订双边投资条约,促进资本的国际流动,从而带动经济发展;另一方面,投资者与东道国之间的投资争端有快速增长的趋势,1987年只有一起投资争议案件,在之后的五六年时间里为零,而进入21世纪后,投资争议案件呈现逐渐增长的趋势,在2015年达到最高,大约有80起投资争议案件。[③] 需要指出的是,这些争议解决数据是针对投资仲裁而言的,但事实上,投资者与东道国之间的投资争议不仅可以通过仲裁的方式解决,还可以通过调解、协商以及东道国行政司法体制解决。即便是通过国际仲裁解决,由于仲裁的保密性特点,有些仲裁案件可能并未公布。因此,上述数据不能完全反映投资者与东道国之间争议的完整情况,其真实数据应该大于上述统计数据。但根据这些数据基本可以判断,仲裁是解决投资者与东道国之间投资争议的重要方式。本文认为,导致投资争议案件增加的原因主要有两个:第一,国际投资条约的广泛签订一方面促进了跨境投资的快速发展,另一方面也使争议发生的概率相应增加。目前大约90%的双边投资条约属于第一代双边投资条约,[④]对当代社会面临的环境问题、人权问题等缺乏相应的规定,因此在东道国采取相应的政策或措施以解决这些国际社会问题时,很有可能触及投资者的利益,这就不可避免地会导致一些争议的发生。另外,第一代双边投资条约的东道国一般都是发展中国家或欠发达国家,他们在签订条约时主要考虑因素是尽可能吸引外国投资,而较为

① UNCTAD, "Bilateral Investment Treaties", https://investmentpolicyhub.unctad.org/IIA, February 6, 2019.

② 联合国贸易和发展会议:《世界投资报告2018》,载联合国贸易和发展会议官网:https://unctad.org/en/PublicationsLibrary/wir2018_overview_ch.pdf,最后访问日期:2019年2月6日。

③ 同上。

④ 所谓第一代双边投资条约,主要是指缔结于20世纪90年代之前的条约,这些条约主要反映了作为资本输出国的工业化发达国家的需求,强调的是对这些国家投资者与投资的提供实质性保护,包括非歧视原则与公平原则,反对东道国采取征收措施等。

克制行使自己作为主权国家的规则制定权，但在经济发展过程中，由于情势变化又不愿或不能完全履行这种克制义务，因此也会导致争议的发生。第二，国际社会对投资者与东道国仲裁机制的熟悉与认可程度的提高也使投资争议数量增长。这方面尤其得益于1965年《关于解决国家与他国国民之间投资争端公约》（以下简称《华盛顿公约》）[①]的签订。《华盛顿公约》是在国际复兴开发银行（世界银行）主持下缔结的、为解决一缔约国与其他缔约国国民间的投资争议的多边国际公约，其目的在于为解决国家和外国私人投资者之间的争议提供便利，促进相互信任的气氛，并鼓励私人资本的国际流动。公约决定在华盛顿成立解决投资争端国际中心（ICSID），作为解决缔约国与其他缔约国国民争议和实施公约的常设机构。1966年，ICSID成立，具有独立的法人资格，并享有公约规定的特权和豁免权。ICSID在成立之后的20年间都没有案件，自1987年才开始管理第一起案件。从后面案件数量的增长来看，ICSID得到了投资者与国家的普遍认可，是目前世界上解决投资者与东道国投资争端的主要机构。近几十年来，国际社会不断对其进行完善，以更好地服务投资者与东道国，促进国际投资的良性流动，在对投资者的保护与促进东道国经济发展之间取得最大平衡。即便如此，投资者与东道国之间的投资仲裁机制在实践中面临来自各方面的检视甚至猛烈批判。为进一步完善该机制，国际社会做了很多努力，这些努力来自各个方面，包括政府间与非政府间的国际组织，前者如ICSID、联合国国际贸易法委员会（United Nations Commission on International Trade Law，UNCITRAL）、UNCTAD，后者如国际律师协会（International Bar Association，IBA）、国际商事仲裁委员会（International Council for Commercial Arbitration，ICCA），以及很多知名的国际仲裁机构。根据UNCITRAL第三工作组的调研，目前投资仲裁主要存在以下三个问题：[②]（1）投资仲裁裁决的一致性、连贯性、可预见性以及正确性；（2）仲裁员的指定以及仲裁员的公正性与独立性；（3）投

① https://icsid.worldbank.org/en/Pages/icsiddocs/ICSID-Convention.aspx, August 25, 2019.

② UNCITRAL, "Report of Working Group Ⅲ", http://undocs.org/en/A/CN.9/964, March 12, 2019.

资仲裁程序的费用和耗时。针对这些问题,国际社会提出了不同的解决方案,这些方案互相关联,但又侧重不同。针对第一个问题提出的解决方案包括设立投资仲裁上诉机制,本文将针对该问题进行论述,探讨该机制是否可行。

二、投资仲裁裁决不一致的样态及成因

一致性是指在某个法律体系下判决结果具有内在的连贯性和协调性,这种一致性能使法律适用具有可预见性,从而保障法律体系的公信力。相反,如果在相同的法律体系下判决结果互相矛盾,就会损害法律适用的可预见性,从而导致对该法律的怀疑。在国际投资仲裁领域,仲裁裁决的不一致性已经受到广泛关注,很多学者试图通过对有关裁决进行分析找出导致这种不一致的原因,并试图提出解决方案。[①] 有学者将这种不一致性归纳为四种情况[②]:

第一,对相同条约作出不同解释。有些投资保护条约在实践中被多次援引,而不同的仲裁庭在裁决不同案件时可能对同一条约作出不同解释,比如《北美自由贸易协定》(North American Free Trade Area,NAFTA)和《能源宪章条约》(Energy Charter Treaty,ECT),这两个条约在实践中多次被作为解决投资者与东道国争议的准据法。

第二,对不同条约中相同或类似用语作出不同解释。由于很多双边投资条约都是以一定的条约范本签订的,因此在用语方面有相同或类似的现象。在投资仲裁中,当事人往往援引之前仲裁庭作出的对自己有利的条约解释结论,但

① See, e. g., Gabrielle Kaufmann-Kohler, "Is Consistency a Myth?" in Emmanuel Gaillard, Yas Banifatemi (eds.), Int'l Arbitration Inst, Precedent in International Arbitration, Juris Publishing, 2008, pp. 137-148; Susan D Franck, "The Legitimacy Crisis in Investment Treaty Arbitration: Privatizing Public International Law Through Inconsistent Decisions" 73 *Fordham L Rev* 1521, 2005; Charles N. Brower, Charles H. Brower Ⅱ and Jeremy K. Sharpe, "The Coming Crisis in the Global Adjudication System" 19 Arb Intl 415, 2003; ICSID Secretariat, "Possible Improvements of the Framework for ICSID Arbitration, Annex, at 3 (22 October 2004)", https://icsid.worldbank.org/en/Documents/resources/Possible%20Improvements%20of%20the%20Framework%20of%20ICSID%20Arbitration.pdf, March 12, 2019.

② Lise Johnson and Lisa Sachs, "Inconsistency's Many Forms in Investor-State Dispute Settlement and Implications for Reform", http://ccsi.columbia.edu/files/2018/11/Inconsistencies_ISDS_Briefing-Note_11.28.18.pdf, March 12, 2019.

是国际投资仲裁中尚未确立先例原则,因此各个仲裁庭具有独立解释条约的权力,不受之前裁决的约束,这也导致了裁决的不一致。

第三,对东道国就适用条约的意图作出不同解释。在根据 NAFTA 提出的投资仲裁中,这种情况时有发生,这促使美国、加拿大和墨西哥成立了 NAFTA 自由贸易委员会,专门就条约有关术语作出有约束力的解释。①

第四,国际法或国内法与公众期望不一致,导致裁决缺乏一致性。这种不一致性是一个新产生的现象,也是颇具争议的一个问题。由于公众对环境保护、公共健康、劳工权益以及人权保障等问题日益关注,可能导致仲裁庭对相应日益复杂的国际法或国内法作出不一致的解释。

IBA 分委员会在 2018 年 11 月发布的报告中也对投资仲裁裁决的不一致情形做了分析。② 该报告认为,首先,在投资仲裁中,条约起草者故意将很多法律用语的外延设定得较为宽泛,以使其能够适用于广泛情形,这就为不同的解释打开了方便之门。其次,在投资仲裁中,当事人可以自由指定仲裁员,组成仲裁庭,将不同的案件置于不同的仲裁机构或仲裁庭管辖,这种非集中性(decentralized)也可能导致裁决的不一致。最后,相对国际贸易以及其他领域仲裁的发展,投资者与东道国投资仲裁发展的历史很短,很多制度尚处于形成和完善当中,这也不可避免地导致裁决缺乏一致性。

此外,国际投资自身的特点也进一步放大了裁决不一致的问题。比如,东道国的某一项措施可能影响来自不同国家的投资者,这些投资者可能根据其母国与东道国签署的双边投资条约提起仲裁,组成不同的仲裁庭。这些仲裁庭可能对同样的措施以及类似的事实问题作出不同的解释,从而作出不同的裁决结果。这种情形加剧了对投资仲裁裁决结果不一致的批判。另外,由于国际投资

---

① NAFTA Free Trade Commission,"North American free Trade Agreement Notes of Interpretation of Certain Chapter 11 Provisions (31 July 2001)", https://www.iisd.org/pdf/2001/trade_nafta_aug2001.pdf, February 6, 2019.

② IBA Subcommittee on Investment Treaty Arbitration,"Consistency, efficiency and transparency in investment treaty arbitration (November 2018) 6", https://www.ibanet.org/LPD/Dispute_Resolution_Section/Arbitration/Default.aspx, February 6, 2019.

仲裁涉及东道国的国际形象和社会公共利益,甚至还可能涉及东道国官员的政治廉洁问题,因此一旦发生争议,往往受到较高关注度,公众要求对投资仲裁程序以及裁决结果予以公布,提高透明度。很多ICSID仲裁裁决在ICSID网站上都能找到详细信息,包括仲裁案件的立案时间、仲裁庭的组成、有关仲裁程序令,以及裁决结果等。这些公开的信息一方面满足了东道国国民对政府行为的知情权,但是另一方面也使仲裁裁决置于广泛监督之下,尤其是很多学者和实务人士对裁决所作的批判性研究,加剧了公众对国际投资仲裁裁决不一致的不满。

一方面是对国际投资仲裁裁决不一致的强烈批判,但另一方面也有学者提出,不一致性是国际投资仲裁所固有的特点,认为消除这种不一致性不利于仲裁庭以更精确、更诚实和更透明的方式对案件作出裁决。[①] 不过大部分观点认为,对国际投资规则采取一致性的解释是一种理想状态,国际社会应当采取相应的措施达成此目标。在"萨伊博姆诉孟加拉国案"(Saipem v. The People's Republic of Bangladesh)中,虽然仲裁庭并不认为之前其他仲裁庭的裁决对其具有约束力,但认为应当对之前的裁决予以适当参考(due consideration),并明确表示确保裁决的一致性是仲裁庭的职责,是实现国际社会(包括国家和投资者)对法治确定性正当期望的必然要求。[②] 但是这种观点也远未获得一致认可,在"伯灵顿资源诉厄瓜多尔案"(Burlington Resources v. Ecuador)中,该仲裁庭的首席仲裁员和"萨伊博姆诉孟加拉国案"为同一个人,即加布里埃尔(Gabrielle Kaufmann-Kohler)教授,但是该仲裁庭就裁决一致性问题并未能达成一致观点,作为边裁之一的布丽奇特(Brigitte Stern)教授明确表示,她的职责是根据案件自身的情况作出裁决,而不受制于任何明显的判例法发展趋势的

---

① Thomas Schultz, *Against Consistency in Investment Arbitration' in Zachary Douglas, Joost Pauwelyn, and Jorge E Vinuales (eds.) The Foundations of International Investment Law: Bringing Theory into Practice*, Oxford University Press 2014.

② *Saipem SpA v The People's Republic of Bangladesh*, Decision on Jurisdiction, 21 March 2007, ICSID Case No ARB/05/07, ¶, 67.

影响。[①]

综上可以看出,对国际投资仲裁裁决不一致的正当性问题的讨论远未结束,并可以预见,该讨论在未来很长一段时间内还将继续。本文认为,消除这种不一致性是不可能的,也不符合仲裁的基本理念,我们只能在适当的范围内控制不合理的不一致性。

三、应对投资仲裁裁决不一致的救济机制

目前国际投资仲裁大致可以分为ICSID仲裁与非ICSID仲裁:ICSID仲裁有其自成体系的机制,包括救济机制与裁决的执行机制;而非ICSID仲裁主要是通过国际知名仲裁机构进行管理的仲裁,当事人在这种情况下享有的救济机制主要依靠仲裁地法院和裁决执行地法院提供。

(一)ICSID仲裁的救济机制

如前所述,目前大部分投资仲裁都是在ICSID进行的,根据《华盛顿公约》的规定,当事人就裁决享有如下救济机制:

第一,请求对裁决作出解释。根据《华盛顿公约》第50条之规定,当事人可以请求ICSID秘书长对裁决作出解释。

第二,请求对裁决进行审查。《华盛顿公约》第51条规定,裁决作出后,如果当事人发现某些事实可能会实质性地影响裁决结果,那么该当事人可以请求对裁决进行审查,只要这些事实在仲裁庭作出裁决时不为仲裁庭或申请人所知悉,或者申请人对该事实不知情并非出于其疏忽。

第三,请求撤销仲裁裁决。根据《华盛顿公约》的规定,当事人在满足下列情形之一时可以请求秘书长撤销仲裁裁决:(1)仲裁庭的组成不恰当;(2)仲裁庭明显超越权限;(3)仲裁庭成员具有腐败行为;(4)仲裁程序严重背离根本的程序规则;(5)裁决未能陈述据以作出的理由。

需要注意的是,无论是对裁决进行解释还是审查,抑或请求撤销,在性质上

---

① *Burlington Resources v Ecuador*, Decision on Liability, 14 December 2012, ICSID Case No. ARB/08/5,¶,187.

都不属于对裁决进行上诉。在对裁决作出解释或审查时,如果秘书长同意申请,该解释或审查应当由作出裁决的仲裁庭进行。事实上,在实践中请求该救济的案件数量非常有限。① 对于撤销裁决,则应当组成新的三人特设委员会对裁决进行审查,特设委员会成员应当从ICSID仲裁专家名单中指定。审理的结果可能导致裁决部分或全部被撤销,也可能维持仲裁庭的裁决。在裁决被部分或全部撤销时,裁决相应地被认定为无效,该争议应当提交新的仲裁庭裁决。另外,在撤销程序中,特设委员会不得对裁决的事实问题进行审理,也就是说,只能就公约规定的撤销事由进行审查。事实上,该撤销程序设置的初衷就是确保仲裁程序的完整性与正当性。② 可以说ICSID有其自成体系较为完善的争议解决机制,该机制随着实践的发展也在不断地改革完善。

(二)非ICSID仲裁的救济机制

尽管绝大部分投资者与东道国投资仲裁是通过ICSID解决的,但是也有一部分案件当事人选择在国际商会(International Chamber of Commerce ,ICC)、瑞典斯德哥尔摩商会仲裁院(Arbitration Institute of the Stockholm Chamber of Commerce, SCC)以及常设仲裁法院(Permanent Court of Arbitration,PCA)解决争议,或者组成临时仲裁庭根据UNCITRAL仲裁规则解决争议。这些仲裁机构的仲裁规则和UNCITRAL仲裁规则都没有设置内部上诉程序,仲裁裁决属于一裁终局,也就是说,当事人不可能就事实问题提起上诉,当事人享有的救济机制主要是请求仲裁地法院撤销裁决。与ICSID仲裁不同,在这些仲裁机构或根据UNCITRAL仲裁规则进行临时仲裁时需要确定仲裁地,仲裁地的法院对撤销裁决具有管辖权。各国规定撤销裁决的事由虽不完全相同,但一般说来属于程序性的,并且没有对仲裁裁决的当事人做出区分,从这个角度来看,投资者与东道国的投资仲裁此时具有很强的商事仲裁特征。鉴于UNCITRAL《国际商事仲裁示范法》在世界范围内得到的广泛认可,其规定的撤销裁决的事由

---

① Lucy Reed, Jan Paulsson and Nigel Blackaby, *Guide to ICSID Arbitration* , Kluwer Law International 2011,pp. 160-162.

② Ibid. ,p. 162.

值得参考[①]:(1) 提出申请的当事人提出证据,证明有下列任何情况:①第 7 条所指仲裁协议的当事人有某种无行为能力情形;或者根据各方当事人所同意遵守的法律或在未指明法律的情况下根据本国法律,该协议是无效的。②未向提出申请的当事人发出指定仲裁员的适当通知或仲裁程序的适当通知,或因他故致使其不能陈述案情。③裁决处理的争议不是提交仲裁意图裁定的事项或不在提交仲裁的范围之列,或者裁决书中内含对提交仲裁的范围以外事项的决定;如果对提交仲裁的事项所作的决定可以与对未提交仲裁的事项所作的决定互为划分,仅可以撤销含有对未提交仲裁的事项所作的决定的那部分裁决。④仲裁庭的组成或仲裁程序与当事人的约定不一致,除非此种约定与当事人不得背离的本法规定相抵触;无此种约定时,与本法不符。(2)法院认定有下列任何情形:①根据本国的法律,争议事项不能通过仲裁解决;②该裁决与本国的公共政策相抵触。将该条规定与《承认及执行外国仲裁裁决公约》(以下简称《纽约公约》)关于拒绝承认与执行外国仲裁裁决的事由进行比较发现,两者基本是一致的,审查的内容基本属于程序性事项,不涉及实体问题的审理,从而保证仲裁裁决的终局性。

综上可以看出,在国际投资仲裁领域,当事人只能就仲裁程序问题提出救济,不得对实体问题申请再审,也没有所谓的上诉机制可供援引,正是在这种背景下,有人提出了设立上诉机制的方案。那么,仲裁程序中的上诉机制能否解决裁决不一致的现象呢?其可行性有多大?本文将进一步对此进行论述。

四、上诉机制的合理性与可行性研究

在投资仲裁中设置上诉机制的讨论并非这一两年才开始的,早在 2004 年 ICSID 改革其程序规则时就正式提出设置上诉机制的建议,但该建议并未得到 ICSID 成员国的积极支持,因此只能作罢。2018 年 ICSID 在其修改建议中没有

---

① 联合国国际贸易法委员会:《国际商事仲裁示范法》第 34 条第 2 款,载联合国国际贸易法委员会官网:https://www.uncitral.org/pdf/chinese/texts/arbitration/ml-arb/ml-arb-c.pdf,最后访问日期:2019 年 2 月 6 日。

再次将设置上诉机制作为改革议案提出,但是关于该问题的讨论一直在持续。① 归纳起来,设立上诉机制的模式主要有两种:一是在双边投资条约中设立仲裁上诉机制,该机制约束的对象比较固定,就是双边条约的东道国和另一缔约国的投资者;二是设立多边投资仲裁上诉机制,该机制为常设性的,可以解决所有投资者与东道国之间的投资争议。无论是常设性上诉机制还是临时性上诉机制,其审理的对象都是仲裁裁决。尽管学者们对设立上诉机制提出了诸多建议和议案,论证其合理性与可行性,但是本文认为,设立投资仲裁上诉机制,无论是从法理上还是从实践上均不可能实现其设立目标,不具有可行性。②

(一)仲裁裁决的终局性问题

一裁终局是仲裁的一个基本原则,也是相对诉讼而言的一大优势,其目的是使争议能够快速低廉地解决。该原则在《纽约公约》、UNCITRAL《国际商事仲裁示范法》、《华盛顿公约》以及国际主要的仲裁机构仲裁规则中得到了充分肯定。该原则也被世界各国所广泛认可,这从《纽约公约》和《华盛顿公约》缔约国的数量以及世界各国国内仲裁立法对UNCITRAL《国际商事仲裁示范法》的广泛参考可以证明。在投资仲裁中,投资者对一裁终局原则也高度认可,认为该原则是国际仲裁的一个基本特征。③ 当然,一裁终局并不意味着无视裁决的一致性与正确性,事实上,在投资仲裁中东道国或公众对裁决的正确性更为

---

① 讨论该问题的文献不少,2015年后发表的具有代表性的文章是:Gabrielle Kaufmann-Kohler and Michele Potestà,"Can the Mauritius Convention serve as a model for the reform of investor-State arbitration in connection with the introduction of a permanent investment tribunal or an appeal mechanism? Analysis and roadmap"。

② 当然也有很多学者对设立投资仲裁上诉机制持否定态,具体可以参考 Jean E. Kalicki, Anna Joubin-Bret (eds.), Brill Nijhoff,"Reshaping the Investor-State Dispute Settlement System, Journeys for the 21st Century", 2015。

③ Loukas Mistelis and Emilia Onyema,"International arbitration: Corporate attitudes and practices", http://www.arbitration.qmul.ac.uk/media/arbitration/docs/IAstudy_2006.pdf, February 8, 2019; *Loukas Mistelis and Rutger Metsch*, "2015 International Arbitration Survey: Improvements and Innovations in International Arbitration', http://www.arbitration.qmul.ac.uk/media/arbitration/docs/2015_International_Arbitration_Survey.pdf, January 29, 2019; Stavros Brekoulakis and Adrian Hodis,"2018 International Arbitration Survey: The Evolution of International Arbitration", http://www.arbitration.qmul.ac.uk/media/arbitration/docs/2018International-Arbitration-Survey-report.pdf, January 29, 2019.

关注。那么,裁决的一致性与正确性是同一个问题吗?它们是否可以通过设立仲裁上诉机制实现呢?本文认为值得商榷。

就裁决的一致性与正确性而言,这属于性质不同的两个问题。如前所述,一致性是指在相同的法律体制下,就相同的案件作出同样的裁决。在不考虑裁决作出者的情况下,一致性的实现需要一定的前提条件,那就是相同的法律和相同的案件事实。但是在国际投资中,目前并不存在像世界贸易组织(World Trade Organization,WTO)体制下相对统一的法律制度,这从目前多达3000多个投资条约可见一斑,这说明国际投资法律体系具有碎片化特征,这主要是由于各国经济发展程度和投资环境不同造成的。那么一致性的前提之一——相同的法律制度在国际投资仲裁中是不具有普遍性的,因此不可避免地导致裁决不一致。在国际投资仲裁中,遭到广泛批评的关于裁决不一致的案件主要涉及阿根廷。[①] 阿根廷在2001年遭遇重大经济危机,政府采取了一系列措施应对危机,从而大范围引发了投资争议。[②] 在这些案件中,阿根廷提出的主要抗辩事由是国家危急免责,但是不同仲裁庭作出了不同裁定。之后阿根廷对几个裁决提出撤销请求,但均被特设委员会驳回。[③] 在这几个案件中,阿根廷依据的撤销理由是仲裁庭的组成不当,但是特设委员会却保持了决定的一致性,认为其无权审查案件可能涉及的实体问题。不过特设委员会的决定和推理却遭到了批判,认为其没有很好地行使《华盛顿公约》第52条规定的审查职能,在一定程度上混淆了撤销和上诉职能的根本区别。[④] 另外,投资条约中的有些法律用语本身就不易达成一致解释,比如公平待遇(fair and equitable treatment)原

① 有学者将该问题纳入投资仲裁"平行程序"中讨论,认为裁决不一致的现象是由于平行程序导致的。参见肖军:《规制冲突裁决的国际投资仲裁改革研究——以管辖权问题为核心》,中国社会科学出版社2017年版,第23~24页。

② 根据ICSID网站,目前有50件仲裁案件是针对阿根廷提出的,大部分已经结案。载https://icsid.worldbank.org/en/Pages/cases/AdvancedSearch.aspx,最后访问日期:2019年3月10日。

③ 比如ICSID Case No. ARB/03/17, Case No. ARB/03/23, Case No. ARB/03/19。

④ Ba Duong (Donny) Trinh, "Arbitral Tribunal Not Properly Constituted: What is the Role of an ICSID Committee?", http://arbitrationblog.kluwerarbitration.com/2019/02/14/arbitral-tribunal-not-properly-constituted-what-is-the-role-of-an-icsid-committee/, March 10, 2019.

则、充分保护与保障(full protection and security)原则、透明度(transparency)原则、武断与歧视(arbitrary and discrimination)等。这些法律概念外延丰富,往往需要结合案件的具体情况进行解释。其实缔约国在缔结有关条约时也未必不清楚这些概念在实践中可能导致不同的解释,但是为了尽可能涵盖实践中可能发生的情形,于是有意选择这些较为宽泛甚至模糊的法律概念。这种立法技巧一方面反映了国际投资实践发展的需要,但另一方面也导致了不同仲裁庭可能作出不同的解释,从而产生裁决不一致的情形。

裁决不一致是否意味着裁决不正确呢?或者反过来说,裁决一致就是正确的呢?本文认为不能简单地作出肯定回答。裁决正确与否应当根据个案判断,需要检视的问题包括案件事实是否清楚、证据是否确凿、法律适用是否正确,而这些标准往往具有一定的主观性,在一定程度上取决于当事人律师的抗辩能力以及对仲裁庭的影响力,当然仲裁员自身的能力也会影响其裁决的作出。那么在这种情况下,很难将不同仲裁庭作出的裁决进行横向比较,从而得出哪个裁决是正确的,哪个是错误的。也就是说,裁决不一致并不必然缺失正当性,裁决一致也不必然说明裁决是正确的。从前述特设委员会对阿根廷撤销请求的决定就可以看出,一致的决定并不意味着免受挑战。而设立上诉机制的目的是想解决裁决的不一致性,从而实现裁决的正确性。那么,在目前国际投资法体系下,即便存在上诉机制,也很难说上诉审的法官或仲裁员能作出所谓正确的裁决。另外,上诉审的法官或仲裁员无论是专职的还是临时的,都面临着任职资格的问题。如何确保这些人士比现有仲裁员的水平更高、更有能力作出所谓正确的裁决,恐怕并非易事,因为目前活跃在国际投资仲裁界的仲裁员普遍都具有较高的法律水平与专业素养。如果上诉机制能制定出一套更先进、更完善的选择法官或仲裁员的机制,那么该机制事实上可以直接用于解决目前导致投资仲裁被批评的一个问题,即仲裁员的指定与任职资格,而无须再大动干戈地设立仲裁上诉机制。正如IBA的2018年报告所指出的,“常设的或半常设的上诉机制并不能确保条约解释的精确性”,其他机制,比如国家之间设立的有约束力的联合解释机制,也可能会取得裁决的一致性和精确性。[①] 因此,解决问题的关键是要找到导致问题产生的根本原因。导致目前仲裁裁决缺乏一致性的根本原因,是国际投资条约体系的分散性、碎片化和重叠性,如果要从根本上解决问题,各国应当将其旧的双边条约予以现代化,要么修订,要么重新签订。[②]

由此可见,仲裁上诉机制并不一定能取得其设立的主要目标,即裁决的一致性与正确性,但是该机制却有可能对投资仲裁产生其他负面影响。比如,败诉的一方当事人可能利用上诉机制拖延程序,使仲裁裁决无法得到执行,从而使本已遭遇诟病的冗长昂贵的投资仲裁雪上加霜。另外,上诉机制还有可能迫使投资者放弃仲裁,转而诉诸东道国国内救济或者其他争议解决渠道(如欧盟力推的国际投资法院),这从长远来看不利于投资仲裁的发展,最终的结果是影响投资者的积极性,不利于资本的国际流动,也就不利于东道国经济的发展,使国际投资陷入恶性循环。

(二)上诉机制对当事人意思自治的限制

意思自治是仲裁的另一个基本原则,相对诉讼而言,仲裁当事人享有高度自治权,包括是否将争议提交仲裁,选择临时仲裁还是机构仲裁,选择仲裁地、仲裁语言,指定仲裁员,选择仲裁程序规则等。但是在目前设计的上诉机制中,当事人将丧失选择仲裁员的权利,对仲裁地或程序规则也可能没有选择的余地。那么这对当事人,尤其是对投资者来说,上诉机制完全不同于仲裁,该机制具有强烈的司法特征,而当事人之所以选择仲裁,其目的就是想避免司法中东道国太强的主权特性,使其争议能通过民间的相对平等的方式得以解决。因此,上诉机制的设立有悖于仲裁的另一基石:当事人意思自治原则。

---

① IBA Subcommittee on Investment Treaty Arbitration (n 36) 29-30. 不过 UNCITRAL 第三工作组认为在条约开始执行后缔约国很少也很难再做出联合解释,载 https://undocs.org/en/A/CN.9/930/Add.1/Rev.1,最后访问日期:2019 年 1 月 8 日。

② UNCITRAL Working Group Ⅲ Secretariat, "Possible reform of investor-State dispute settlement (ISDS): Consistency and related matters", 28 August, 2018, para. 30.

(三)上诉机制设想尚未取得国际社会广泛认可

美国在2002年《两党贸易促进授权法案》(Bipartisan Trade Promotion Authority Act of 2002)中要求政府在进行贸易协定谈判时应当加入关于建立"旨在提供对贸易协定中的投资条款作出协调一致解释的上诉机制或类似机制"的条款。[①] 该法案的这一要求在美国随后缔结的一些自由贸易协定中得到了体现。另外,美国2004年双边投资协定范本(2004 US Model BIT)通过附件D再次重申了这一要求,根据该附件的规定,美国要求在双边投资协定生效之日起3年内,双方应当就投资者与东道国争议解决条款考虑设置上诉机制。[②] 美国这一做法似乎对其他国家也有所影响,比如2015年中国和澳大利亚签订的自由贸易协定中就有类似条款,要求缔约双方在协定生效后3年内启动关于建立双边上诉机制的谈判。[③] 然而有意思的是,美国在其2012年双边投资协定范本中将附件D予以删除,从而改变了之前要求设立投资者与东道国争议解决上诉机制的做法。[④] 换句话说,美国在谈判双边投资协定时,并不要求其他国家考虑设置双边上诉机制。但是对于多边上诉机制,美国2012年范本与2004年范本一样,要求缔约方考虑将争议解决置于多边上诉机制之下,如果国际社会将来能够设置这样的多边上诉机制的话。[⑤] 由此可见,美国已经放弃了设置双边上诉机制的想法,但是对多边上诉机制依然抱有期望。[⑥] 然而美国在2018年11月30日签署的《美国—墨西哥—加拿大协议》(the United States-Mexico-Canada Agreement, USMCA)[⑦]中,似乎偏离了其自2002年到2012年

---

① *Bipartisan Trade Promotion Authority Act of* 2002, 19 USC § 3801-3813 (West Supp 2003).

② 2004 US Model BIT, Annex D, https://www.state.gov/documents/organization/117601.pdf, January 8, 2019.

③ 《中澳自由贸易协定》第9.23条。该协定于2015年6月16日签署,于同年12月20日生效。

④ 2012 US model BIT, https://ustr.gov/sites/default/files/BIT%20text%20for%20ACIEP%20Meeting.pdf, January 8, 2019.

⑤ 2004 US Model BIT (n 66) Article 28.10; 2012 US Model BIT (n 68), Article 28.10.

⑥ 美国在进行《跨太平洋伙伴关系协定》(Trans-Pacific Partnership Agreement, TPP)的谈判时也不要求就该TPP本身设置上诉机制,而是考虑是否能设立一个多边上诉机制。不过美国已于2017年1月30日宣布退出TPP。

⑦ 该协议的目的是取代NAFTA,尚未生效。

关于设立双边或多边上诉机制的实践,与2012年到2016年在TPP中的做法也不一致,主要表现在:第一,USMCA对是否设立上诉机制审查仲裁庭就协议项下投资者与东道国争议作出的裁决未作规定;第二,USMCA对是否就设立再审机制进行谈判未作要求,也未有鼓励;第三,USMCA偏离投资仲裁最显著的规定,是取消了美国和加拿大之间投资者与东道国投资仲裁的做法,对于美国和墨西哥之间投资者与东道国的投资仲裁也做了明显限制。从美国关于投资仲裁的实践来看,我们似乎可以得出以下结论:美国对目前投资仲裁的实践并不满意,其试图通过设立投资仲裁上诉机制以消除其不满,但似乎这种努力并没有达到其目的,因此转而试图在很大程度上否定投资仲裁。

相对美国的做法来说,欧盟似乎更激进。[①] 欧盟委员会试图通过设立一个多边投资法院(包含上诉机制)来取代现有的投资者与东道国投资仲裁机制。[②]尽管欧盟在其与其他国家的投资协定谈判中都试图加入该内容,[③]但是并没有明确使用"投资法庭"(investment court)这样的字眼。事实上,是采用"投资法院"还是"仲裁庭",不仅是名称上的问题,它还关涉判决或裁决的执行问题。如果是"投资法院"作出的判决,该判决是否能够依据1958年《纽约公约》在缔约国得到执行?考虑到执行上可能存在的困难,欧盟提出设立"多边上诉仲裁庭"(Multilateral Appeals Tribunal, MAT)的概念,以暂时取代多边投资法庭的说法。但是无论如何,这些所谓的多边机制的运转都取决于有多少其他国家参与,否则很可能沦为双边救济机制。

此外,作为国际上解决投资者与东道国投资争议的主要国际机构,ICSID也在积极探索如何保障仲裁裁决的一致性。早在2004年,ICSID在其公布的ICSID仲裁机制改革公开讨论稿中就包含了设立上诉机制的建议,但是成员国

---

① 比如,在与日本进行自由贸易协定谈判时,欧盟委员会表示:对欧盟而言,ISDS已经死亡。建立多边投资法院是其在所有欧盟协议中的诉求。

② European Commission, "The Multilateral Investment Court Project", http://trade.ec.europa.eu/doclib/press/index.cfm?id=1608, January 24, 2019.

③ The concluded EU's FTAs with Canada, Mexico, Singapore and Vietnam. The European Commission is negotiating similar agreements with Chile, China, Indonesia, Japan, Malaysia, Myanmar and the Philippines.

认为讨论该建议为时尚早。[①] 2018年,ICSID再次公布ICSID仲裁机制改革讨论稿,但是此次没有包含设立上诉机制的建议。ICSID秘书长解释,关于设立上诉机制的愿望在成员国中并未取得充分一致。[②]

从美国、欧盟以及ICSID的实践可以看出,国际社会关于设立上诉机制的建议不仅没有达成一致意见,似乎还有放缓之趋势。本文认为,之所以出现这种情况,是因为上诉机制具有以下缺陷或问题:第一,上诉机制违背了仲裁的一些基本原则和理念,比如一裁终局和当事人意思自治等,模糊了仲裁与诉讼的界限。第二,在目前国际投资法律体系碎片化的状态下,上诉机制不仅无法取得裁决的一致性,更不可能保障裁决的正确性,这将导致设置该机制的目的落空。第三,可能导致争议解决更加耗时昂贵,在有上诉机制可以求助的情况下,败诉一方当事人无论出于何种目的,往往都会选择上诉。这种情况可能在商事争议中不太可能出现,因为商事主体的目的是逐利,但是在投资仲裁中,如果东道国败诉,不上诉似乎无法给公众一个满意的交代,似乎说明政府或政府有关官员在案件中可能有渎职行为,甚至让人怀疑是否存在腐败行为,东道国唯有通过上诉机制以证其清白。第四,上诉机制的设立本身也面临诸多困难。设置双边上诉机制的建议基本不会得到采纳,因为该机制和临时仲裁庭的功能基本一致,仅就个案根据某个特定的双边投资条约作出裁决,无法实现裁决在世界范围内的一致性。而多边上诉机制面临更多挑战,其设立的前提是能得到世界各国的普遍认可,而这一点非常困难。我们从ICSID被签署、批准、生效以及到正式受理案件的过程就可以看出,一个多边机制要得到世界的普遍认可是一个漫长的过程,而ICSID得到认可还有赖于世界银行的有力支持。而目前所谓的多边上诉机制似乎并没有这样的政府间组织作为基础,其得到认可的过程必将

---

① Meg Kinnear, "Appeal, Review, Annulment … What's it all about?", http://isdsblog.com/2015/10/23/icsid-guest-post-appeal-review-annulment-whats-it-all-about/, January 8, 2019.

② Crina Baltag, "Interview with Meg Kinnear, Secretary General of the International Centre for Settlement of Investment Disputes", http://arbitrationblog.kluwerarbitration.com/2018/04/15/interviews-with-our-editors-interview-with-meg-kinnear-secretary-general-of-the-international-centre-for-settlement-of-investment-disputes/, January 8, 2019.

更加困难。此外,该机制还涉及诸多法律上的障碍,比如该机制作出的决定在性质上属于仲裁裁决还是法院判决,根据什么法律承认与执行,是否还有撤销机制,该机制是否具有独立法律人格,是否享有豁免,是常设的还是临时的,仲裁员或法官的指定程序能否体现当事人尤其是投资者的意思,他们应当具备怎样的任职资格,等等。由此可见,设立上诉机制产生的问题远比它能解决的问题多,因此,其可行性是相当值得探讨的。

五、促进仲裁裁决一致性的建议

国际社会为促进投资仲裁裁决一致性所做的探讨和提出的建议是值得肯定的,无论是设立上诉机制,还是成立国际投资法庭,都有其合理性。但如前所述,这些改革措施尚无法达成广泛认可。诚然,解决投资仲裁裁决不一致问题绝非易事,但是我们绝不能完全否定投资仲裁的积极作用,抛弃投资仲裁。我们需要做的是采取一切可行措施,尽量弥补其缺陷,为此,本文认为可以从以下几个方面对投资仲裁制度予以完善。

(一)制定统一的投资协定范本

如前所述,导致投资仲裁裁决缺乏一致性的主要原因是仲裁庭对不同投资协定中的法律用语作出不同解释,在目前存在 3000 多个双边投资协定或多边条约的情况下,这种情况不可避免。这些条约签订的时间可能不同,有所谓的第一代双边投资协定,也有所谓的现代投资协定,因此,即便这些条约的用语一致,但是由于其签署的历史背景不同,因此可能具有不同的意思。要想较为彻底地解决该问题,最佳的办法是各国对现有双边投资协定进行修订,签署内容一致的投资协定。但是,显然这是一种理想状态,各国由于经济发展水平不同,法律环境和制度存在差异,对外资的需求也不一样,因此不可能签署内容完全一致的投资协定。但是这不影响国际社会就双边投资协定提供示范范本,这种做法绝非新鲜事物,比如美国不定期地更新其双边投资协定范本。当然美国提供的范本主要是从其本国立场出发,不具有普遍代表性。要在国际范围内制定投资协定范本,有关国际组织可以发挥其作用。比如,UNCITRAL 就国际商事仲裁制定了示范法,该示范法得到世界各国的广泛认可,在很大程度上作为各国国内仲裁立法的蓝本。在这方面取得显著成果的还有国际统一私法协会(International Institute for the Unification of Private Law,UNIDROIT)制定的《国际商事合同通则》等。在国际投资法领域,UNCTAD一直致力于对国际投资的研究,因此可以担负起该任务,制定双边投资协定范本,当然条件成熟时可以拟定多边投资条约,如同国际社会通过谈判达成的WTO协定一样。UNCTAD制定的范本对成员国不具有法律约束力,仅供参考,但是由于该范本是基于对各国投资环境以及全球投资趋势的实证研究拟定的,因此它具有广泛的代表性,也容易为世界各国所接受。

(二)双边投资协定重述

虽然解决裁决不一致最理想的方法是签订统一的投资协定,避免国际投资法律体系碎片化现象,但是显然在短时间内还无法实现该目标。但是这不影响国际社会对现有双边投资协定中的主要法律条文作出相对统一的解释,只是该解释工作应由国际组织统一行使。具体设想类似于美国的法律重述,我们知道美国是判例法国家,为了对司法实践进行总结,并对法理发展趋势做出预测,美国法学会组织专家学者对司法判例和有关学说理论进行梳理并归纳总结,即所谓的重述。虽然该重述不属于立法,也并非司法,不具有法律约束力,但它对司法实践的指导意义非常重大,不容忽视。那么在国际投资仲裁领域,也可以设立一个专家委员会对投资协定中普遍适用的规定或法律用语作出解释,该解释应当建立在对有关仲裁裁决进行梳理分析基础之上,并形成类似于指南的文献,供仲裁庭在实践中参考。尽管这种指南本身对仲裁庭不具有法律约束力,但是由于其结合仲裁实践和专家委员会的专业知识,因此具有很强的说服力,仲裁庭在实践中如果要背离该指南,应当予以充分的说理。如前所述,虽然在投资仲裁领域没有先例制度,但是仲裁庭在实际审理案件时往往会对之前仲裁案件的说理予以参考,投资者与东道国的律师也不会忽视之前裁决的推理,往往选取对自己有利的裁决或推理提供给仲裁庭。因此,在这种背景下,对投资协定进行重述是可能的,该工作依然可以由UNCTAD牵头,这为其制定投资协定范本也是大有裨益的。其实,对双边投资协定进行解释也早有实践,比如美国、加拿大和墨西哥就 NAFTA 的解释成立了贸易协定解释委员会,并且该委员会作出的解释对投资者与东道国具有约束力。需要注意的是,UNCTAD 成立的专家委员会在人选方面应当考虑以下因素:专家应当具有很高的国际法水平,熟知条约解释方法,具有地域、法律教育以及性别的多元性。

(三)加强仲裁员职业道德规范

正所谓仲裁的好坏取决于仲裁员的好坏,因此各国都要求仲裁员公道正派和公正独立,要求仲裁员对可能影响其公正性与独立性的情形予以披露。在投资仲裁领域,仲裁员缺乏多元性引起广泛重视,甚至遭到批评。[①] 缺乏多元性主要表现在仲裁员国籍集中在欧洲和北美,某些仲裁员被多次指定从而表现出一定的情感偏向性(如投资者友好型或东道国友好型)。另外,仲裁员身份的多重性和随时转换性也遭到批评,这主要是因为国际投资仲裁中很多仲裁员兼具律师身份,他们可能在 A 案中担任仲裁员,但同时在 B 案中担任律师,这种身份的重叠和角色的交错可能会影响他们在仲裁中的立场与倾向,从而对投资条约作出具有倾向性的解释,背离条约法解释规则,因为在 A 案中的裁决结果可能影响 B 案的结果,这无疑会影响案件裁决的正确性和一致性。鉴于此,UNCITRAL 第三工作组提出加强仲裁员职业道德规范的建议,提高仲裁员的公正性与独立性。[②] 此外,目前国际社会对仲裁员的专业素养没有明确规定,这可能也是导致仲裁裁决不一致的一个原因。投资仲裁与一般的商事仲裁不同,它不仅涉及对投资者与东道国政府或机构签订的投资合同的解释,还涉及对国际条约的解释,前者需要仲裁员具备合同法知识,后者需要其具备扎实的国际法知识,特别是国际公法中关于条约法和国家责任方面的专业知识。此外,由于投资争议往往涉及的是基础设施建设(包括航空、铁路、公路和桥梁建设等)、能源开采以及大型工程等,这需要仲裁员具备对这些领域争议特点能

① UNCITRAL,"Report of Working Group Ⅲ, A/CN. 9/WG. Ⅲ/WP. 152, paragraphs 19 - 26", https://undocs. org/A/CN. 9/WG. Ⅲ/WP. 151, January 8, 2019.

② UNCITRAL,"Report of Working Group Ⅲ, A/CN. 9/WG. Ⅲ/WP. 151", https://undocs. org/A/CN. 9/WG. Ⅲ/WP. 151, January 8, 2019.

够了解的能力,并在必要时进行现场勘察等。由此可见,国际投资仲裁对仲裁员专业能力的要求往往要高于一般国际商事仲裁的要求,这进一步增加了实现国际投资仲裁裁决一致性目标的难度。

六、结论

一方面,投资者与东道国投资仲裁机制在较短的历史发展过程中取得如此广泛的认同实属不易,也说明该机制基本符合投资者与东道国利益,在一定程度上保障了资本的跨境流动,促进了东道国经济发展。另一方面,该机制在运用过程中也暴露出一些问题,比如裁决不一致、仲裁费用较高以及仲裁程序冗长等。导致这些问题的原因是多方面的,既包括国际投资法律体系本身存在的问题,也包括仲裁制度基本原则和固有特征所可能产生的问题。为解决这些问题,国际社会提出了诸多解决方案,包括设立仲裁上诉机制、建立多边投资法庭、优化仲裁程序、改进仲裁规则、提高仲裁员的职业道德水平和专业素养等。毫无疑问,这些方案都具有一定的合理性。但是在决定采取何种解决方案时,不仅要考虑其合理性,还要考虑其可行性,即新的方案所带来的成效应当大于其可能产生的负面影响,这种方案才应纳入考量范围。与此同时,仲裁之所以成为替代诉讼解决争议的一种方式,是因为它与诉讼具有一些根本区别,包括其裁决的终局性与当事人的意思自治,那么在对投资仲裁进行改革时不得完全抹杀仲裁的基本特性,使其具有明显的诉讼特征。因此,设立仲裁上诉机制绝非良方,不具有可行性。同时,还应当认识到投资仲裁与商事仲裁不同,表现在两者涉及的主体、援引的法律依据以及涉及的争议性质等方面,因此在商事仲裁中可由当事人自由约定的一些事项可能在投资仲裁中并不具有可行性。对于建立国际投资法庭,本文认为该机制是相对仲裁而独立存在的诉讼机制,与仲裁不冲突,完全可以与仲裁并存。但是我们也要看到,设立多边投资法庭并非易事,其主要问题包括参与国的数量与判决的执行等,当然在诉讼机制下设立上诉程序则毫无问题,不过这种情形势必增加当事人的诉讼费用和时间成本,如果该机制不具有其他突出优势,则很难取代仲裁成为当事人的首选,不过国家在投资协定中直接排除仲裁而约定诉讼则是另一种争议解决模式。因此，本文认为，对现有投资仲裁进行改革可以从以下两方面着手：一是对投资条约中的主要法律用语进行解释或重述，为仲裁庭提供参考或指南，同时提供统一的投资协定范本供各国参考使用，从而促进投资法律体系的统一化；二是设立投资法庭，直接通过诉讼解决争议，尽管这种方案已经不属于对投资仲裁本身的改革，但也不失为一种选择。

图书在版编目(CIP)数据

仲裁与法律. 第142辑 / 中国国际经济贸易仲裁委员会, 中国海事仲裁委员会, 中国国际商会仲裁研究所主办. -- 北京 : 法律出版社, 2019
ISBN 978-7-5197-3958-4

Ⅰ. ①仲… Ⅱ. ①中… ②中… ③中… Ⅲ. ①仲裁-研究-丛刊 Ⅳ. ①D915.704-55

中国版本图书馆CIP数据核字(2019)第213321号

仲裁与法律·第142辑
ZHONGCAI YU FALÜ · DI-142 JI

中国国际经济贸易仲裁委员会
中国海事仲裁委员会
中国国际商会仲裁研究所
主办

责任编辑 马丽娟
装帧设计 汪奇峰

出版 法律出版社
总发行 中国法律图书有限公司
经销 新华书店
印刷 固安华明印业有限公司
责任校对 马　丽
责任印制 吕亚莉

编辑统筹 法治与经济出版分社
开本 710毫米×1000毫米 1/16
印张 17.5
字数 260千
版本 2019年10月第1版
印次 2019年10月第1次印刷

法律出版社/北京市丰台区莲花池西里7号(100073)
网址/www.lawpress.com.cn
投稿邮箱/info@lawpress.com.cn
举报维权邮箱/jbwq@lawpress.com.cn
销售热线/400-660-8393
咨询电话/010-63939796

中国法律图书有限公司/北京市丰台区莲花池西里7号(100073)
全国各地中法图分、子公司销售电话:
统一销售客服/400-660-8393/6393
第一法律书店/010-83938432/8433　西安分公司/029-85330678　重庆分公司/023-67453036
上海分公司/021-62071639/1636　深圳分公司/0755-83072995

书号:ISBN 978-7-5197-3958-4　**定价**:48.00元